Mel Bay's

Deluxe Bass Chords, Arpeggios & Scales

by Al Hendrickson & Art Orzeck

CONTENTS

CONTENTS BY 5th RELATIONSHIP

INTRO

This encyclopedia of scales and arpeggios is thoroughly comprehensive in its demonstration of all the practical scales and arpeggios. It is everything an electric bass player should desire as a source of reference and as a method which can accompany any other bass method at any level of instruction.

To preserve more usual musical relationships, the presentation of Parts One and Two - Scales and Related Arpeggios, is according to the Fifth Relationship- The Circle of Fifths (p6). In this manner, greater musical meaning is given to practice efforts. The keys do not progress alphabetically. The Contents is listed twice, once by successive pages, and again alphabetically. This was done to make the volume useable as a method or as a source of reference. Part Three, Comprehensive Arpeggios, is presented in abridged form, but the bass player should have no difficulty constructing any arpeggio according to the models given.

The term "Position" is used to indicate any span of 4 frets on the fingerboard. This span is covered bv the player's 4 fingers, and the placement of the 1st finger designates the number of the position. For example, if the 1st finger is in the 5th fret, the player is in the fifth position. See Illustration:

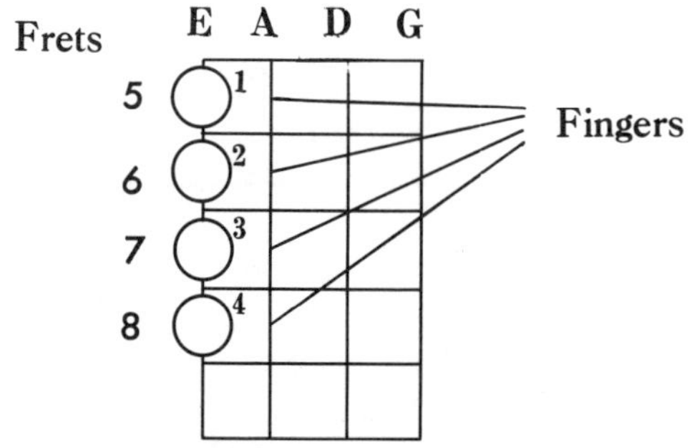

The following remarks will become more meaningful to the student as he engages in the study of scales. Here is presented a formula for finding any particular key or position with respect to a given form (Primary, Secondary, Tertiary, and Quaternary).

MAJOR FORMS

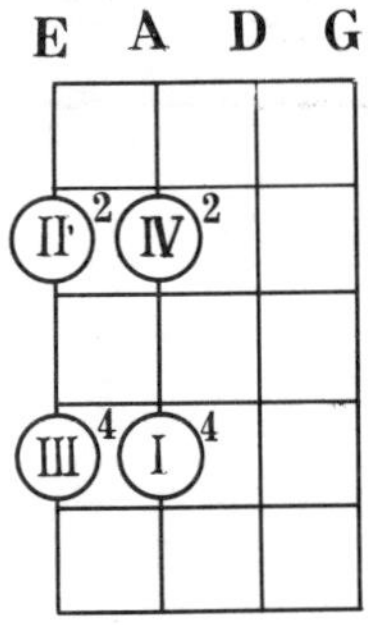

I Primary Major Form: Start with the 4th finger, A String, in any given position.

II Secondary Major Form: Start with the 2nd finger, E String, in any given position.

III Tertiary Major Form: Start with the 4th finger, E String, in any given position.

IV Quaternary Major Form: Start with the 2nd finger, A String, in any given position.

MINOR FORMS

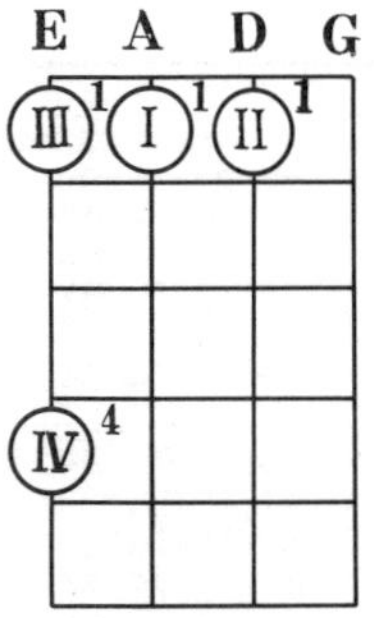

I Primary Minor Form: Start with 1st finger, A String, in any given position

II Secondary Minor Form: Start with 1st finger, D String, in any given position.

III Tertiary Minor Form: Start with 1st finger, E String, in any given position.

IV Quaternary Minor Form: Start with 4th finger, E String, in any given position.

How To Tune The Electric Bass

The student should tune the 1st string, G, to the corresponding G on the piano. This G is just below middle C, the fourth space in the bass staff (see below). Now press the D string at the 5th fret and tune it to a unison with the open G string. Next, press the A string at the 5th fret and tune it to a unison with the open D string. Finally, press the E string at the 5th fret and tune it to a unison with the open A string. Check tuning with harmonics at the 7th 5th and 12th frets and the sound of normal playing.

STRINGS

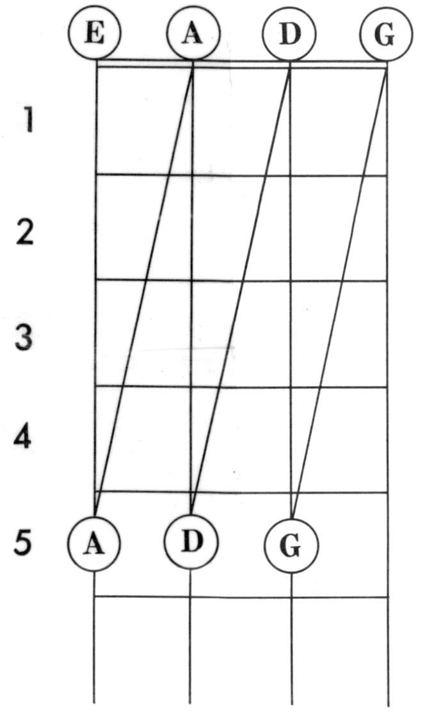

Connecting lines indicate unisons

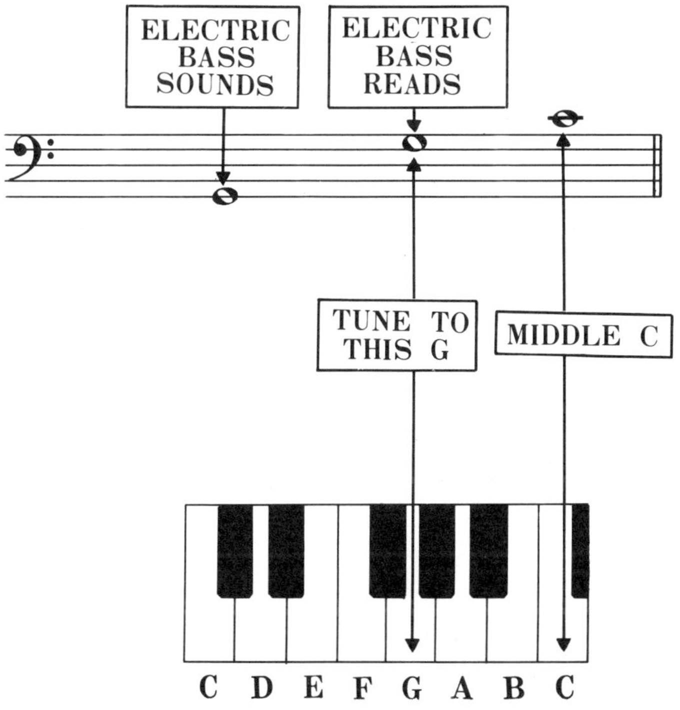

Electric Bass Fingerboard

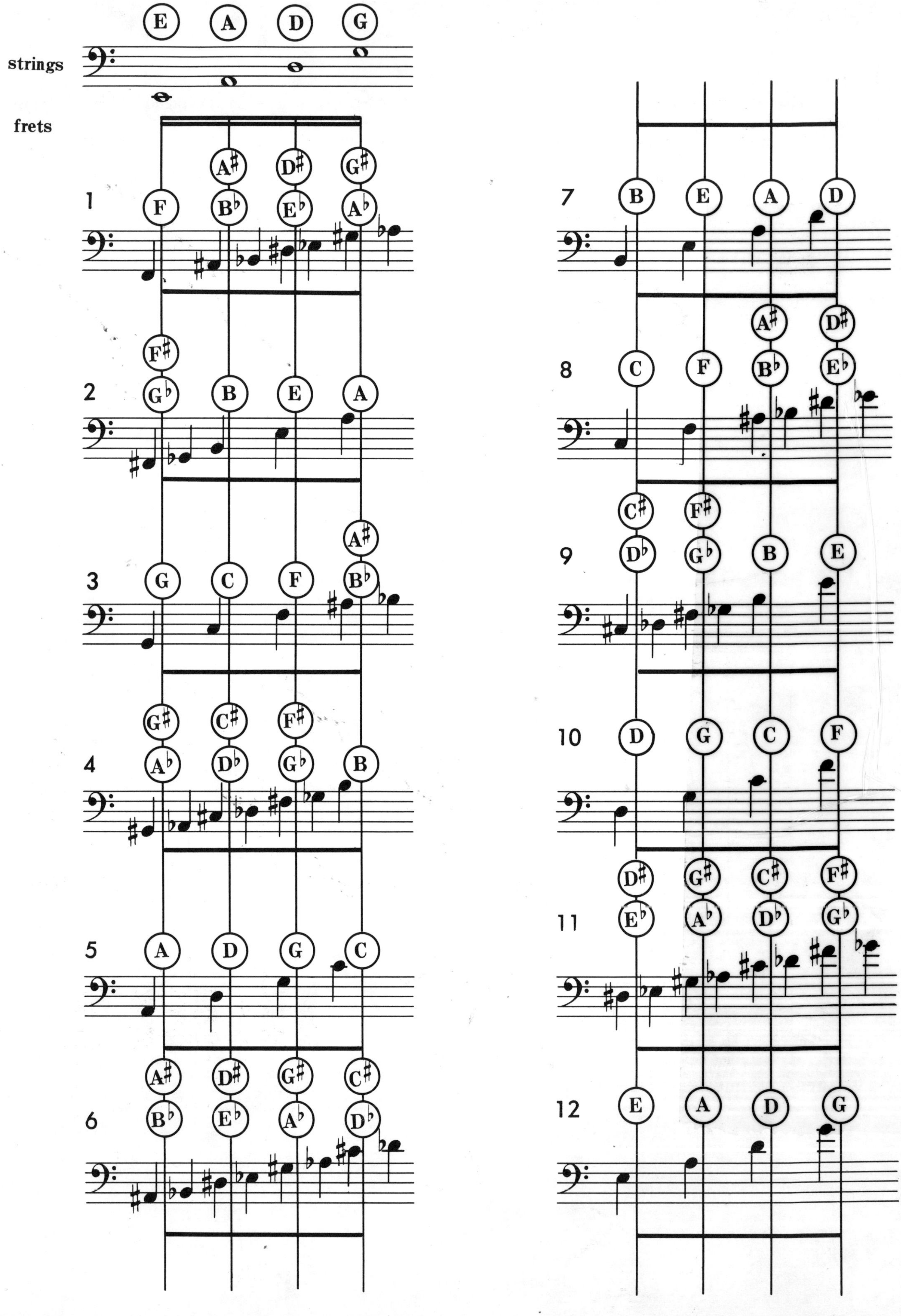

THEORY

The electric bass, like all fretted instruments, has a fingerboard composed of half tones on a musical continuum. There are 12 half tones in the complete one octave chromatic scale (See fingerboard chart on page 4). The scale notes are given letter names A B C D E F G, and are repeated octave after octave (See below) and since some intervals between notes are whole tones, and some are half tones, there are a total of 12 half tones, thus:

A A♯ B C C♯ D D♯ E F F♯ G G♯, A A♯ *etc.*
1 2 3 4 5 6 7 8 9 10 11 12, 1 2

The Electric Bass employs the Bass Staff - F Clef.

It may be apparent that a sharp (♯) raises a given note a half tone. The same chromatic scale can be spelled using flats (♭) to lower each given note a half tone, thus:

A A♭ G G♭ F E E♭ D D♭ C B B♭, A A♭ *etc.*
1 2 3 4 5 6 7 8 9 10 11 12, 1 2

Combining the two, produces a system of enharmonic equivalents:

A A♯(B♭) B C C♯(D♭) D D♯(E♭) E F F♯(G♭) G G♯(A♭)
1 2 3 4 5 6 7 8 9 10 11 12

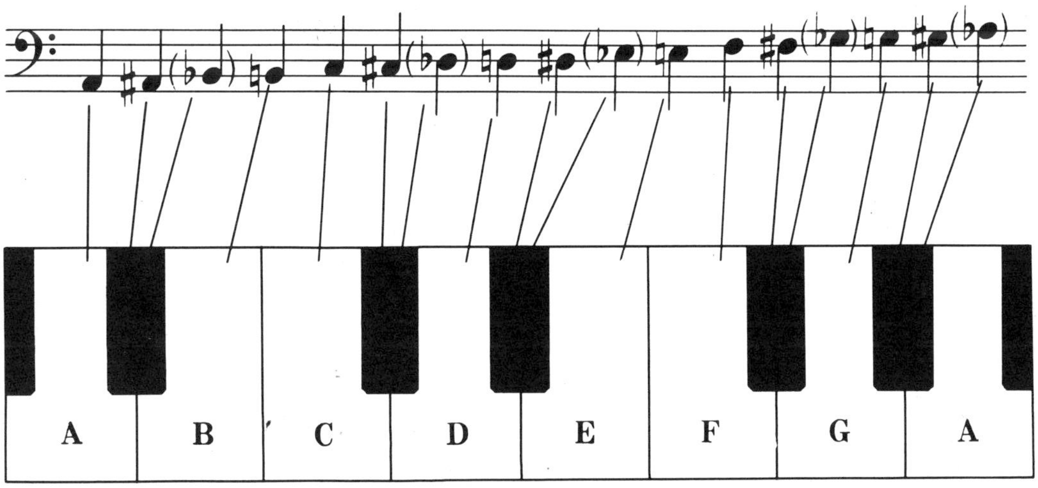

The more obvious piano fingerboard is used to illustrate. Each white and black note is equal to a fret on the bass.

There may be times when an already sharped note may be sharped again. The double sharp sign is indicated so: × Double flatted notes are simply indicated by 2 flats: ♭♭

If a sharp or a flat is to be cancelled out, a natural sign (♮) is employed. For example, to cancel A♯  the natural sign would be employed in this manner: A♮  Similarly, to cancel A♭  the natural sign would be employed in the same manner: A♮ 

SCALES

In current use, there are basically two kinds of diatonic scales, Major and Minor. A diatonic scale may be best demonstrated by referring to the white keys on the piano (see page 5). From C to C, an octave higher, is a major diatonic scale (C Major). From A to A, an octave higher, is a minor diatonic scale (A Minor). There are various ways to alter a minor scale which will be shown later (page 36) when it will become more practically apparent.

Scales are associated with various key signatures. Most musicians accept 15 keys. The Table of Keys, below, illustrates the various keys formed in a Circle of 5ths. The Treble Staff (G Clef) is used to privide additional information. The circle of 5ths is a very important relationship which all musicians employ in daily practice.

Table of Keys

Parts One and Two will include all keys through G♭ (6 flats) and F♯ (6 sharps), Which are enharmonically equivalent. All keys beyond (C♭ and C♯ are omitted since they have other enharmonic equivalents. Part Three, Comprehensive Arpeggios, omits the keys of F♯, G♭, and B, and their relative minors.

Neighboring keys (and the 3 fundamental harmonies of any key) are a fifth away from each other. A fifth is five scale degrees:

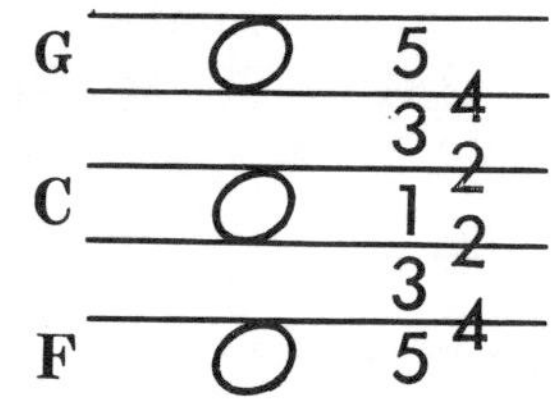

CHORDS AND ARPEGGIOS

The simplest definition of a scale is any two or more notes played by step ($\frac{1}{2}$ or 1 whole tone). For example, the notes C C♯, or C D, constitute a two note scale.

The simplest definition of a chord or arpeggio is any two or more notes played by a skip (3rd or more). For example, the notes C E, or C E♭, are a two note chord or arpeggio. An arpeggio is simply a chord played one note at a time, while the chord is a matter of playing the same notes all at one time.

This volume contains all the arpeggios that a bass player will ever want to use. In theory, an arpeggio can be altered by sharping or flatting any and all of its notes except the root (lowest note in normal construction), forming thereby an "altered chord." The most useable altered arpeggios are presented in this volume.

This volume of scales and arpeggios is not intended to be an encyclopedia of all music in general. The above theoretical comments are some essentials immediately applicable to this volume. The student is advised to obtain a music dictionary for general information. An independent course in harmony would help a great deal.

PICKING EXERCISES

* Play triplets with alternate down-up-down and up-down-up strokes regardless of accent. Play scales (and all those to follow) in both directions, maintaining evenness of rhythm and sound. The object is to play up-strokes as freely as down-strokes.

SIMPLE RHYTHMS

In simple fractions, The lower number indicates the value of one beat. The upper number indicates how many beats are in one measure.

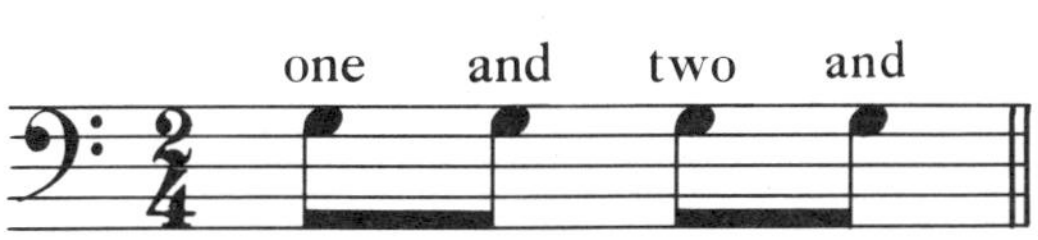

All Simple: 2/2 2/4 3/4 4/4 2/8 3/8 4/8

COMPOUND RHYTHMS

In compound fractions, The lower number indicates the value of a third of a beat. The upper number indicates how many of these 1/3rd beats are in the measure. For example, there are two beats in a 6/8 measure.

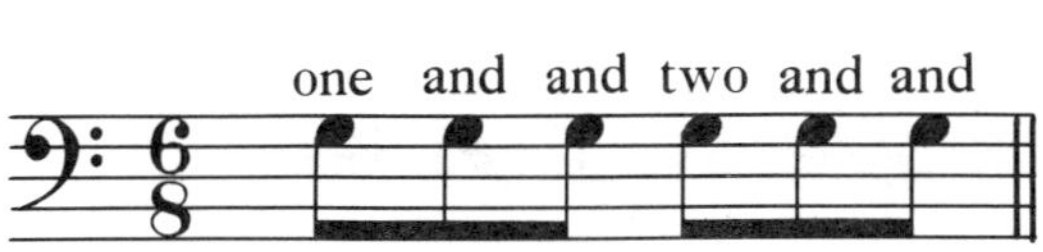

All Compound: 6/4 6/8 9/4 9/8 12/4 12/8

PART ONE - MAJOR FORMS

Scales and Related Arpeggios in All Positions

PRIMARY FORMS

OPEN POSITION - C MAJOR

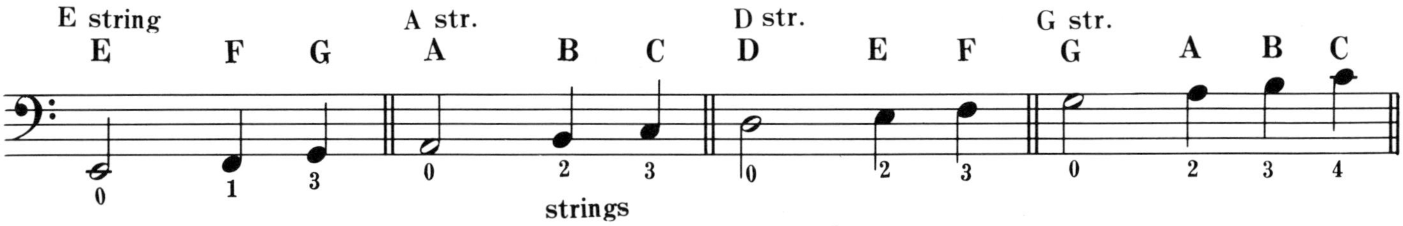

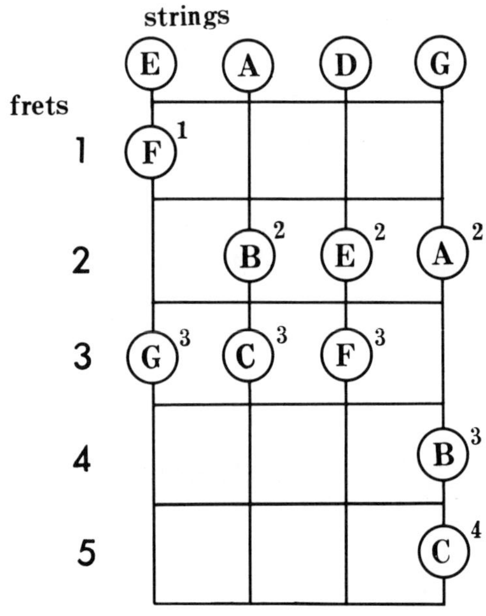

ARPEGGIOS

C

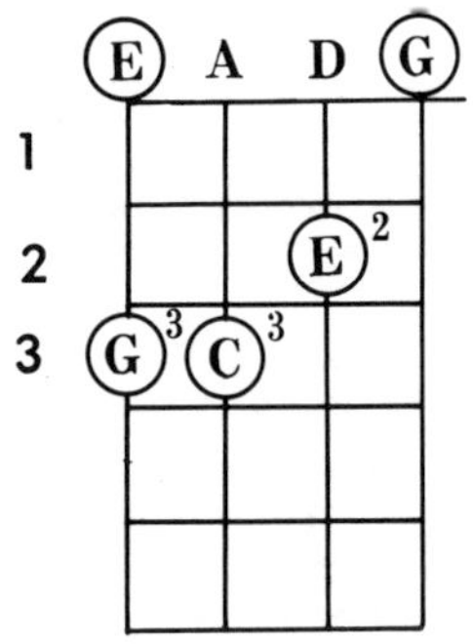

Tonic

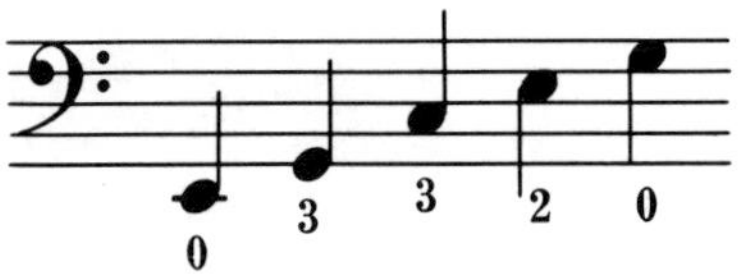

F

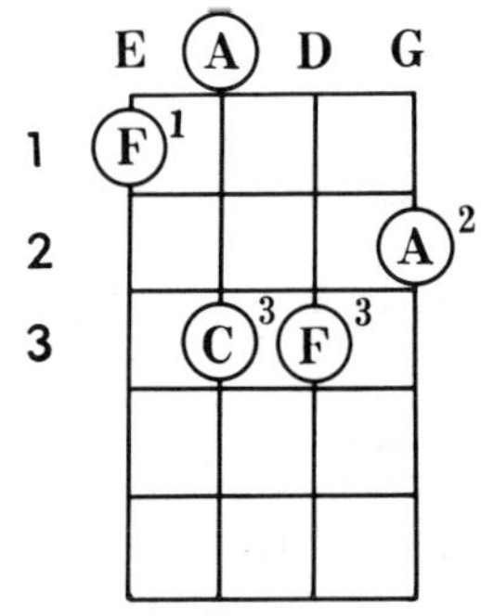

Subdominant

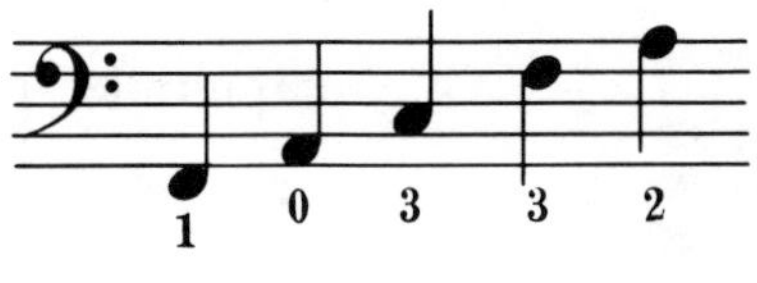

G_7

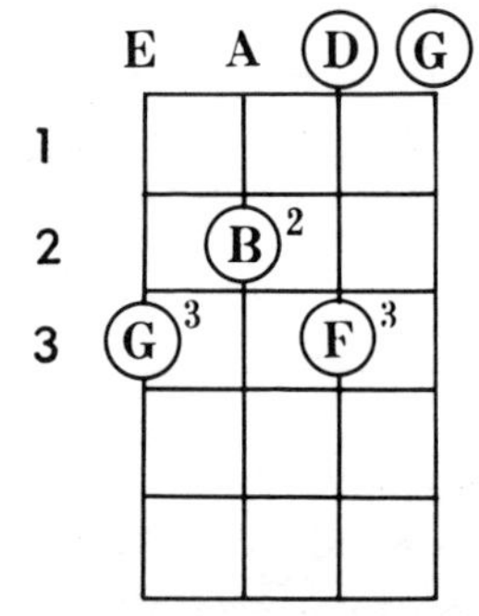

Dominant 7th

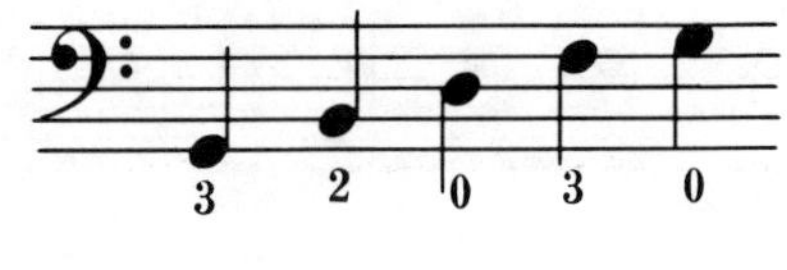

PRIMARY FORMS

F MAJOR

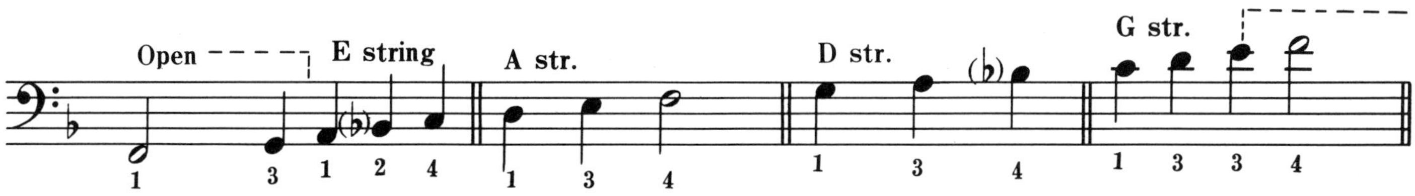

Vth POSITION

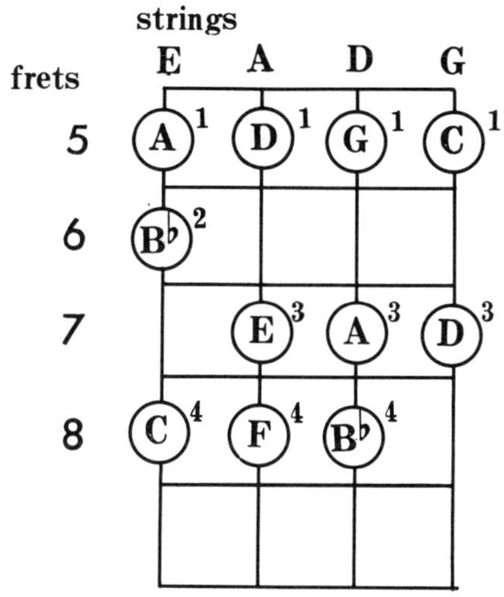

ARPEGGIOS

F

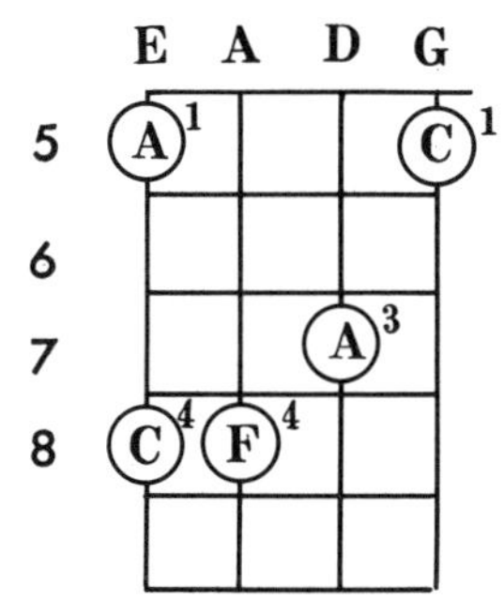

Tonic

B♭

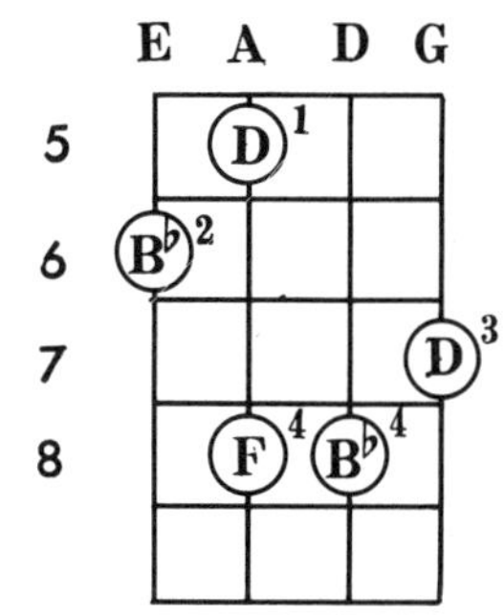

Subdominant

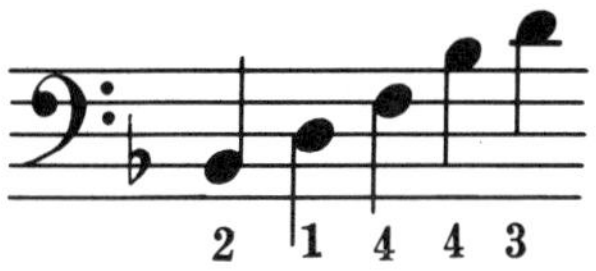

C_7

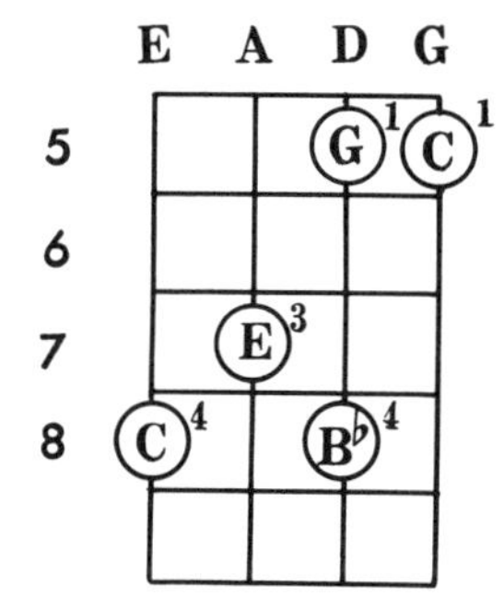

Dominant 7th

G MAJOR

VIIth POSITION

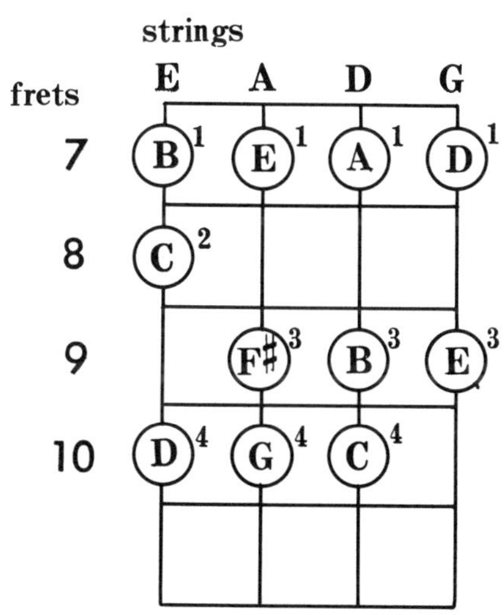

ARPEGGIOS

G

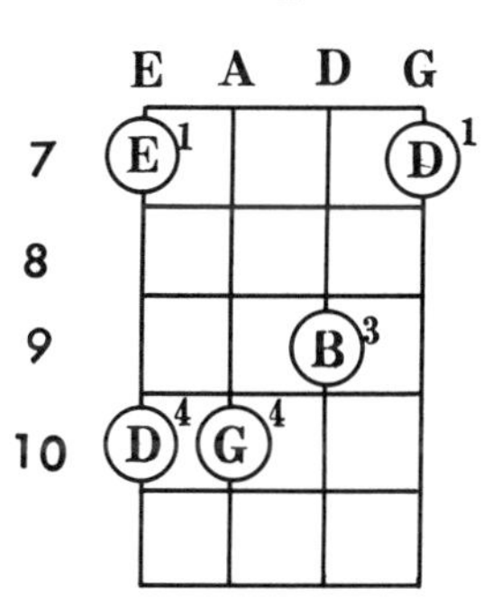

Tonic

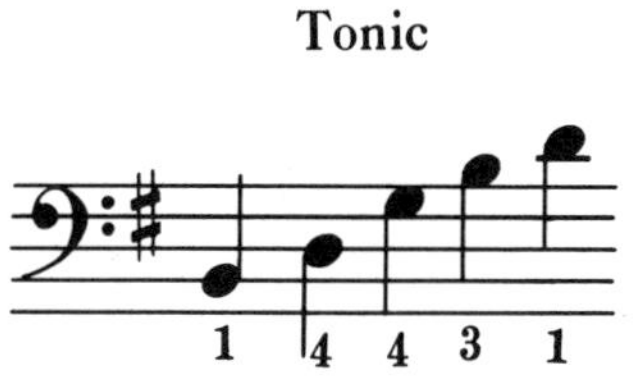

C

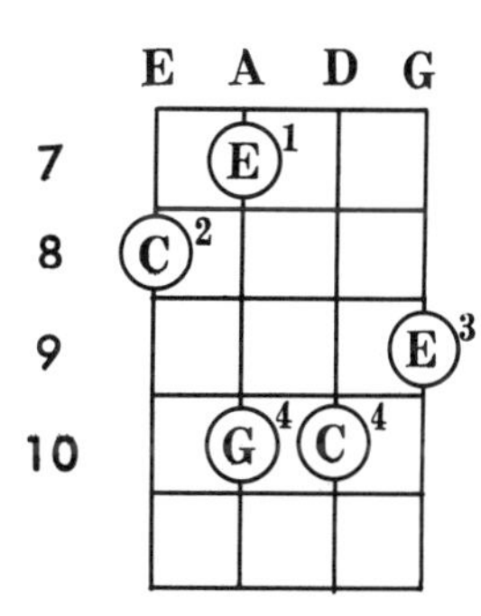

Subdominant

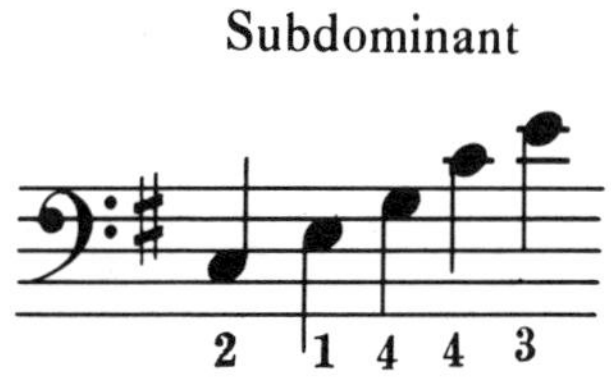

D_7

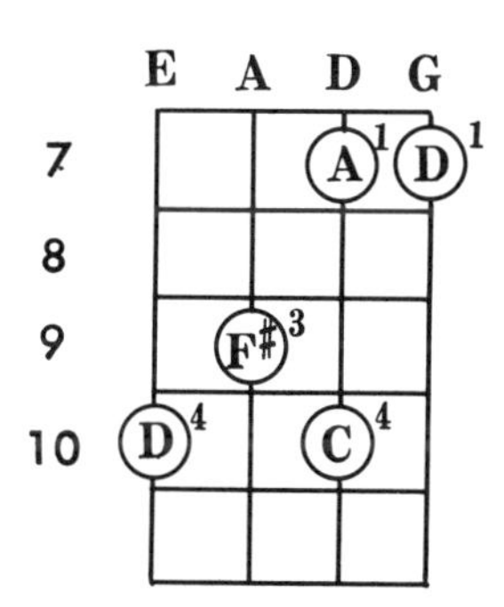

Dominant 7th

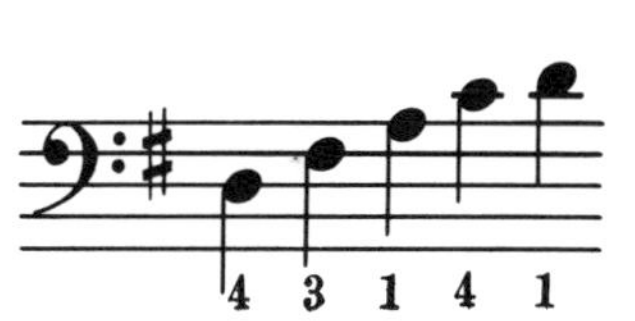

PRIMARY FORMS

B♭ MAJOR

Xth POSITION

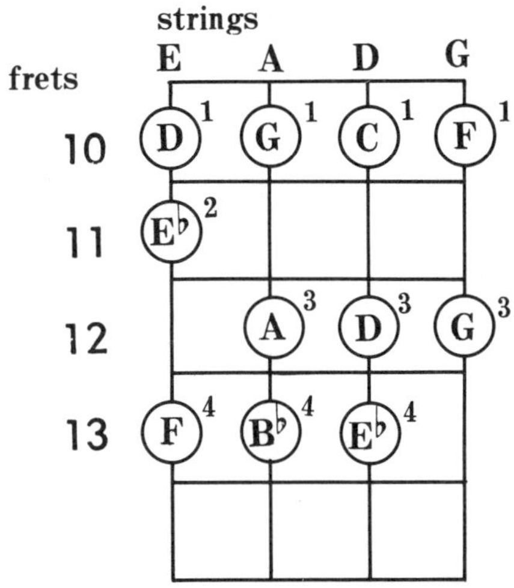

ARPEGGIOS

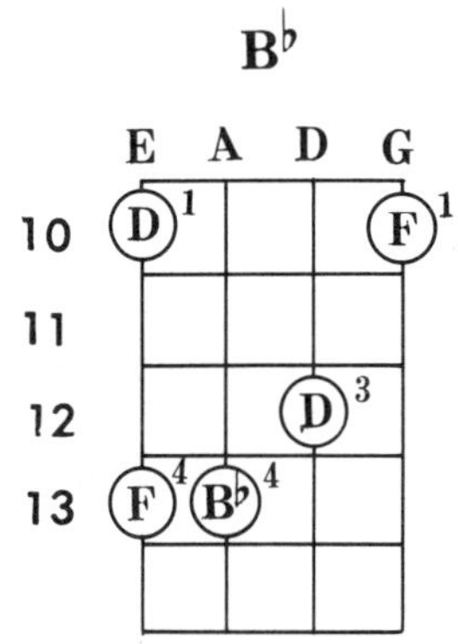

Tonic

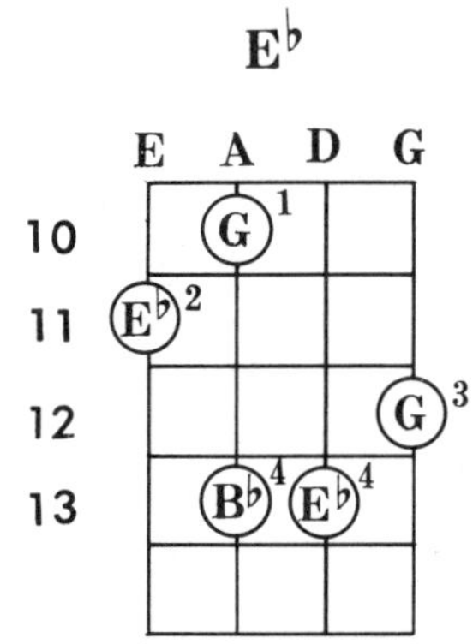

Subdominant

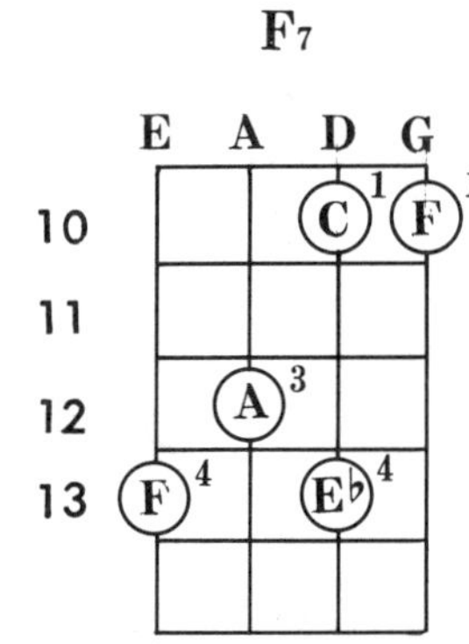

Dominant 7th

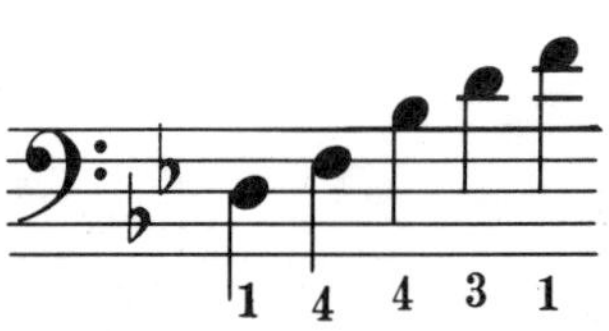

D MAJOR

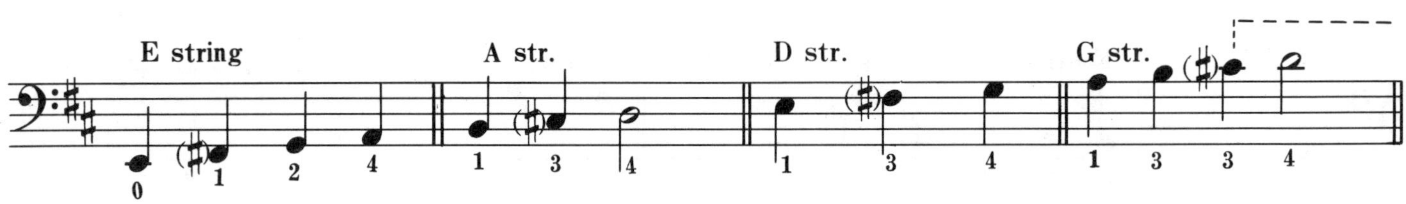

IInd POSITION

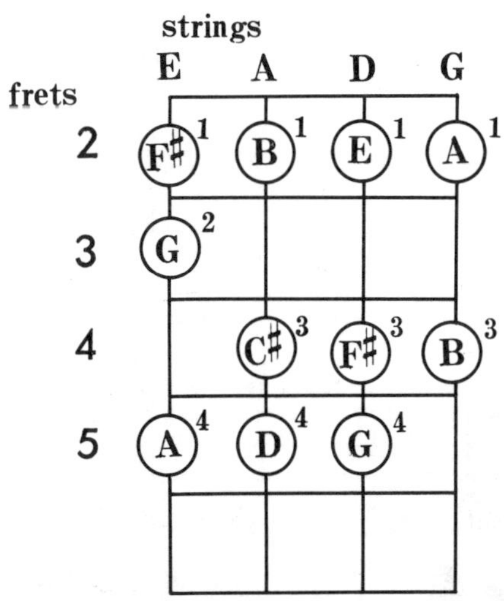

ARPEGGIOS

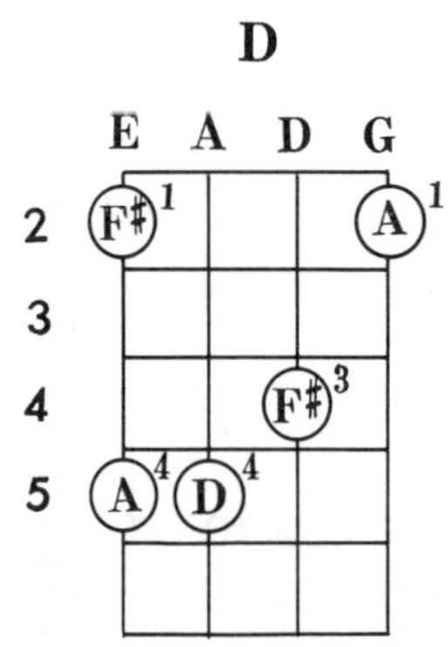

Tonic

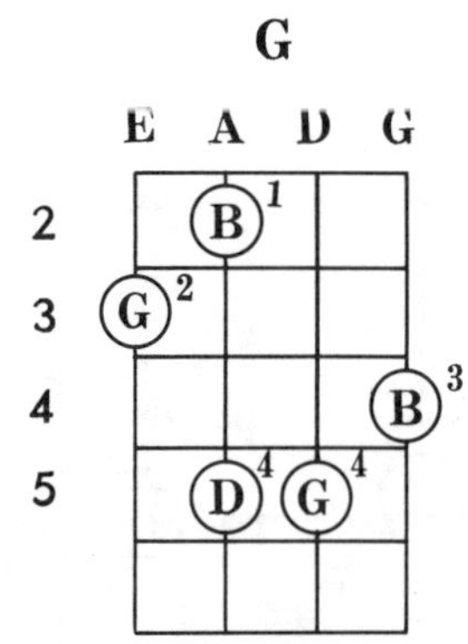

Subdominant

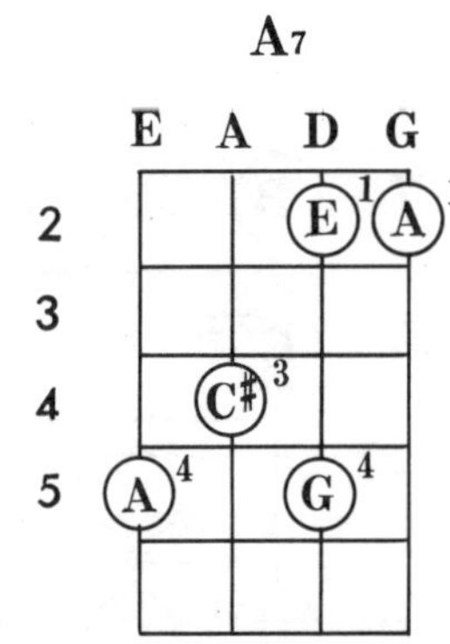

Dominant 7th

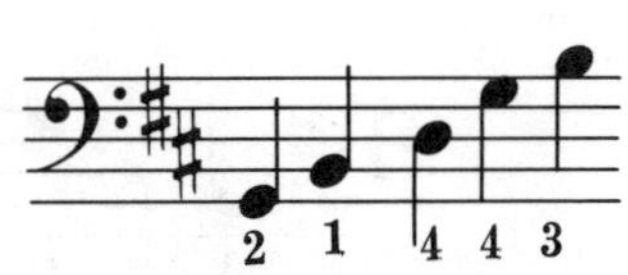

PRIMARY FORMS

E♭ MAJOR

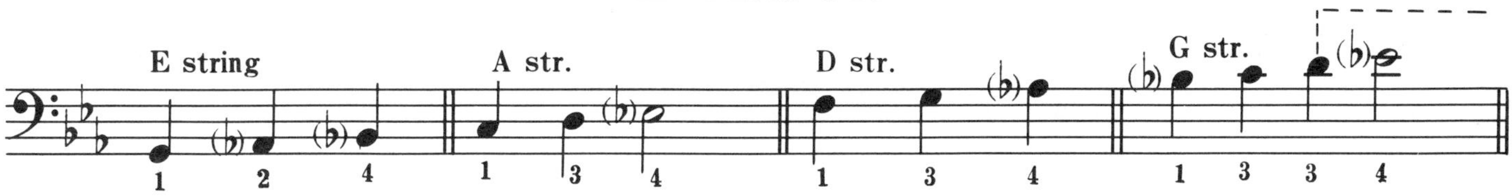

IIInd POSITION

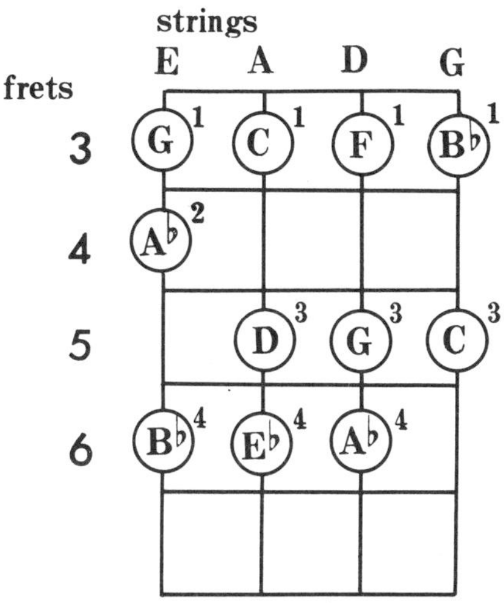

ARPEGGIOS

E♭

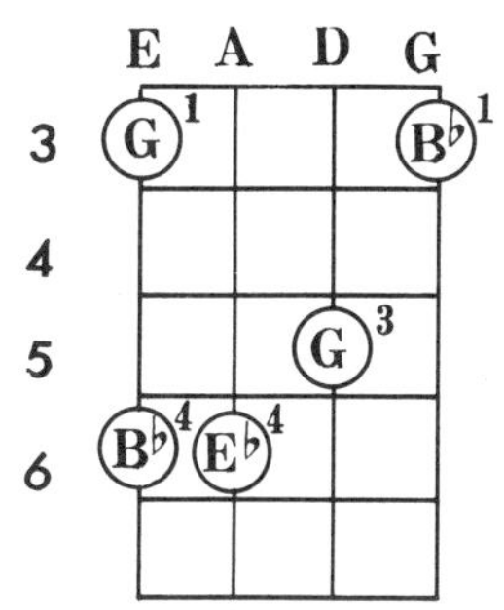

Tonic

A♭

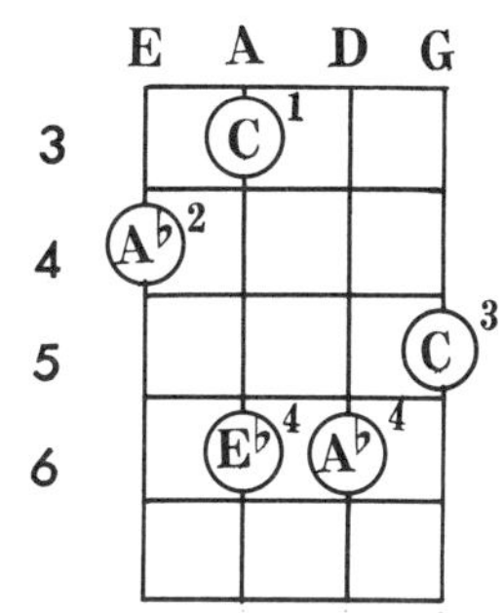

Subdominant

B♭7

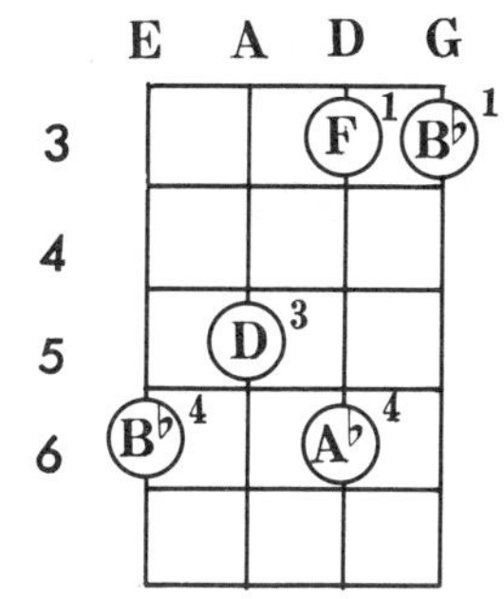

Dominant 7th

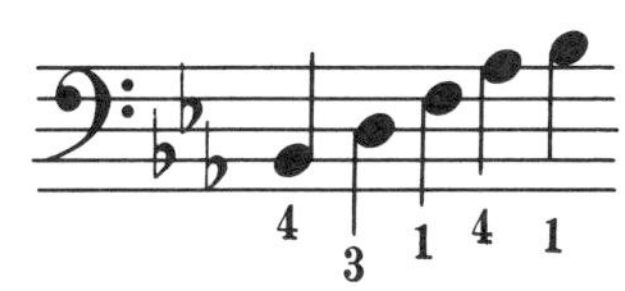

A MAJOR

IXth POSITION

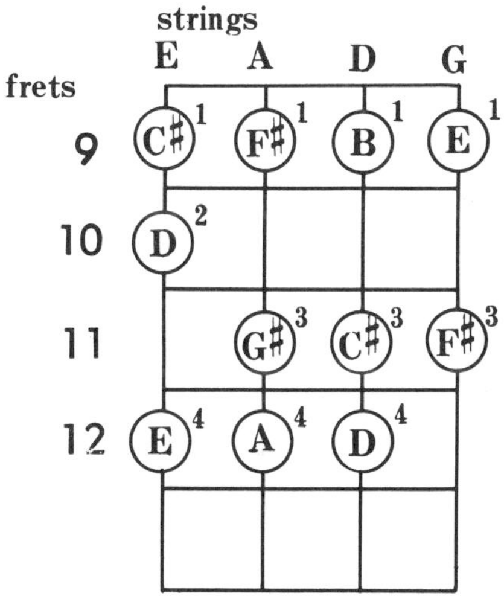

ARPEGGIOS

A

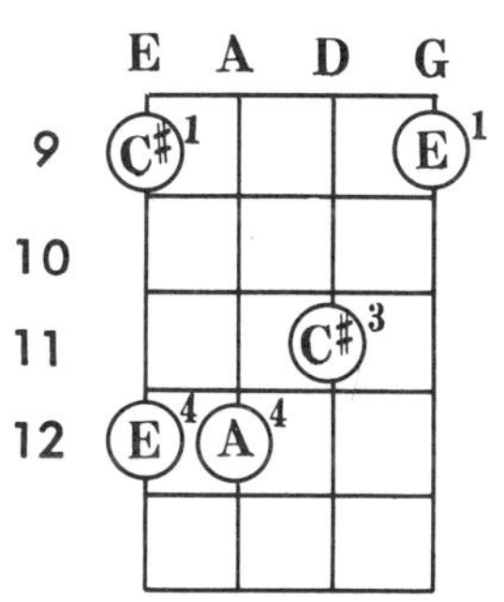

Tonic

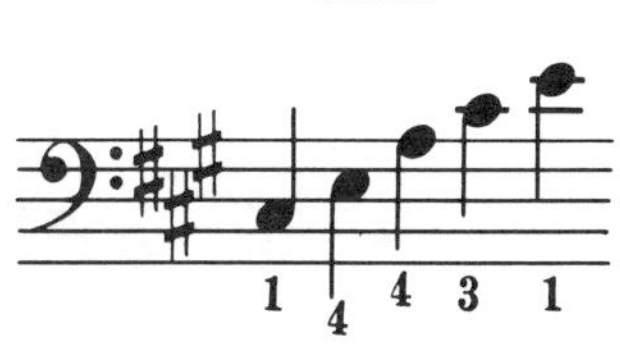

D

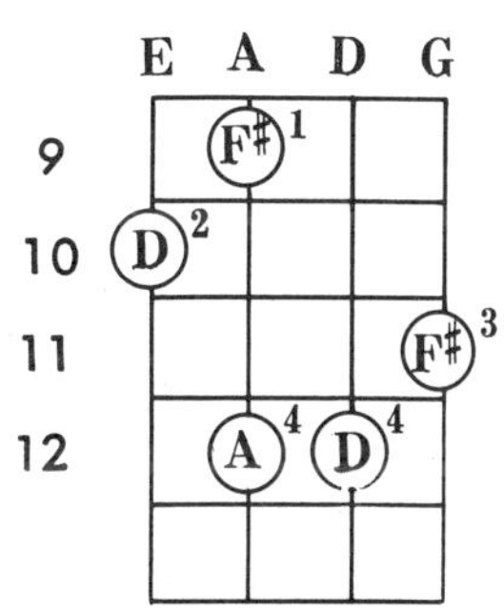

Subdominant

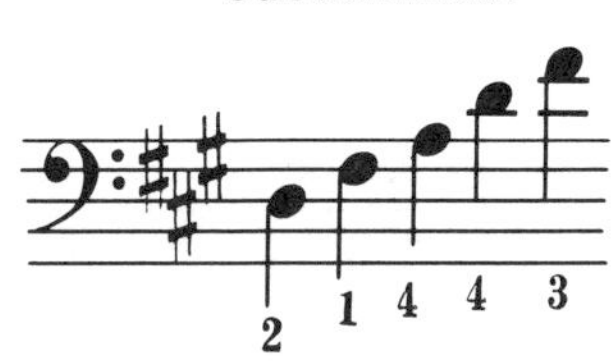

E7

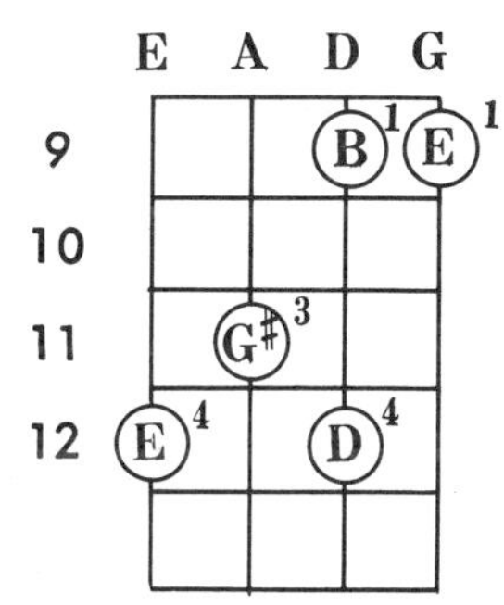

Dominant 7th

PRIMARY FORMS

A♭ MAJOR

VIIIth POSITION

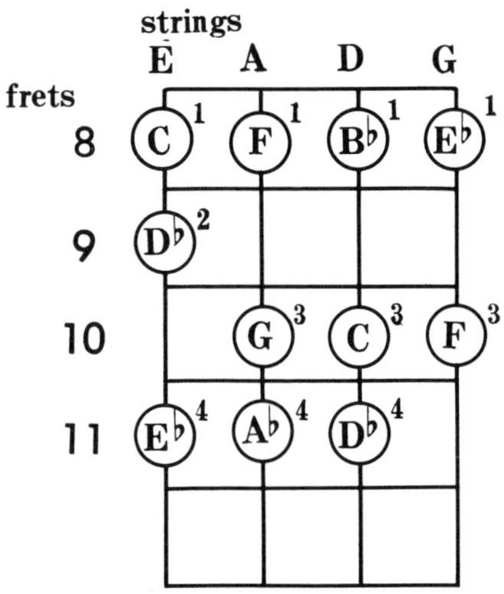

ARPEGGIOS

A♭

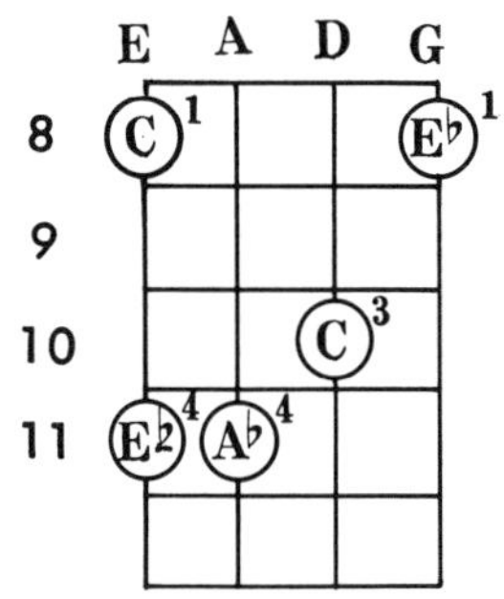

Tonic

D♭

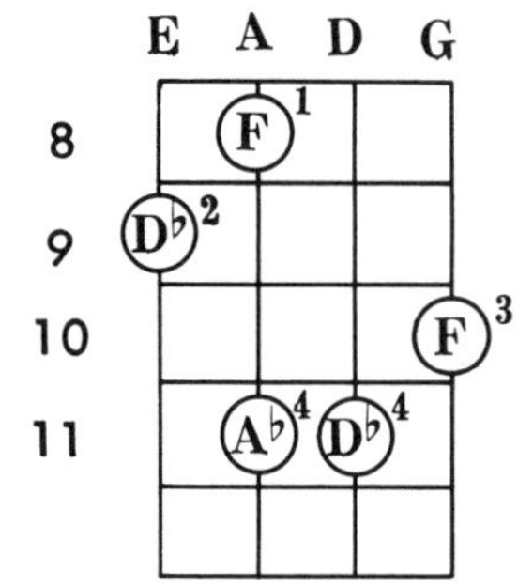

Subdominant

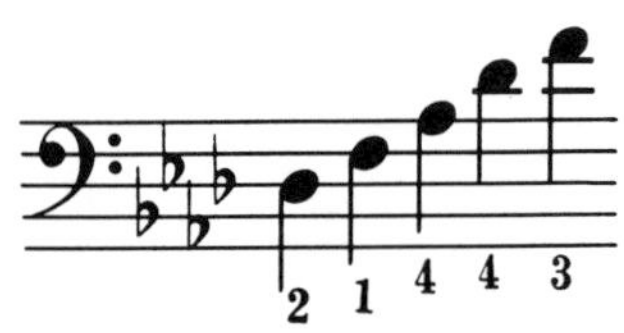

E♭$_7$

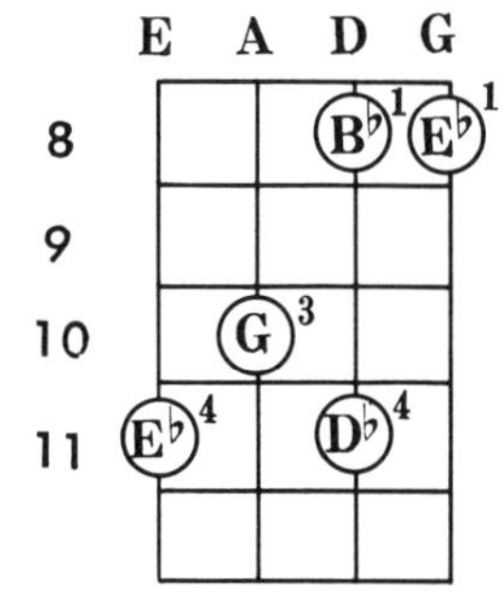

Dominant 7th

E MAJOR

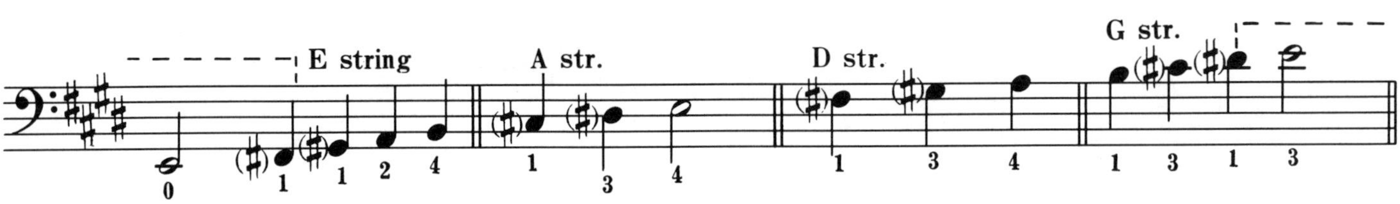

IVth POSITION

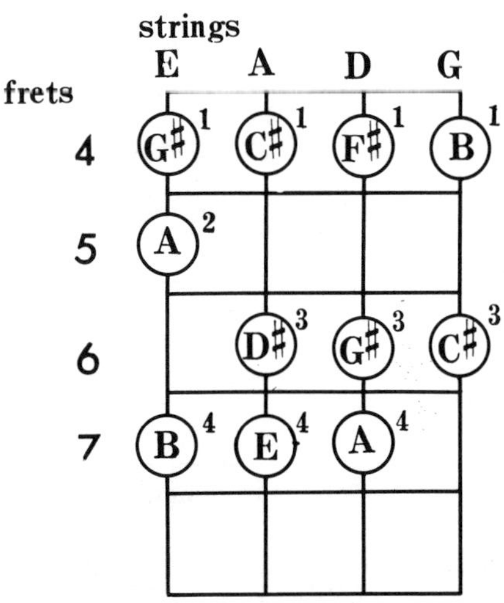

ARPEGGIOS

E

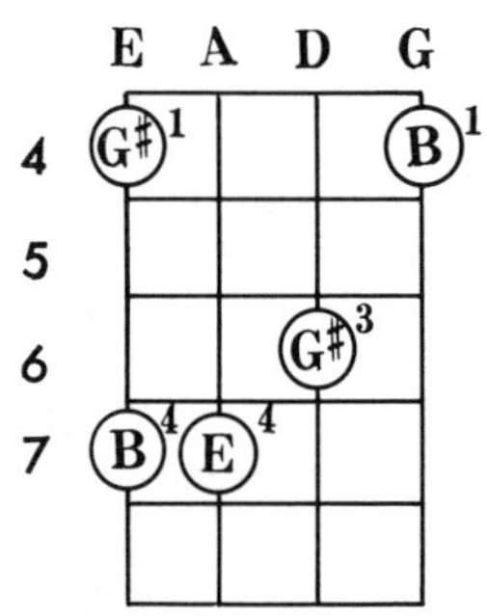

Tonic

A

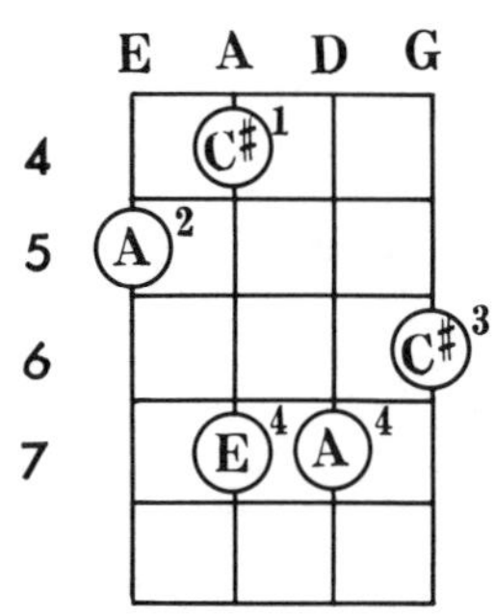

Subdominant

B$_7$

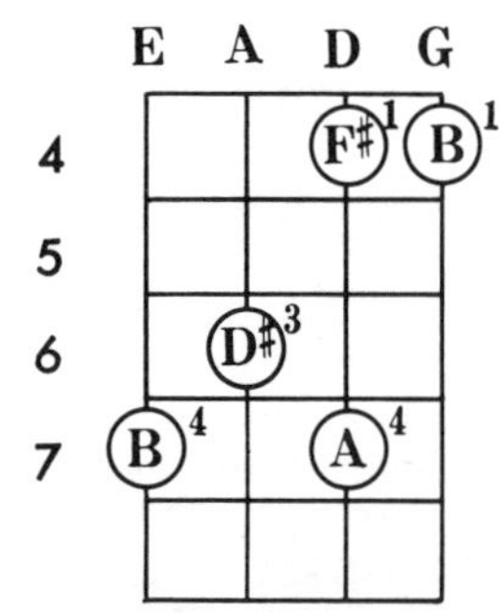

Dominant 7th

PRIMARY FORMS

D♭ MAJOR

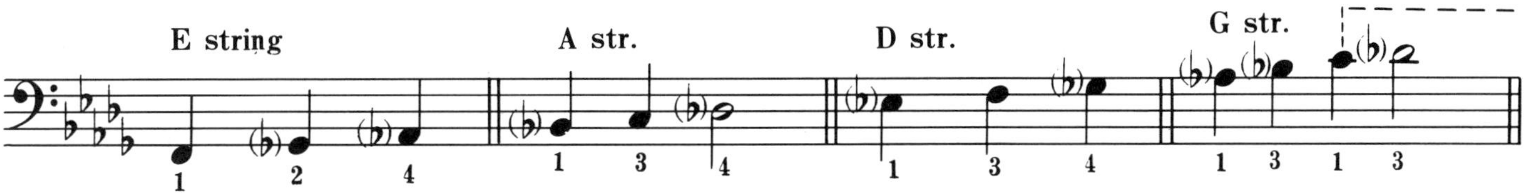

Ist POSITION

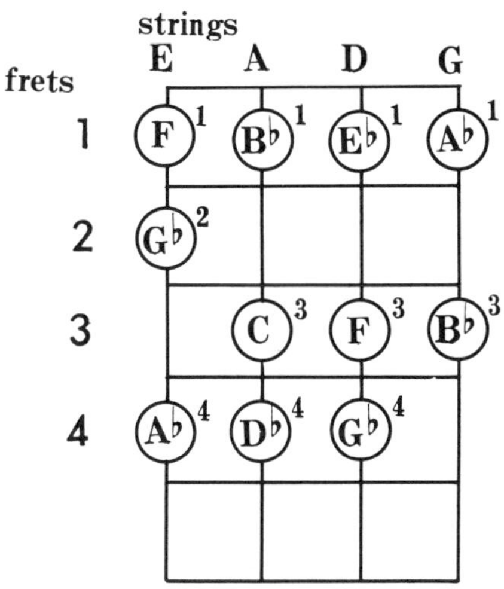

ARPEGGIOS

D♭

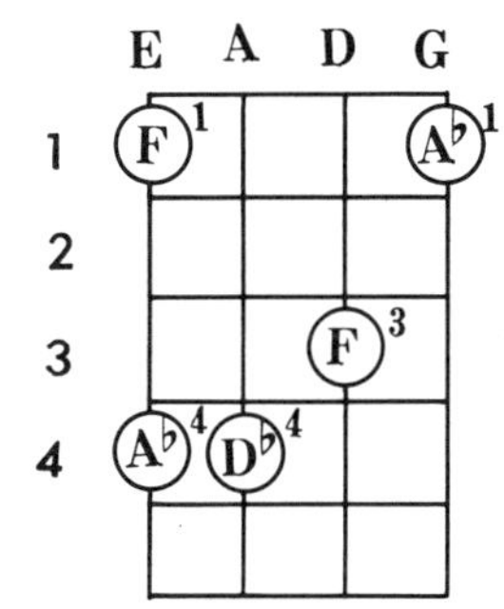

Tonic

G♭

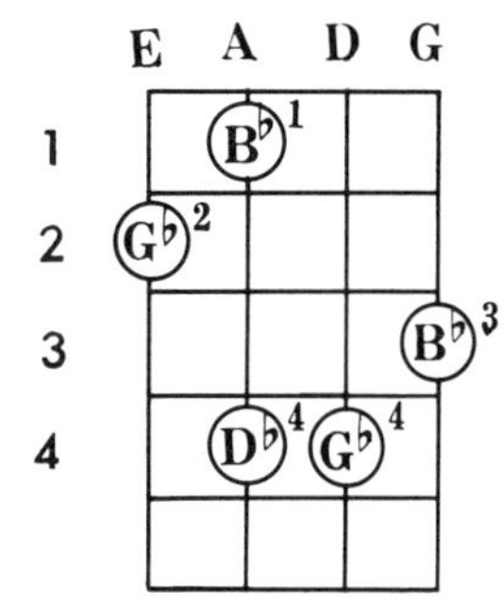

Subdominant

A♭7

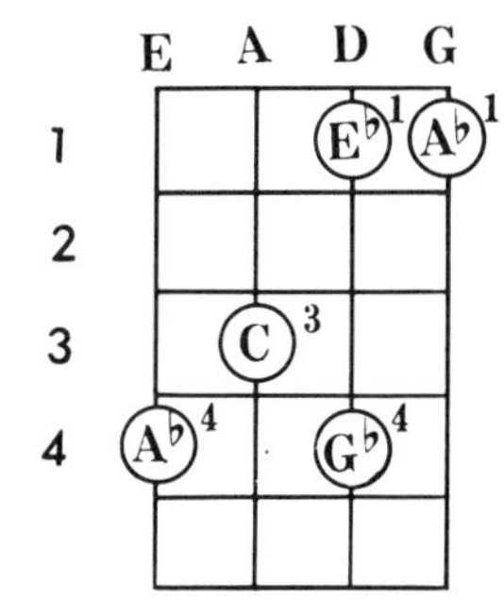

Dominant 7th

B MAJOR

XIth POSITION

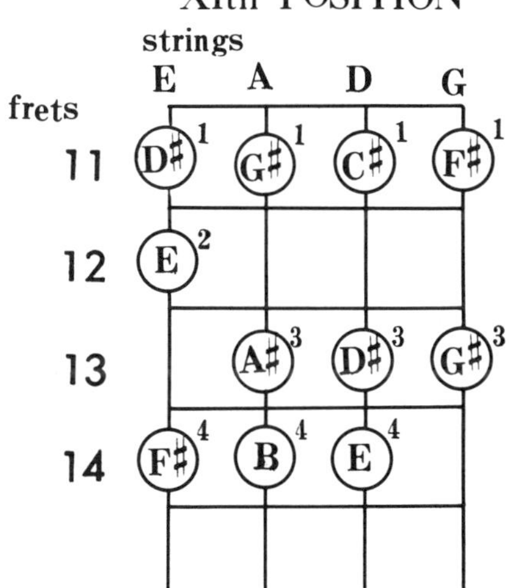

ARPEGGIOS

B

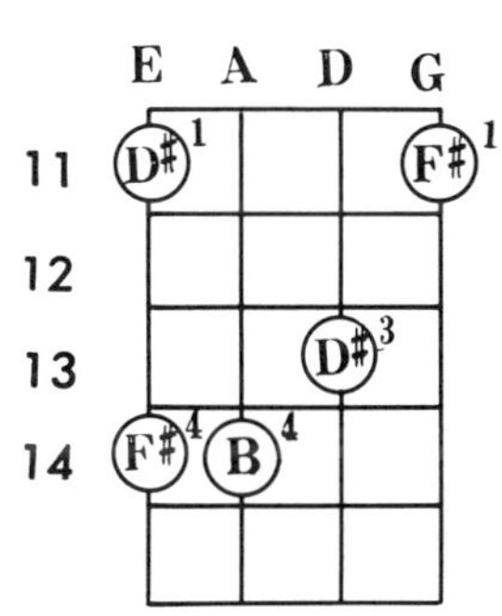

Tonic

E

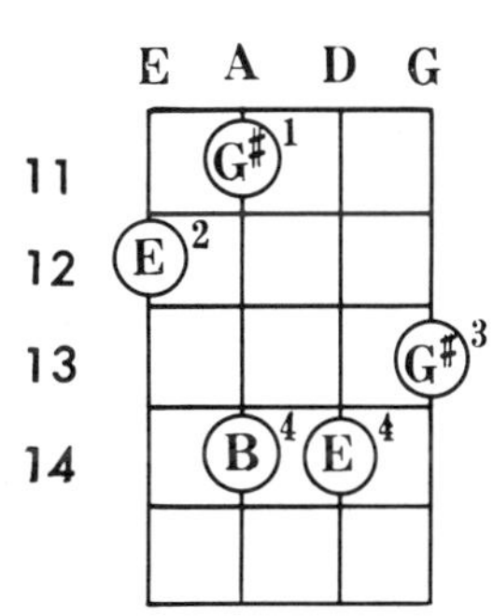

Subdominant

F♯7

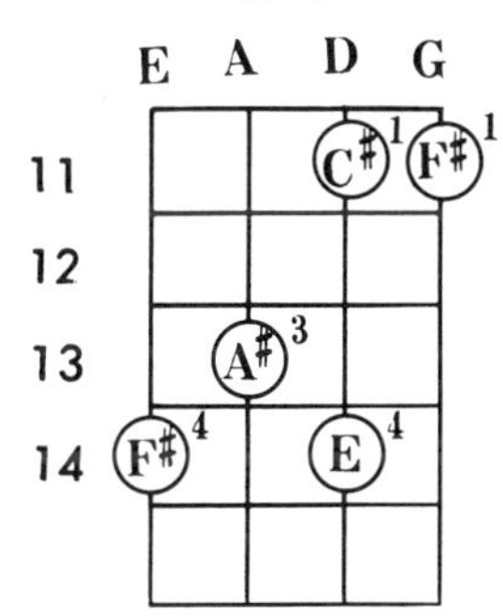

Dominant 7th

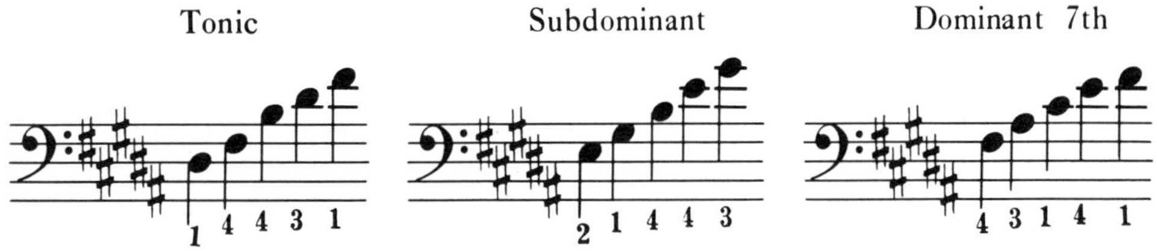

PRIMARY FORMS

G♭ MAJOR

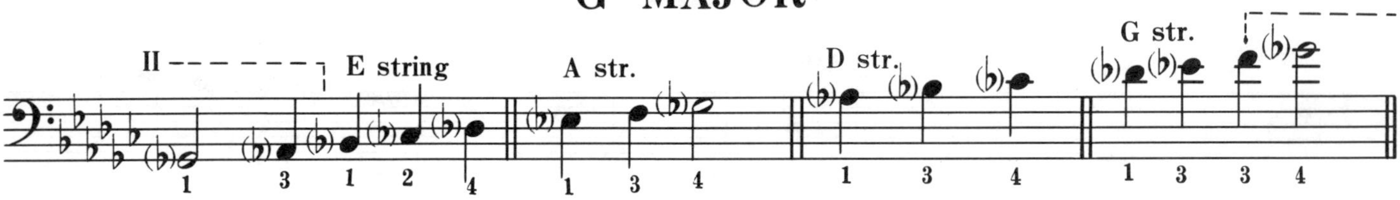

VIth POSITION

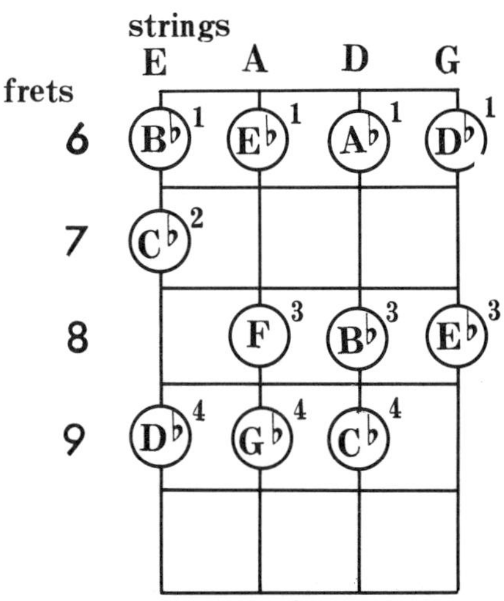

Note that these two keys are enharmonically equivalent.

ARPEGGIOS

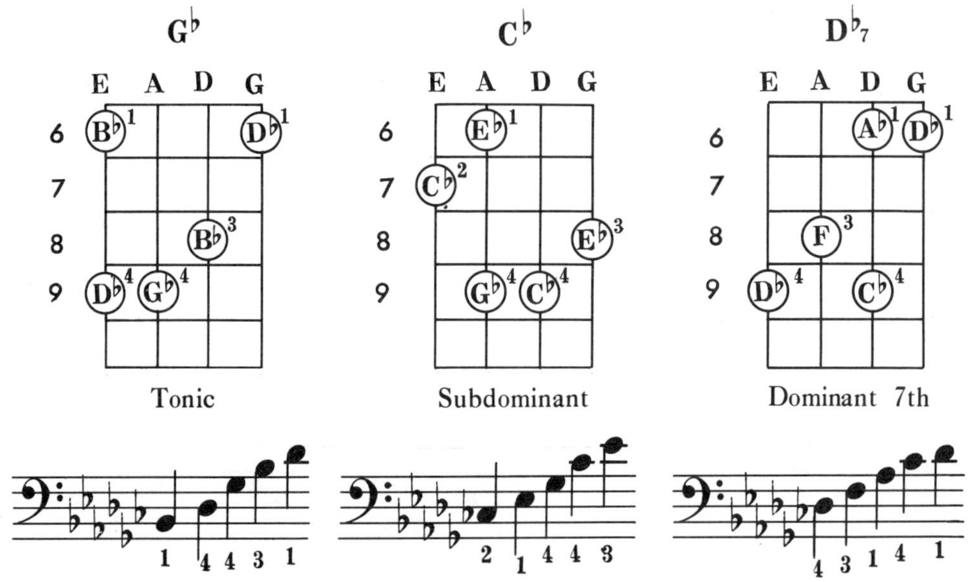

F♯ MAJOR

VIth POSITION

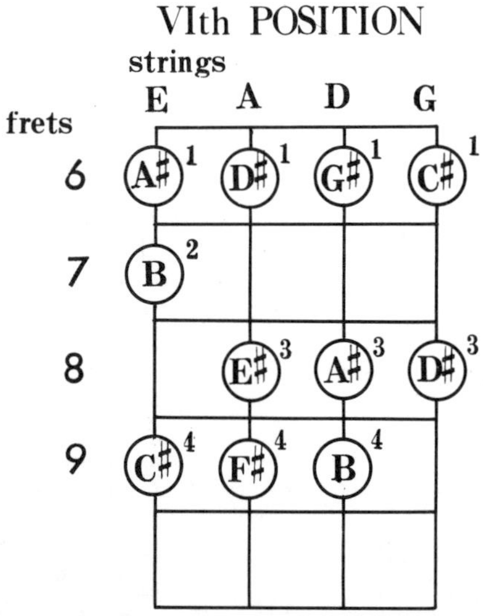

ARPEGGIOS

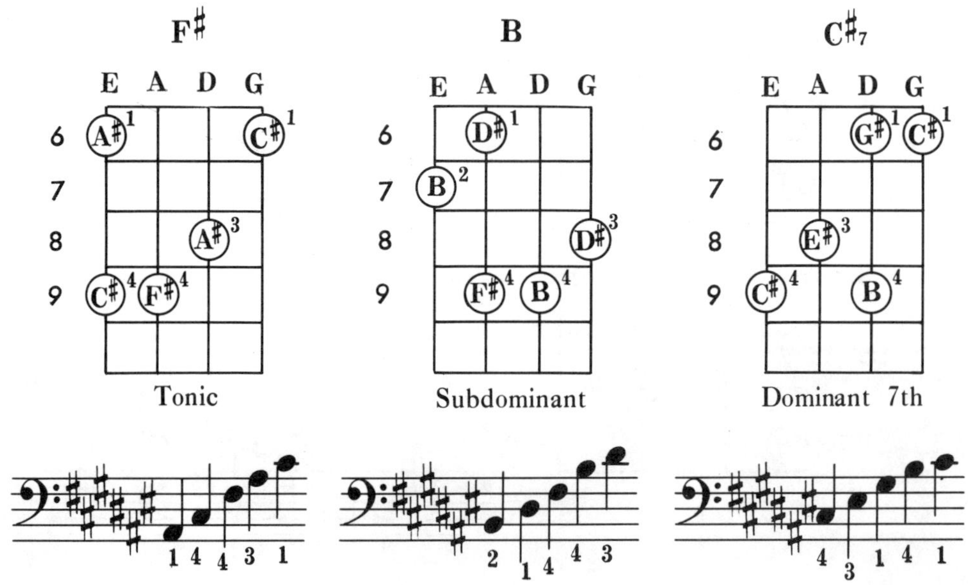

SECONDARY FORMS

C MAJOR

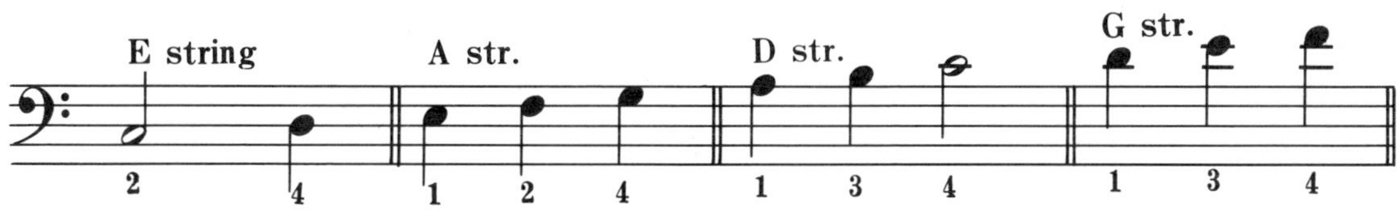

VIIth POSITION

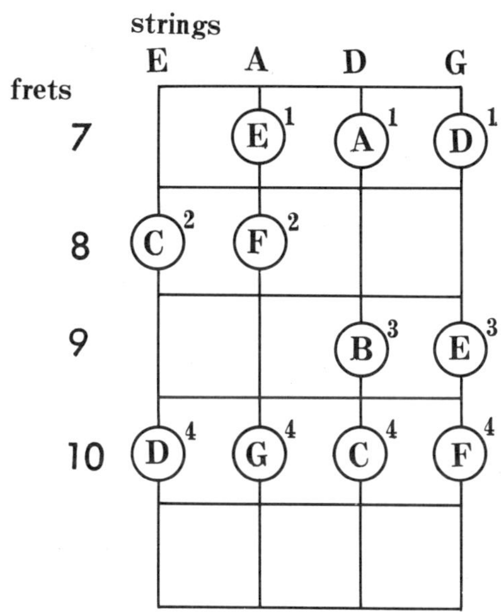

ARPEGGIOS

C

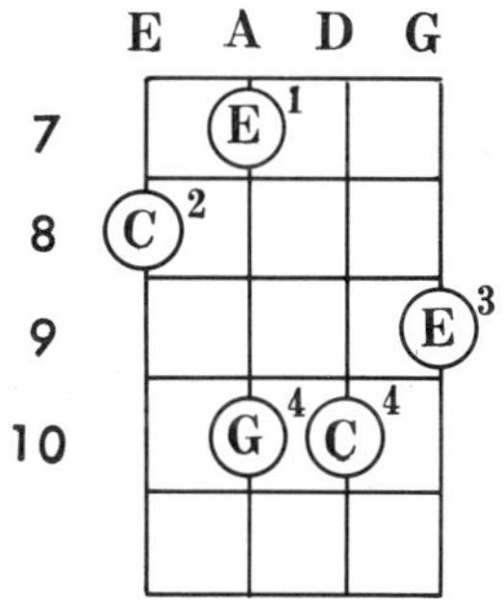

Tonic

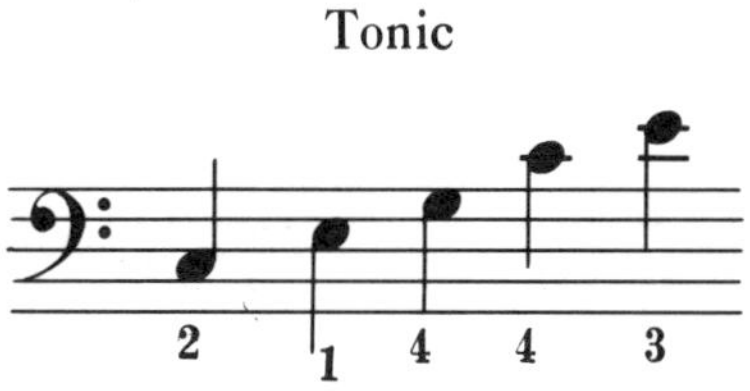

F

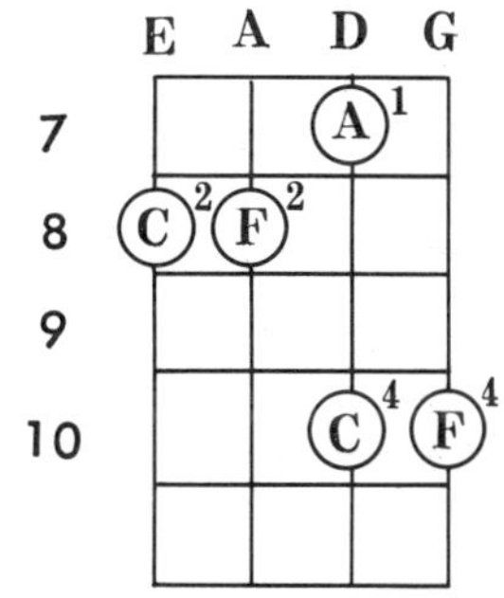

Subdominant

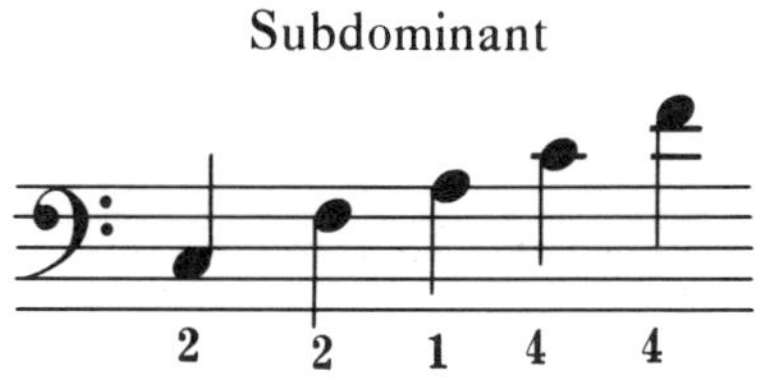

G7

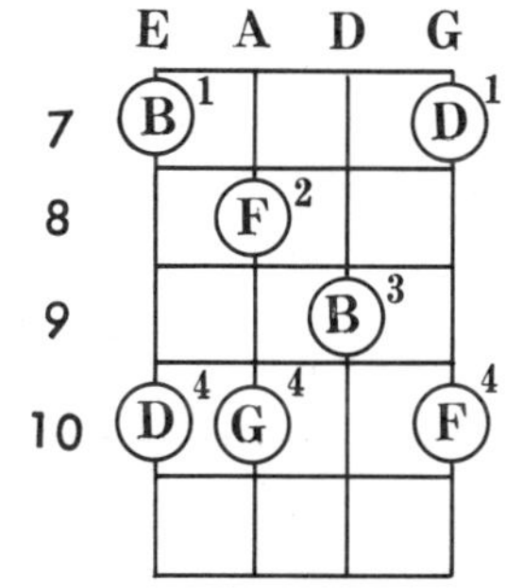

Dominant 7th

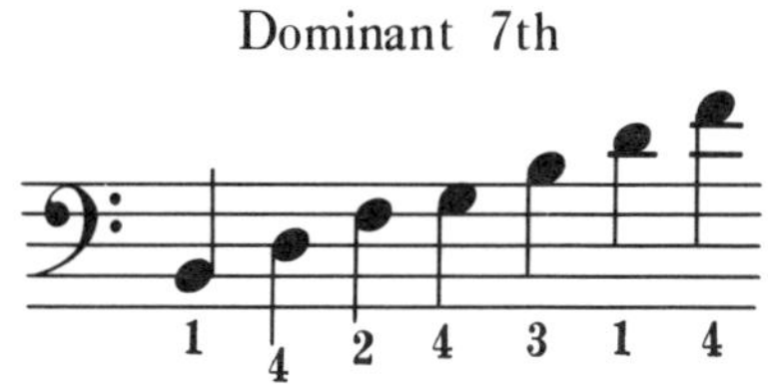

SECONDARY FORMS

F MAJOR

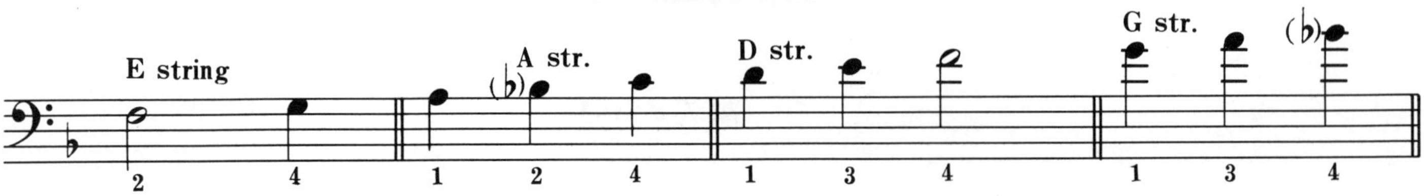

VIIth POSITION

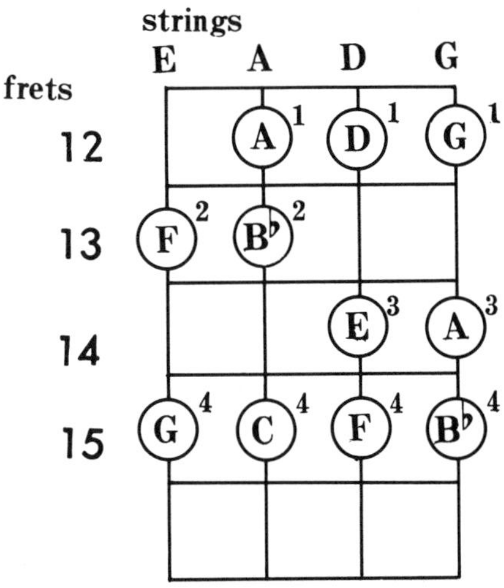

ARPEGGIOS

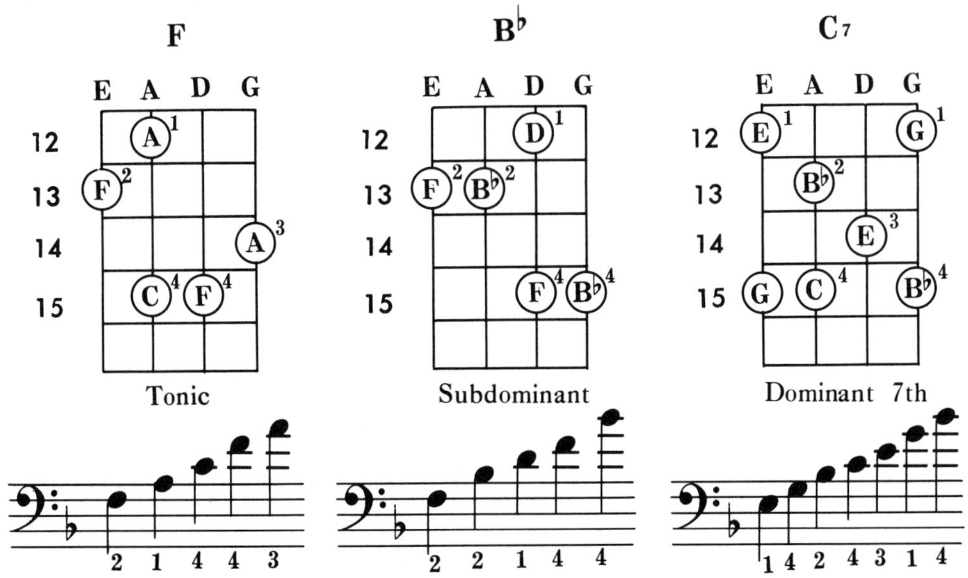

G MAJOR

IInd POSITION

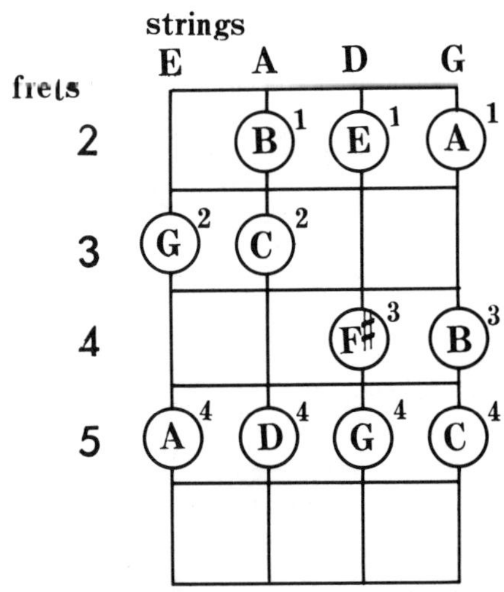

ARPEGGIOS

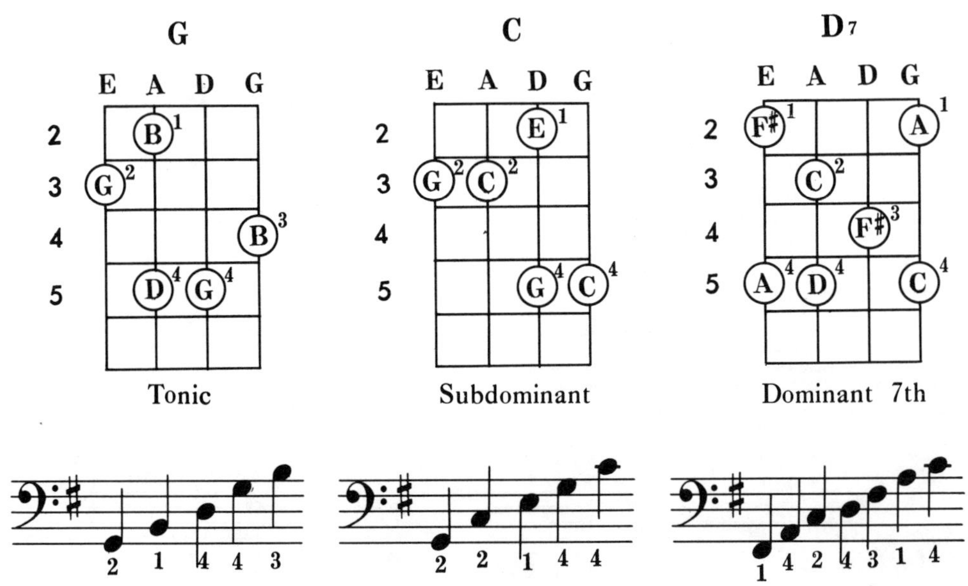

SECONDARY FORMS

B♭ MAJOR

Vth POSITION

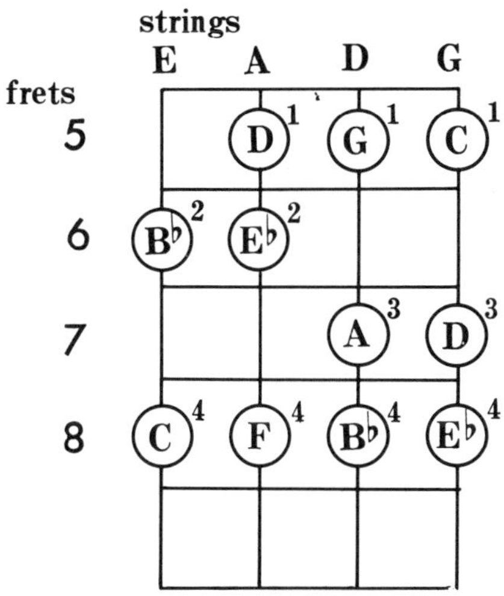

ARPEGGIOS

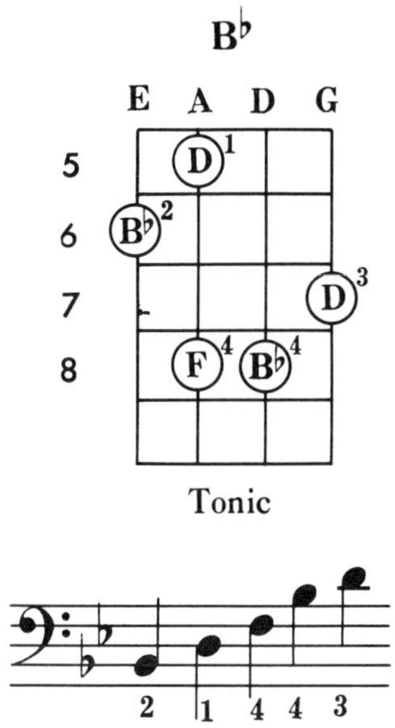

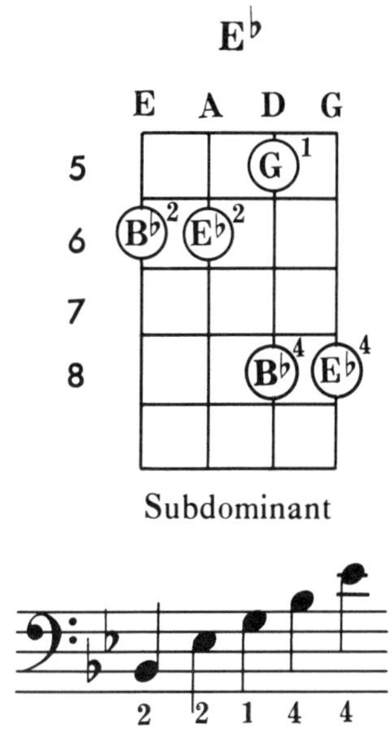

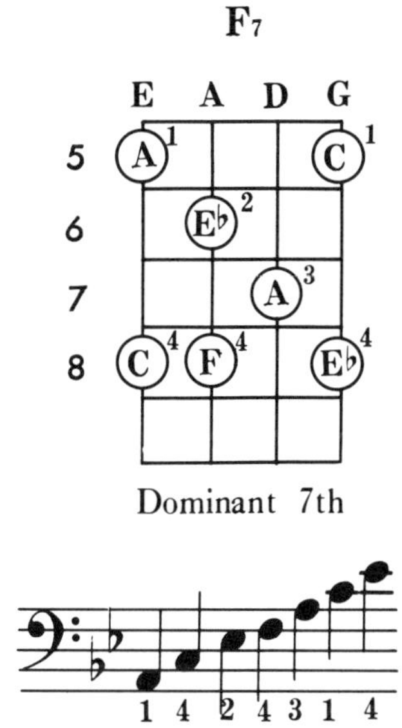

D MAJOR

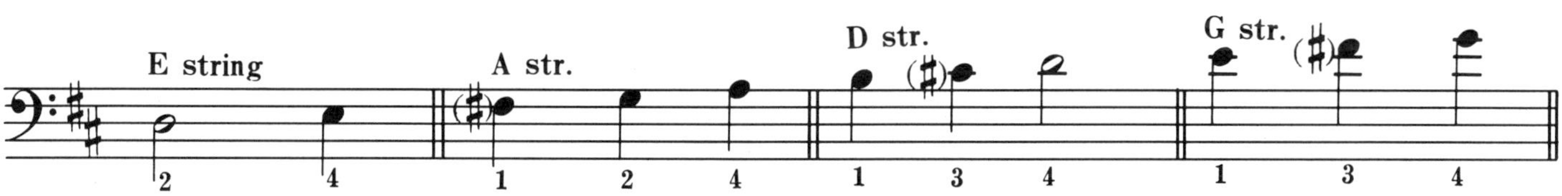

IXth POSITION

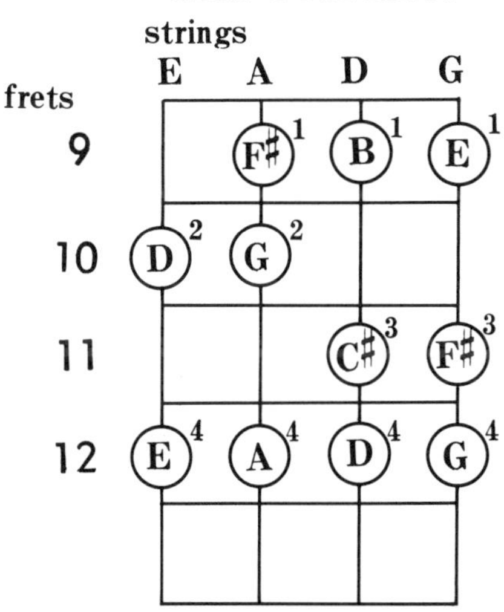

ARPEGGIOS

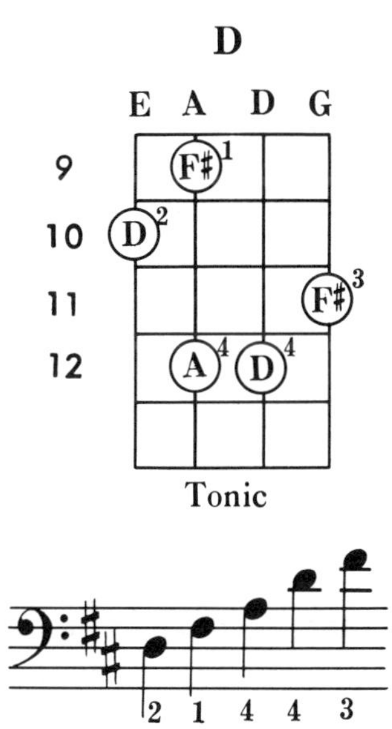

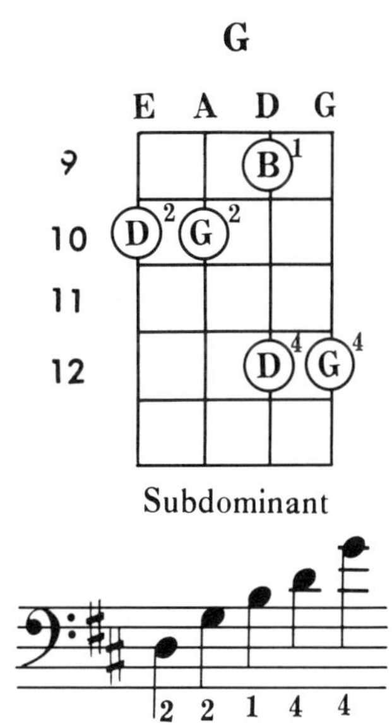

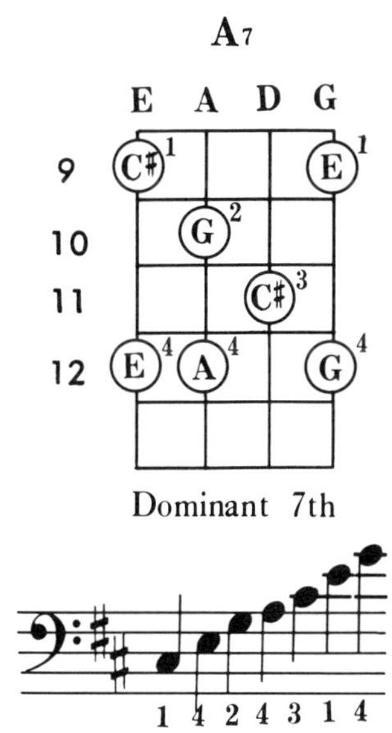

SECONDARY FORMS

E♭ MAJOR

Xth POSITION

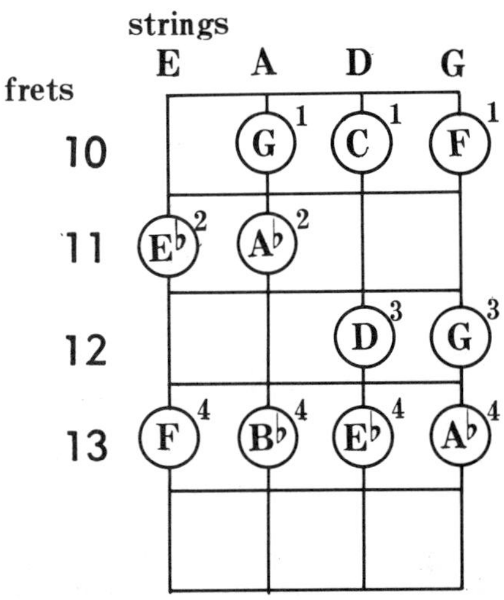

ARPEGGIOS

E♭

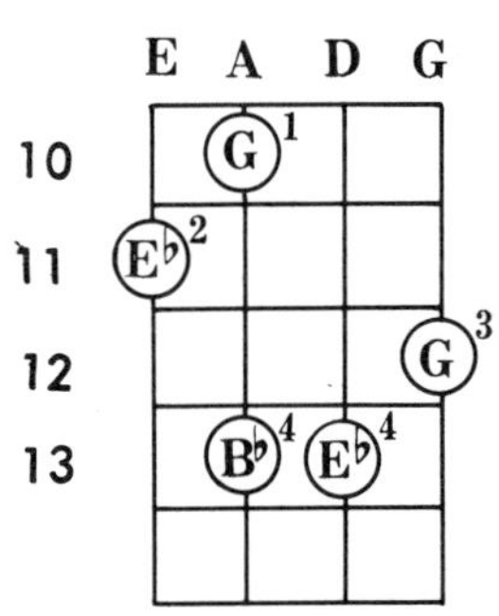

Tonic

A♭

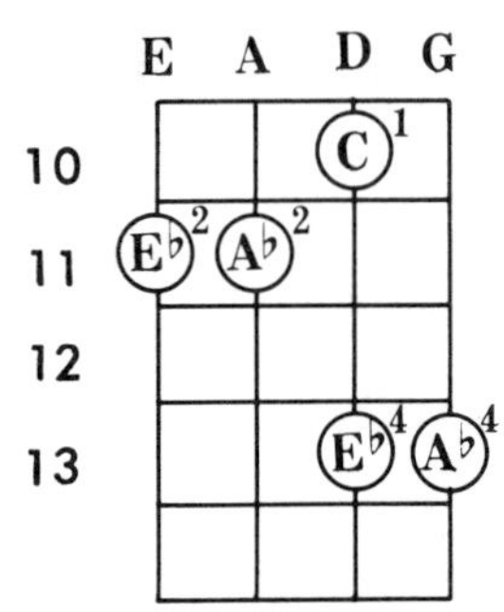

Subdominant

B♭7

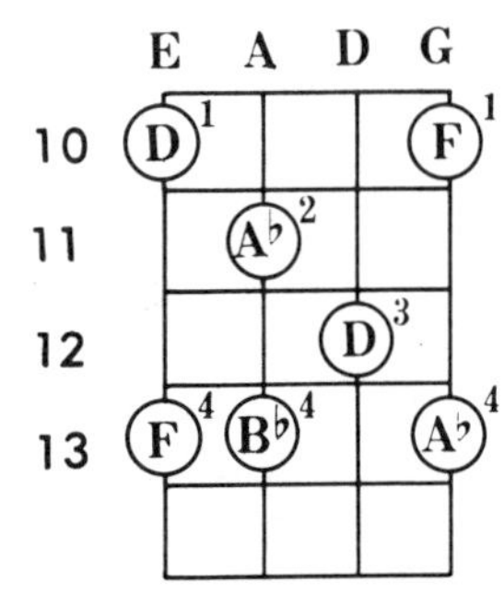

Dominant 7th

A MAJOR

IVth POSITION

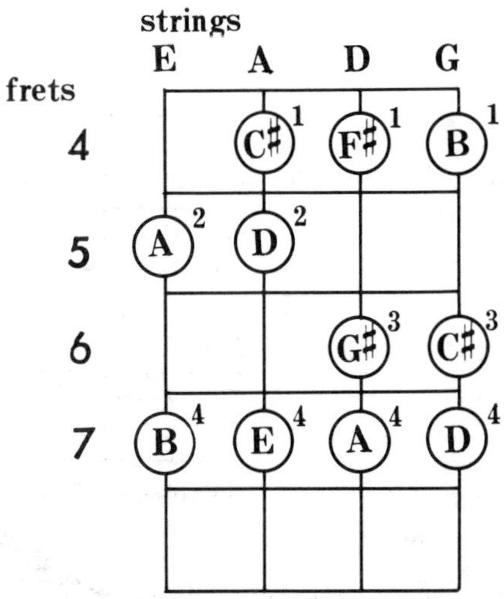

ARPEGGIOS

A

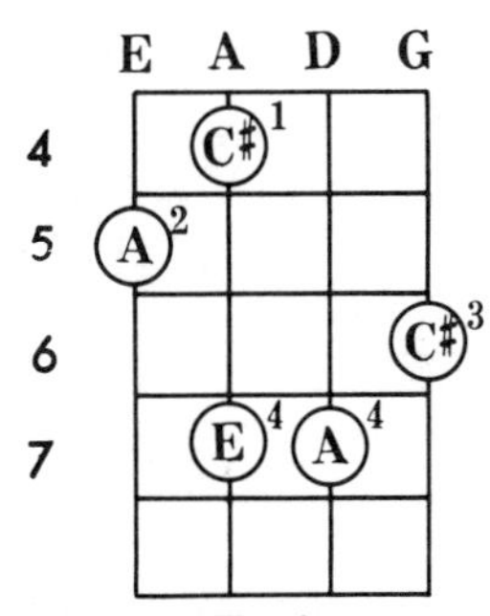

Tonic

D

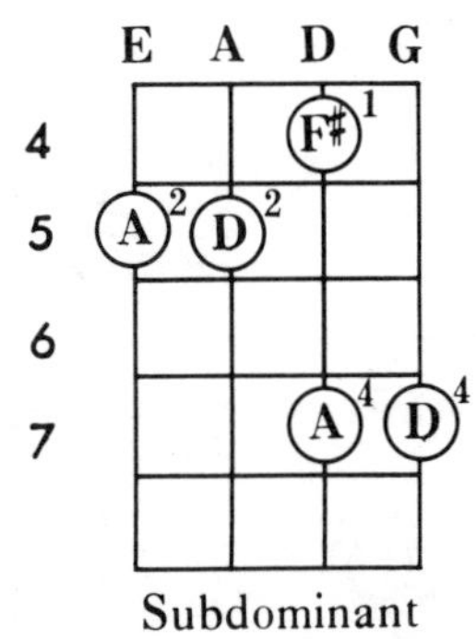

Subdominant

E7

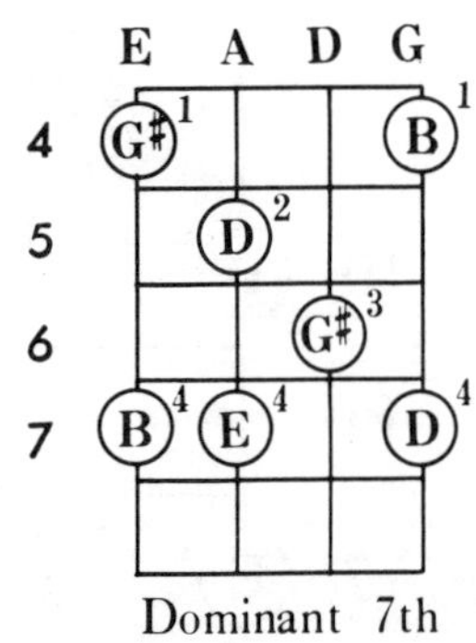

Dominant 7th

SECONDARY FORMS

A♭ MAJOR

IIInd POSITION

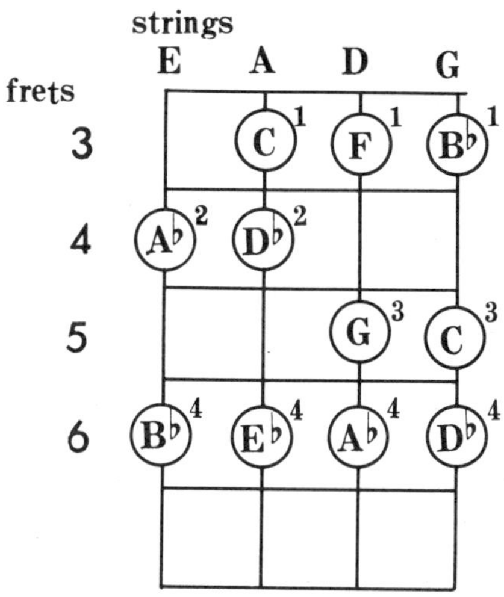

ARPEGGIOS

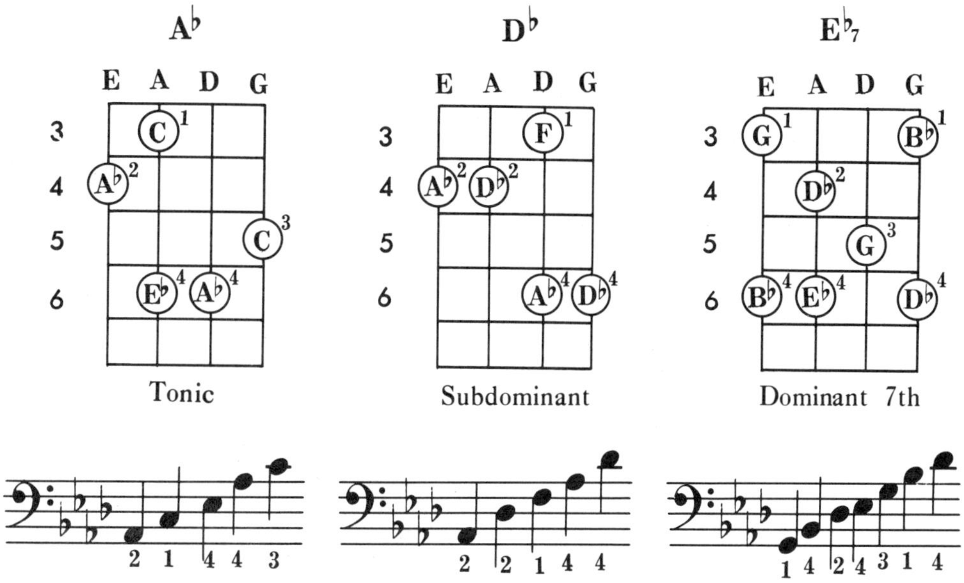

E MAJOR

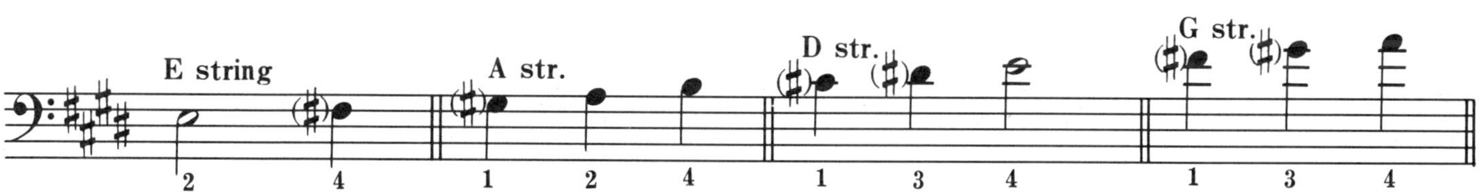

XIth POSITION

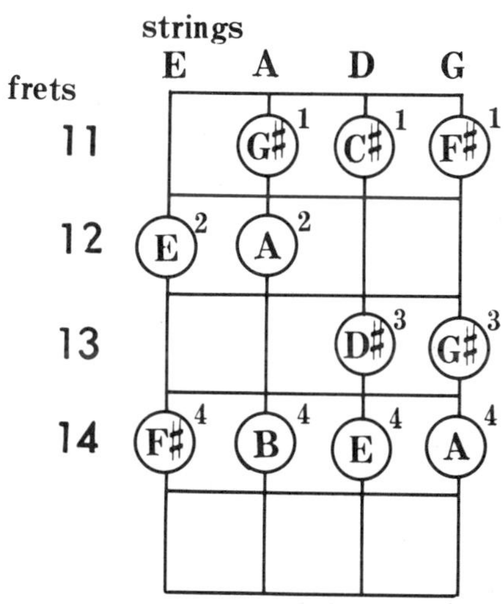

ARPEGGIOS

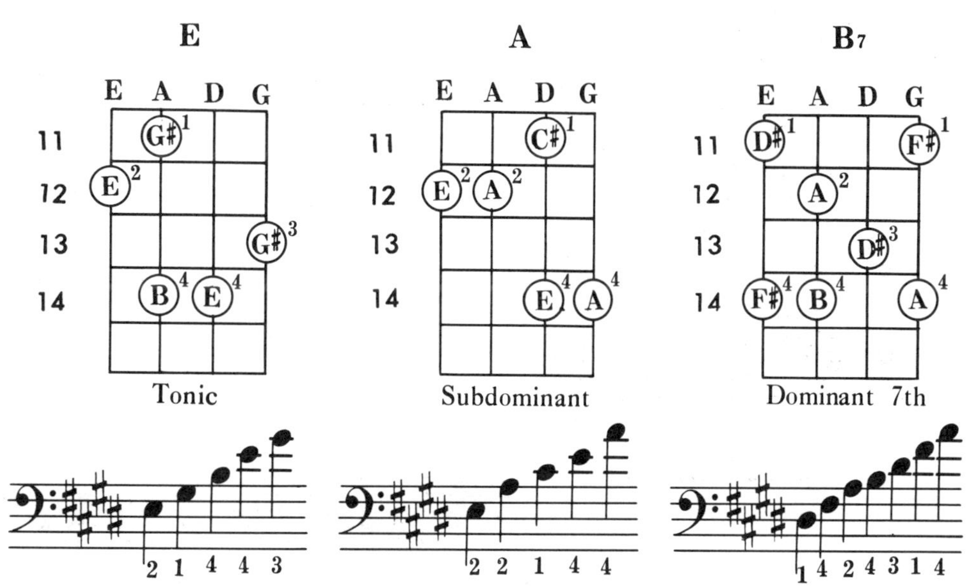

SECONDARY FORMS

D♭ MAJOR

VIIIth POSITION

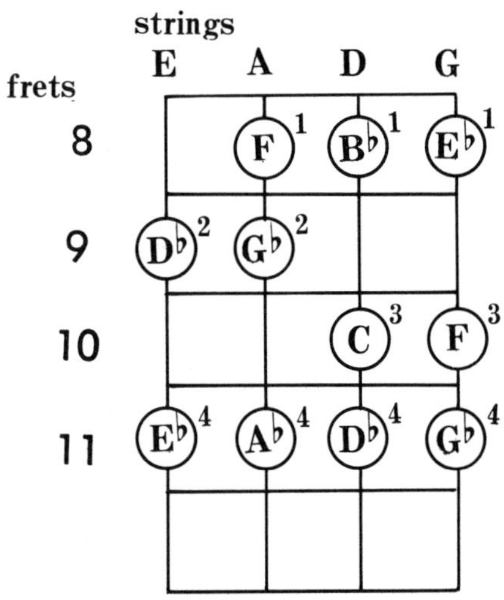

ARPEGGIOS

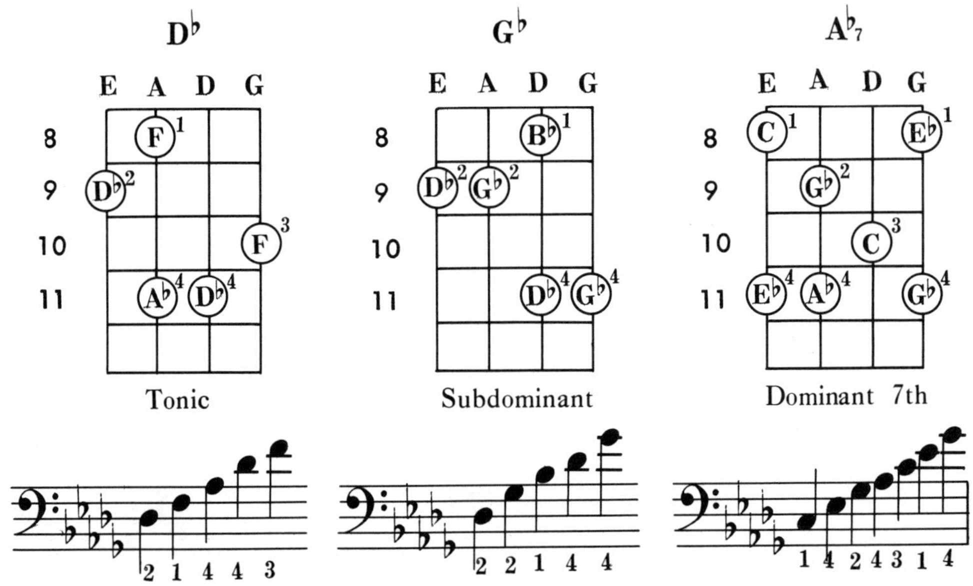

B MAJOR

VIth POSITION

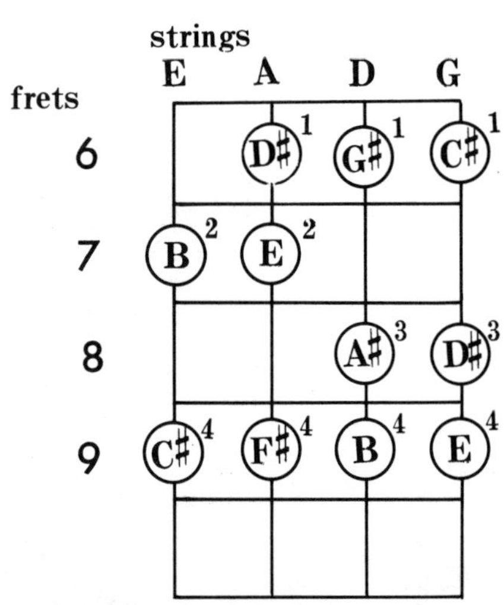

ARPEGGIOS

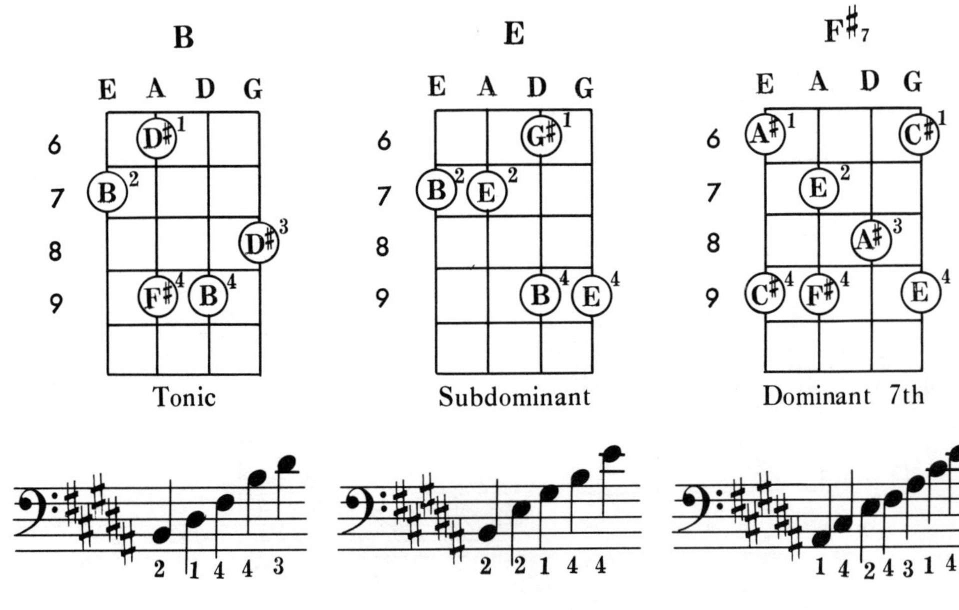

SECONDARY FORMS

G♭ MAJOR

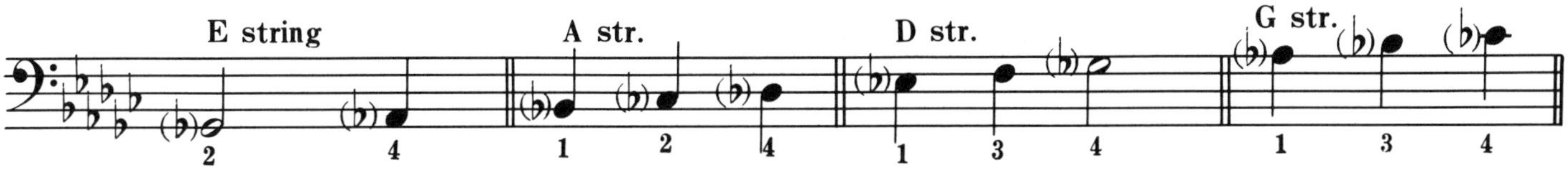

Ist POSITION

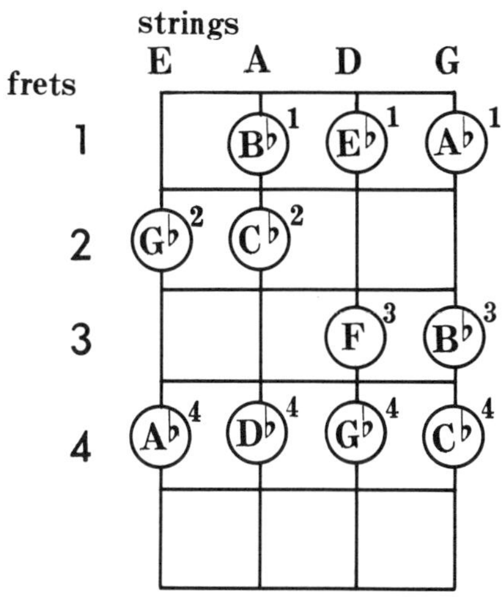

Note that these two keys are enharmonically equivalent.

ARPEGGIOS

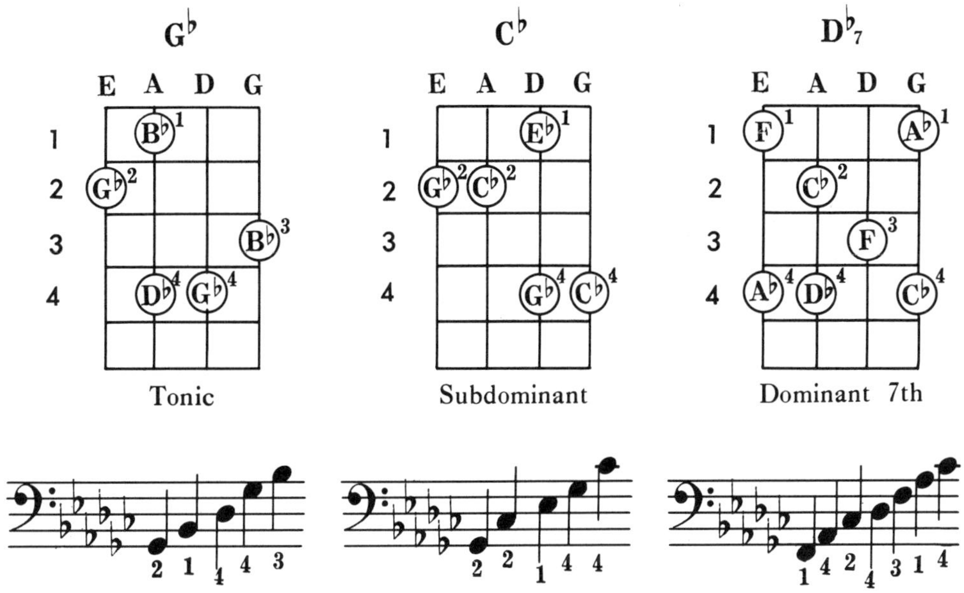

F♯ MAJOR

Ist POSITION

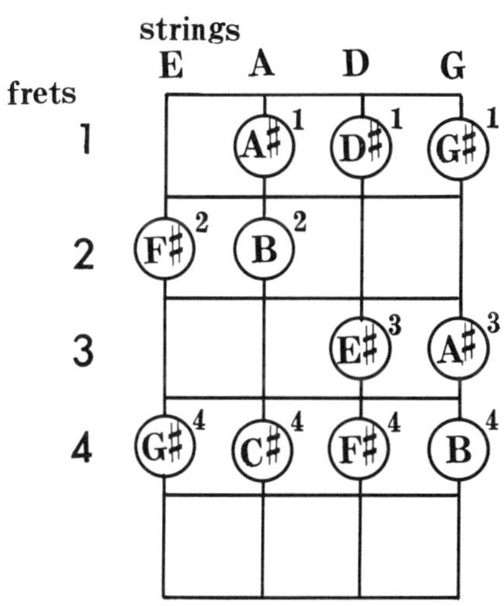

ARPEGGIOS

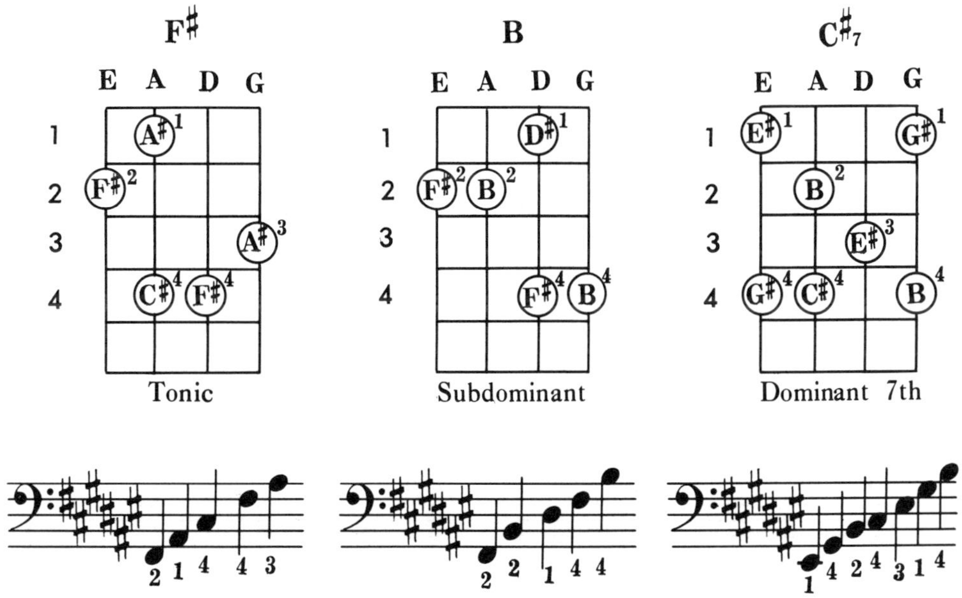

TERTIARY FORMS

C MAJOR

Vth POSITION

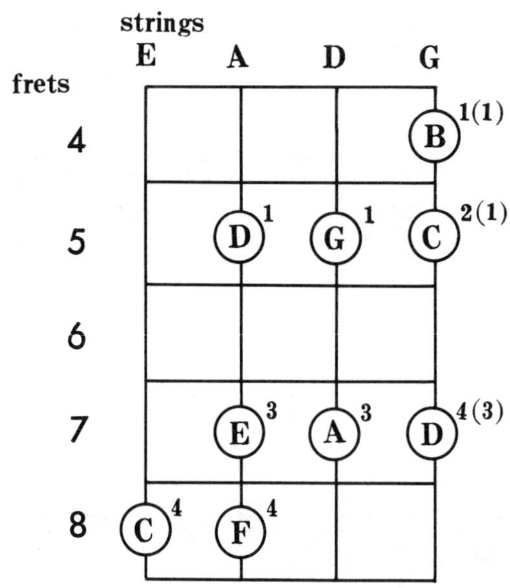

ARPEGGIOS

C

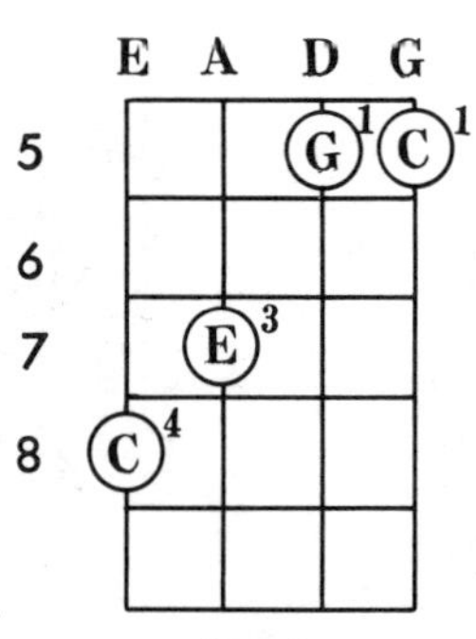

Tonic

F

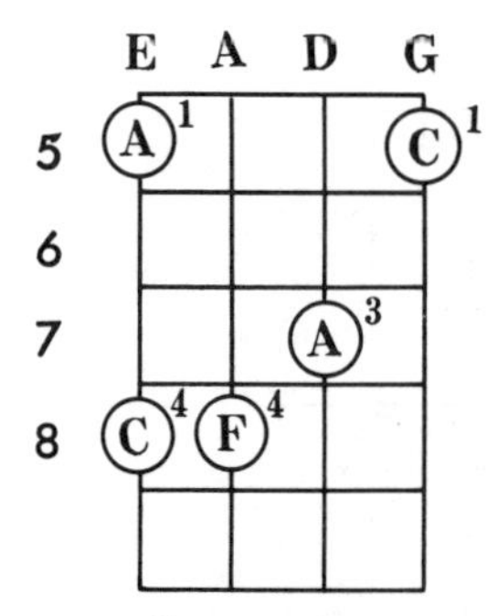

Subdominant

G7

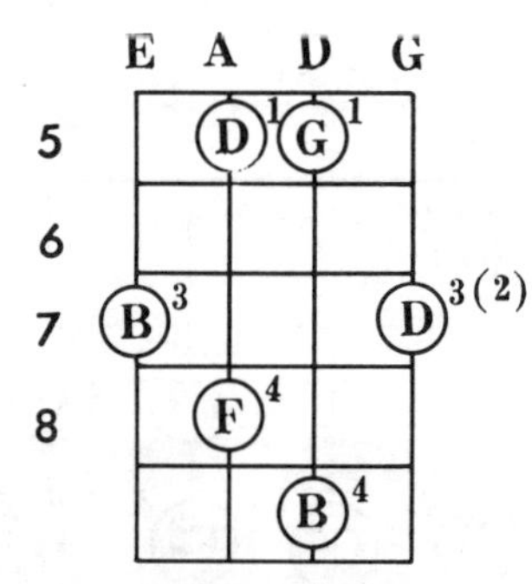

Dominant 7th

TERTIARY FORMS

F MAJOR

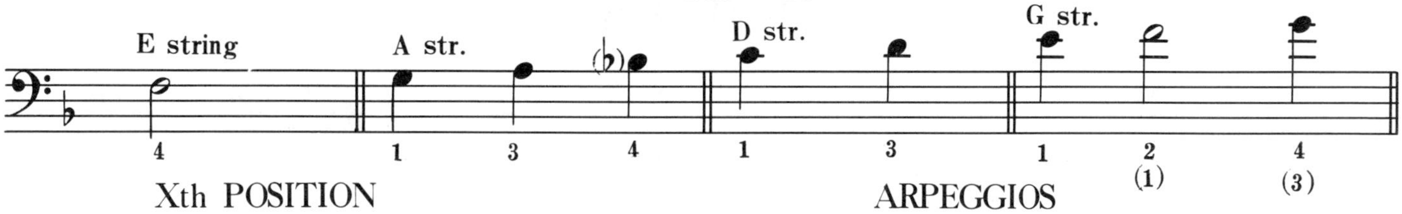

Xth POSITION

ARPEGGIOS

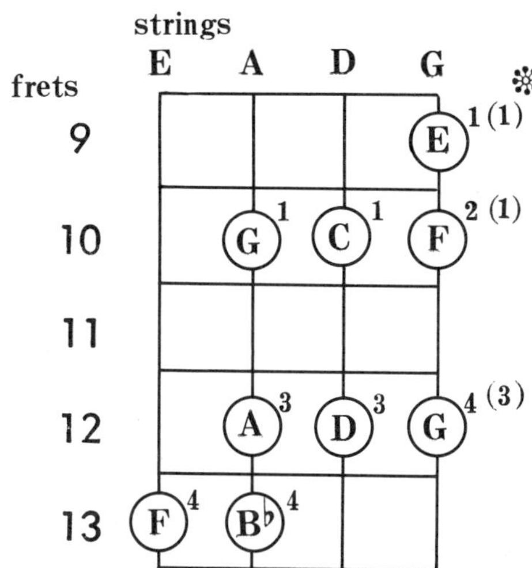

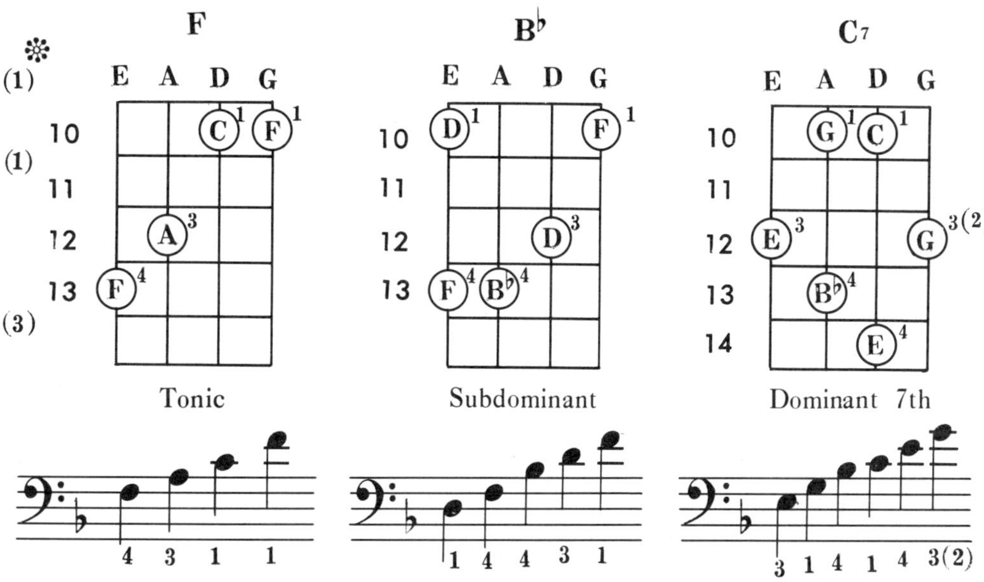

* The extension to a fret beyond the normal position is called a fifth fret stretch. Alternate fingering will depend on particular playing situations.

G MAJOR

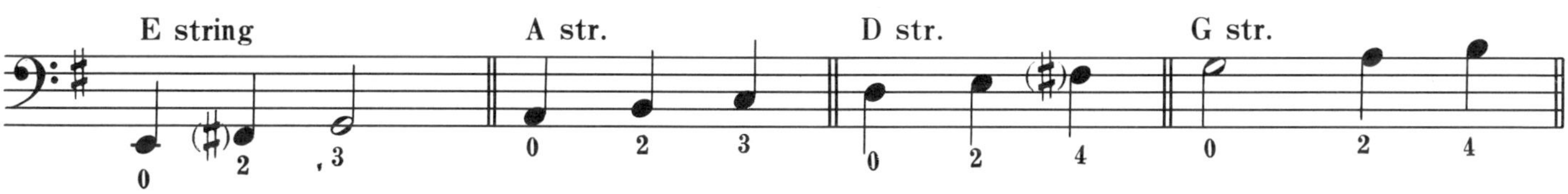

OPEN POSITION

ARPEGGIOS

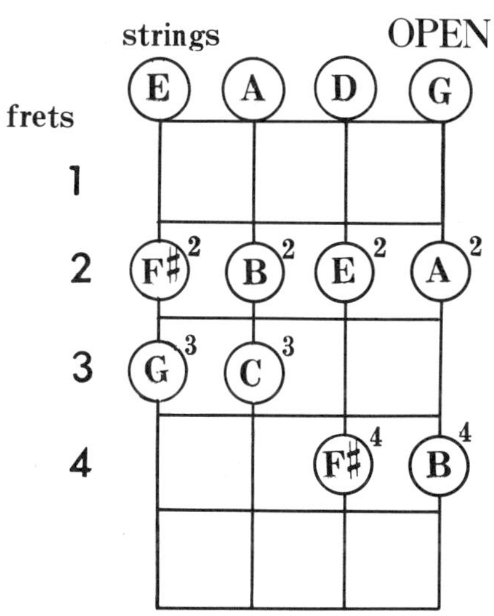

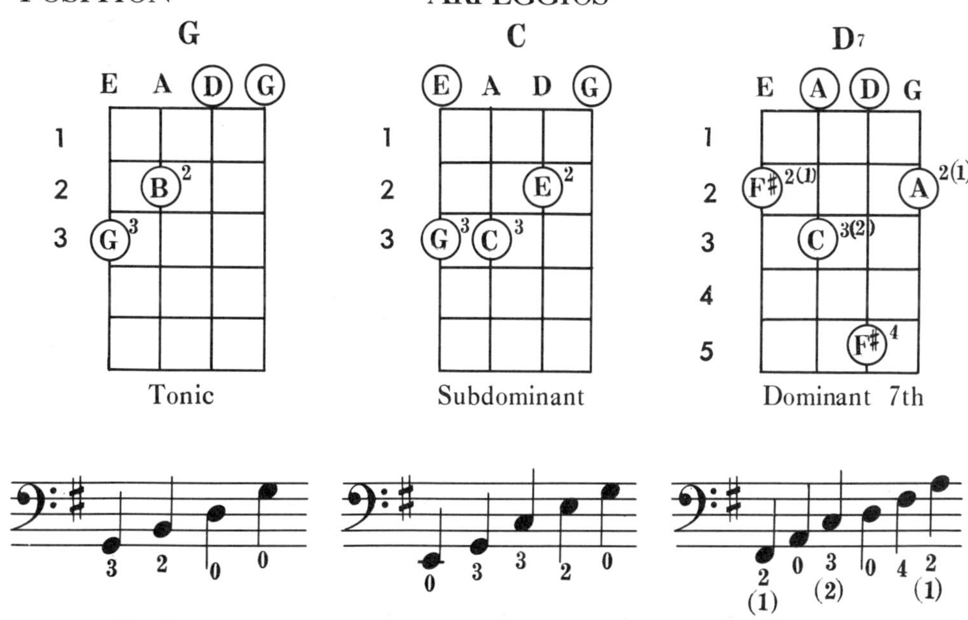

Note that this form departs from the normal tertiary form. It looks like the first presented C scale on page 8 with the exception of F ♯ for F. The tertiary form for G is played precisely as other tertiary forms 1 octave higher in the 12th position. The lower scale is here presented because of its greater useability.

TERTIARY FORMS

B♭ MAJOR

IIIrd POSITION

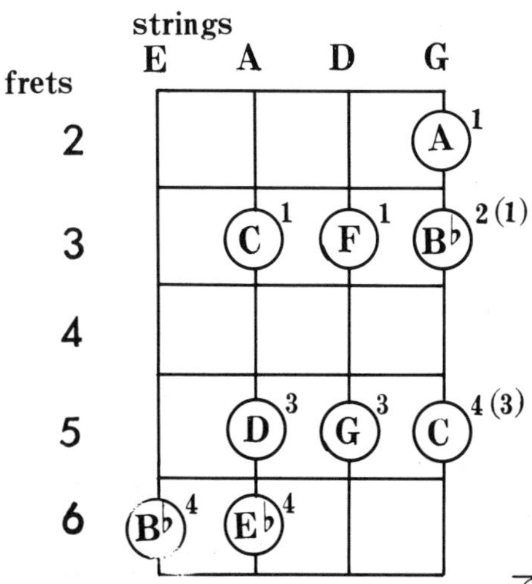

ARPEGGIOS

B♭

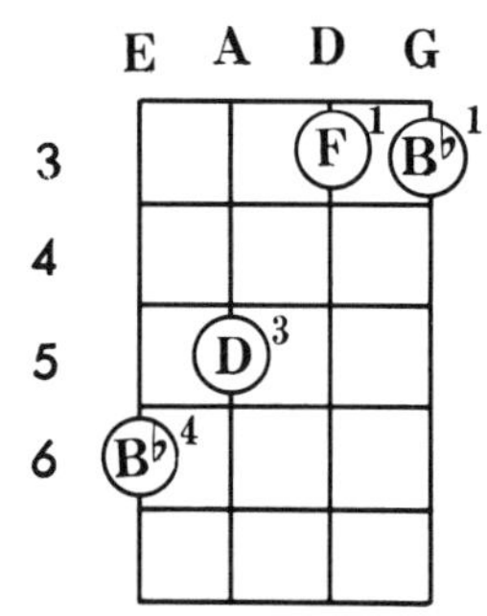

Tonic

E♭

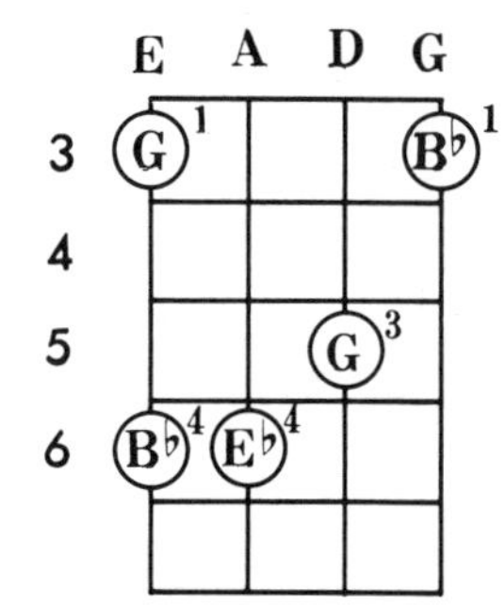

Subdominant

F7

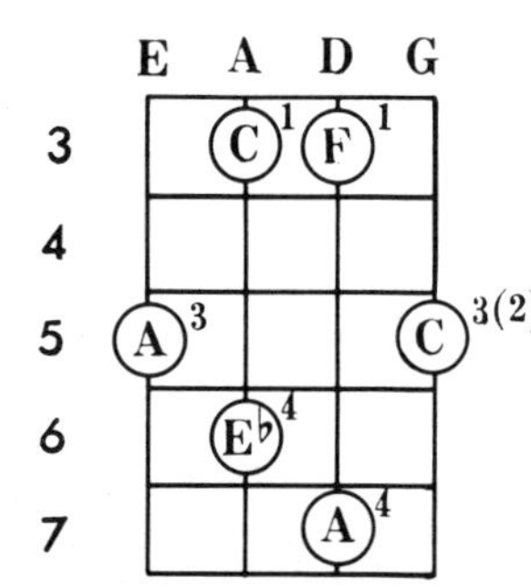

Dominant 7th

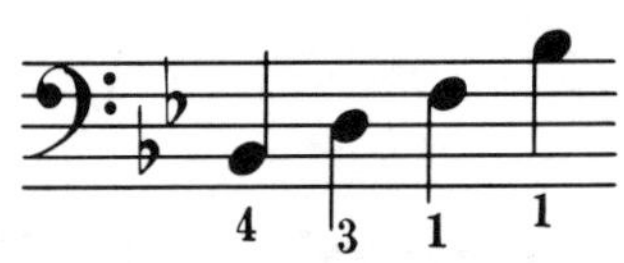

D MAJOR

VIIth POSITION

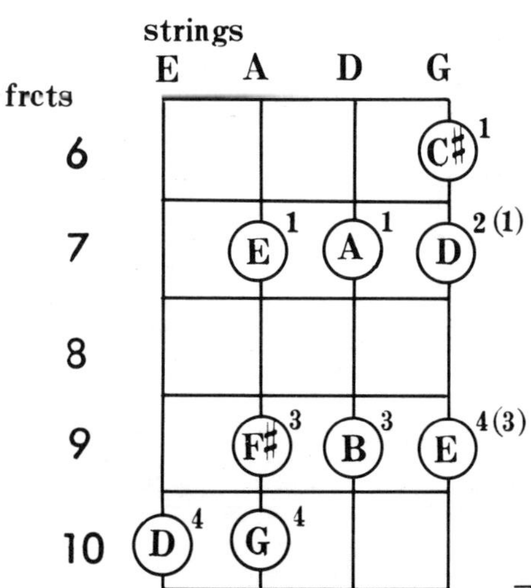

ARPEGGIOS

D

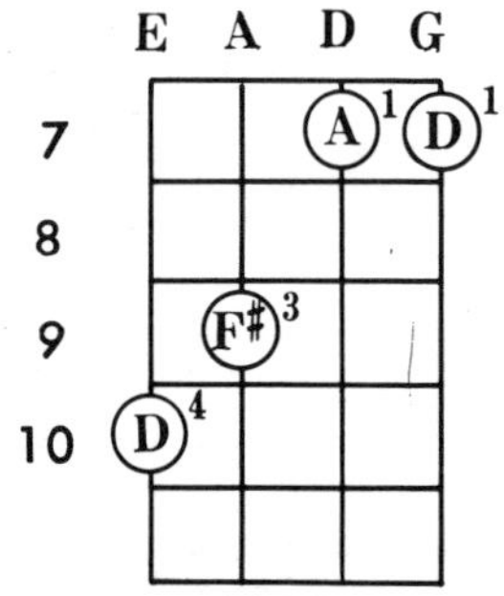

Tonic

G

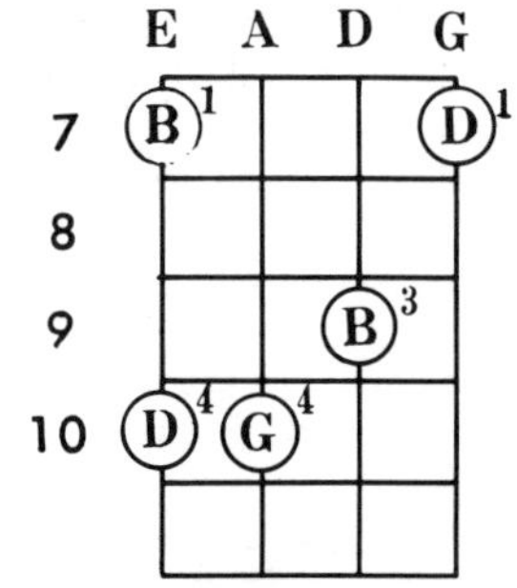

Subdominant

A7

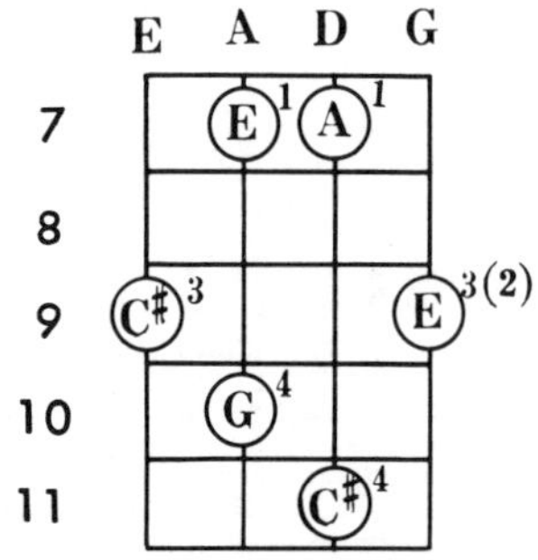

Dominant 7th

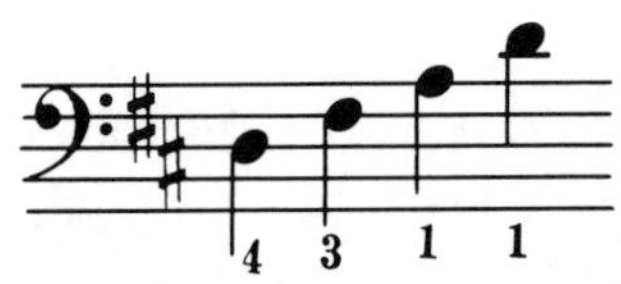

TERTIARY FORMS

E♭ MAJOR

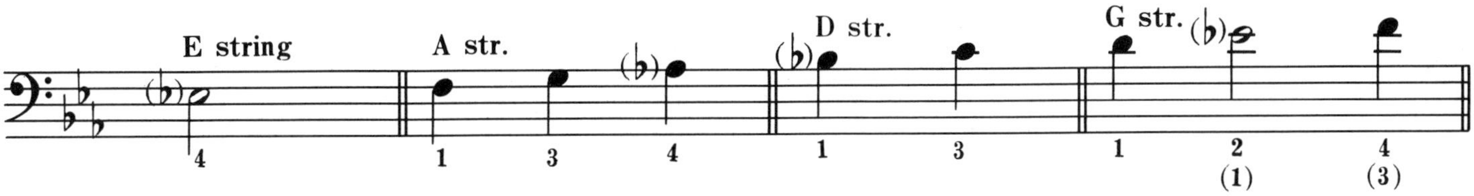

VIIIth POSITION

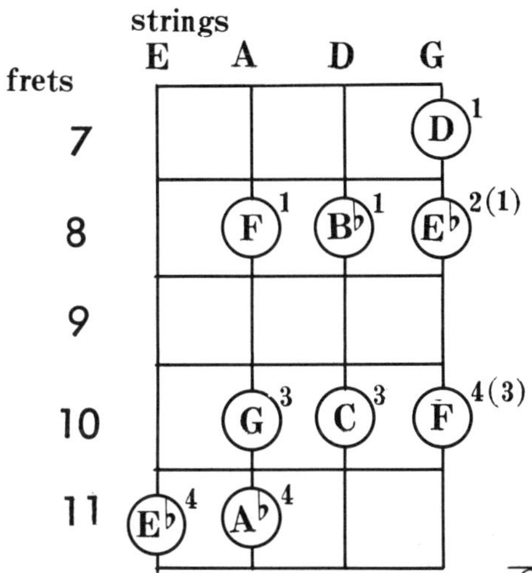

ARPEGGIOS

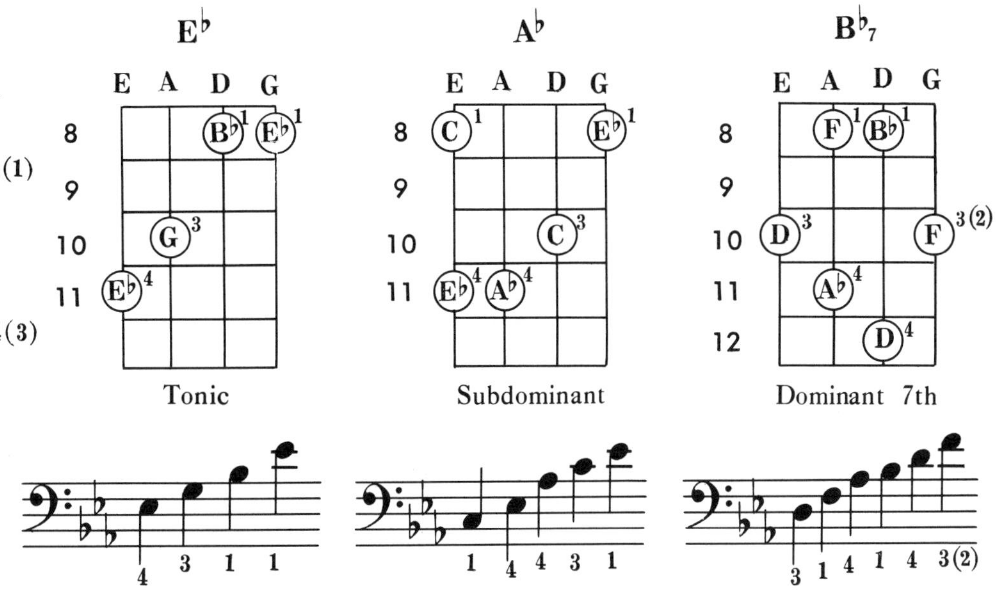

A MAJOR

IInd POSITION

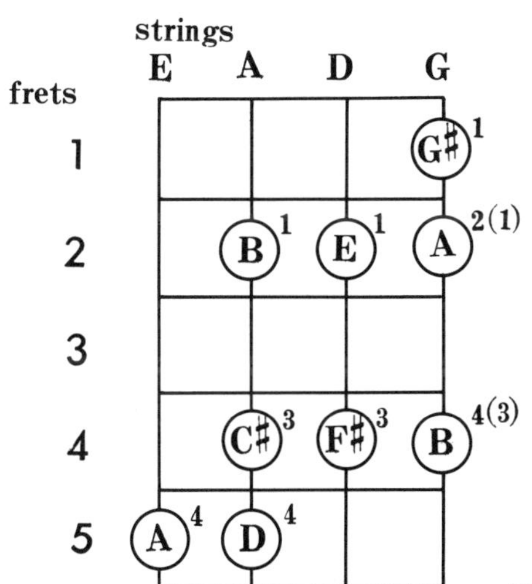

ARPEGGIOS

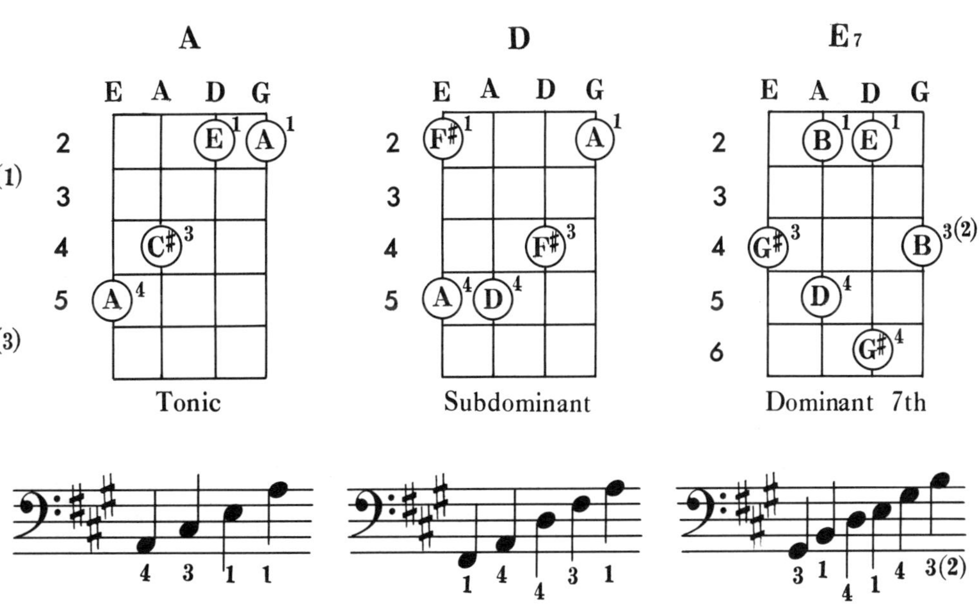

TERTIARY FORMS

A♭ MAJOR

Ist POSITION

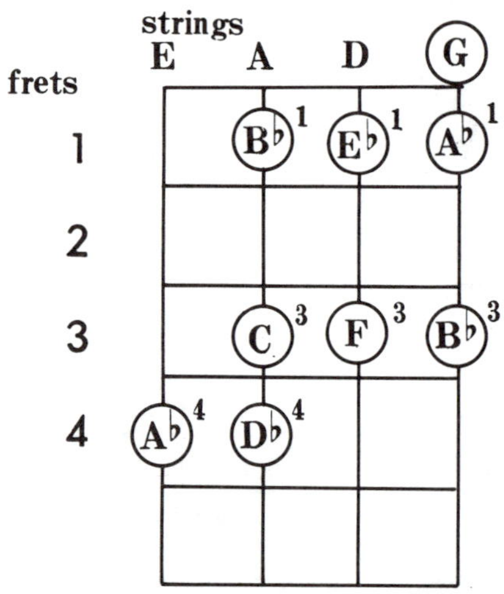

ARPEGGIOS

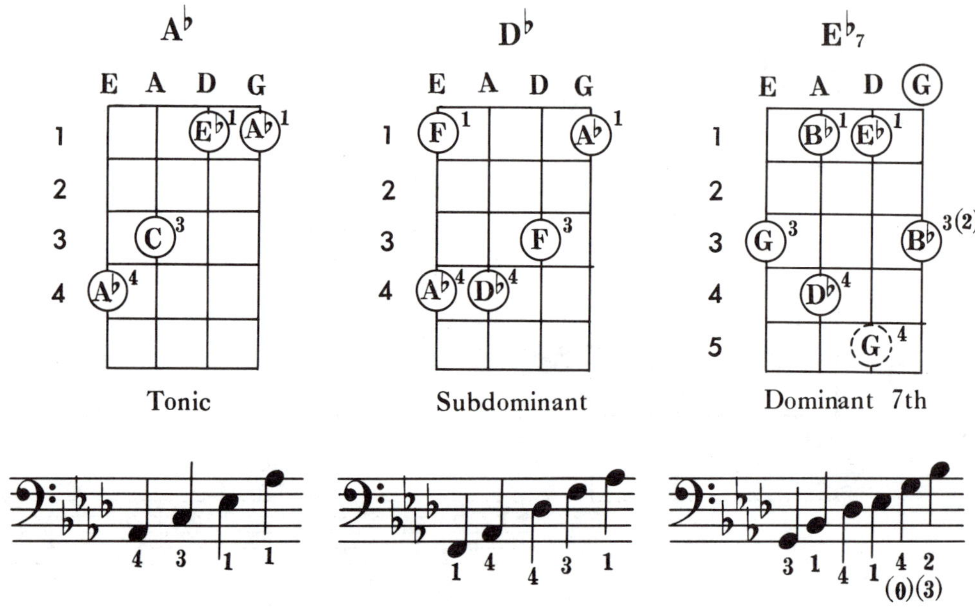

E MAJOR

IXth POSITION

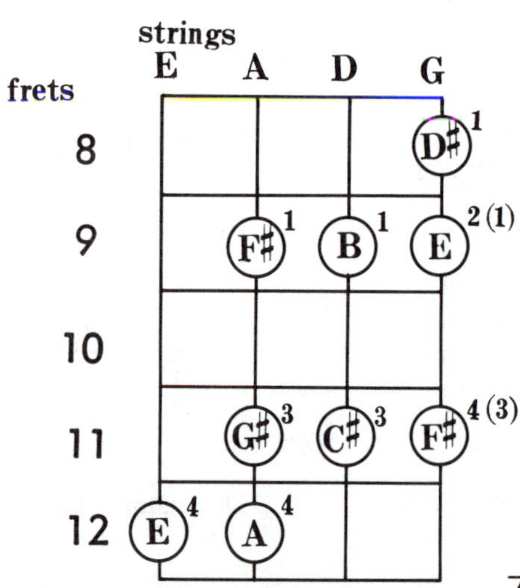

ARPEGGIOS

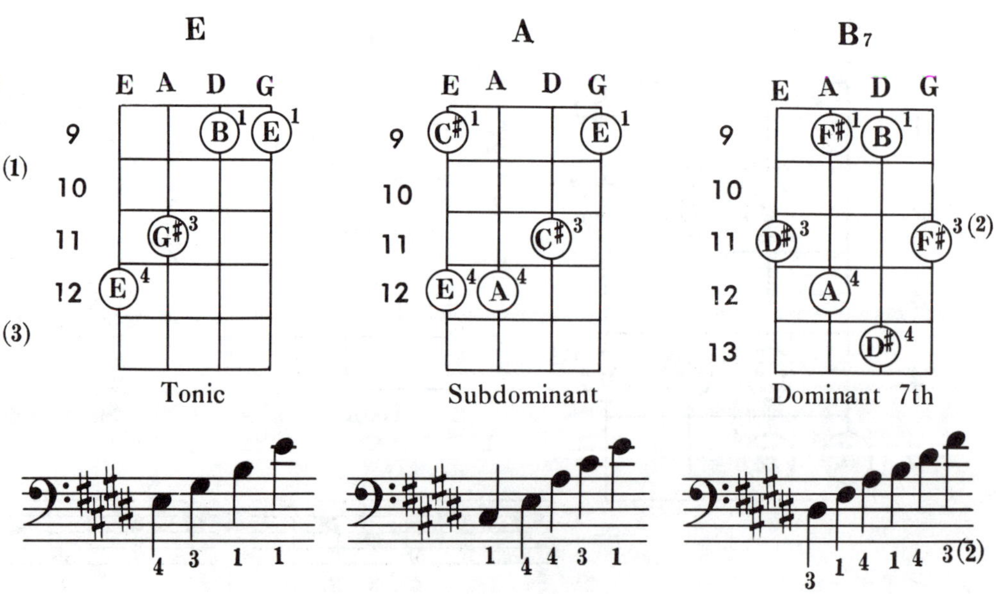

TERTIARY FORMS

D♭ MAJOR

VIth POSITION

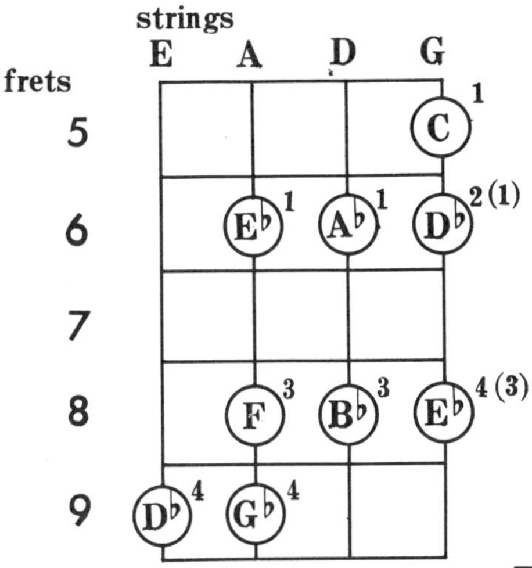

ARPEGGIOS

D♭

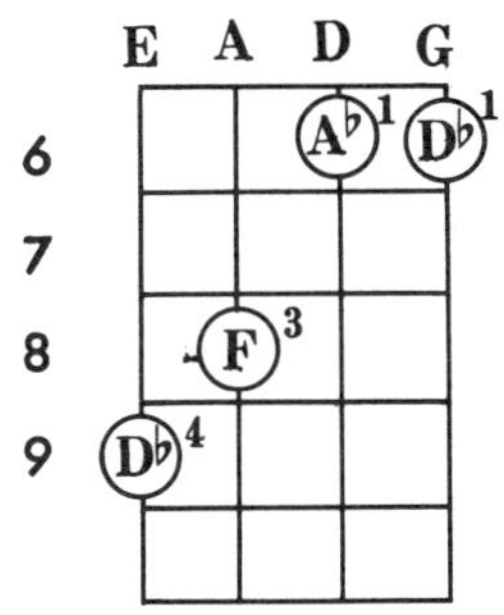

Tonic

G♭

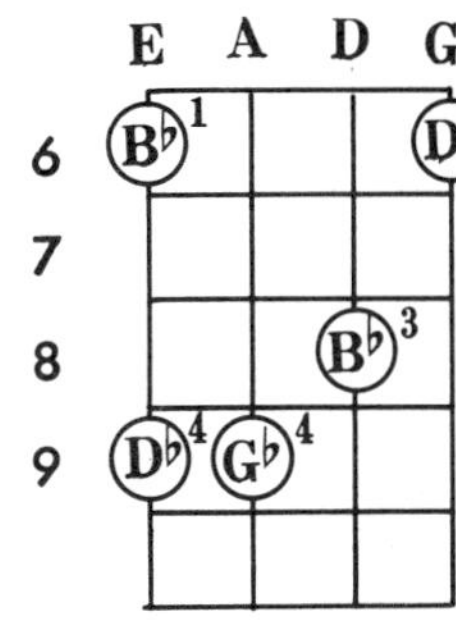

Subdominant

A♭7

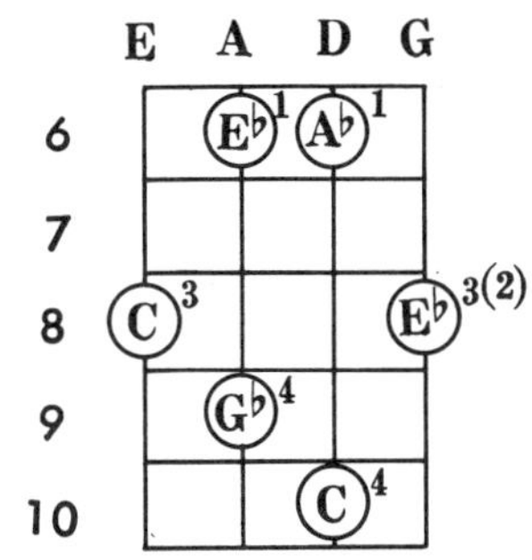

Dominant 7th

B MAJOR

IVth POSITION

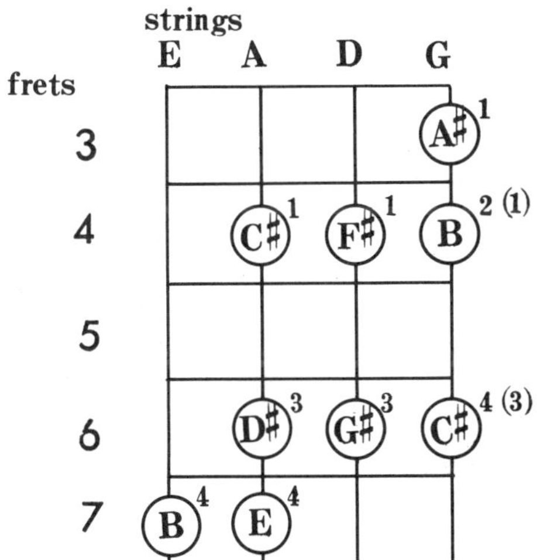

ARPEGGIOS

B

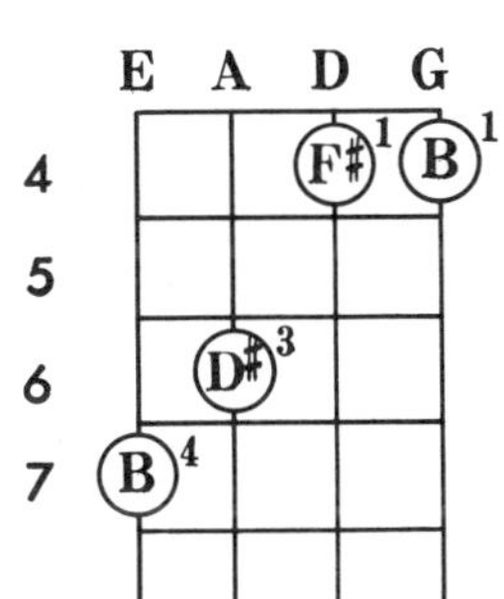

Tonic

E

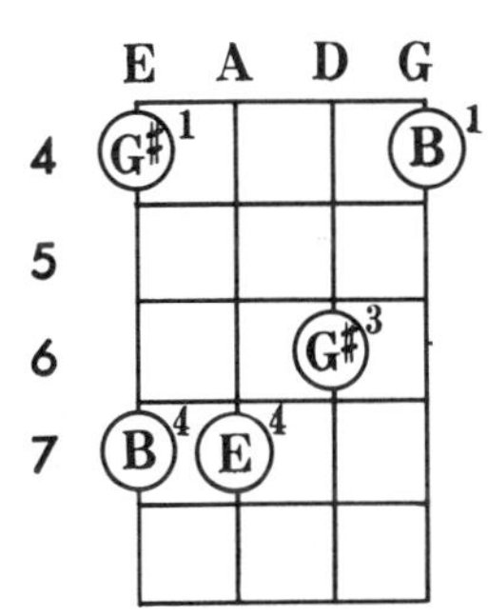

Subdominant

F♯7

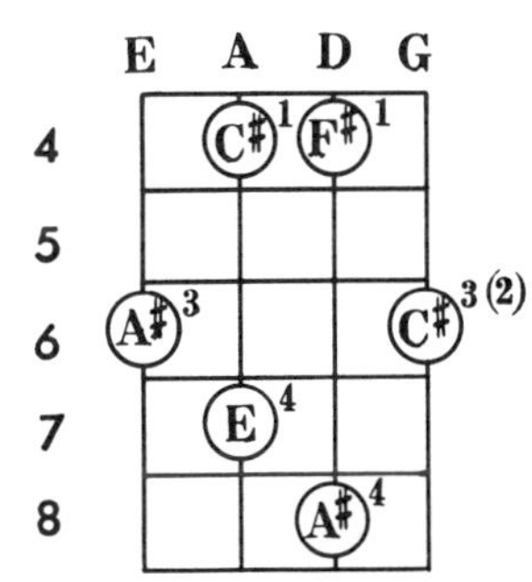

Dominant 7th

TERTIARY FORMS

G♭ MAJOR

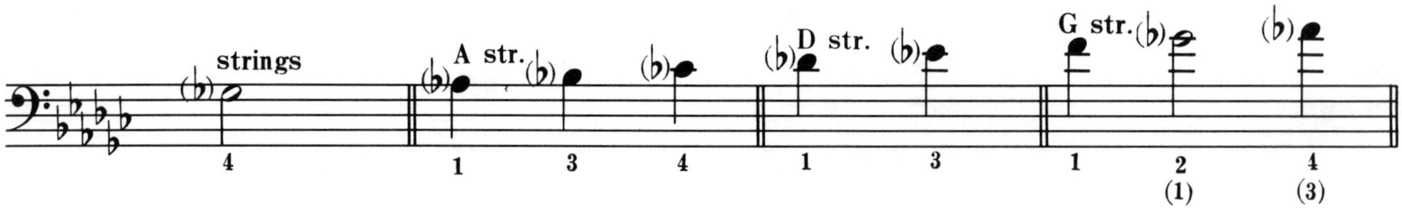

XIth POSITION

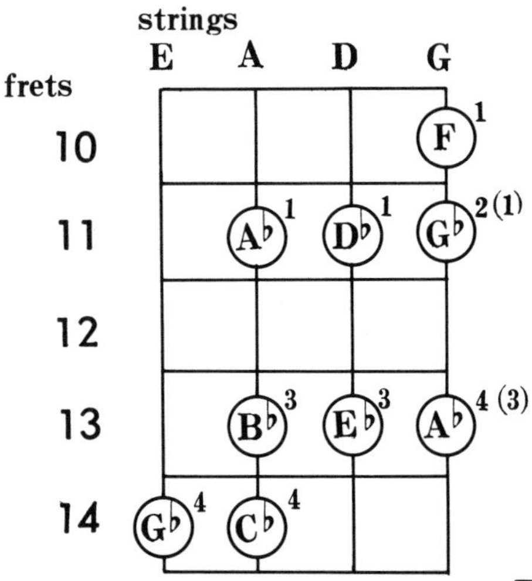

Note that these two keys are enharmonically equivalent.

ARPEGGIOS

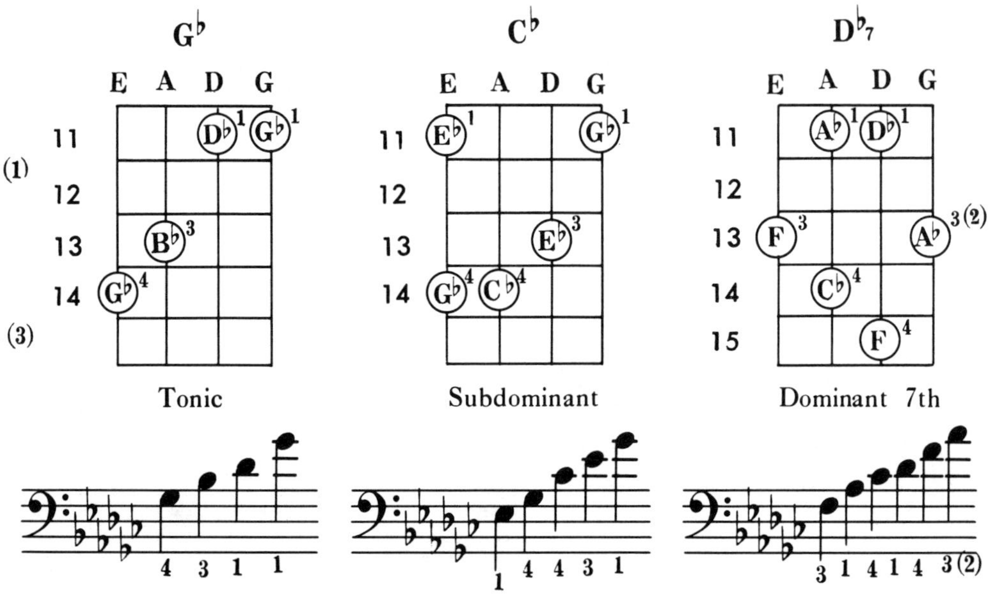

Tonic Subdominant Dominant 7th

F♯ MAJOR

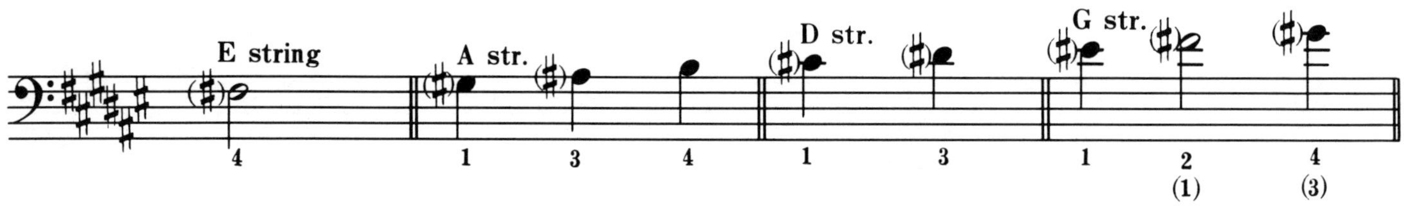

XIth POSITION

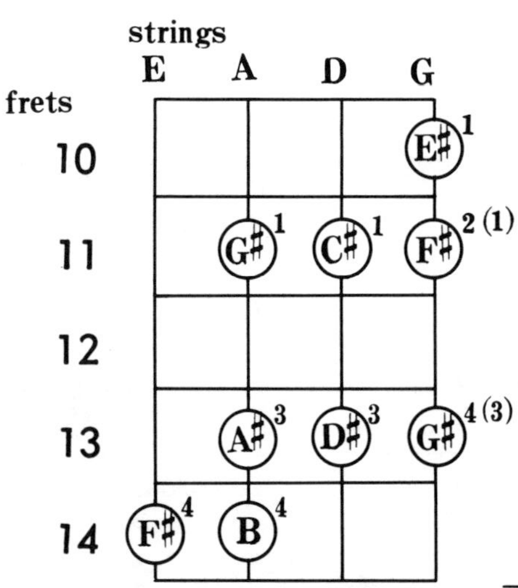

ARPEGGIOS

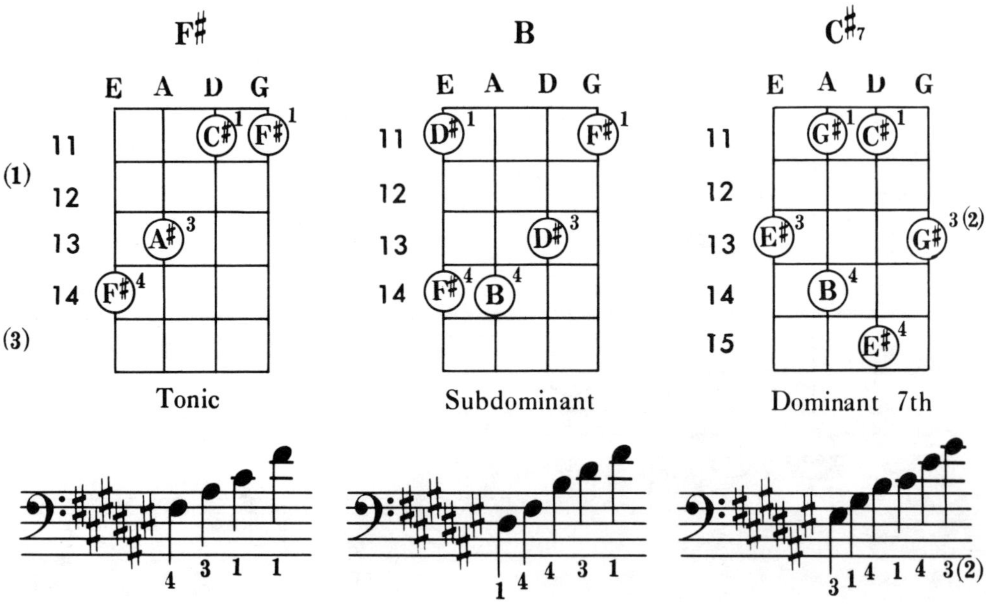

Tonic Subdominant Dominant 7th

QUATERNARY FORMS

C MAJOR

IInd POSITION

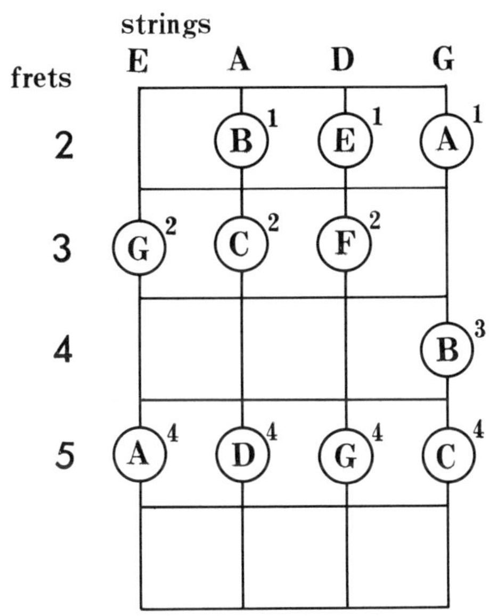

ARPEGGIOS

C

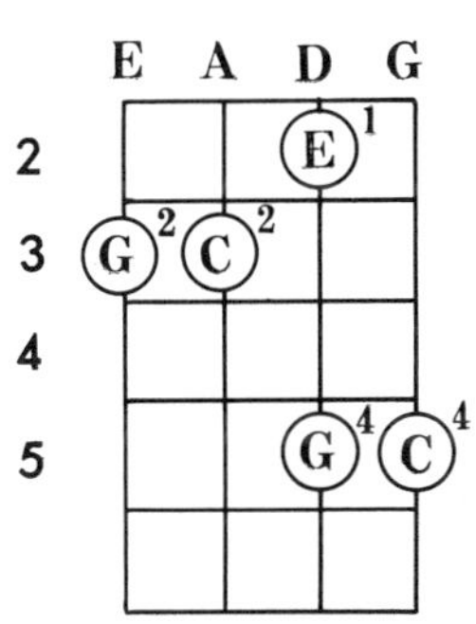

Tonic

F

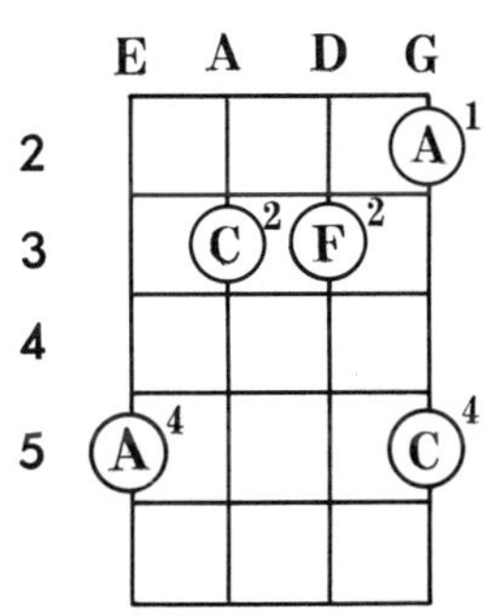

Subdominant

G7

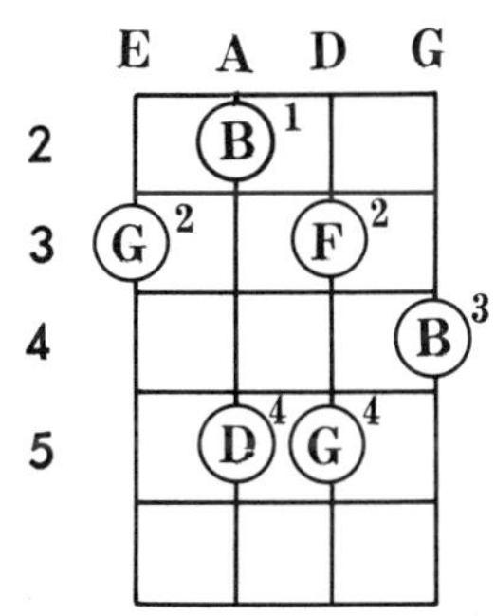

Dominant 7th

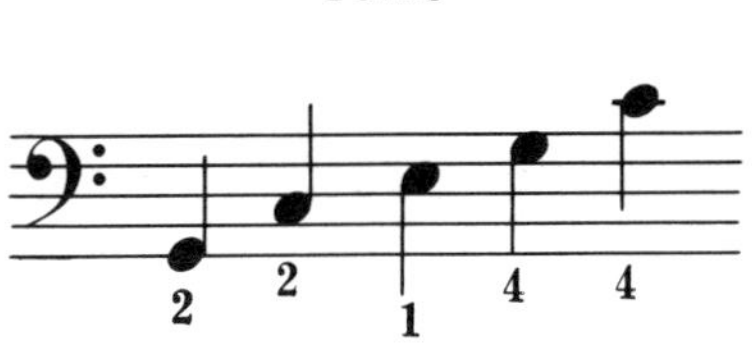

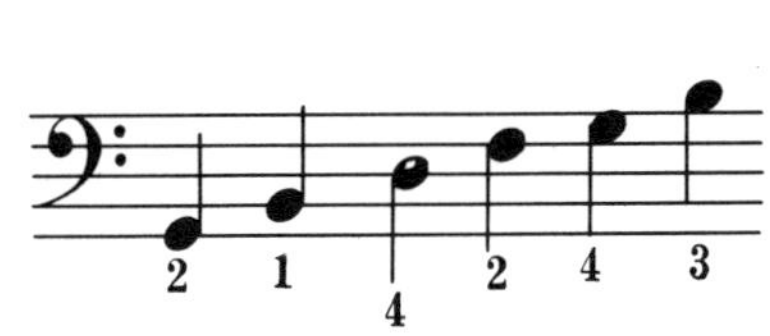

QUATERNARY FORMS

F MAJOR

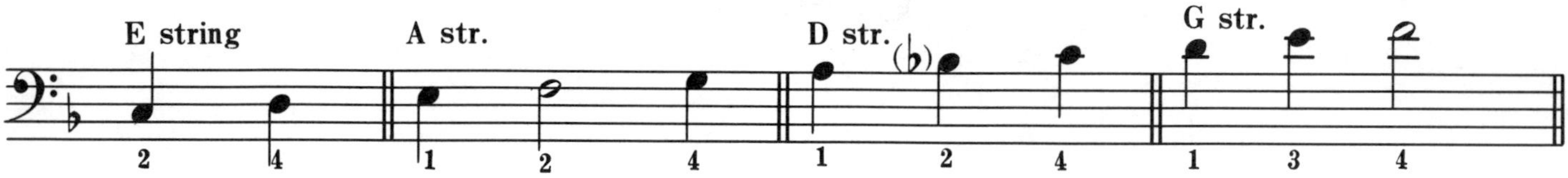

VIIth POSITION

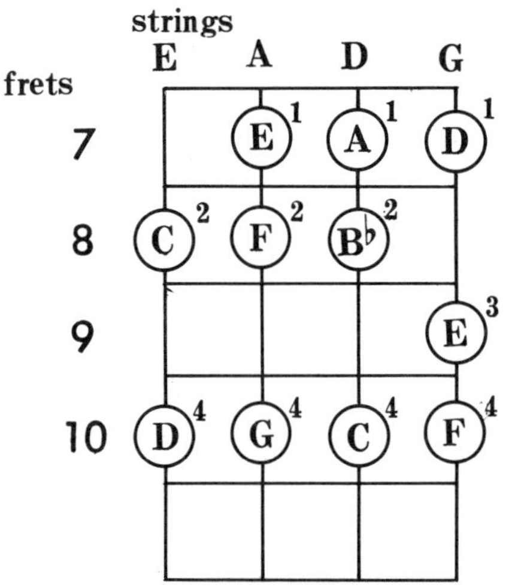

ARPEGGIOS

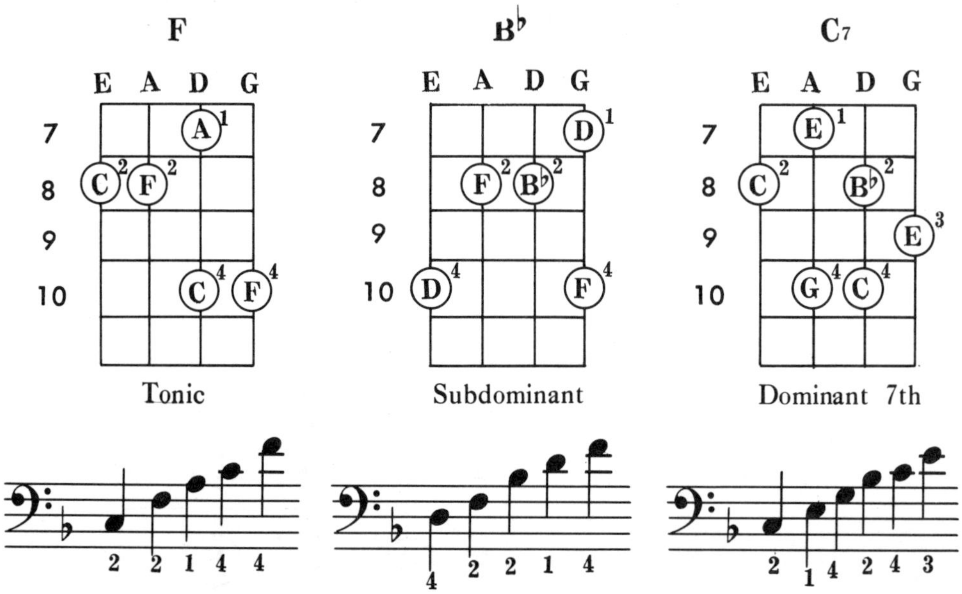

G MAJOR

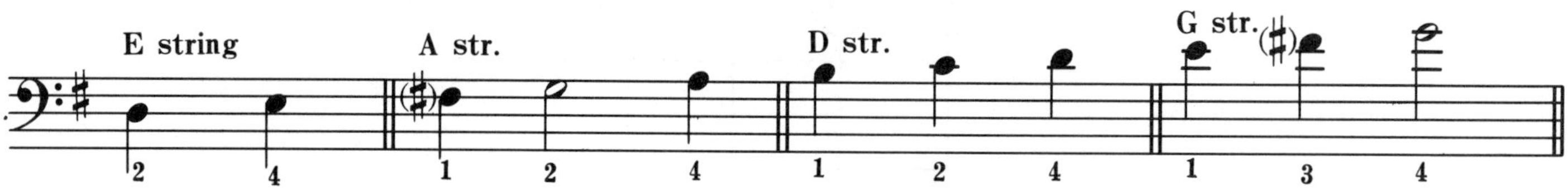

IXth POSITION

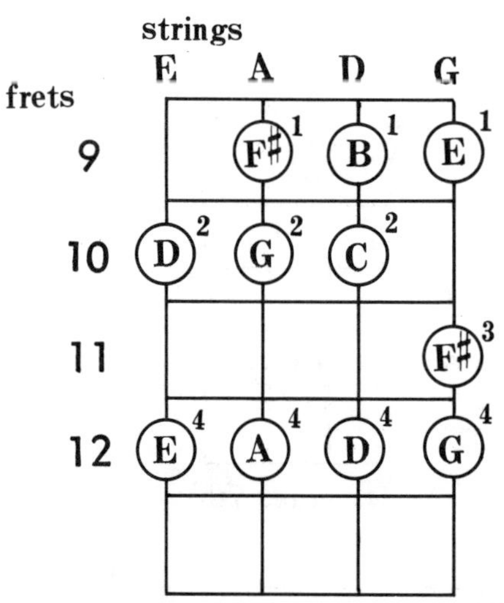

ARPEGGIOS

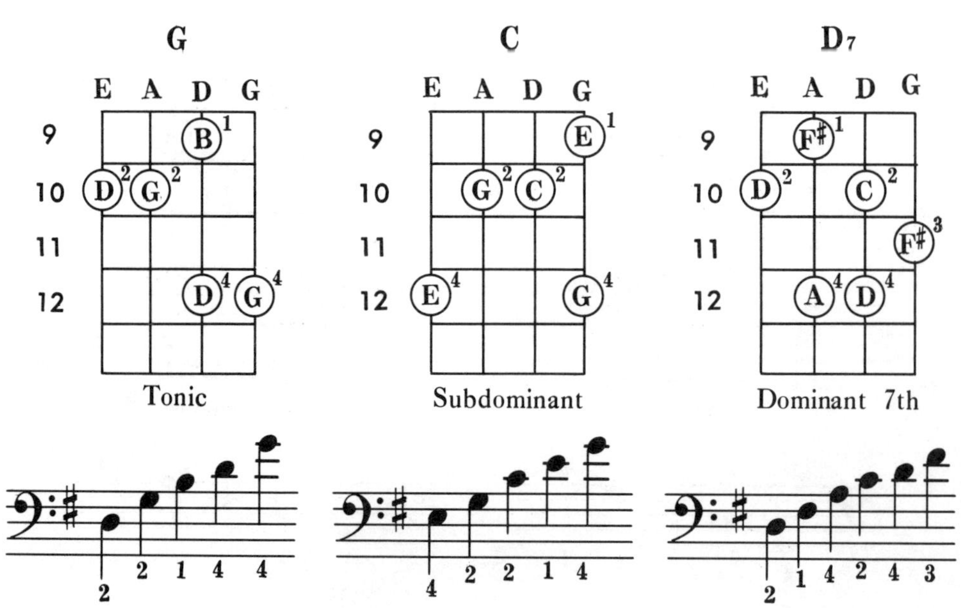

QUATERNARY FORMS

B♭ MAJOR

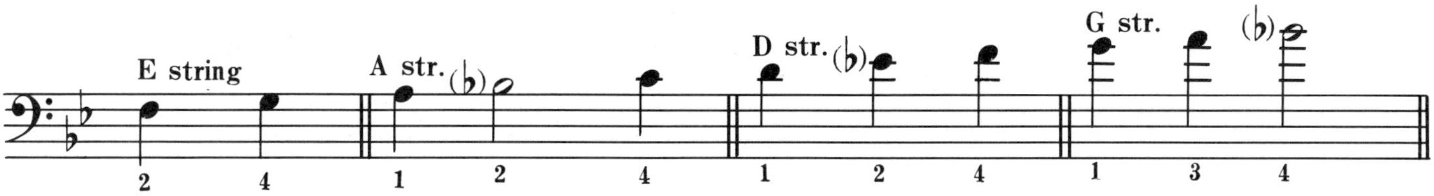

XIIth POSITION

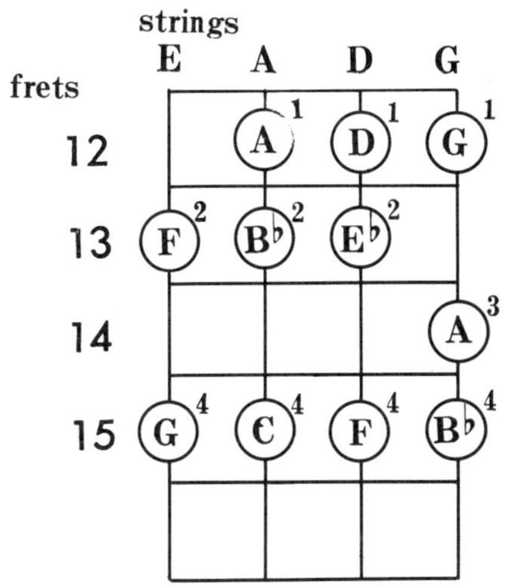

ARPEGGIOS

B♭

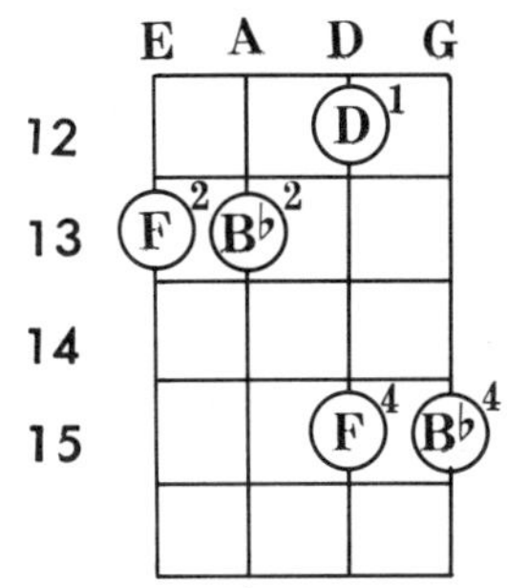

Tonic

E♭

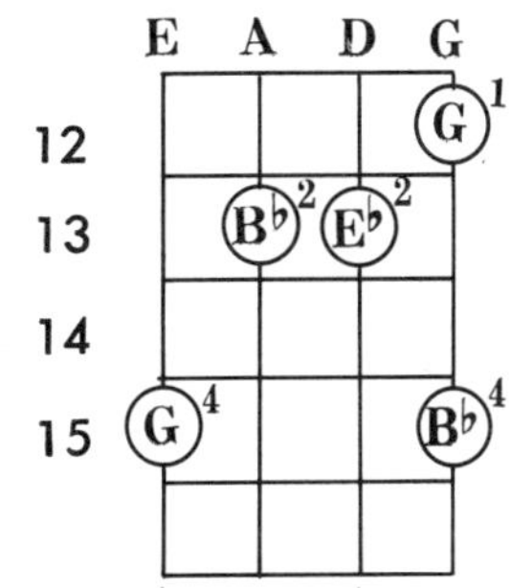

Subdominant

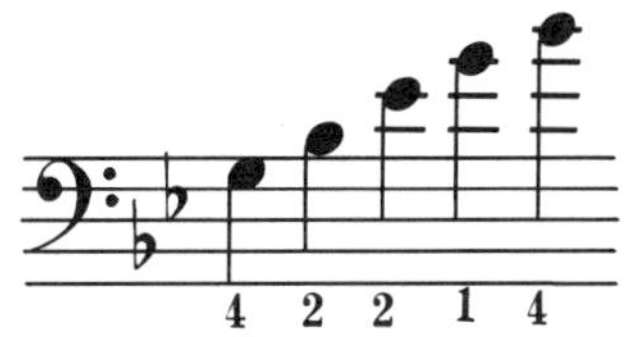

F_7

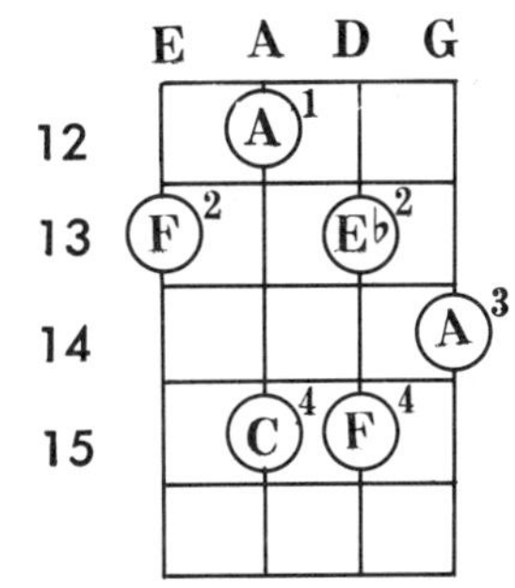

Dominant 7th

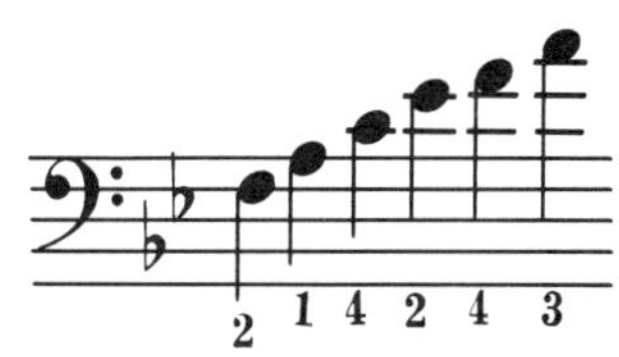

D MAJOR

IVth POSITION

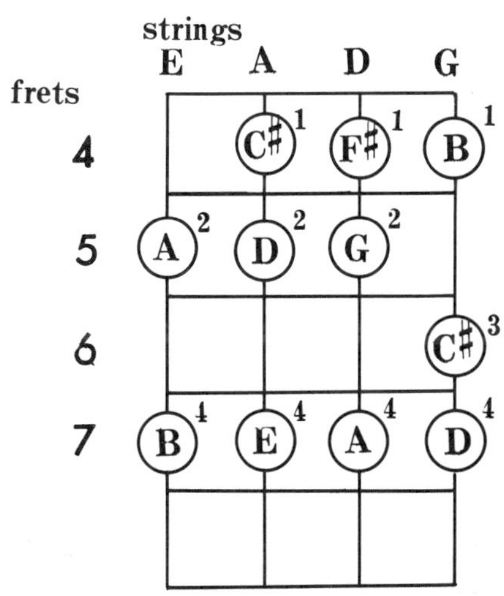

ARPEGGIOS

D

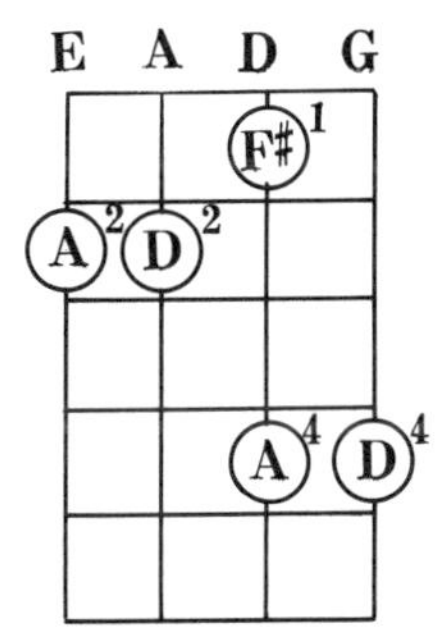

Tonic

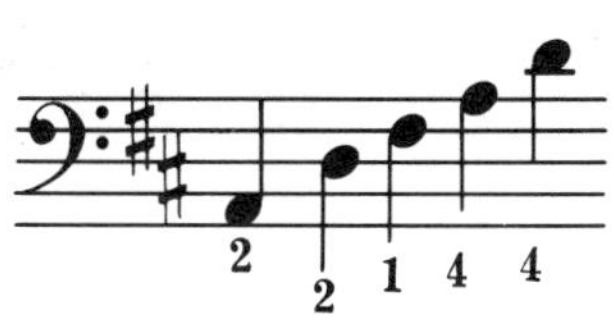

G

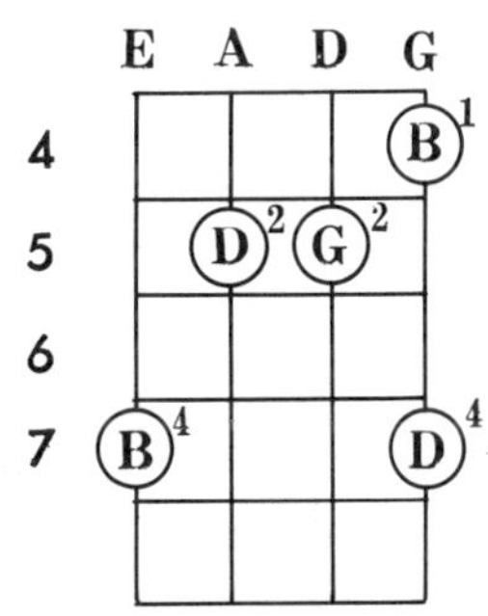

Subdominant

A_7

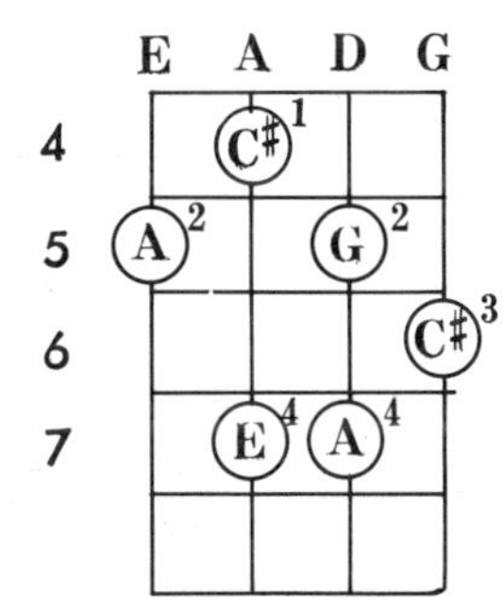

Dominant 7th

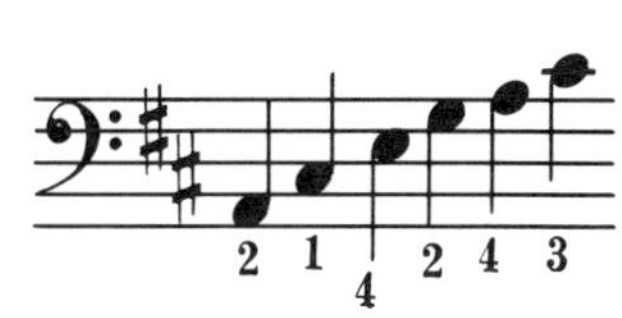

QUATERNARY FORMS

E♭ MAJOR

Vth POSITION

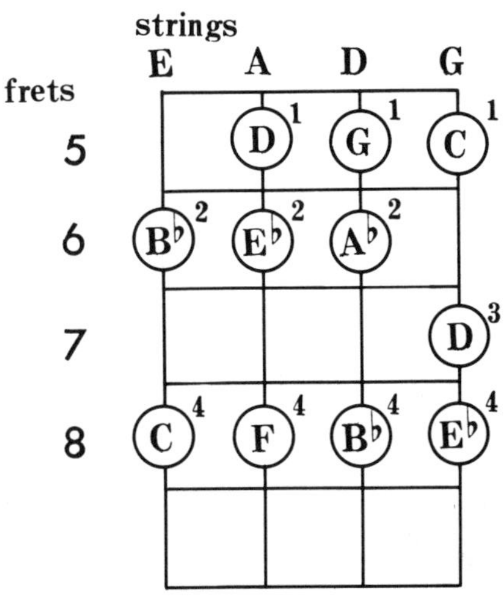

ARPEGGIOS

E♭

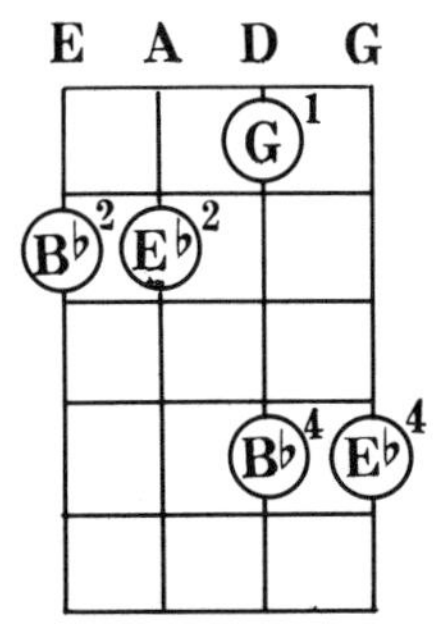

Tonic

A♭

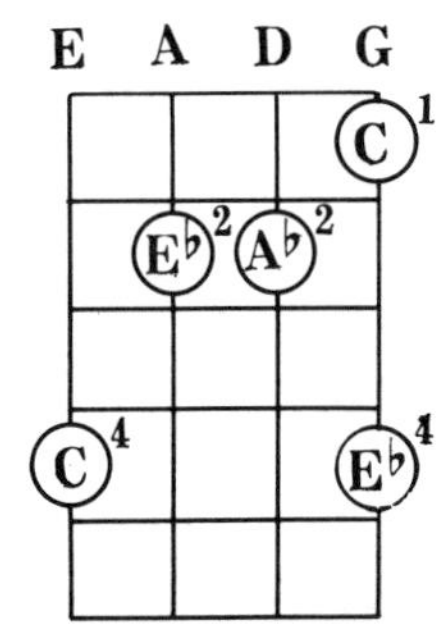

Subdominant

$B^{\flat}_7$

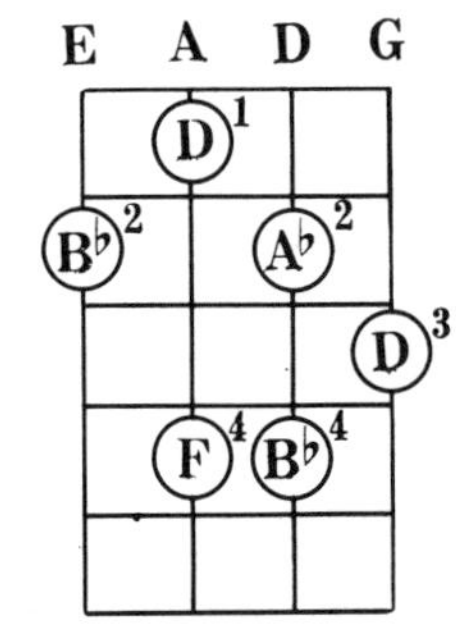

Dominant 7th

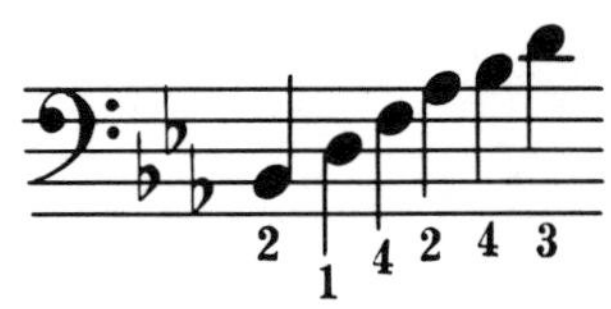

A MAJOR

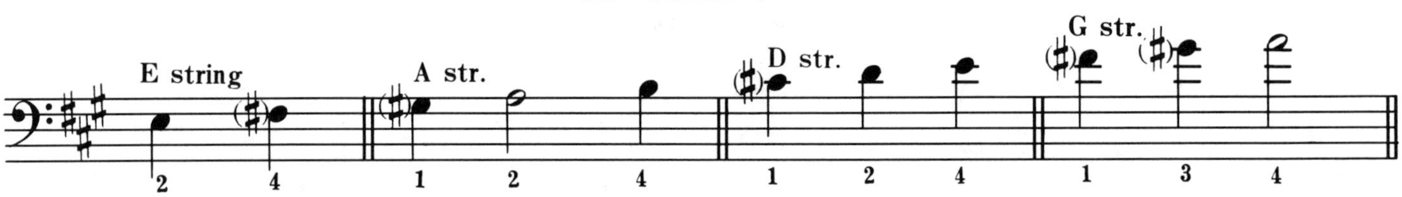

XIth POSITION

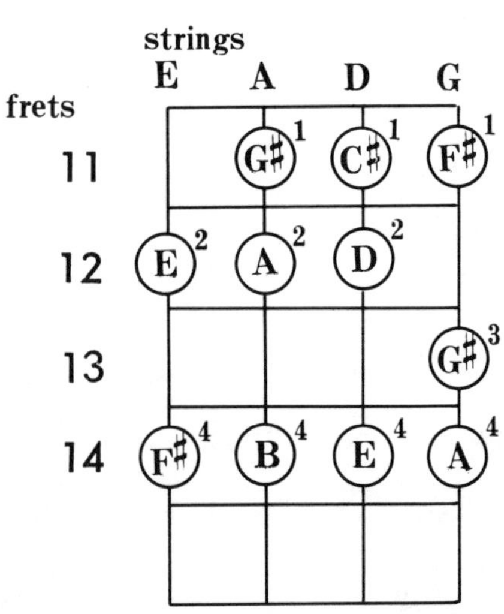

ARPEGGIOS

A

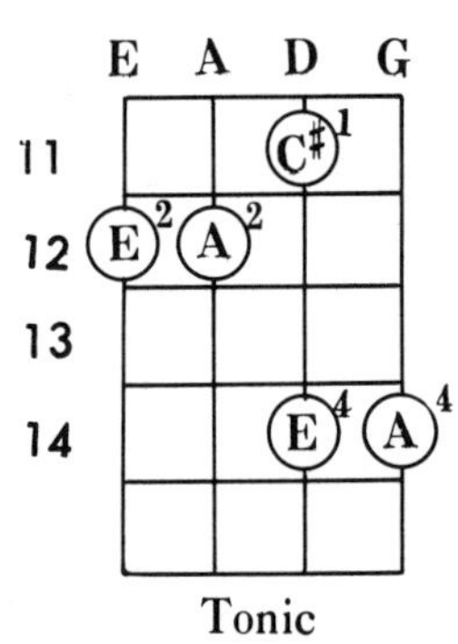

Tonic

D

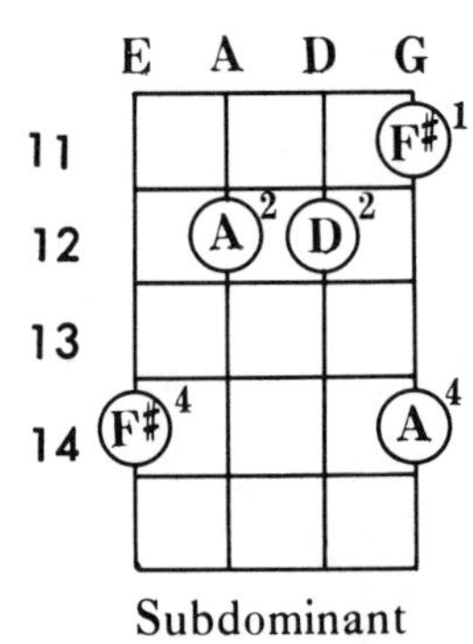

Subdominant

E_7

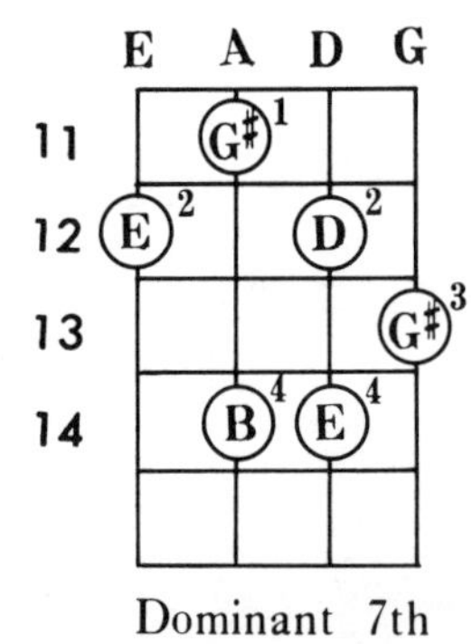

Dominant 7th

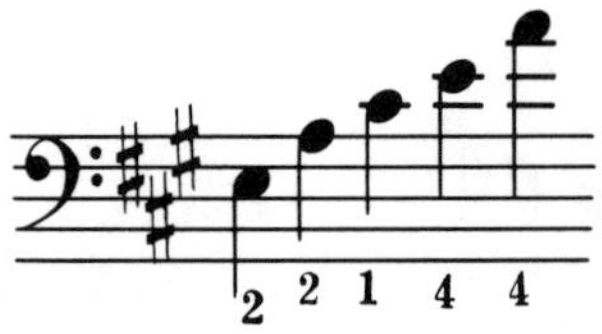

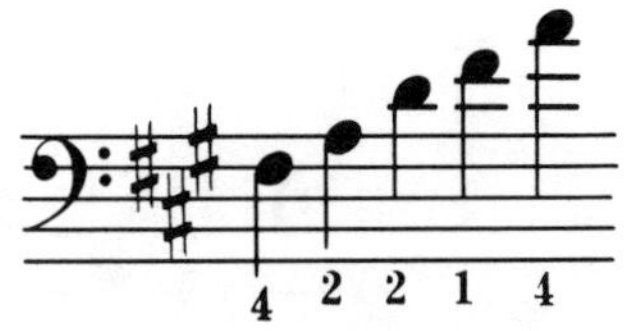

QUATERNARY FORMS

A♭ MAJOR

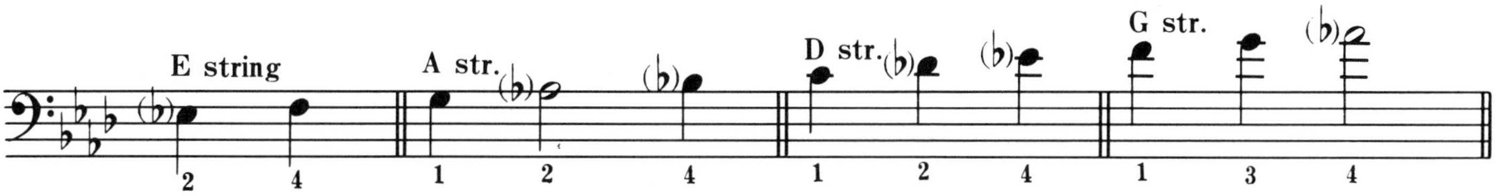

Xth POSITION

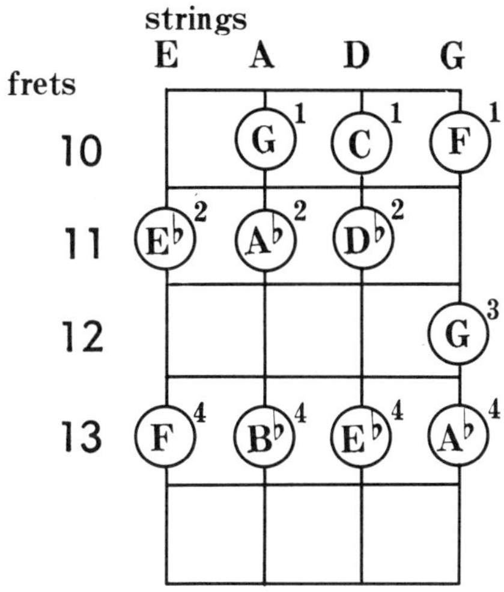

ARPEGGIOS

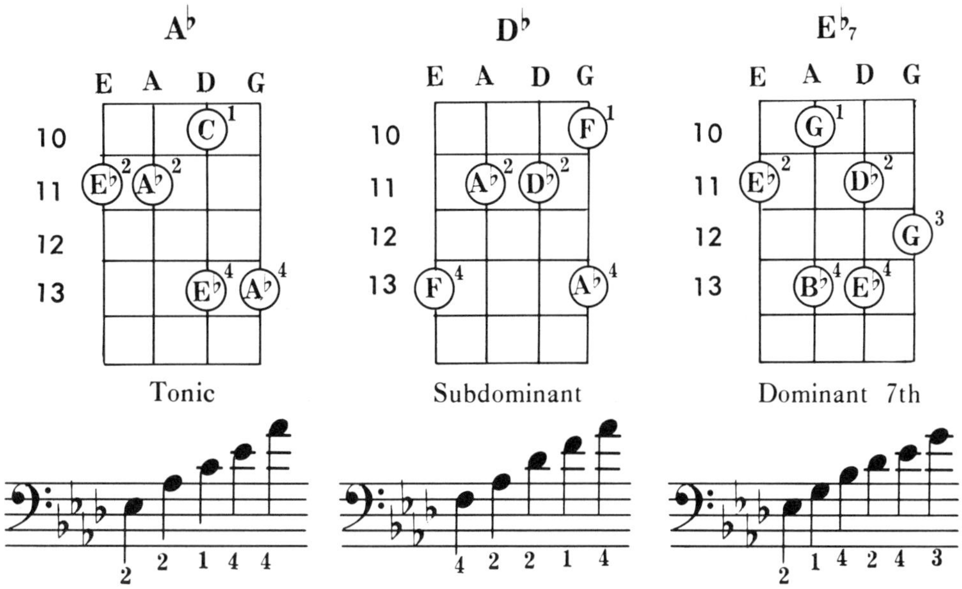

E MAJOR

VIth POSITION

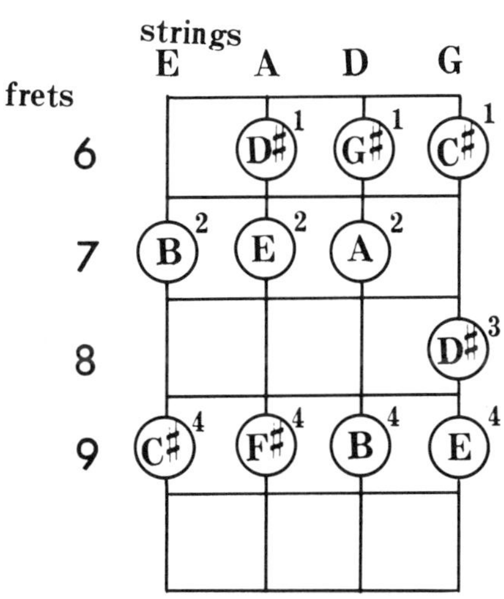

ARPEGGIOS

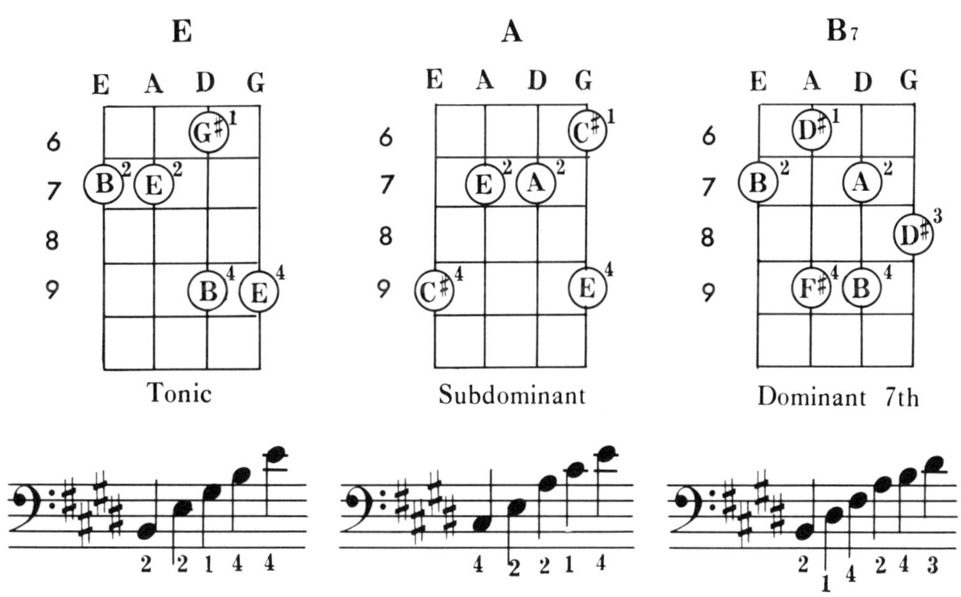

QUATERNARY FORMS

D♭ MAJOR

IInd POSITION

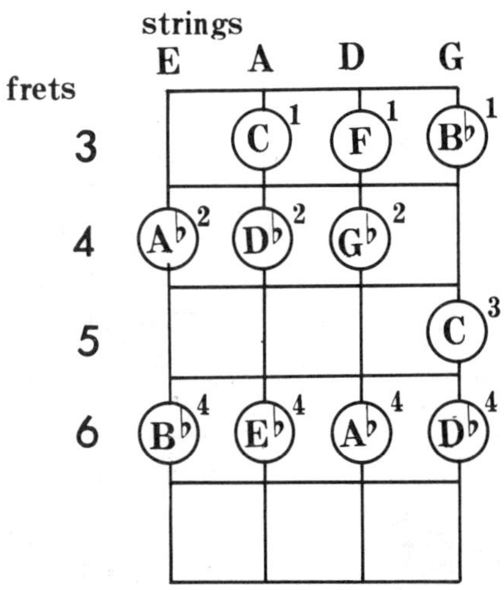

ARPEGGIOS

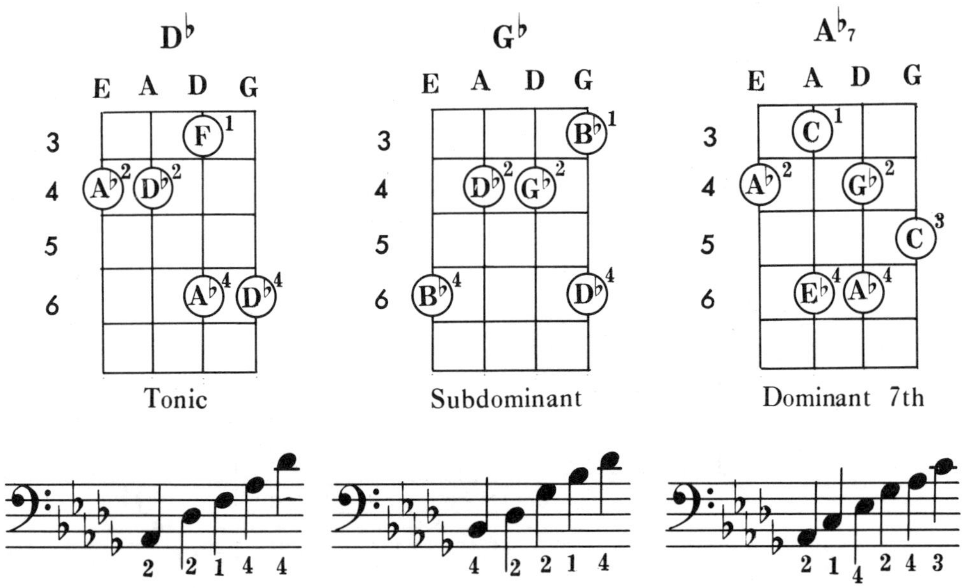

B MAJOR

Ist POSITION

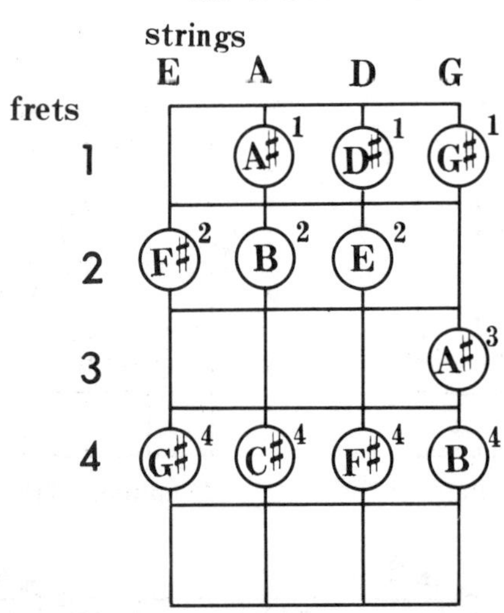

ARPEGGIOS

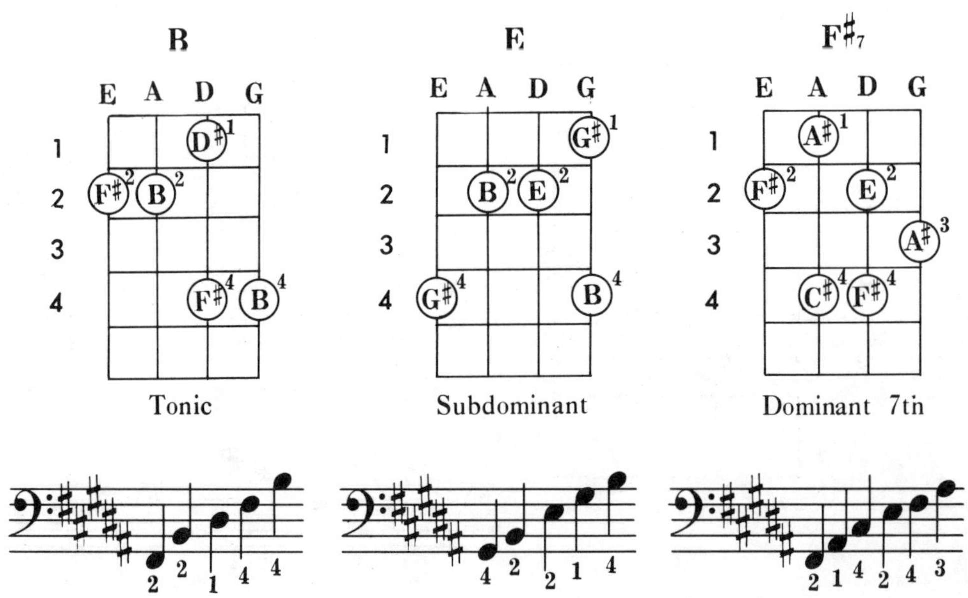

QUATERNARY FORMS

G♭ MAJOR

VIIIth POSITION

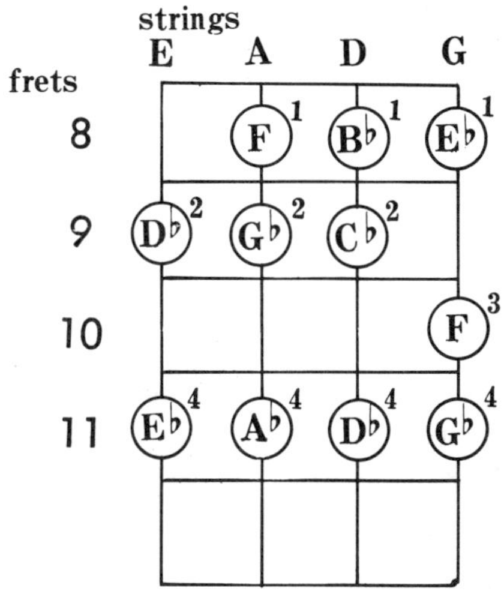

Note that these two keys are enharmonically equivalent.

ARPEGGIOS

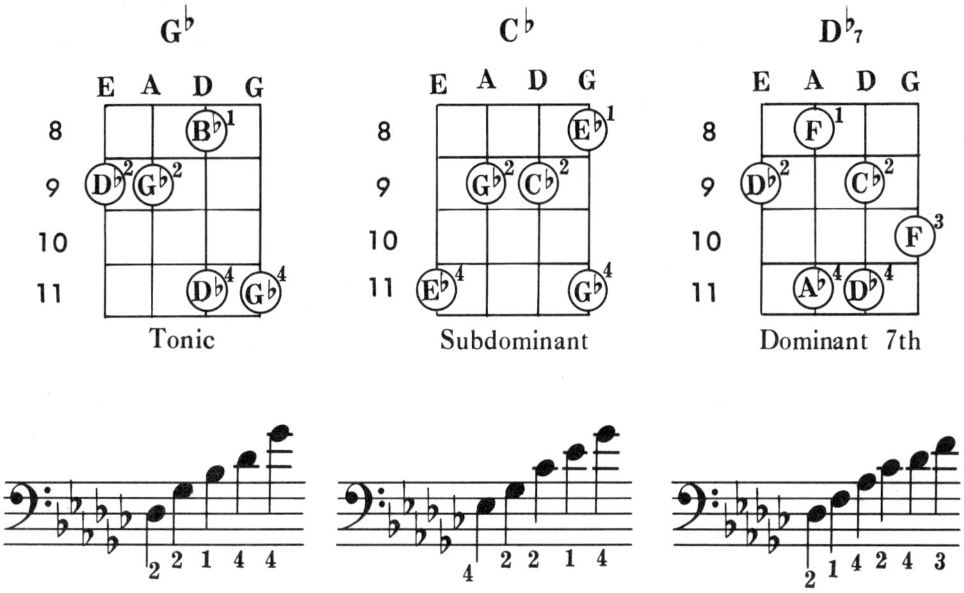

F♯ MAJOR

VIIIth POSITION

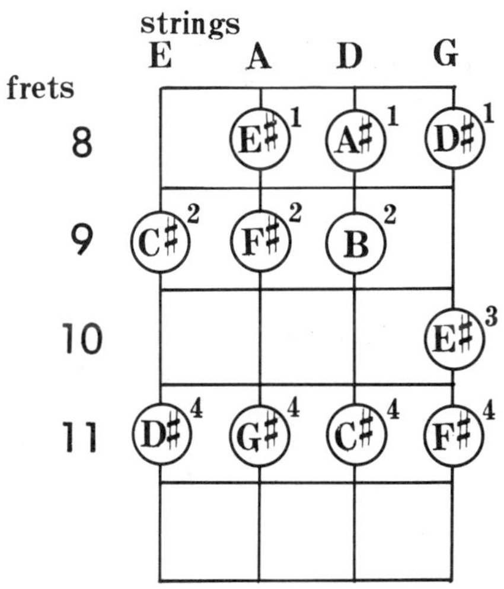

ARPEGGIOS

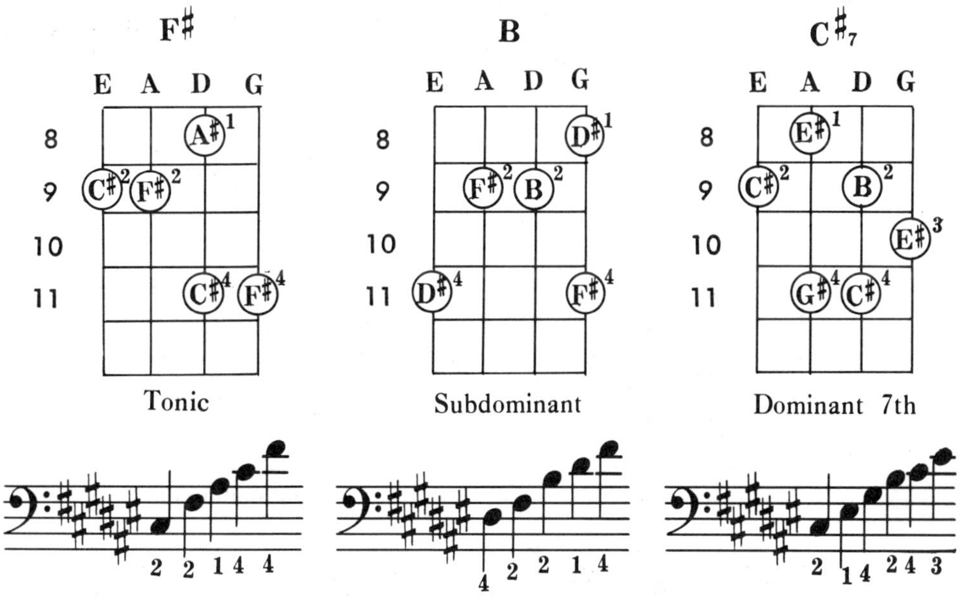

PART TWO - MINOR FORMS

Minor forms-scales and arpeggios-are next considered. Each major key has a relative minor key, located one minor third below the major key. The minor key enjoys the same key signature (sharps or flats) as its relative major key. For example, the relative minor of C major is A minor; the re lative minor of F major is D minor.

PRIMARY FORMS

OPEN POSITION - A MINOR

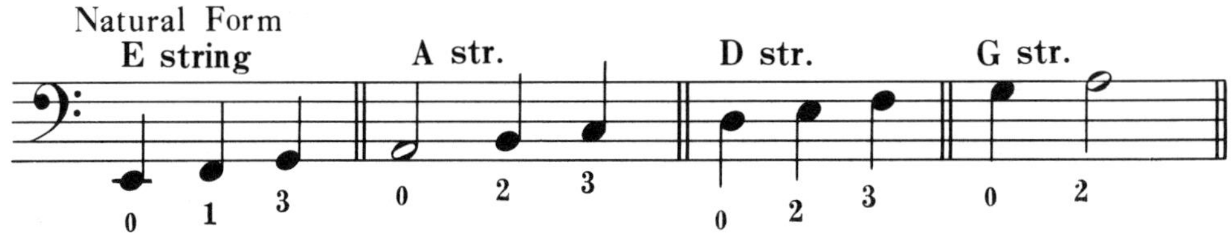

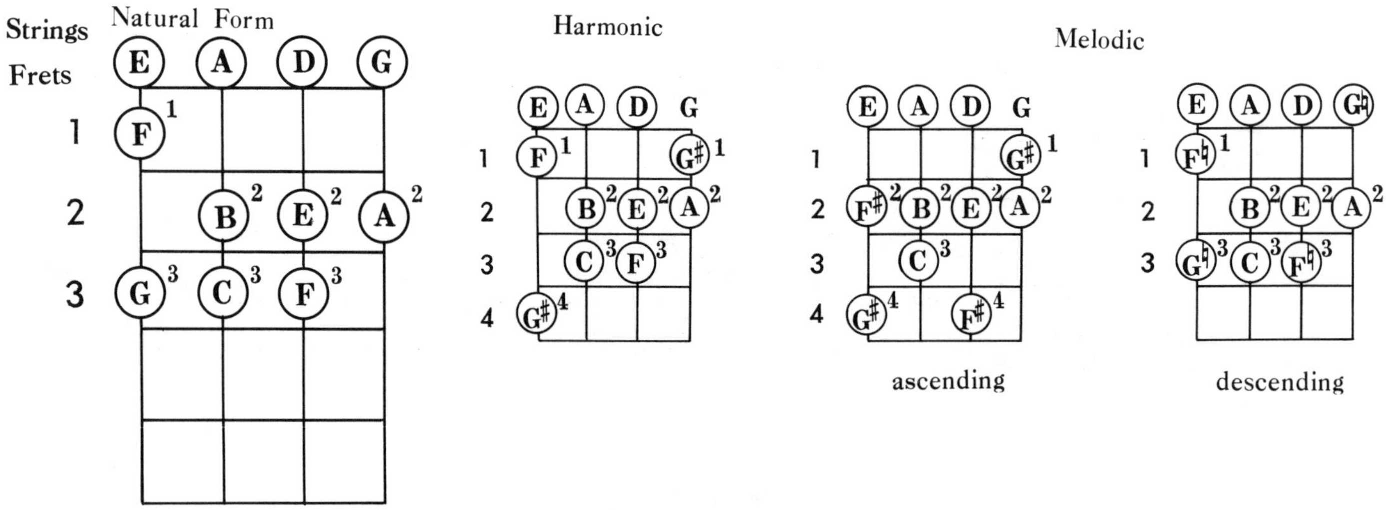

HARMONIC FORM-7th step is raised-in both directions.

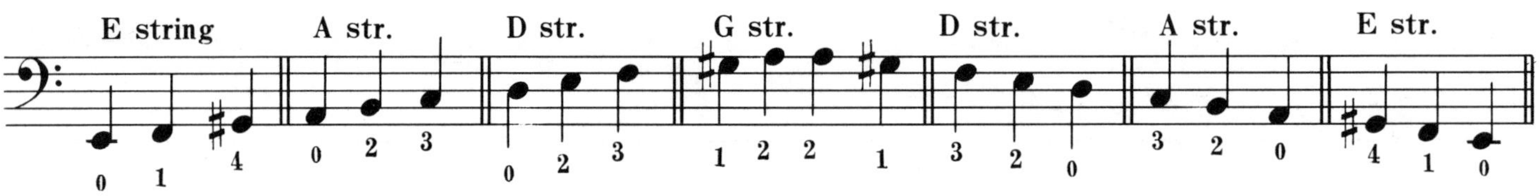

MELODIC FORM-6th and 7th steps raised ascending-6th and 7th steps lowered descending.

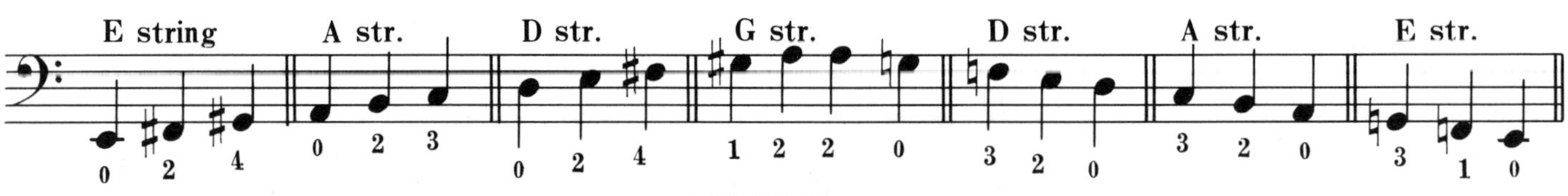

ARPEGGIOS

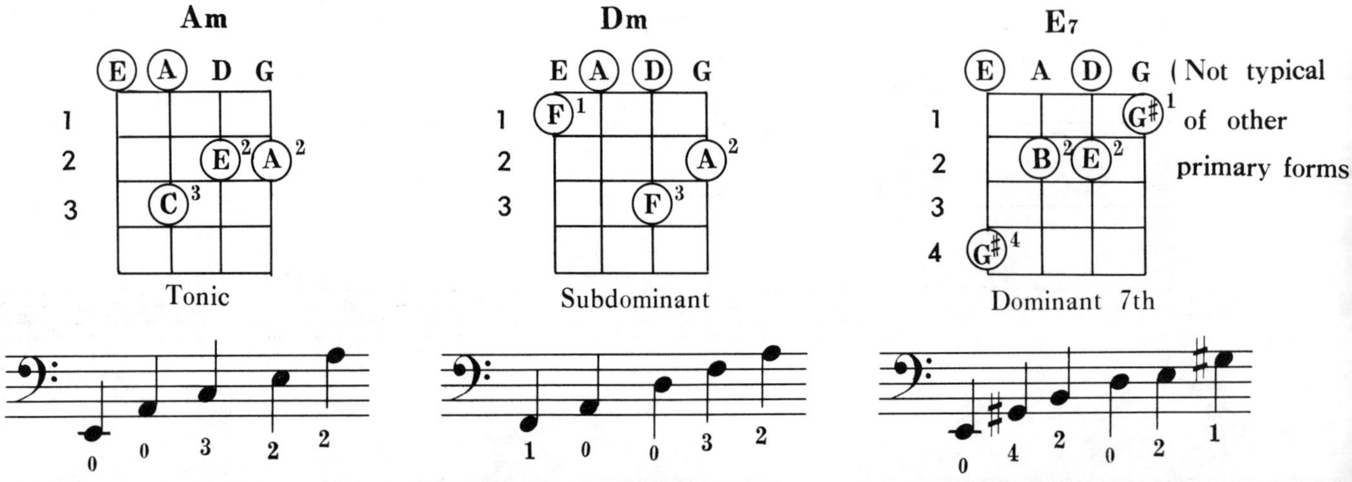

PRIMARY FORMS

D MINOR

HARMONIC

Vth POSITION

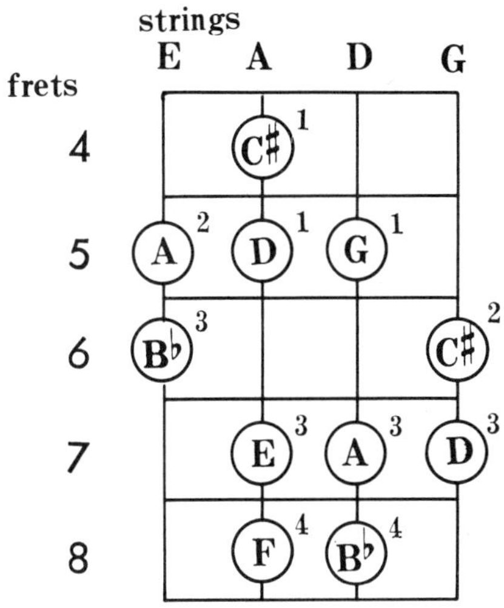

Harmonic

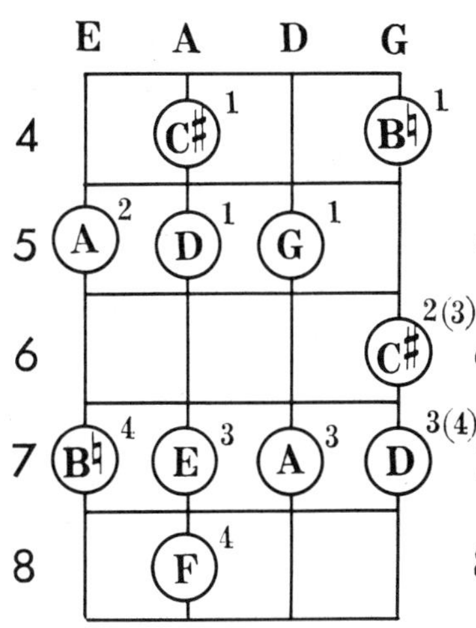

Melodic ascending

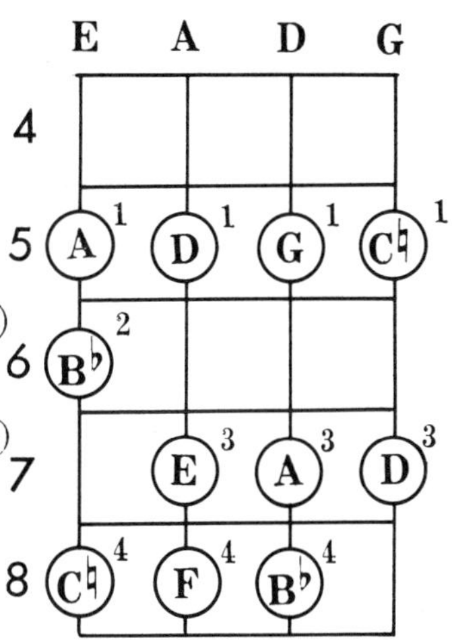

Melodic descending

This form is the same as the natural form, and except for mode or feeling, it is the same as the relative major (F).

MELODIC

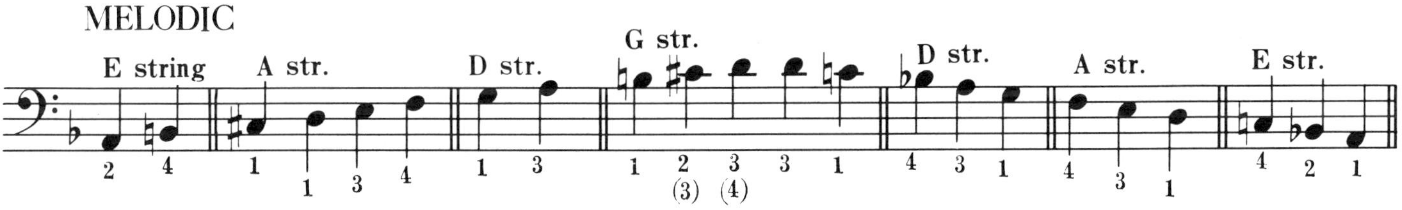

ARPEGGIOS

Dm

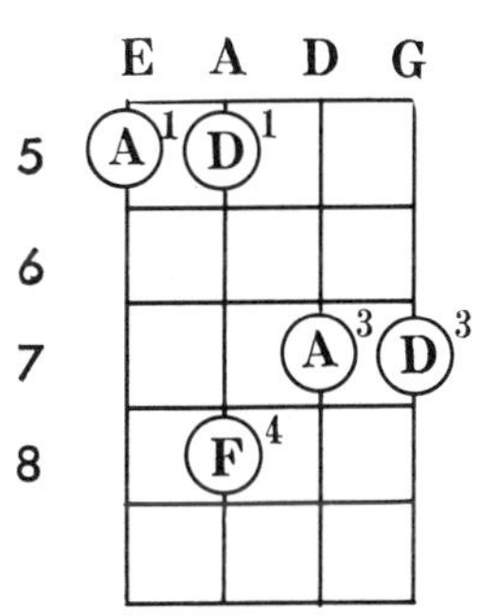

Tonic

Gm

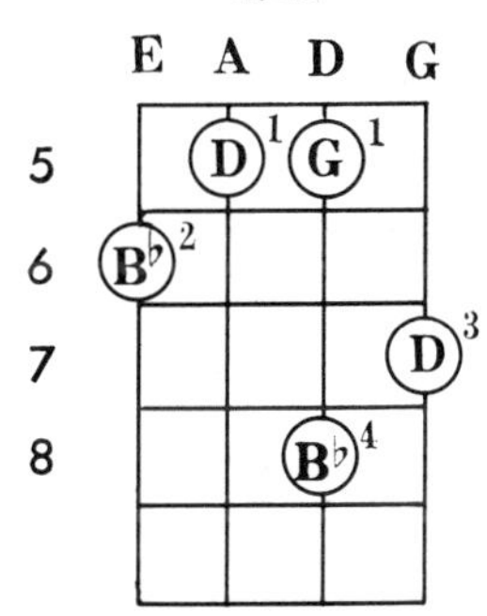

Subdominant

A7

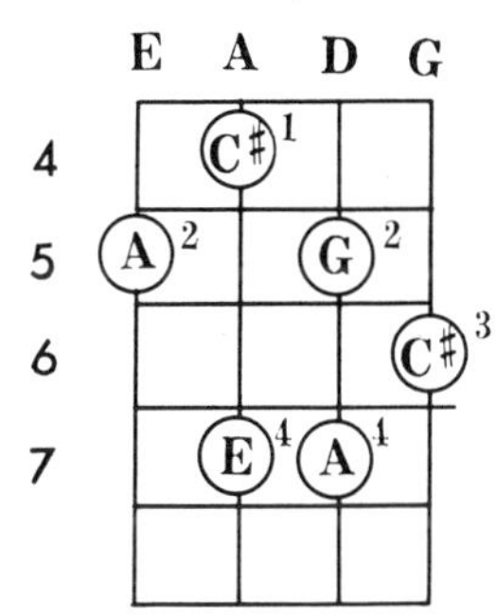

Dominant 7th

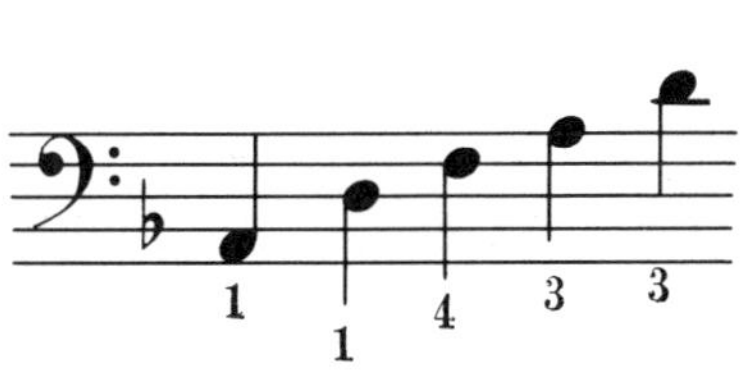

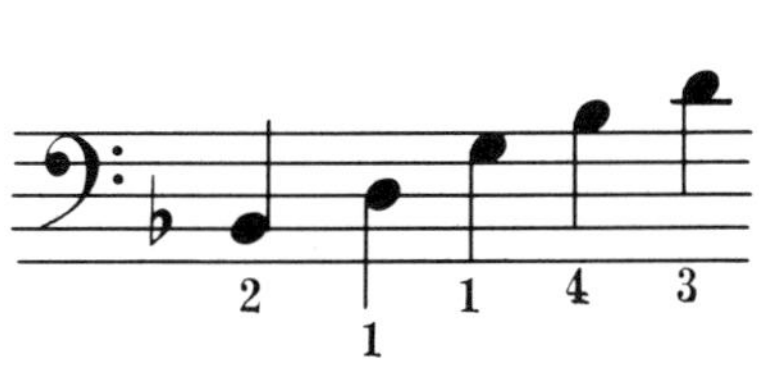

PRIMARY FORMS

E MINOR

HARMONIC

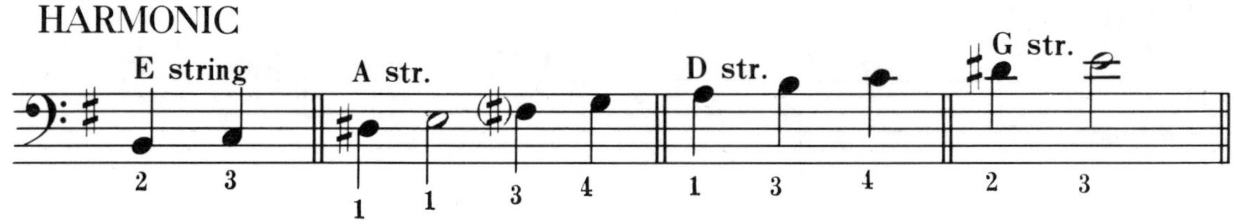

VIIth POSITION

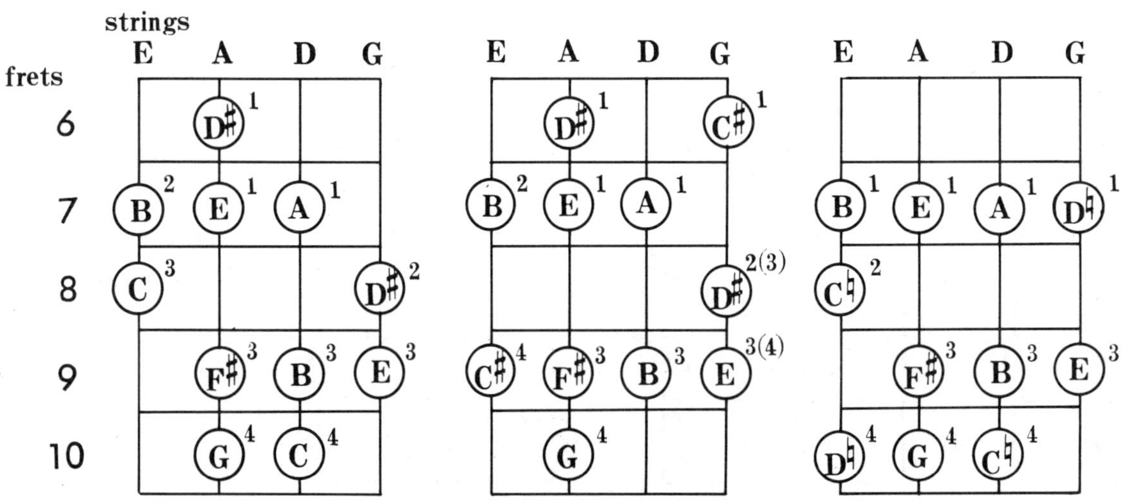

Harmonic Melodic ascending Melodic descending

This form is the same as the natural form, and except for mode or feeling, it is the same as the relative major (G).

MELODIC

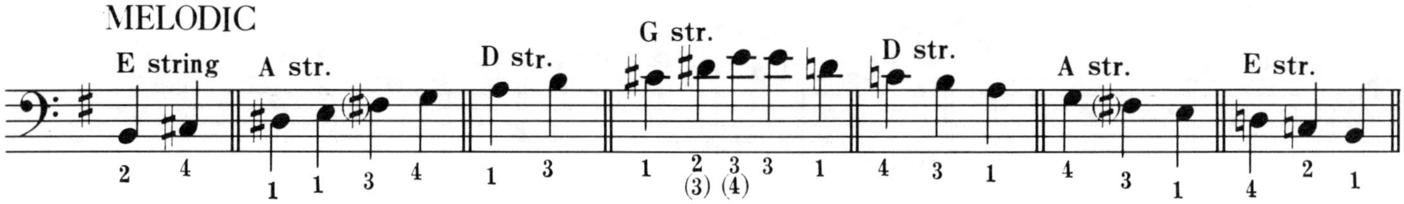

ARPEGGIOS

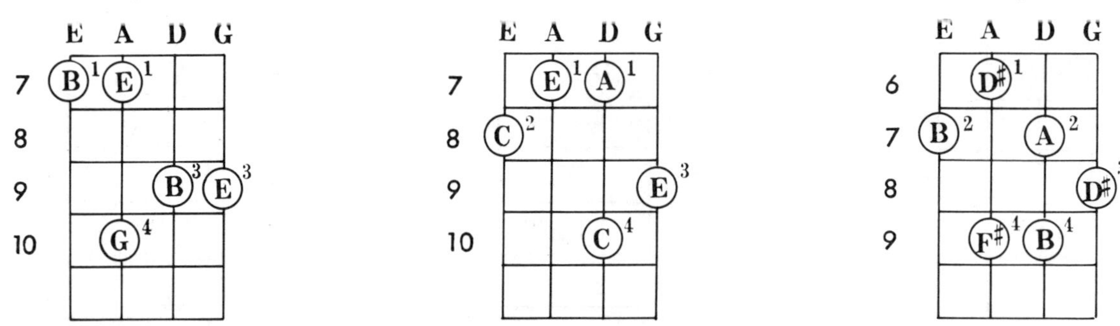

Tonic Subdominant Dominant 7th

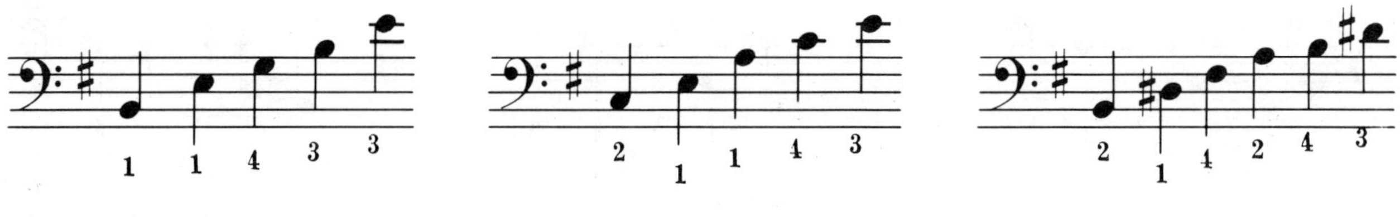

PRIMARY FORMS

G MINOR

HARMONIC

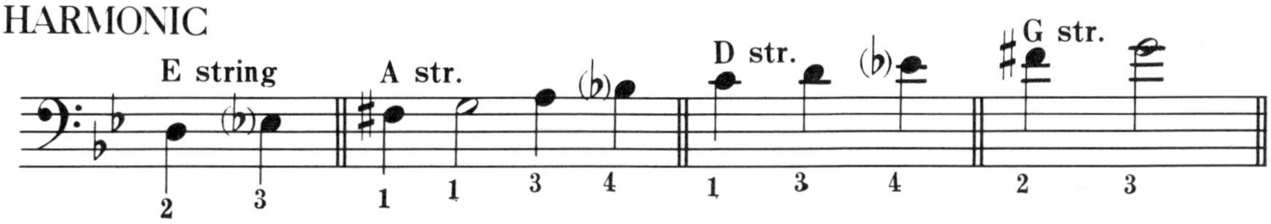

Xth POSITION

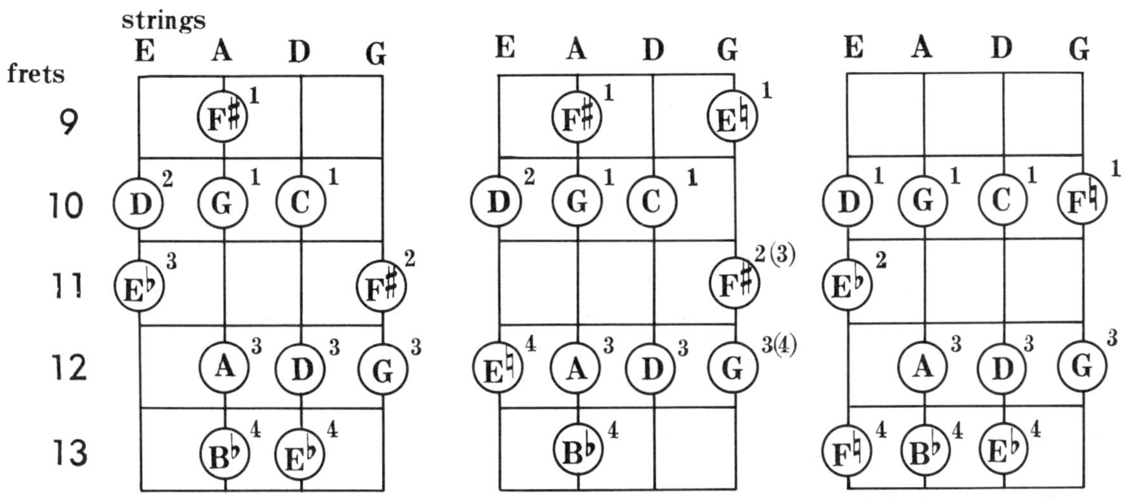

Harmonic — Melodic ascending — Melodic descending

This form is the same as the natural form, and except for mode or feeling, it is the same as the relative major (B♭).

MELODIC

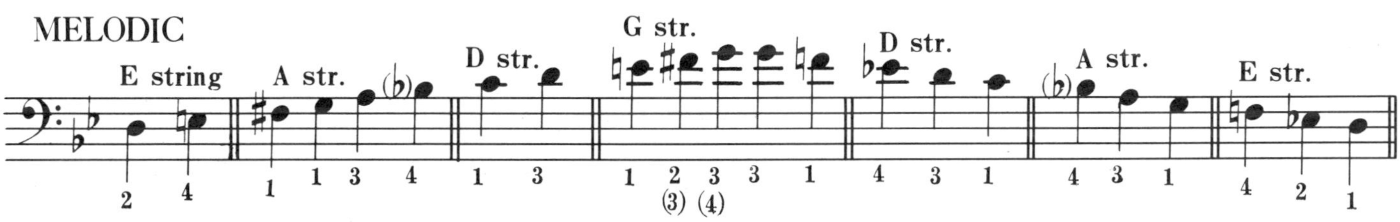

ARPEGGIOS

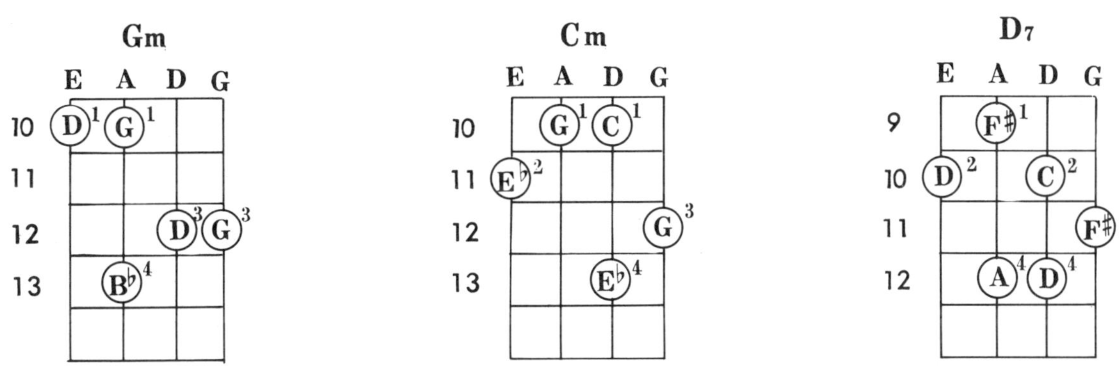

Tonic — Subdominant — Dominant 7th

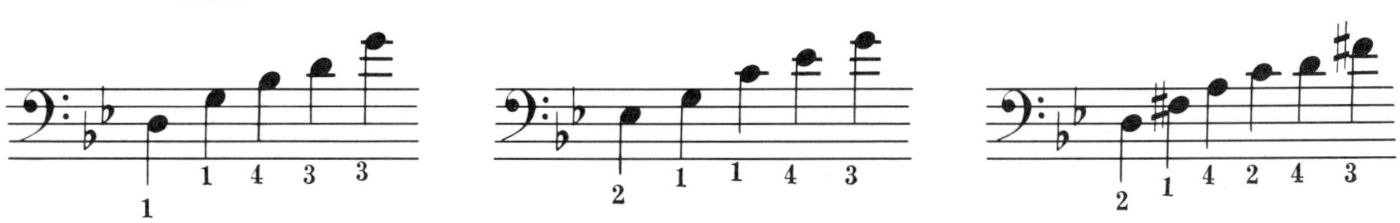

PRIMARY FORMS

B MINOR

HARMONIC

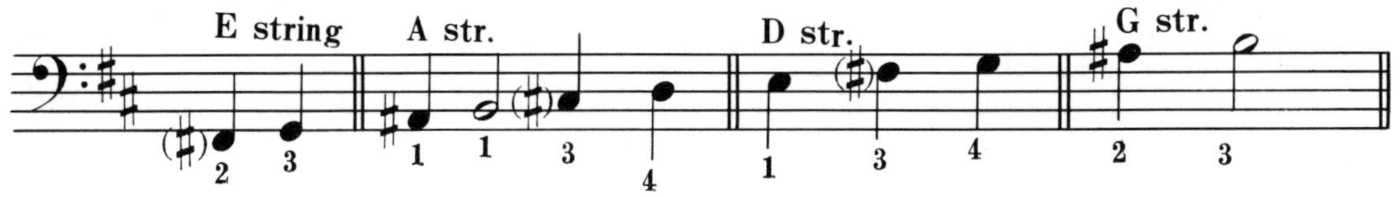

IInd POSITION

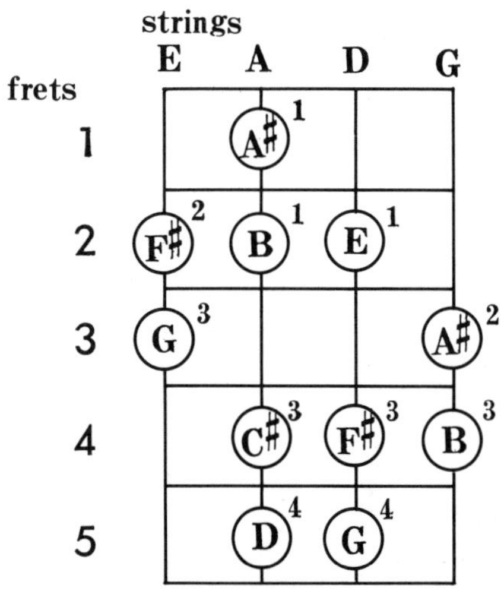

Harmonic

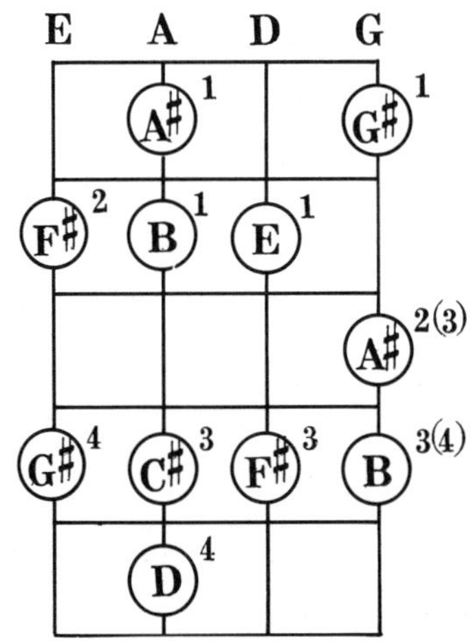

Melodic ascending

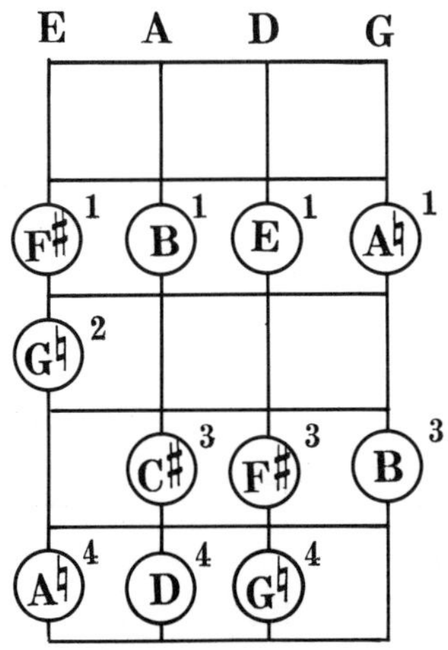

Melodic descending

This form is the same as the natural form, and except for mode or feeling, it is the same as the relative major (D).

MELODIC

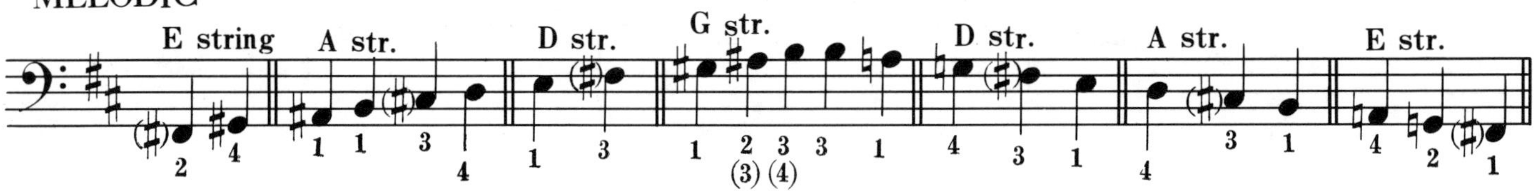

ARPEGGIOS

Bm

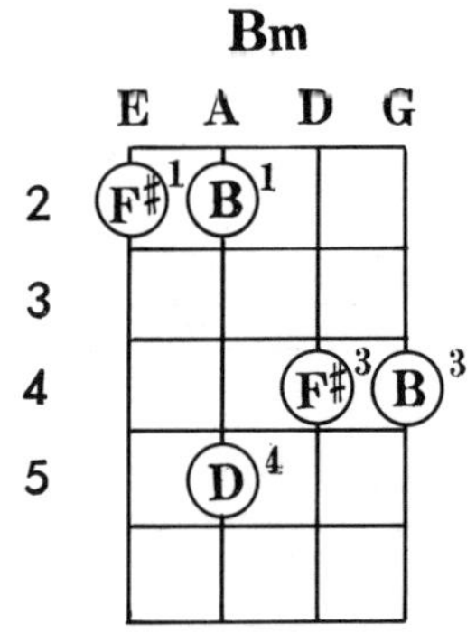

Tonic

Em

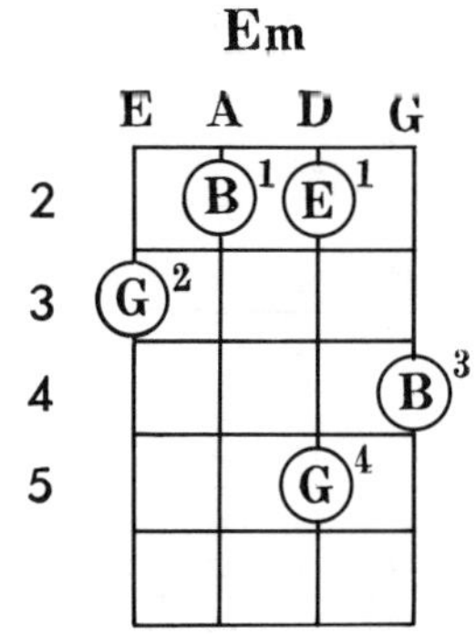

Subdominant

F♯7

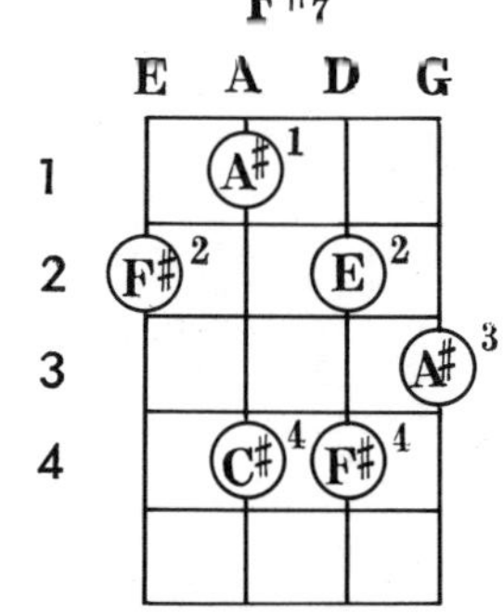

Dominant 7th

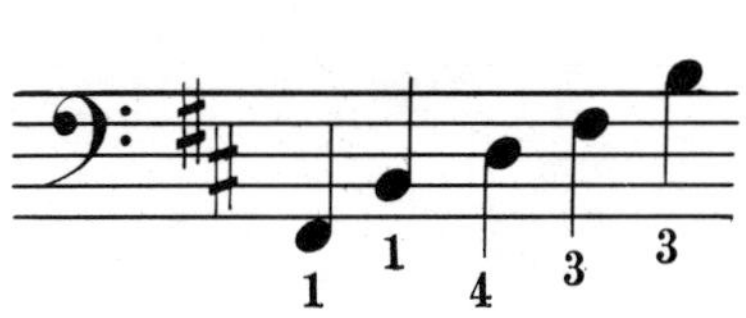

PRIMARY FORMS

C MINOR

HARMONIC

IIIrd POSITION

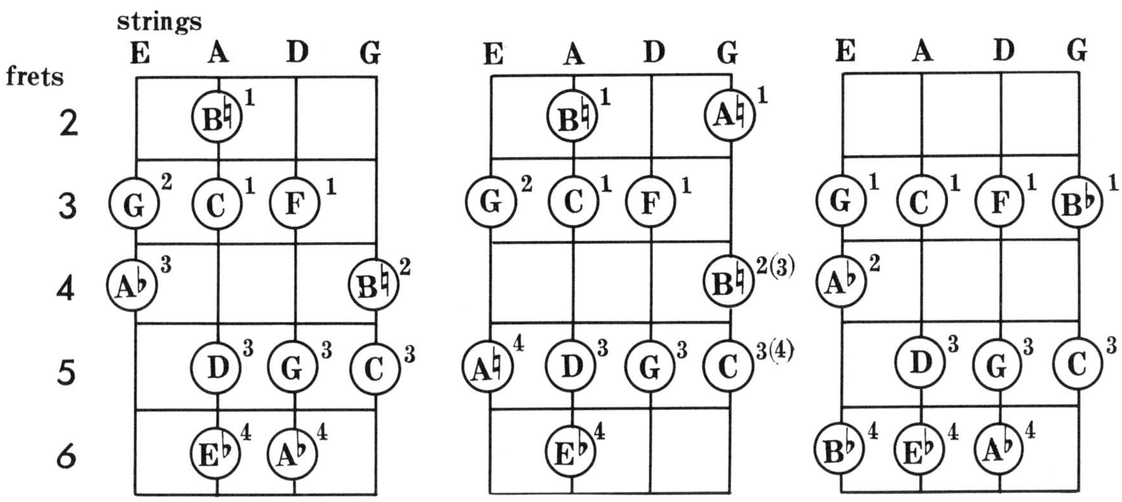

Harmonic — Melodic ascending — Melodic descending

This form is the same as the natural form, and except for mode or feeling, it is the same as the relative major (E♭).

MELODIC

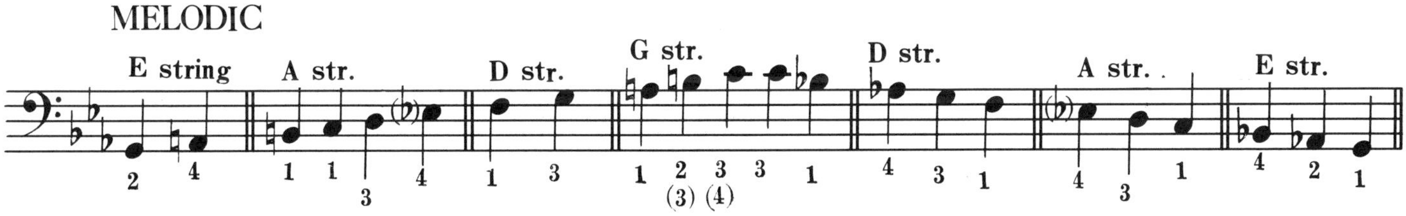

ARPEGGIOS

Cm

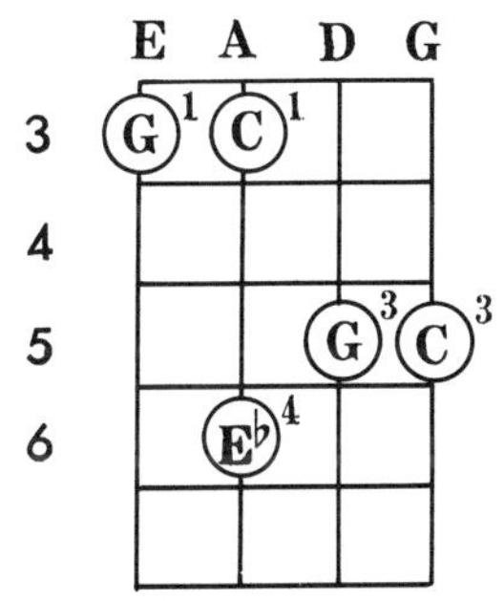

Tonic

Fm

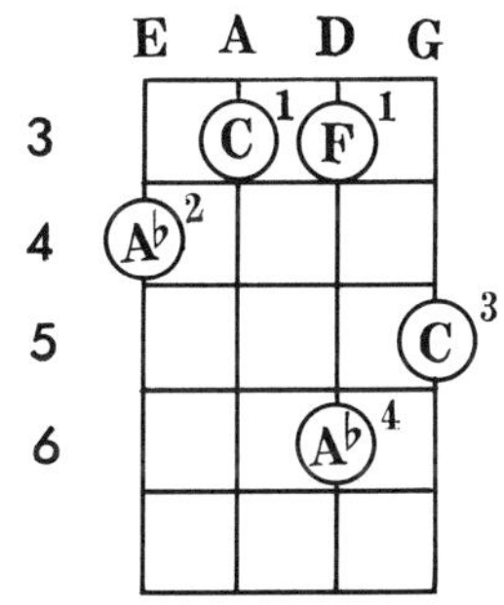

Subdominant

G7

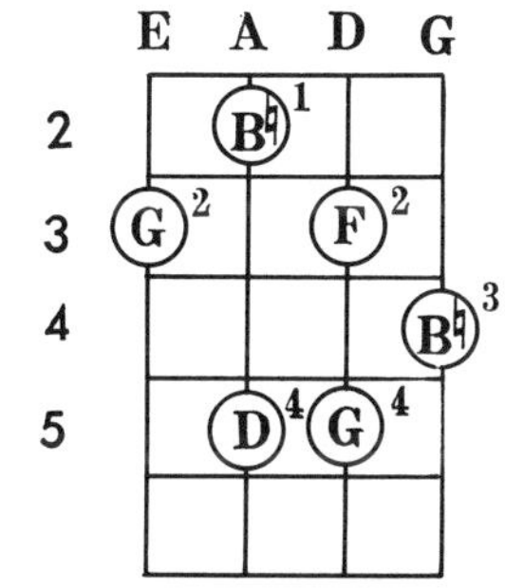

Dominant 7th

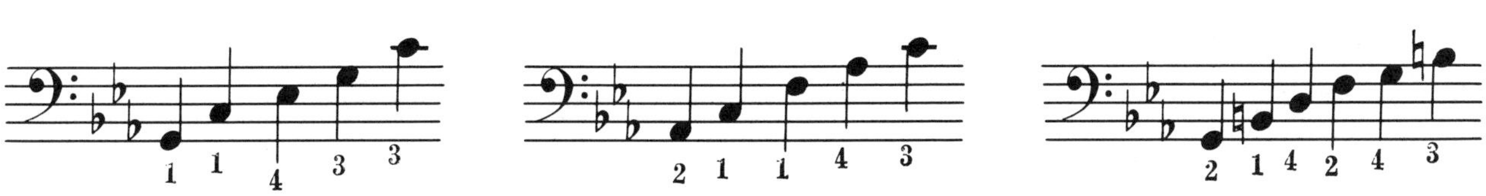

PRIMARY FORMS

F♯ MINOR

HARMONIC

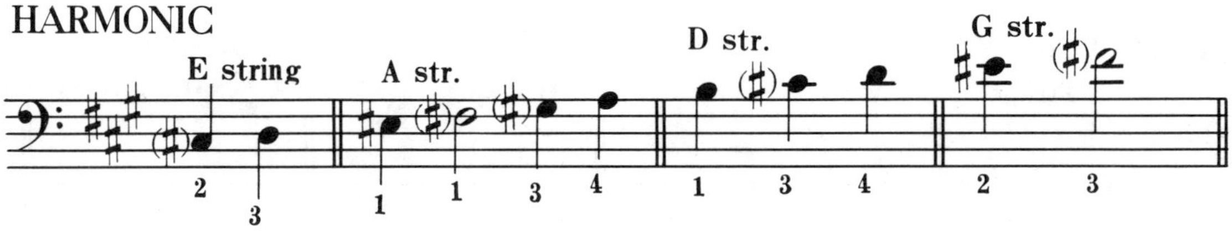

IXth POSITION

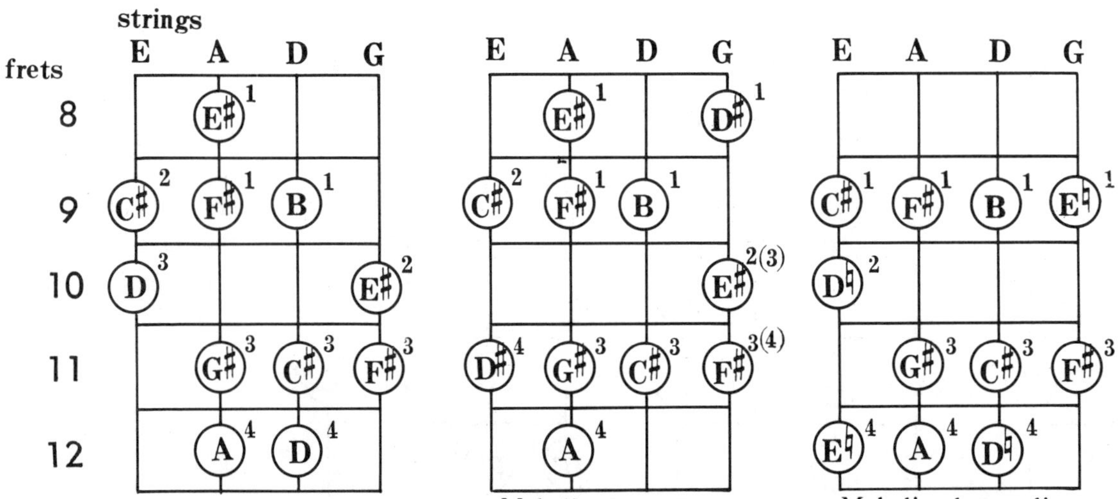

Harmonic

Melodic ascending

Melodic descending

This form is the same as the natural form, and except for mode or feeling, it is the same as the relative major (A).

MELODIC

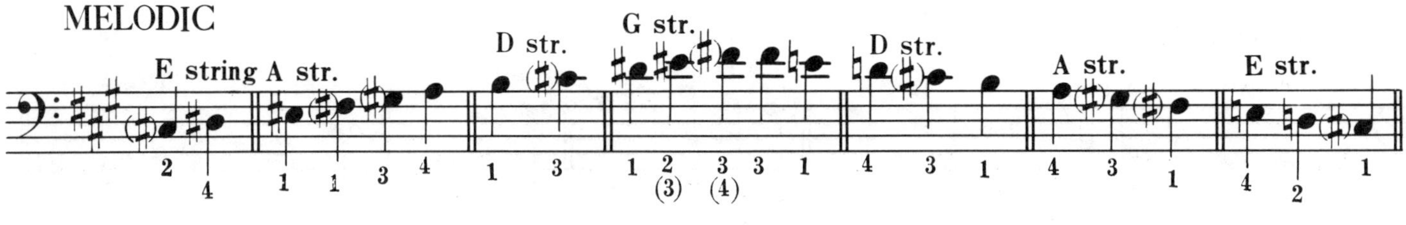

ARPEGGIOS

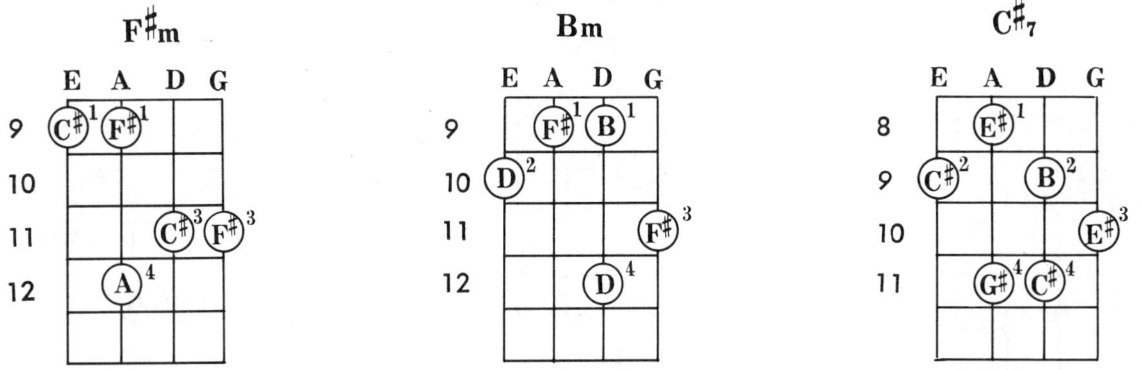

Tonic

Subdominant

Dominant 7th

PRIMARY FORMS

F MINOR

HARMONIC

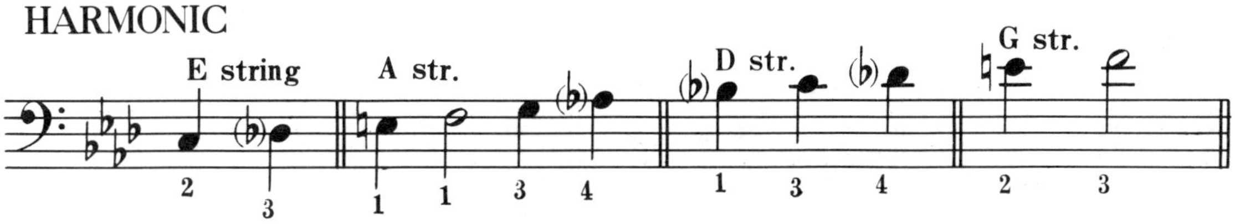

VIIIth POSITION

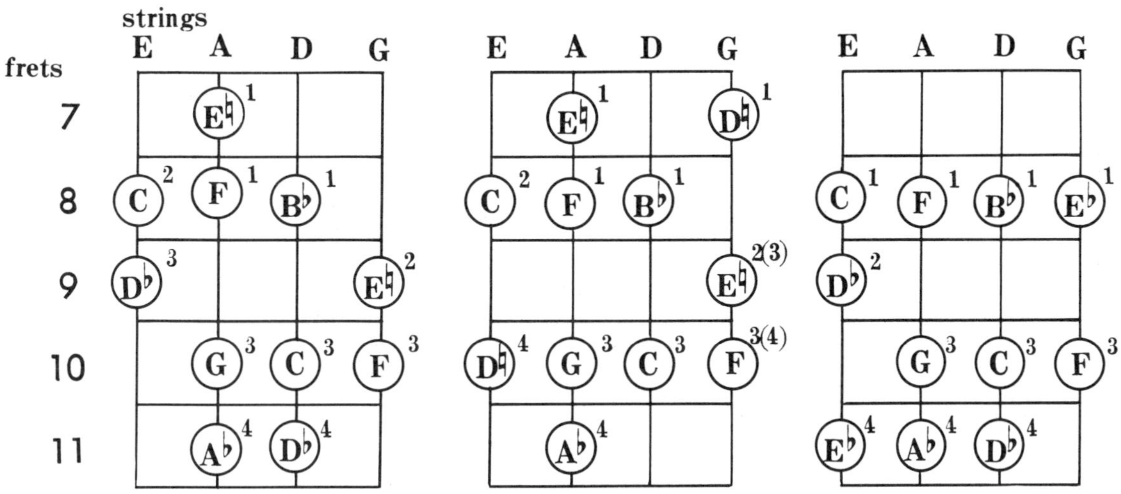

Harmonic — Melodic ascending — Melodic descending

This form is the same as the natural form, and except for mode or feeling, it is the same as the relative major (A♭).

MELODIC

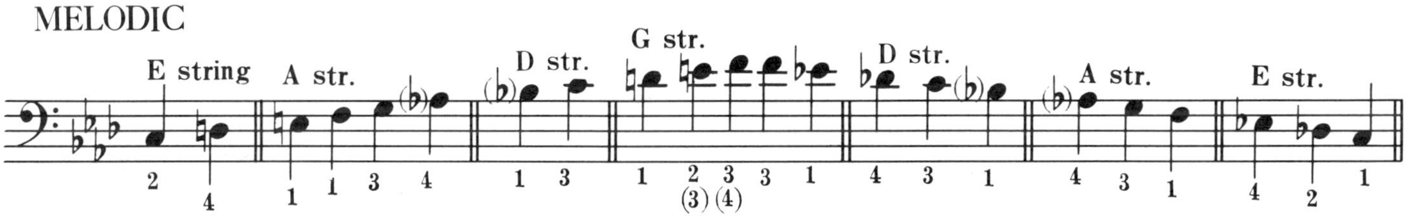

ARPEGGIOS

Fm

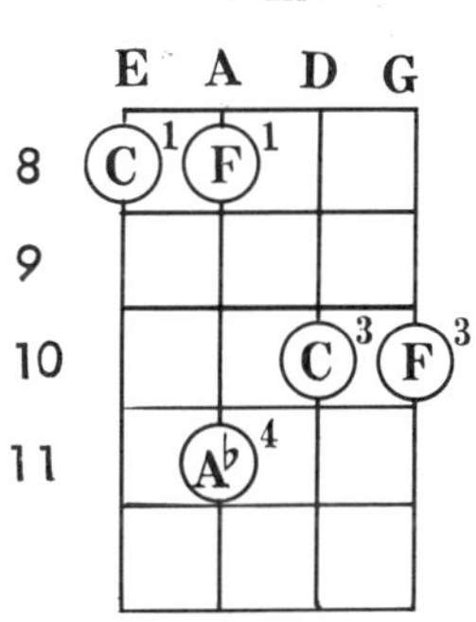

Tonic

B♭m

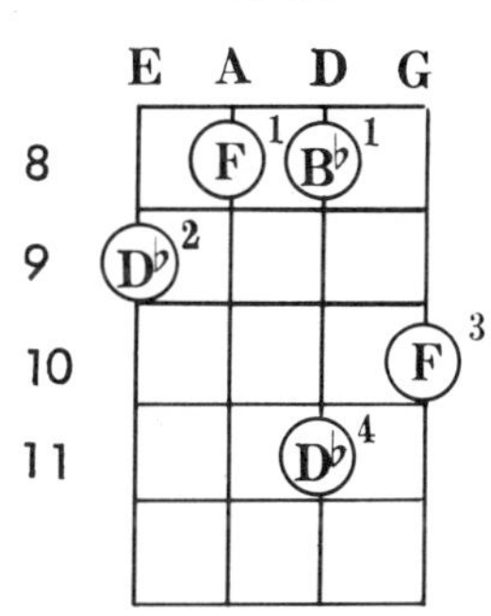

Subdominant

C7

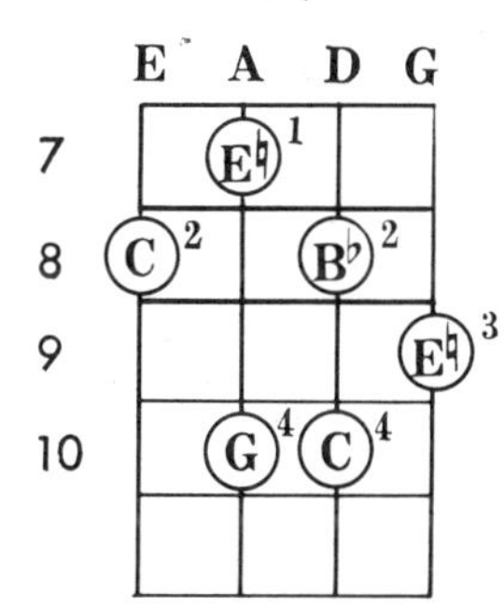

Dominant 7th

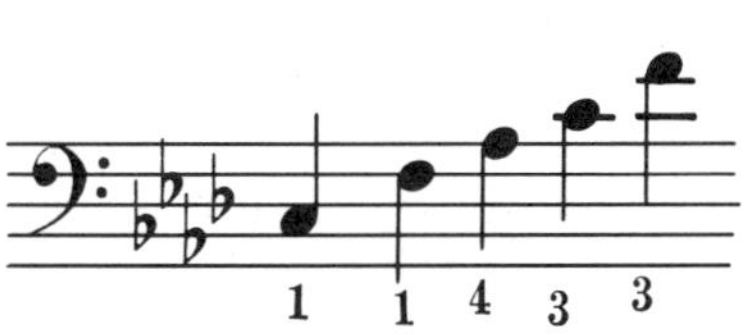

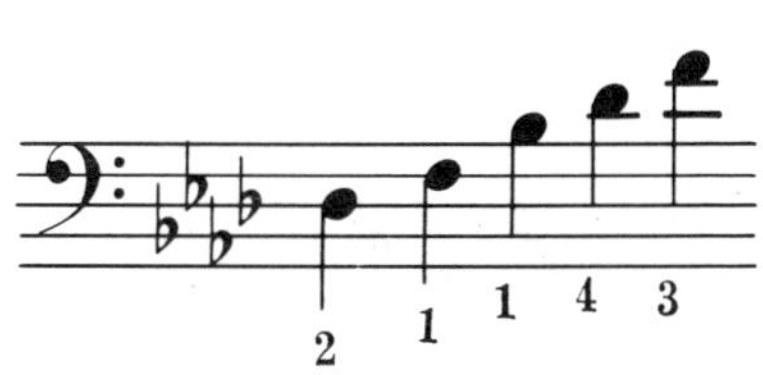

PRIMARY FORMS

C♯ MINOR

HARMONIC

IVth POSITION

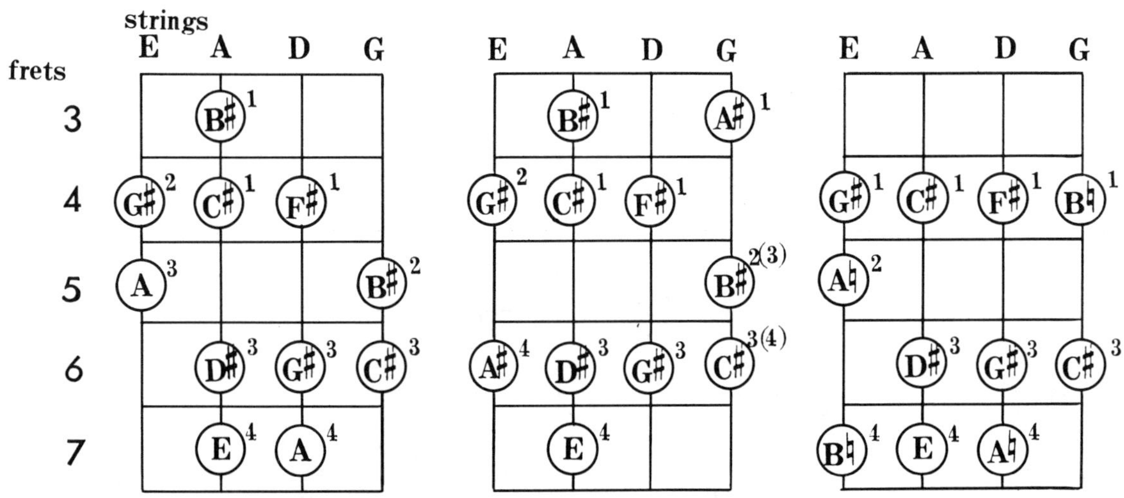

Harmonic — Melodic ascending — Melodic descending

This form is the same as the natural form, and except for mode or feeling, it is the same as the relative major (E).

MELODIC

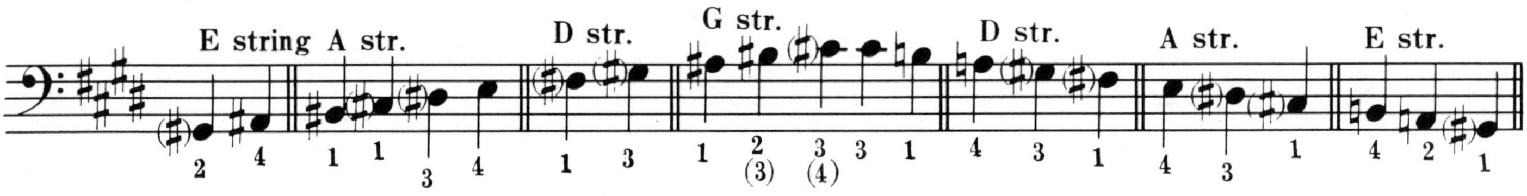

ARPEGGIOS

C♯m — F♯m — G♯$_7$

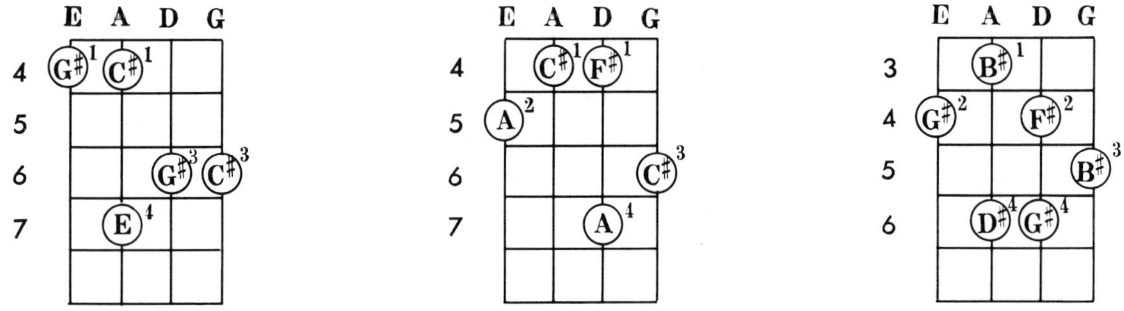

Tonic — Subdominant — Dominant 7th

PRIMARY FORMS

B♭ MINOR

HARMONIC

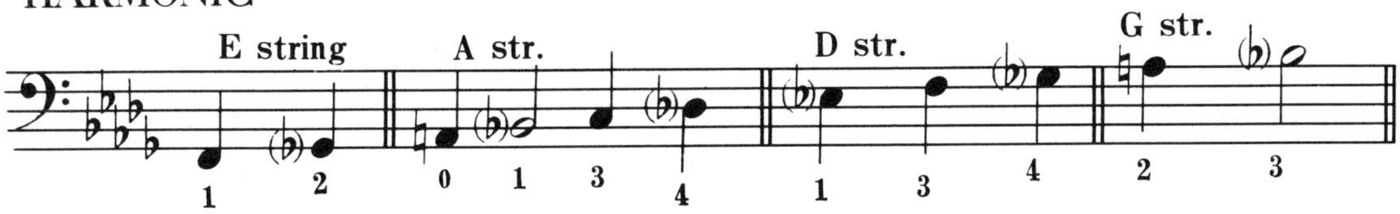

1st POSITION

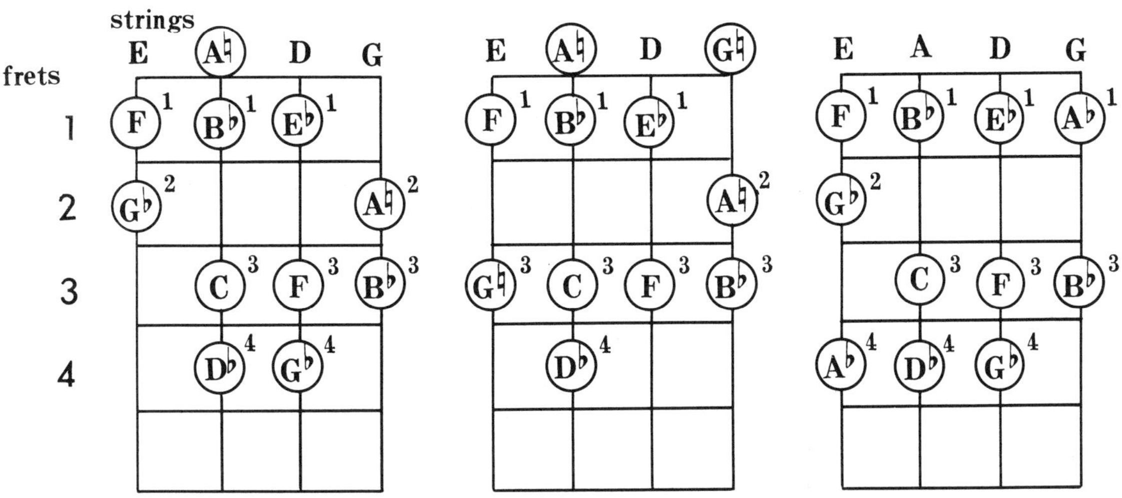

Harmonic Melodic ascending Melodic descending

This form is the same as the natural form, and except for mode or feeling, it is the same as the relative major (D♭).

MELODIC

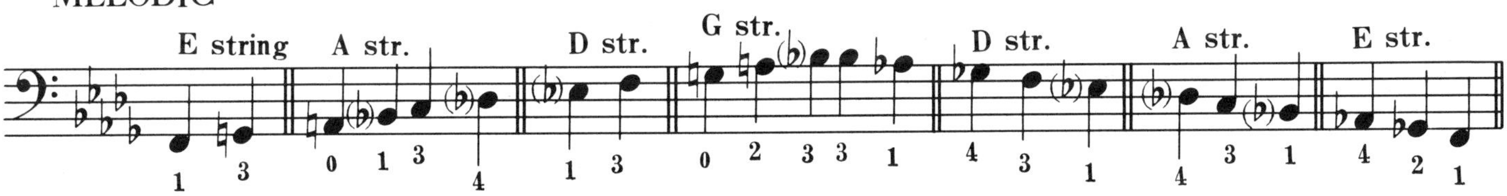

ARPEGGIOS

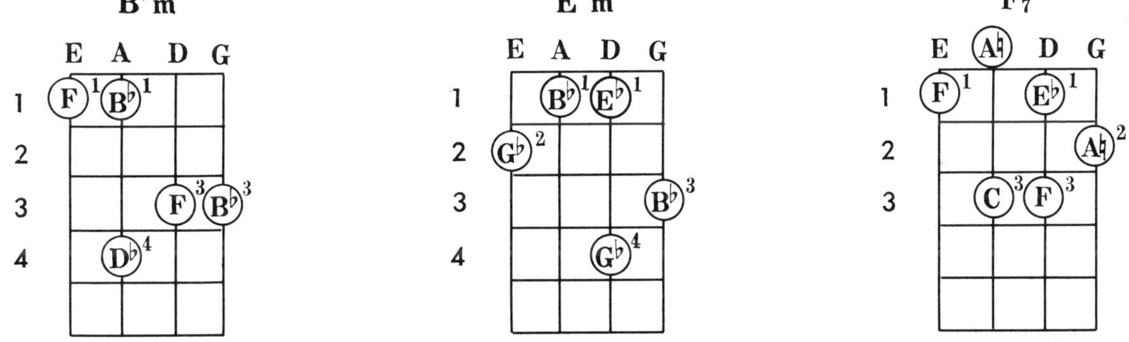

Tonic Subdominant Dominant 7th

PRIMARY FORMS

G♯ MINOR

HARMONIC

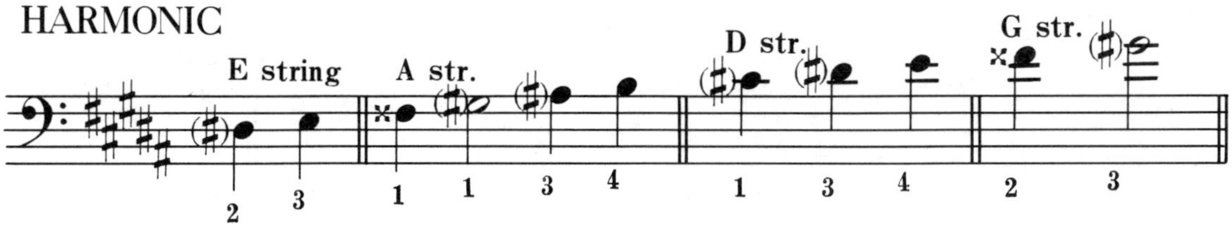

XIth POSITION

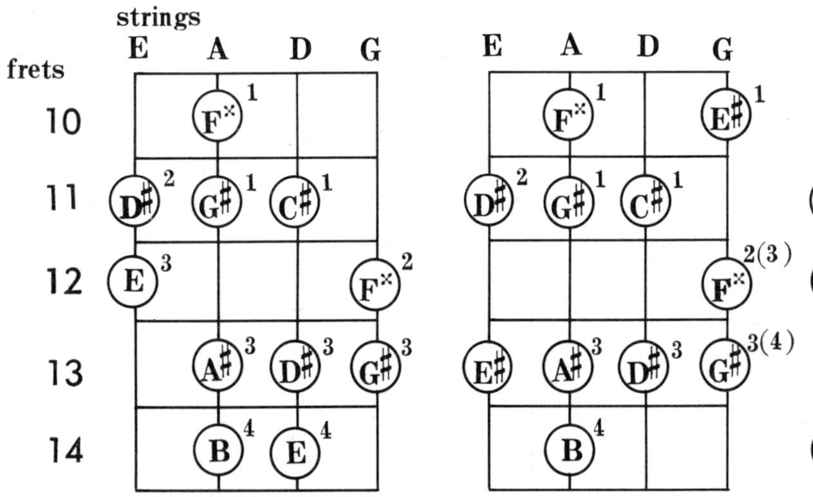

Harmonic | Melodic ascending | Melodic descending

This form is the same as the natural form, and except for mode or feeling, it is the same as the relative major (B).

MELODIC

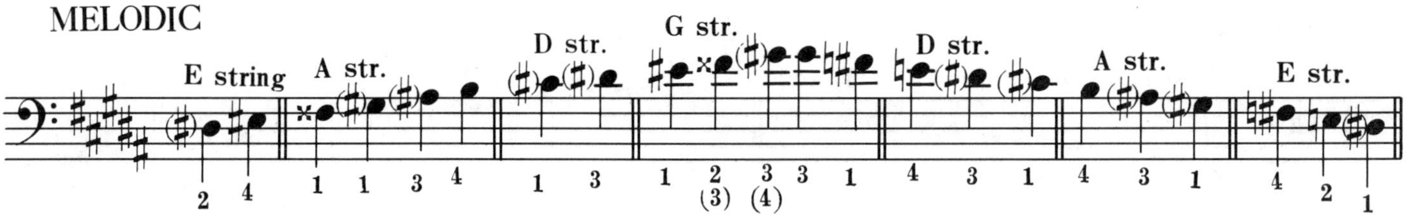

ARPEGGIOS

G♯m

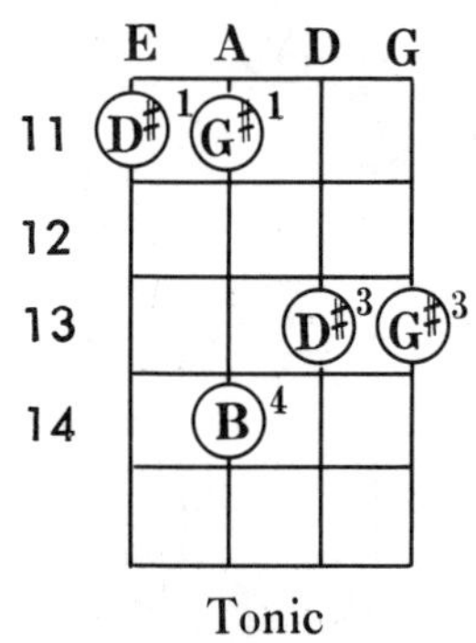

Tonic

C♯m

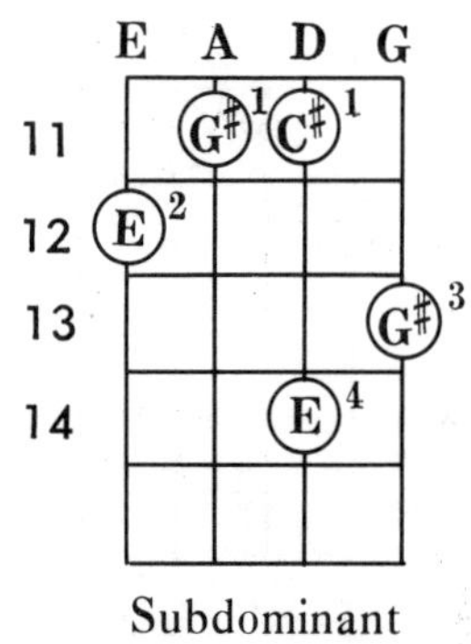

Subdominant

D♯7

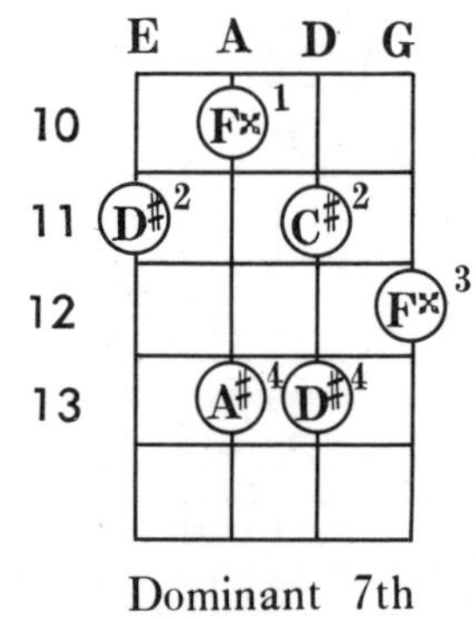

Dominant 7th

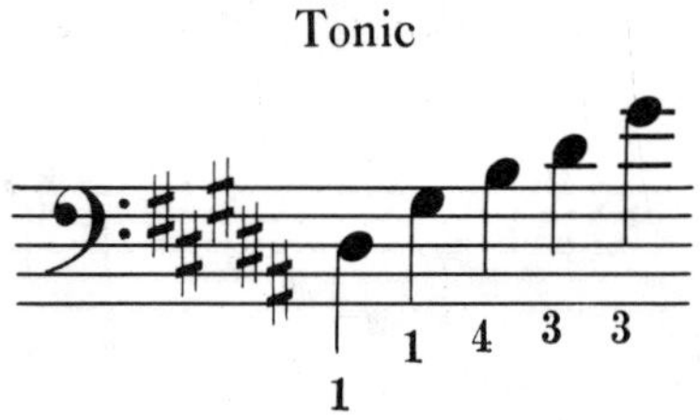

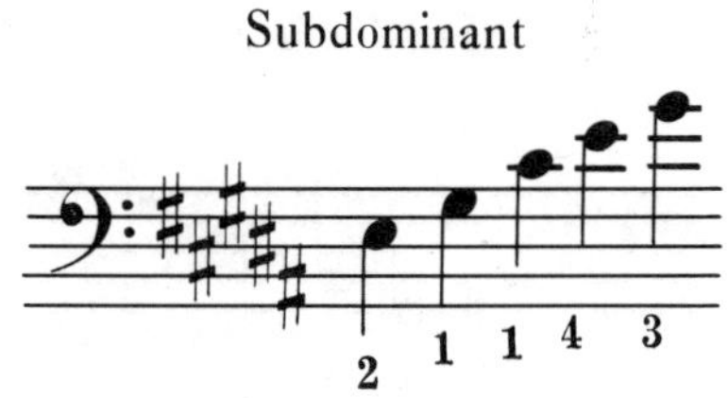

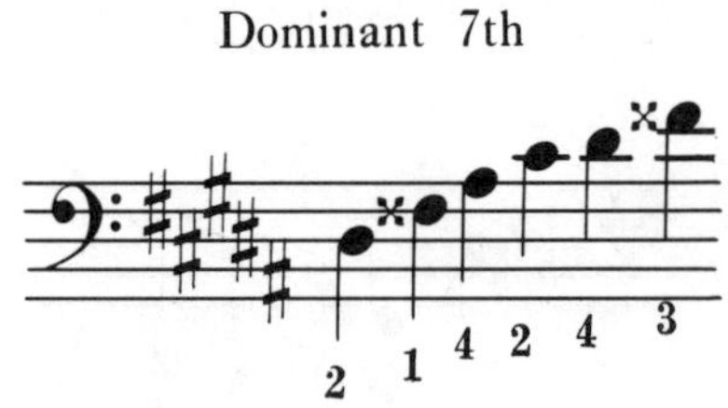

PRIMARY FORMS

E♭ MINOR

This key is enharmonically equivalent to D♯ Minor (p 48).

HARMONIC

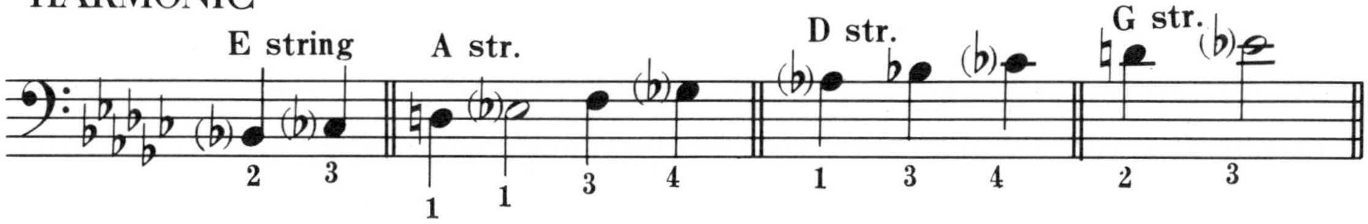

VIth POSITION

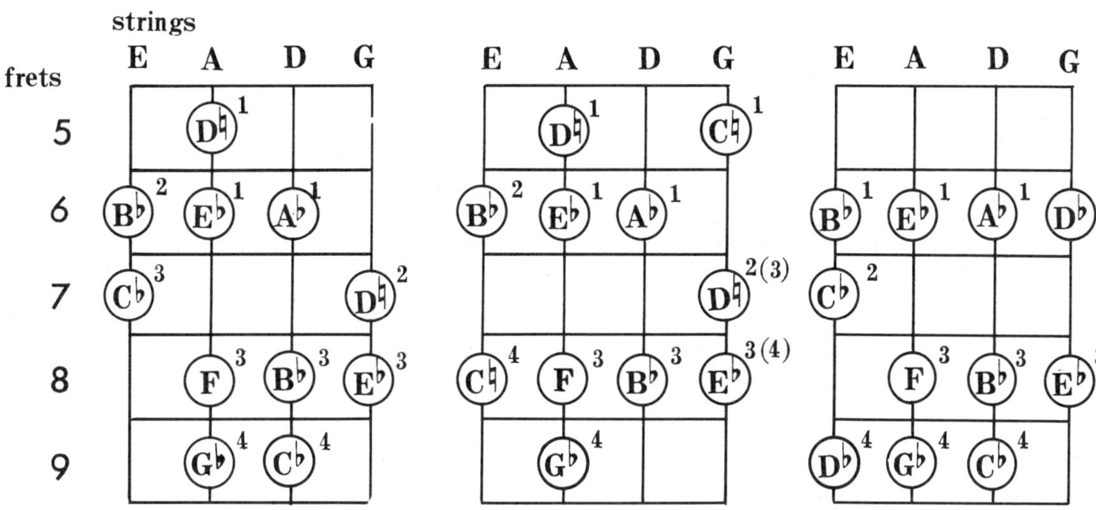

Harmonic — Melodic ascending — Melodic descending

This form is the same as the natural form, and except for mode or feeling, it is the same as the relative major (G♭).

MELODIC

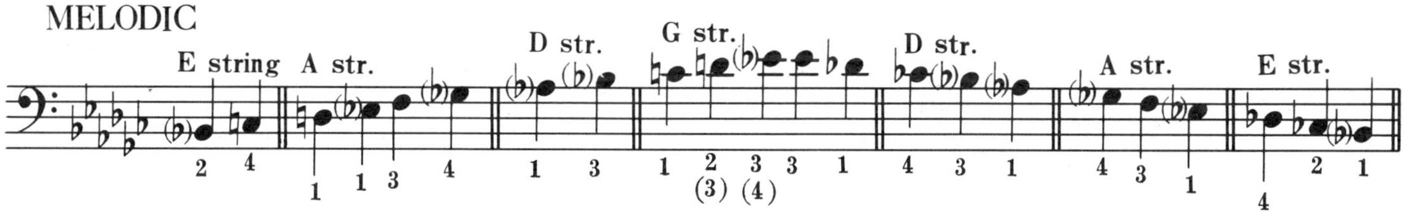

ARPEGGIOS

E♭m

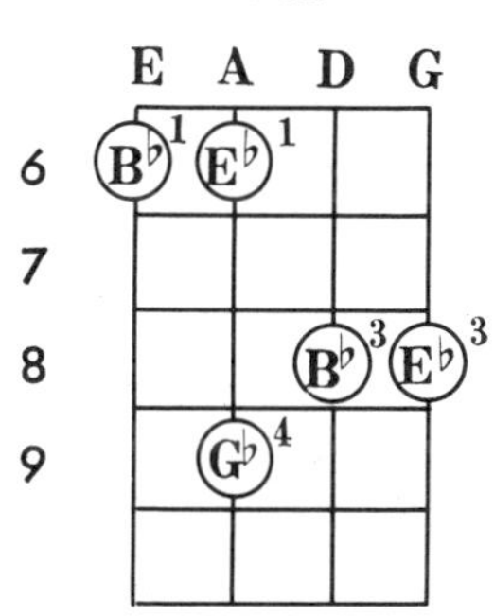

Tonic

A♭m

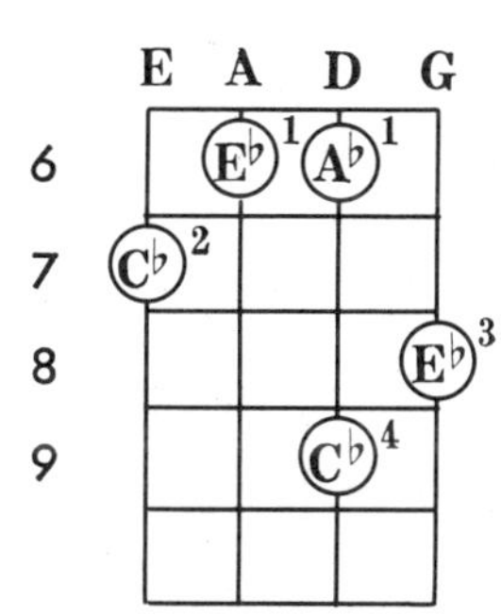

Subdominant

B♭7

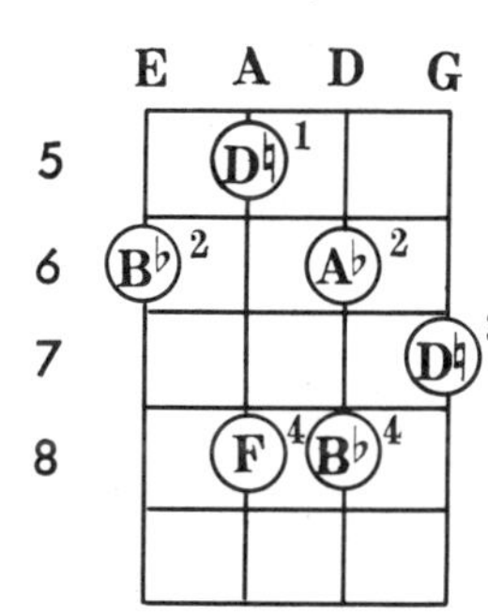

Dominant 7th

PRIMARY FORMS

D♯ MINOR

This key is enharmonically equivalent to E♭ Minor (p. 47).

HARMONIC

VIth POSITION

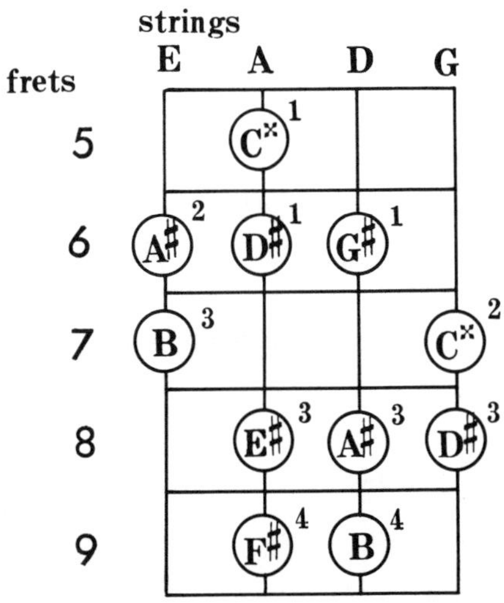

Harmonic

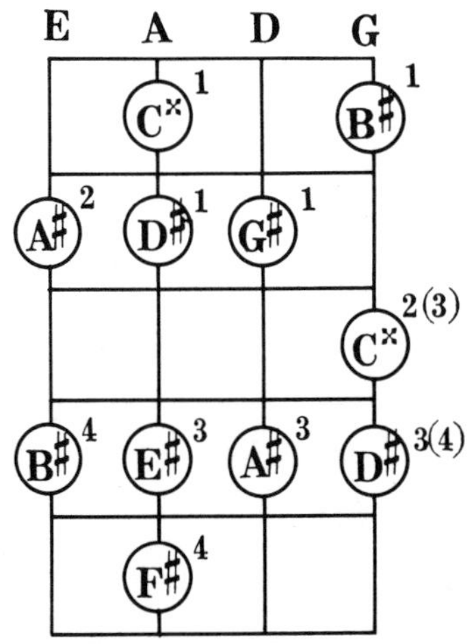

Melodic ascending

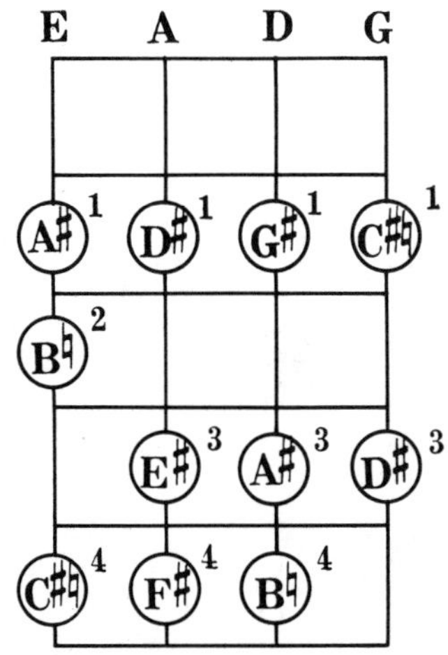

Melodic descending

This form is the same as the natural form, and except for mode or feeling, it is the same as the relative major (F♯).

MELODIC

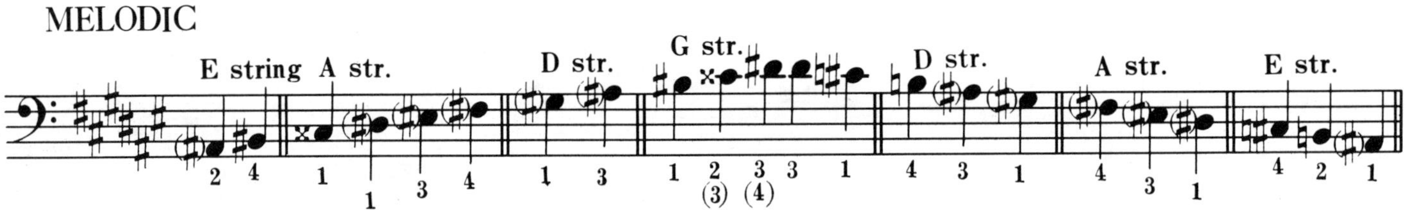

ARPEGGIOS

D♯m

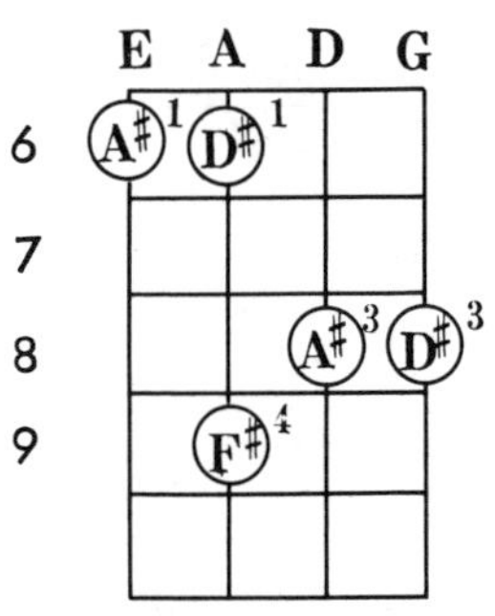

Tonic

G♯m

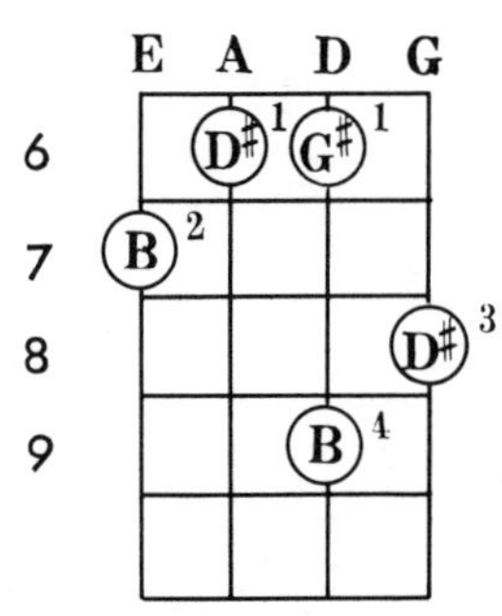

Subdominant

A♯7

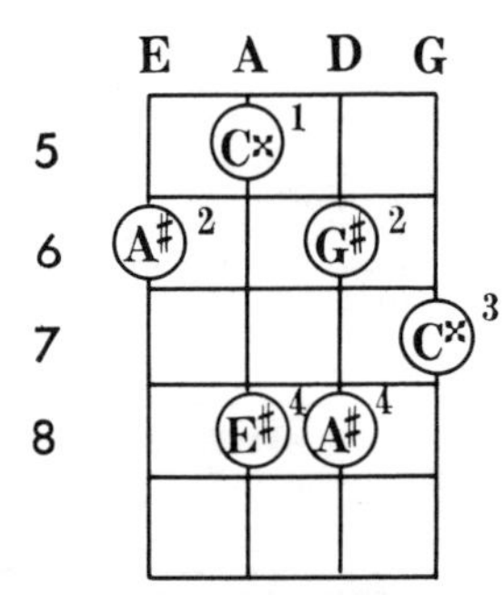

Dominant 7th

SECONDARY FORMS

A MINOR

HARMONIC

VIIth POSITION

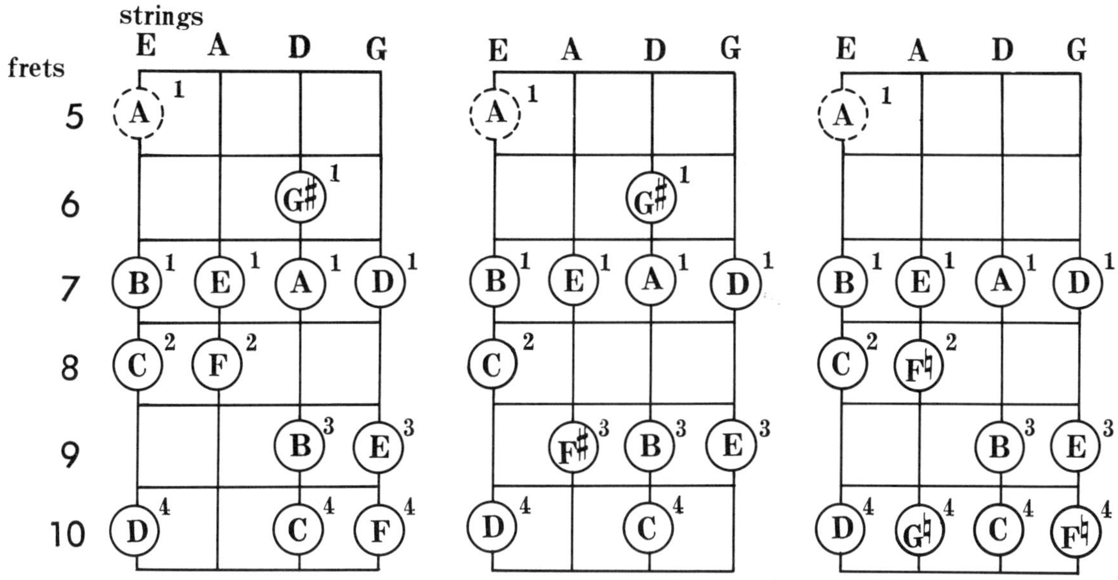

Harmonic — Melodic ascending — Melodic descending

This form is the same as the natural form, and except for mode or feeling, it is the same as the relative major(C).

MELODIC

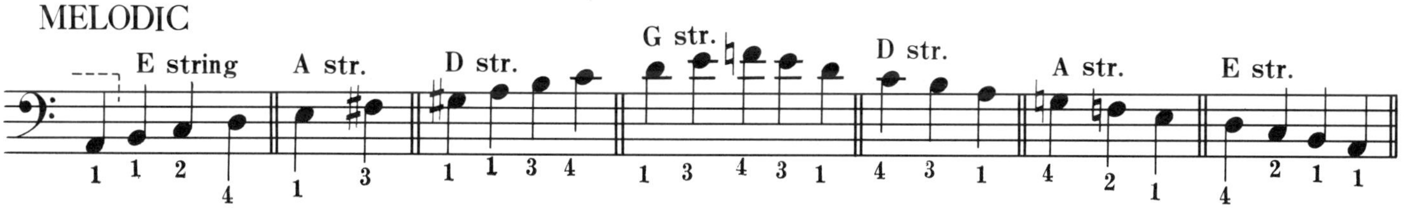

ARPEGGIOS

Am

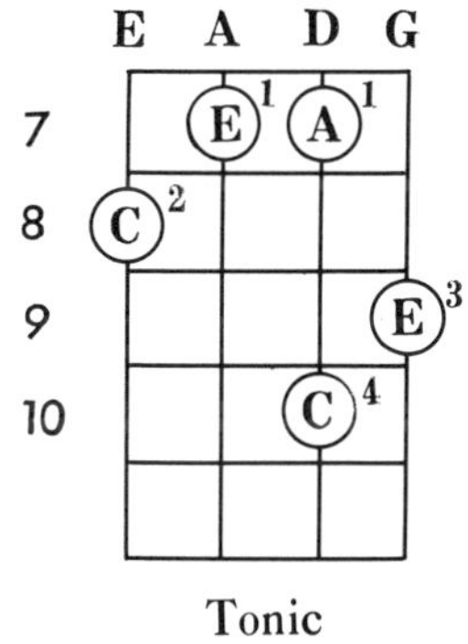

Tonic

Dm

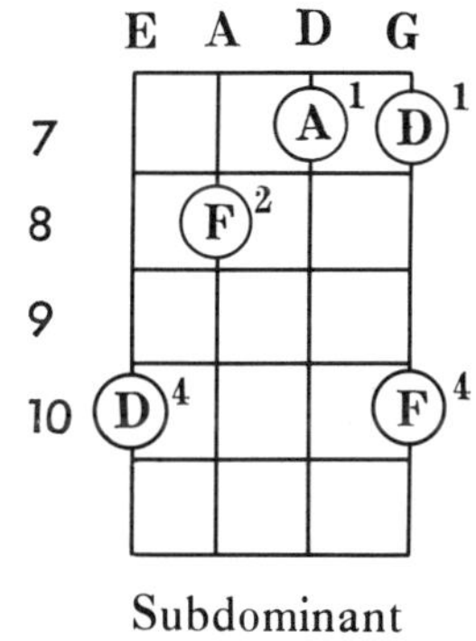

Subdominant

E7

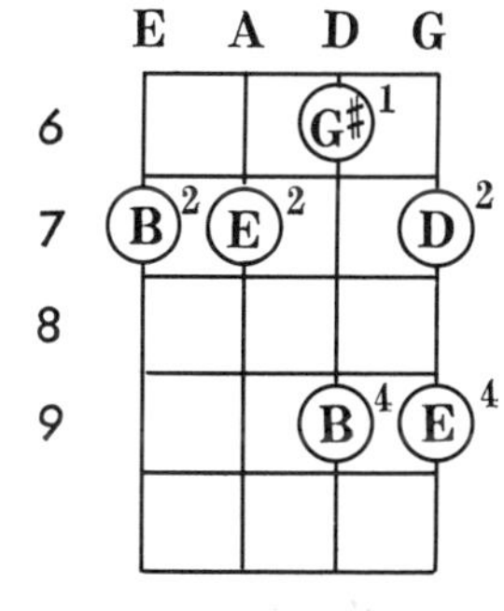

Dominant 7th

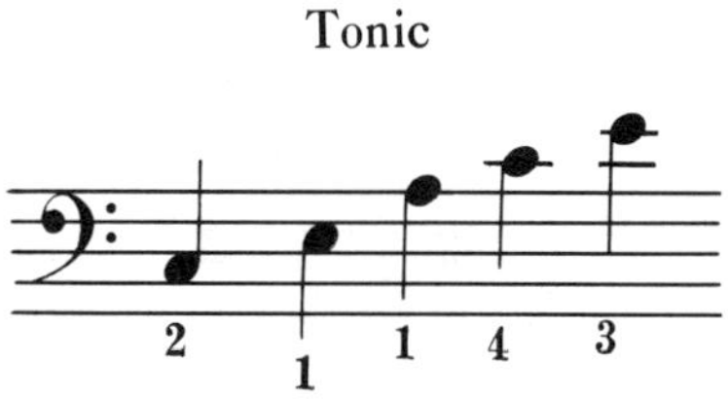

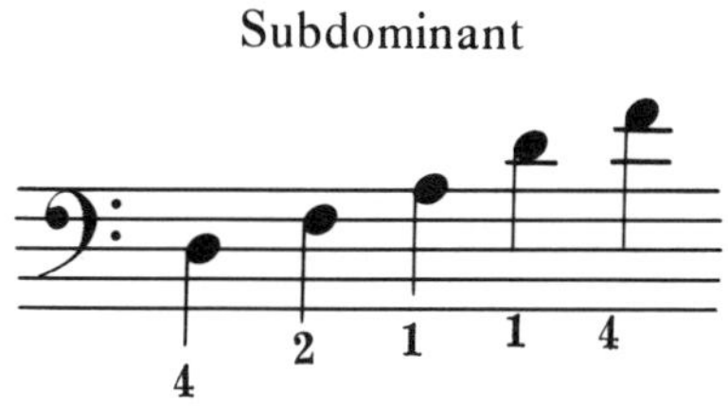

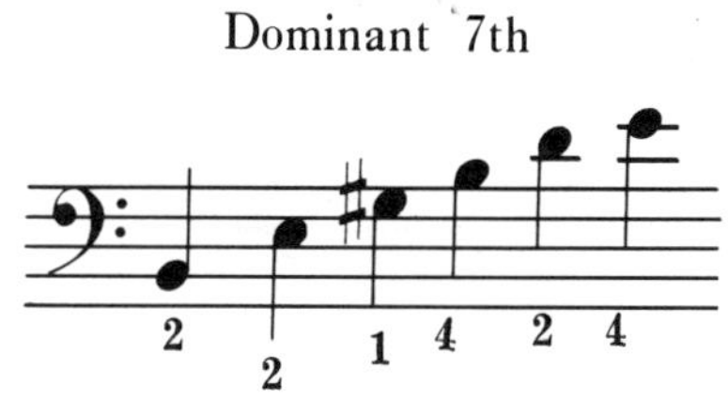

SECONDARY FORMS

D MINOR

HARMONIC

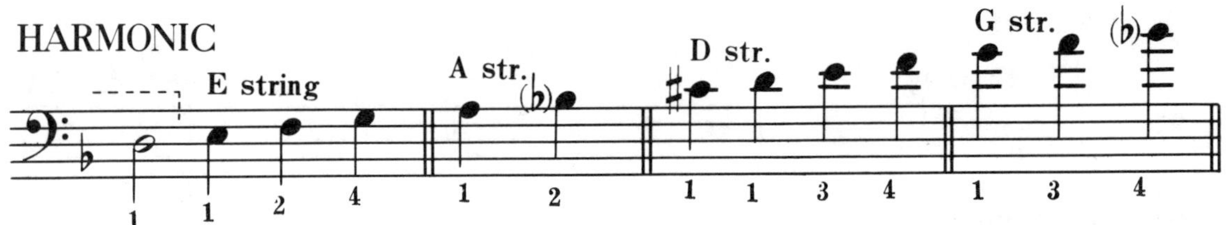

XIIth POSITION

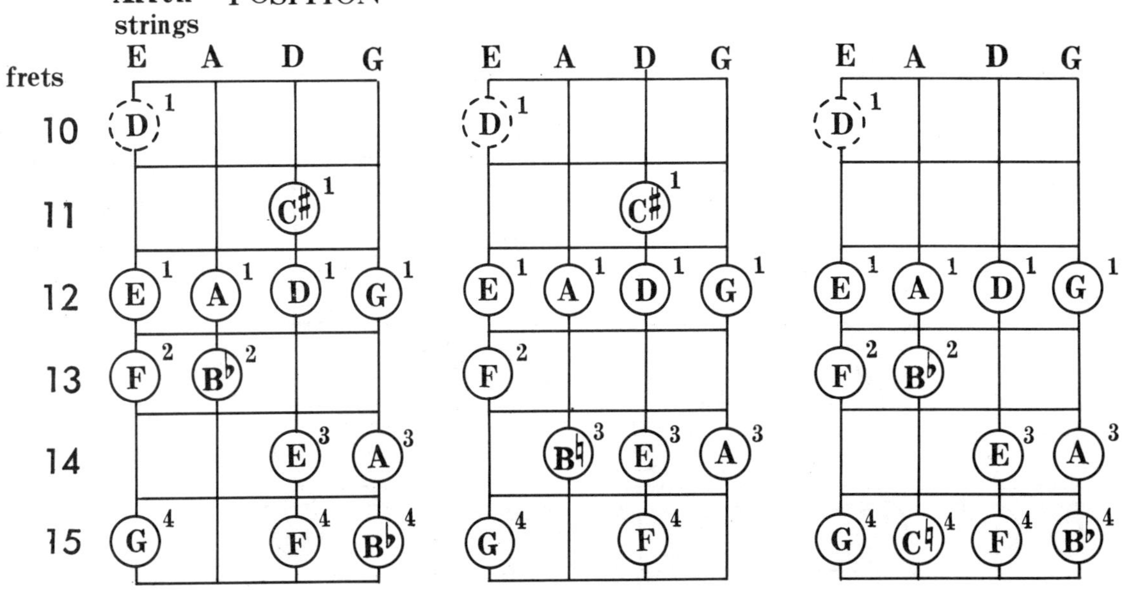

Harmonic | Melodic ascending | Melodic descending

This form is the same as the natural form, and except for mode or feeling, it is the same as the relative major (F).

MELODIC

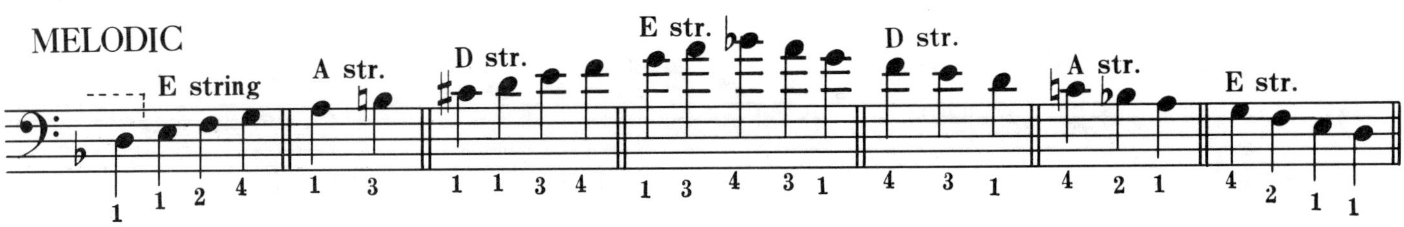

ARPEGGIOS

Dm

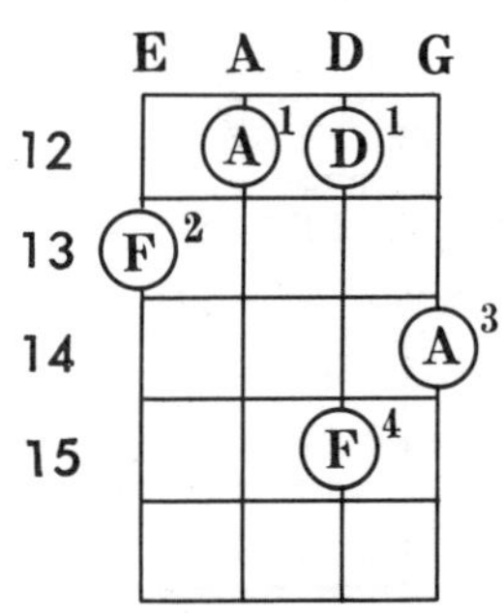

Tonic

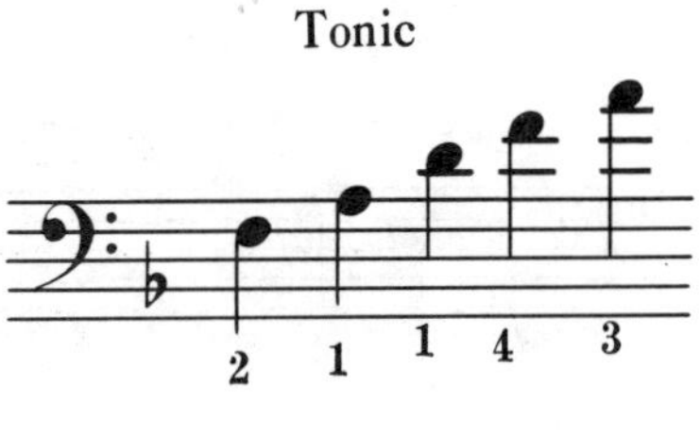

Gm

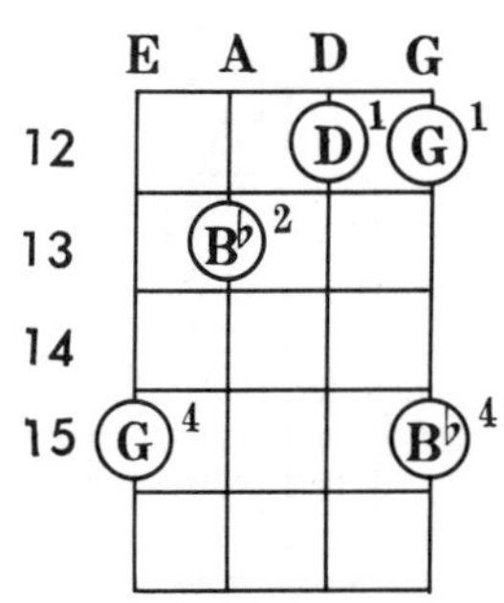

Subdominant

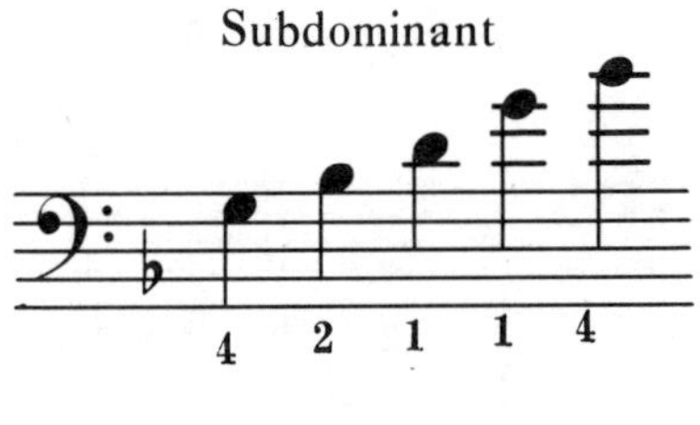

A_7

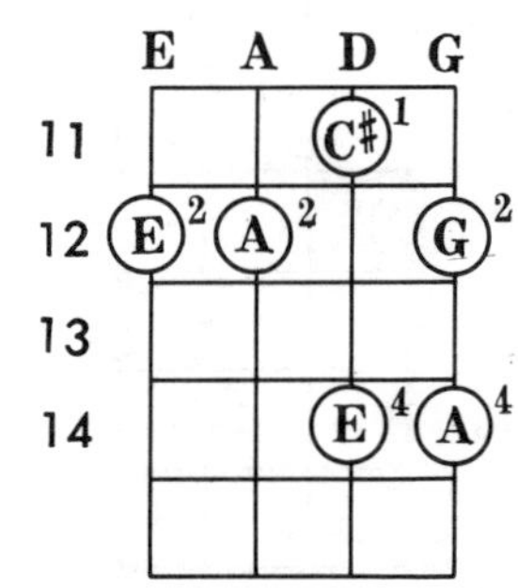

Dominant 7th

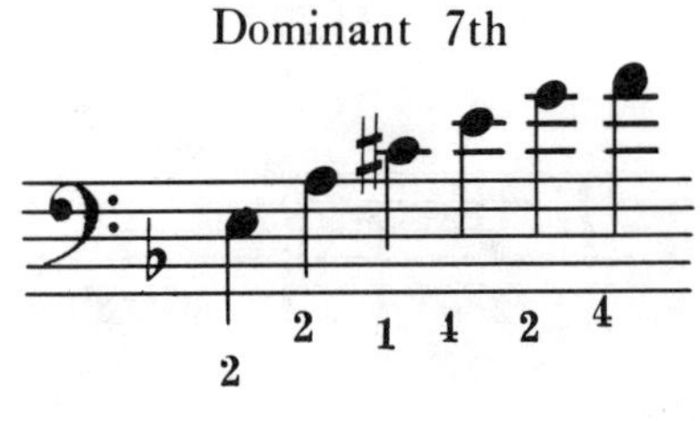

SECONDARY FORMS

E MINOR

HARMONIC

IInd POSITION

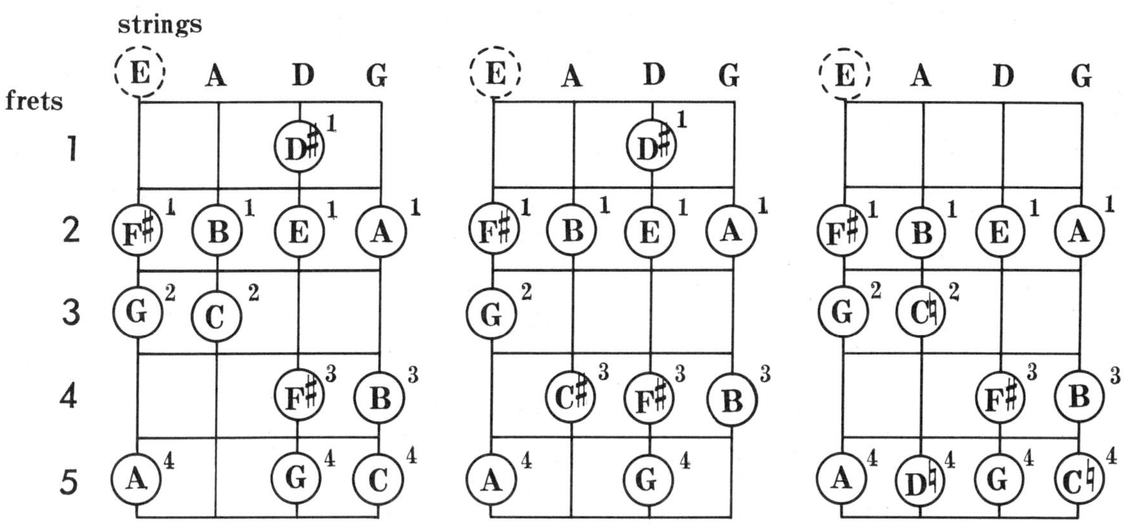

Harmonic — Melodic ascending — Melodic descending

This form is the same as the natural form, and except for mode or feeling, it is the same as the relative major (G).

MELODIC

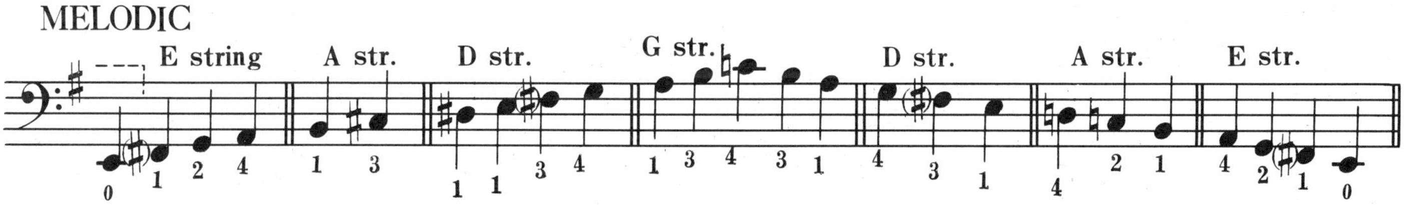

ARPEGGIOS

Em

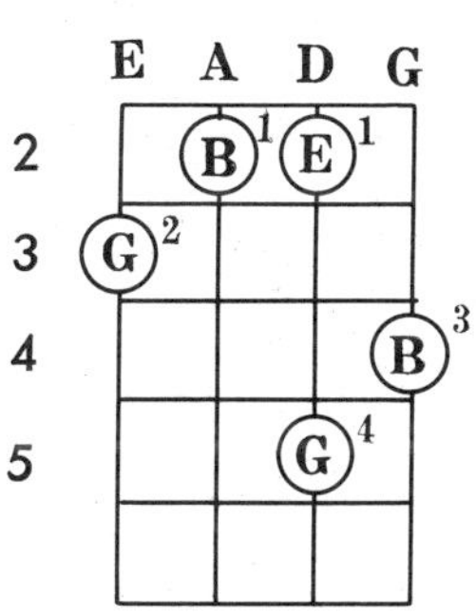

Tonic

Am

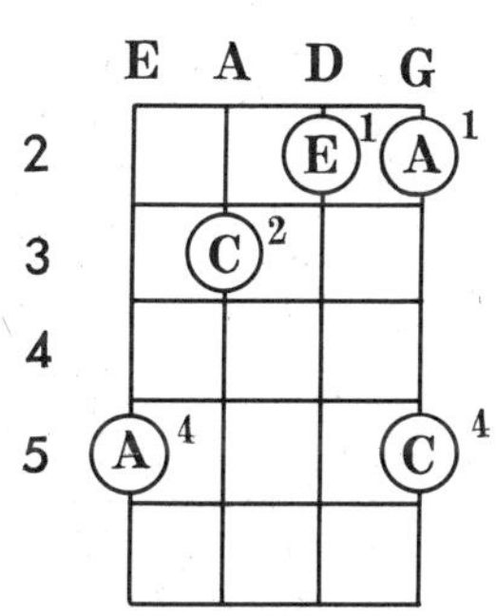

Subdominant

B7

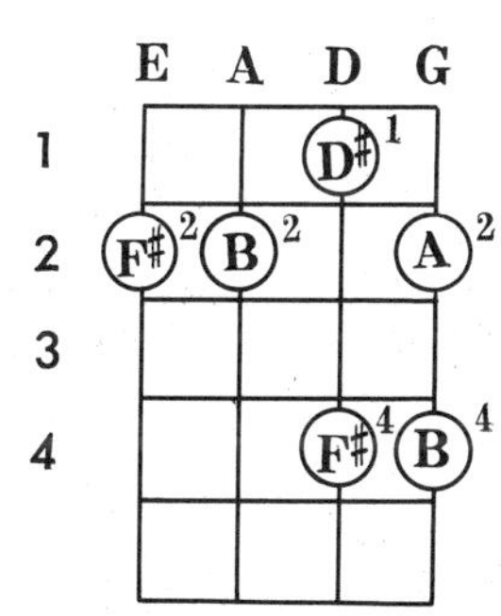

Dominant 7th

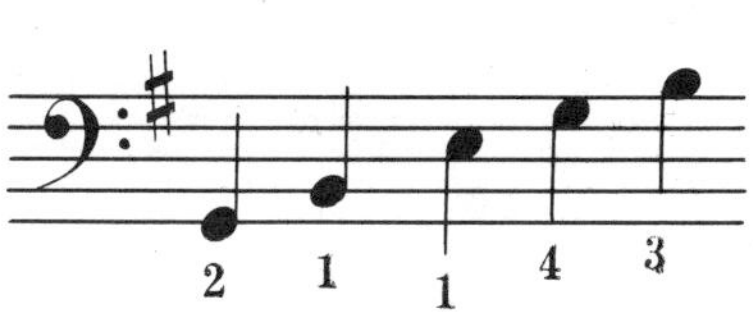

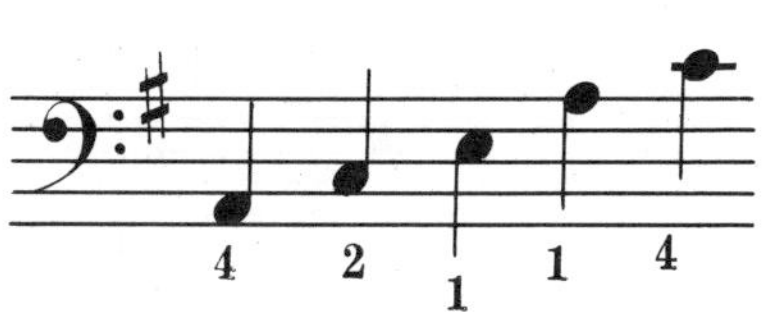

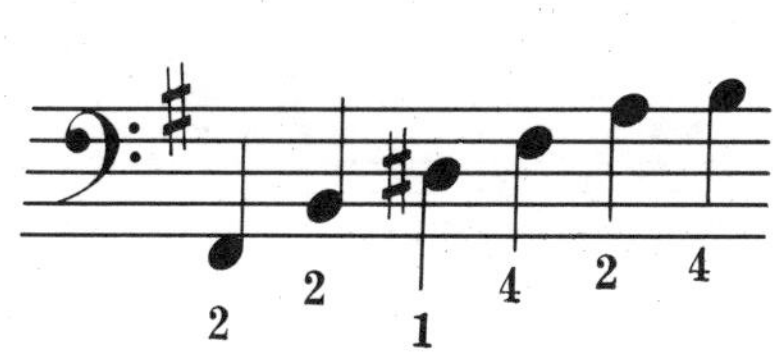

SECONDARY FORMS

G MINOR

HARMONIC

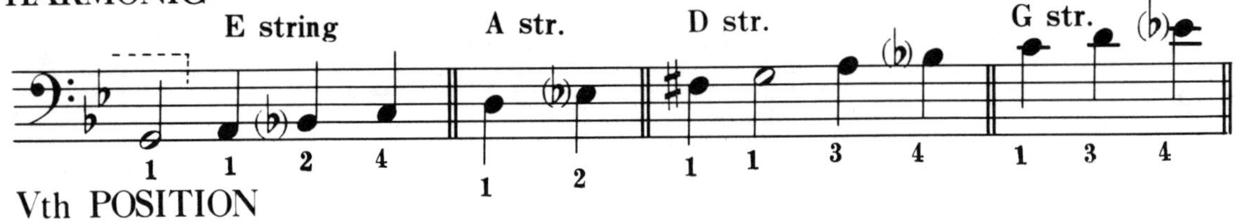

Vth POSITION

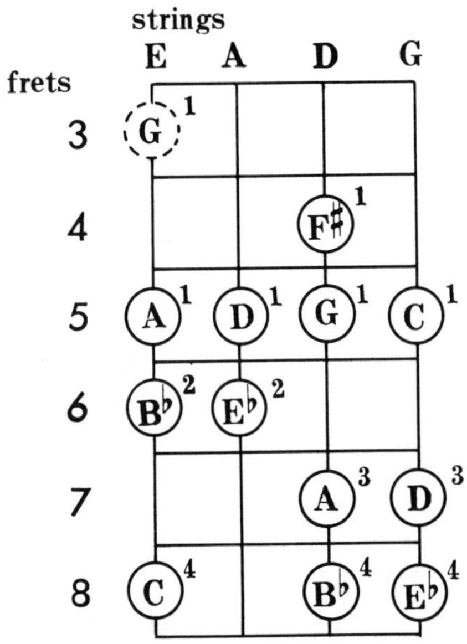

Harmonic

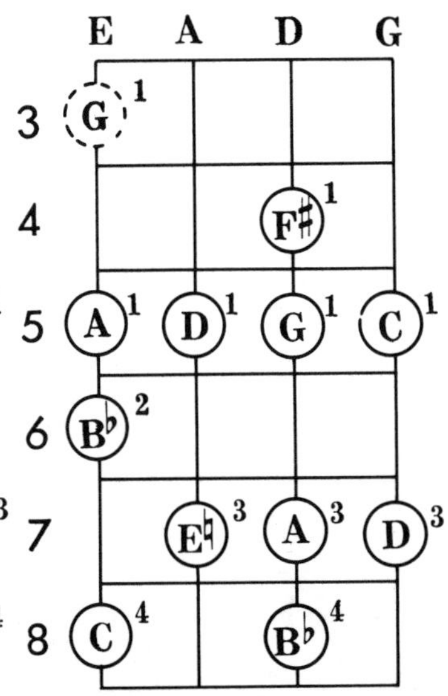

Melodic ascending

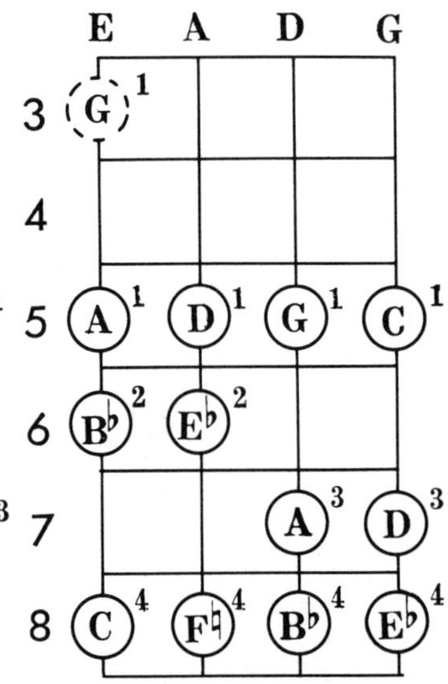

Melodic descending

This form is the same as the natural form, and except for mode or feeling, it is the same as the relative major (B♭).

MELODIC

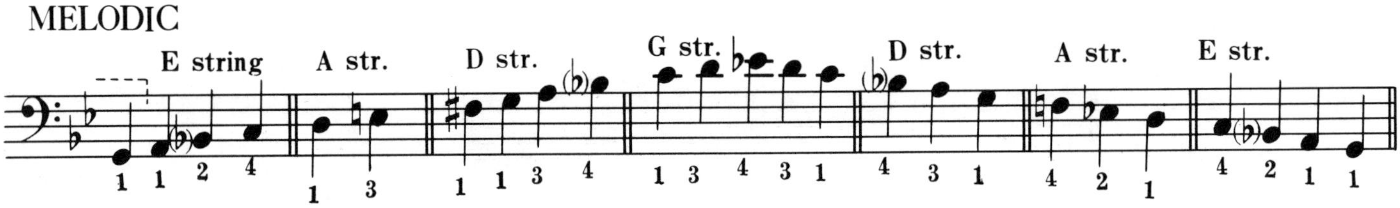

ARPEGGIOS

Gm

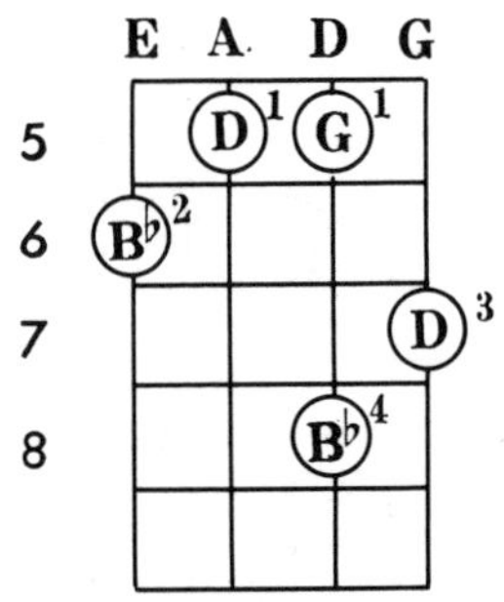

Tonic

Cm

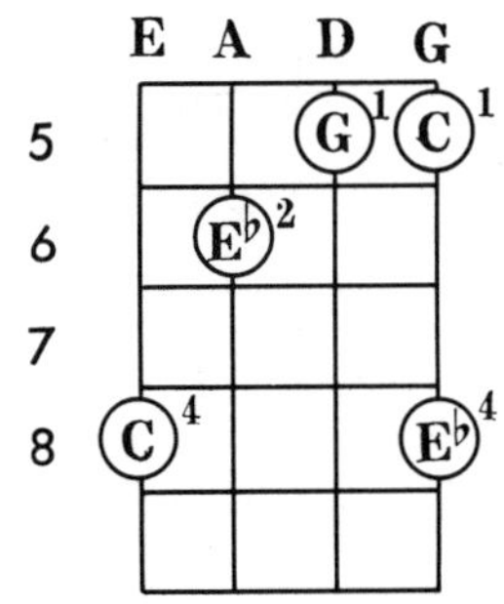

Subdominant

D7

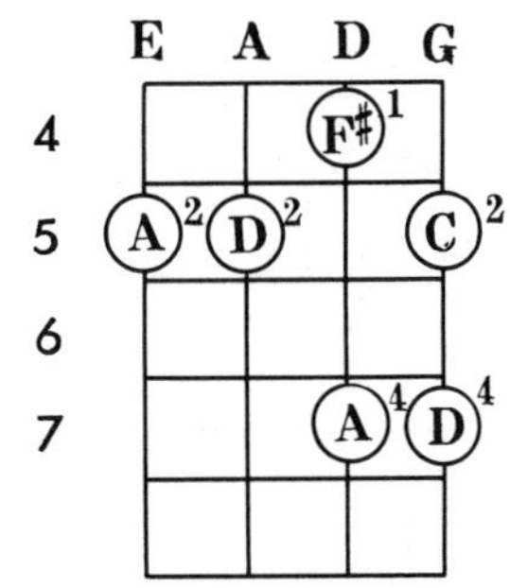

Dominant 7th

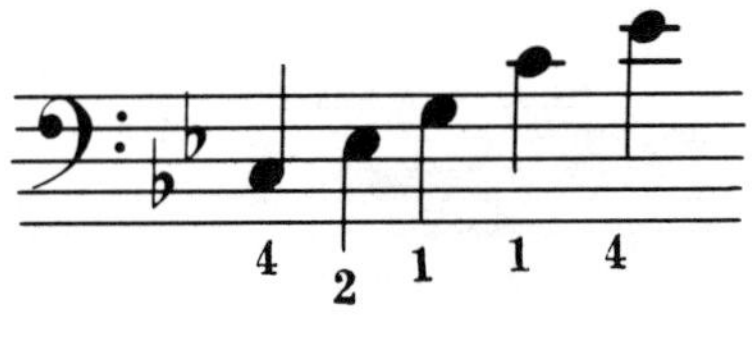

SECONDARY FORMS

B MINOR

HARMONIC

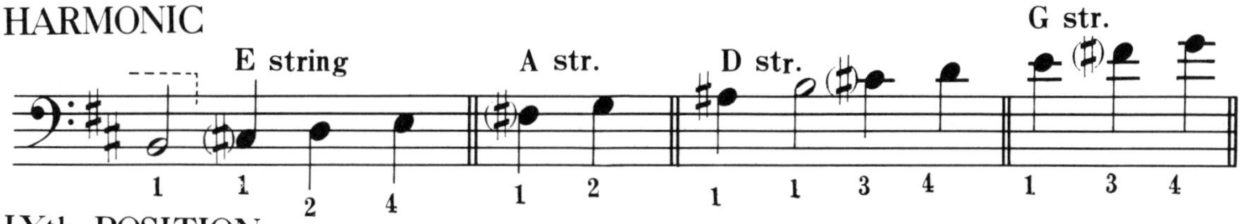

IXth POSITION

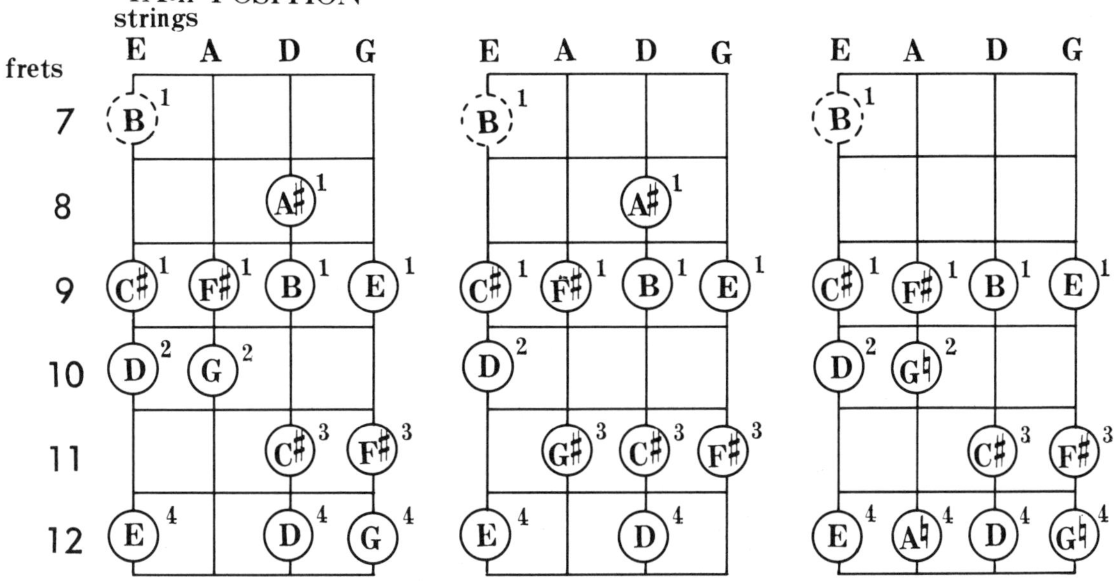

Harmonic　　Melodic ascending　　Melodic descending

This form is the same as the natural form, and except for mode or feeling, it is the same as the relative major (D).

MELODIC

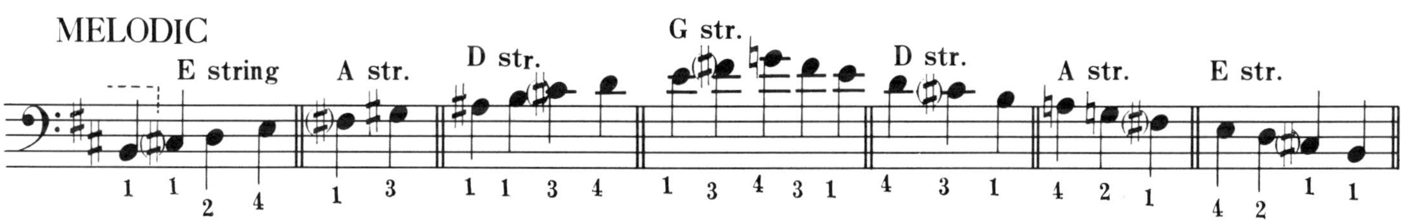

ARPEGGIOS

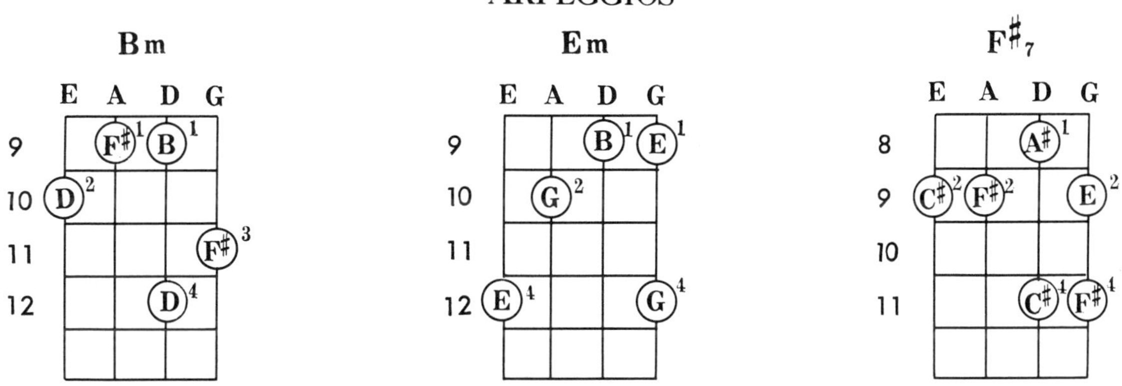

Tonic　　Subdominant　　Dominant 7th

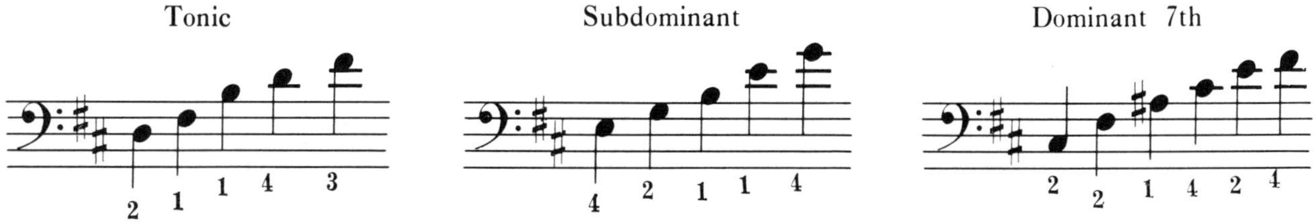

SECONDARY FORMS

C MINOR

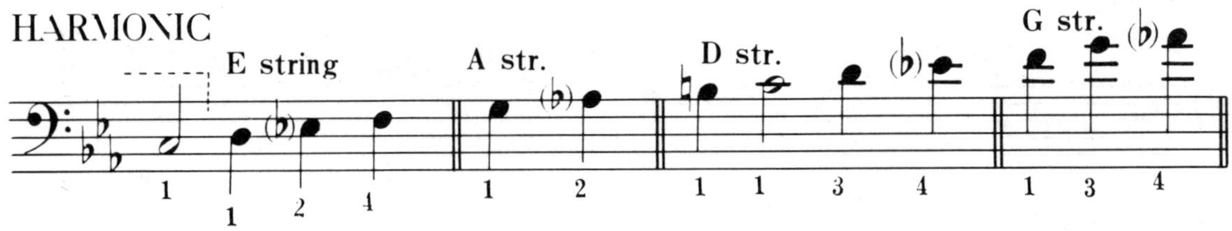

strings Xth POSITION

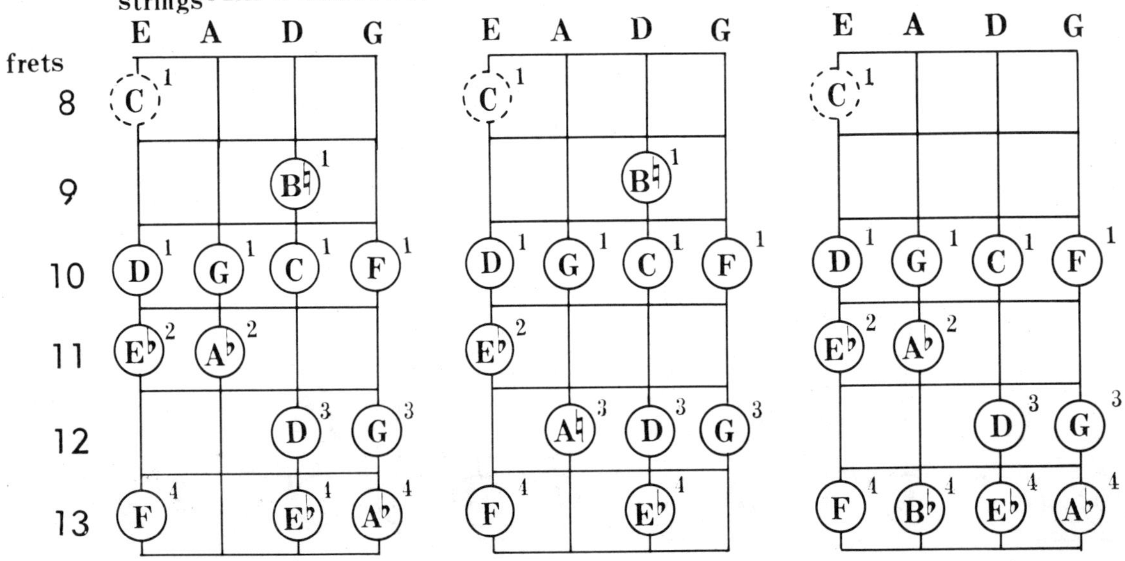

Harmonic   Melodic ascending   Melodic descending

This form is the same as the natural form, and except for mode or feeling, it is the same as the relative major (E♭).

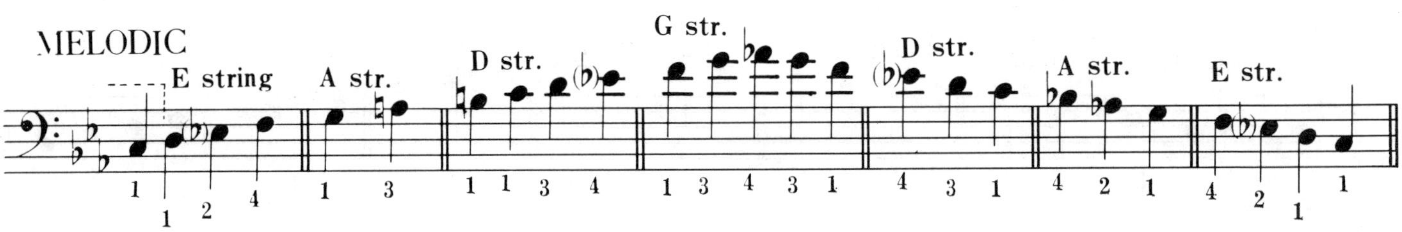

ARPEGGIOS

Cm

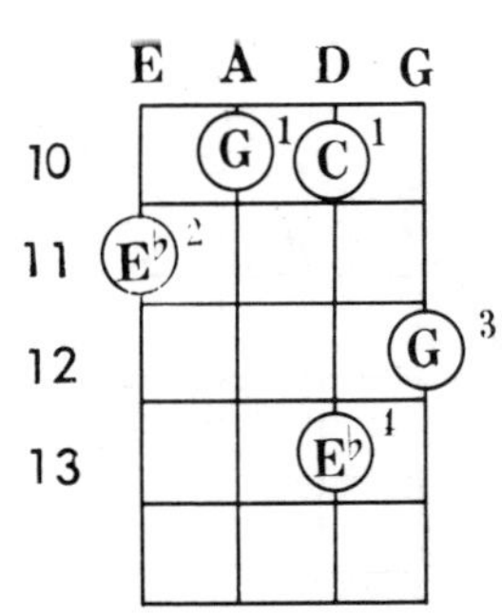

Tonic

Fm

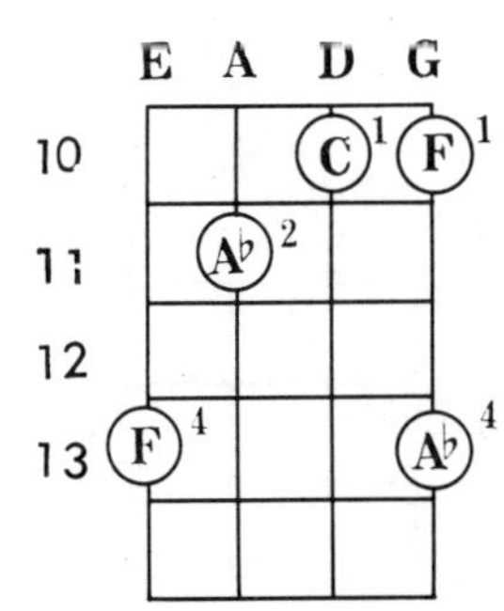

Subdominant

G7

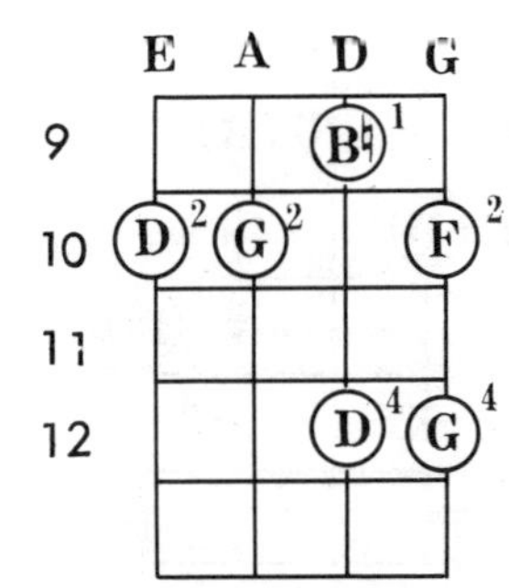

Dominant 7th

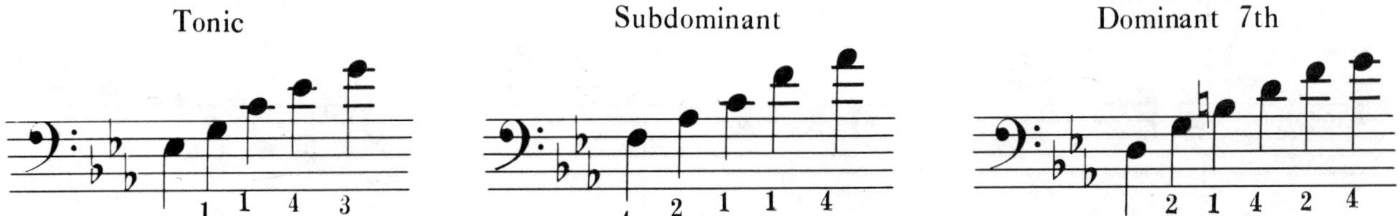

SECONDARY FORMS

F♯ MINOR

HARMONIC

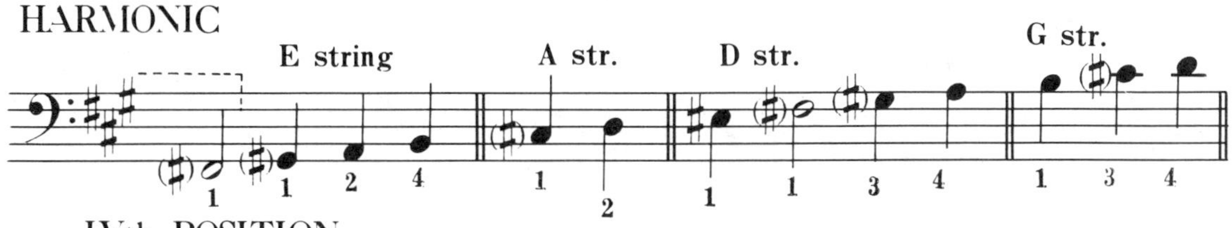

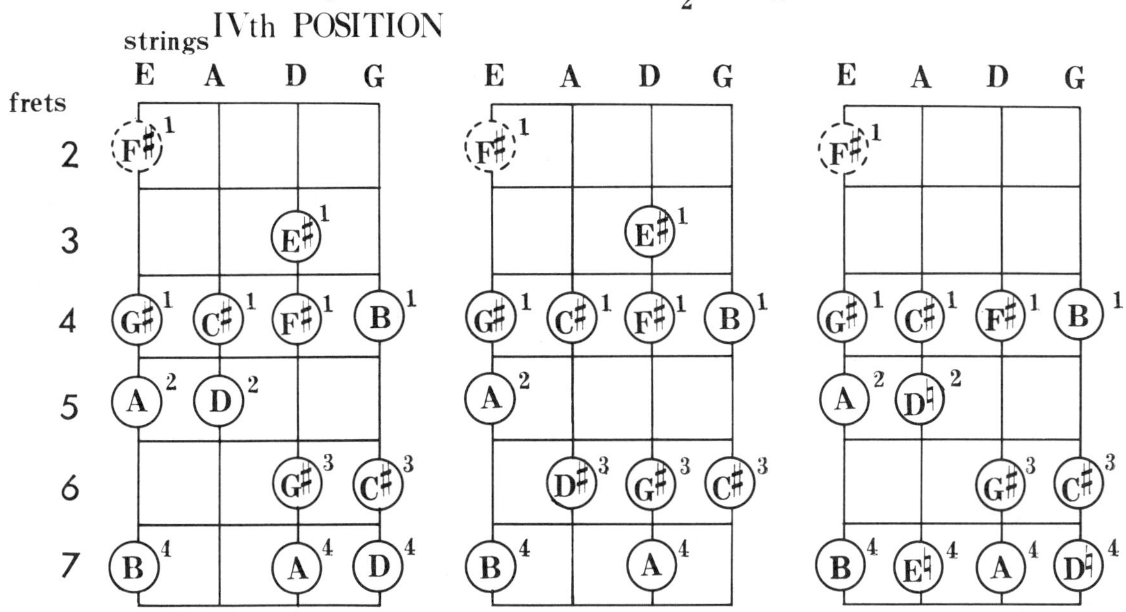

Harmonic | Melodic ascending | Melodic descending

This form is the same as the natural form, and except for mode or feeling, it is the same as the relative major (A).

MELODIC

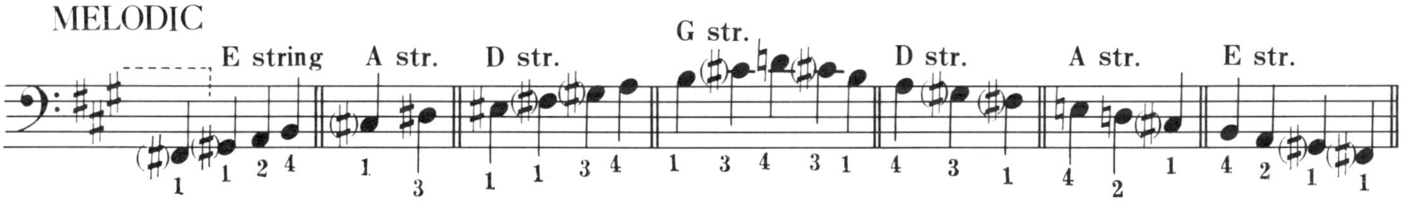

ARPEGGIOS

F♯m

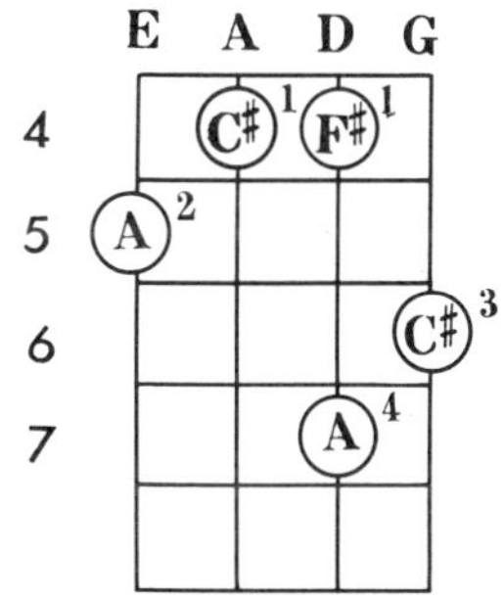

Tonic

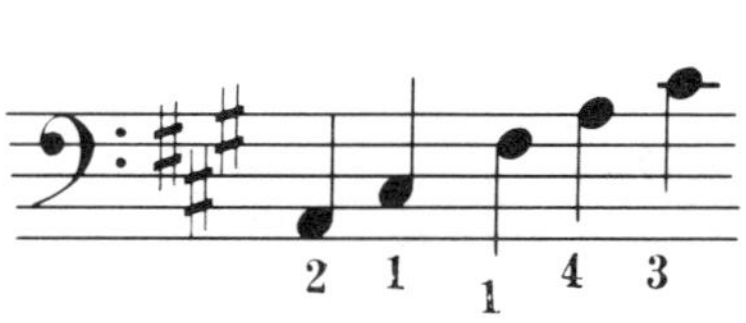

Bm

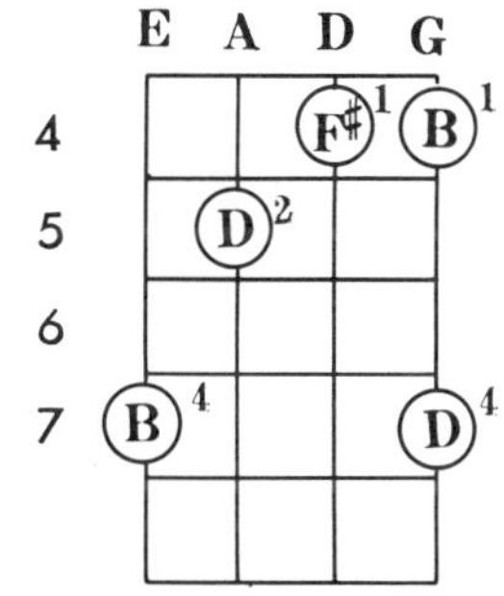

Subdominant

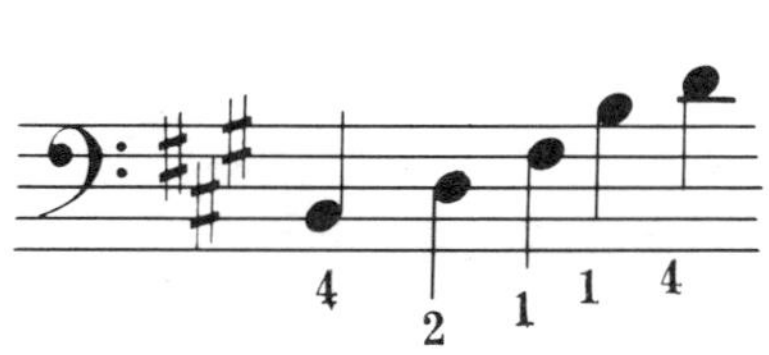

C♯7

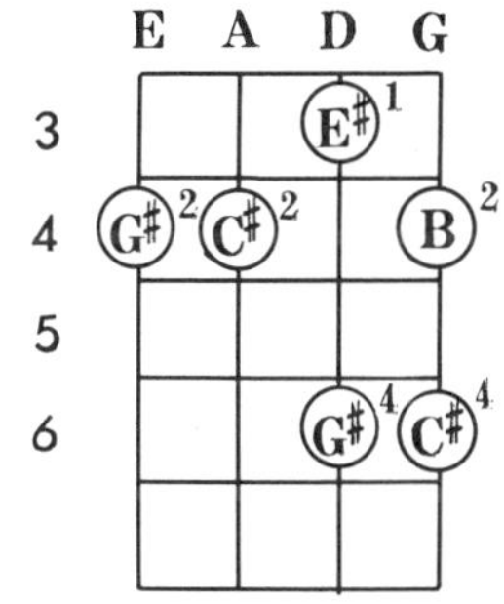

Dominant 7th

SECONDARY FORMS

F MINOR

HARMONIC

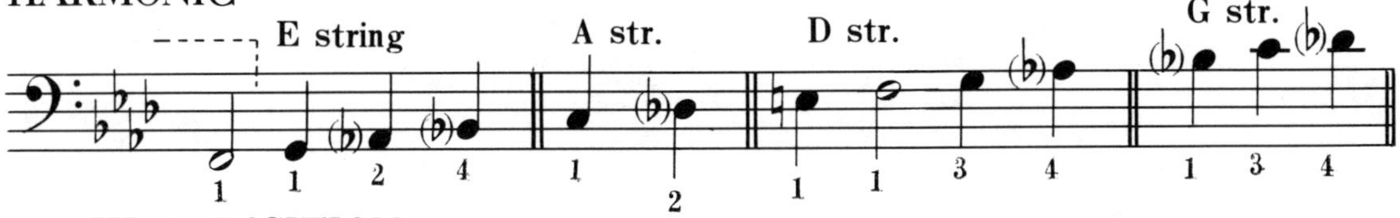

IIInd POSITION

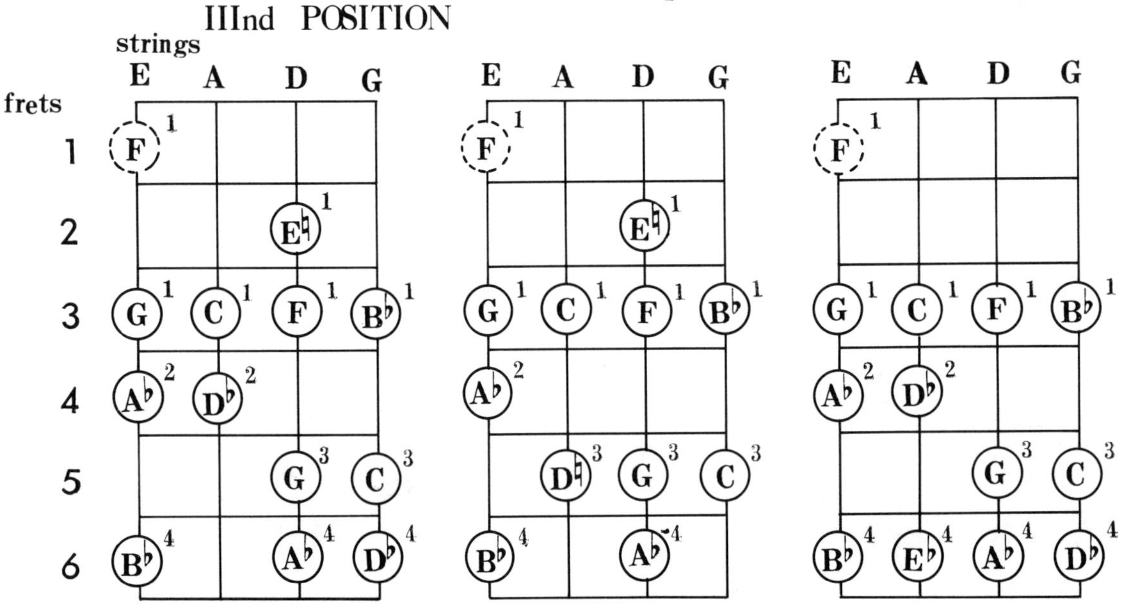

Harmonic Melodic ascending Melodic descending

This form is the same as the natural form, and except for mode or feeling, it is the same as the relative major (A♭).

MELODIC

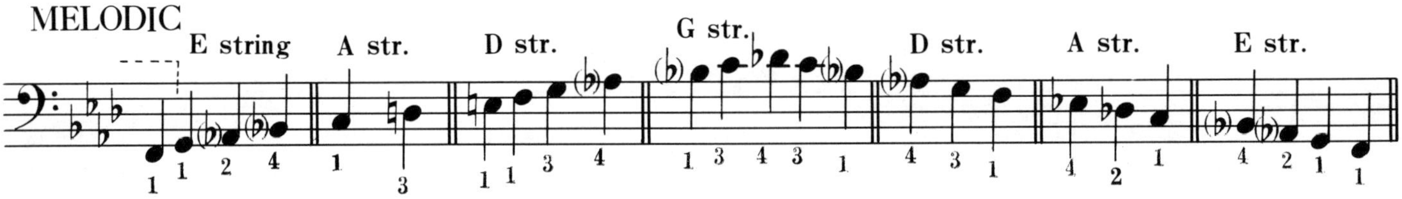

ARPEGGIOS

Fm B♭m C7

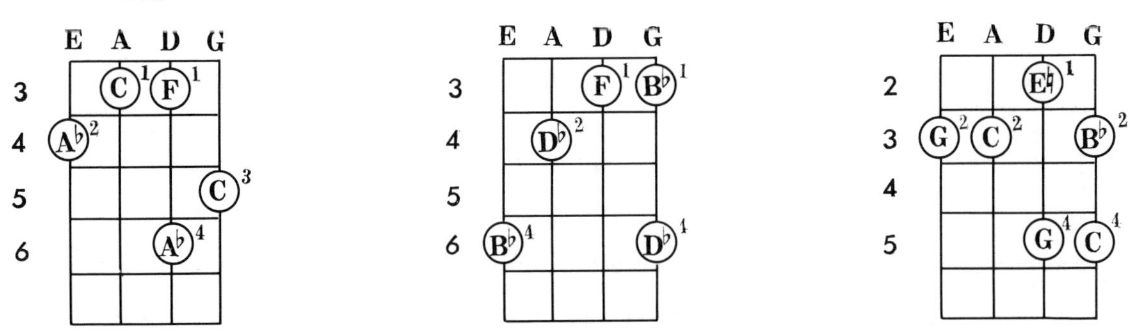

Tonic Subdominant Dominant 7th

SECONDARY FORMS

C♯ MINOR

HARMONIC

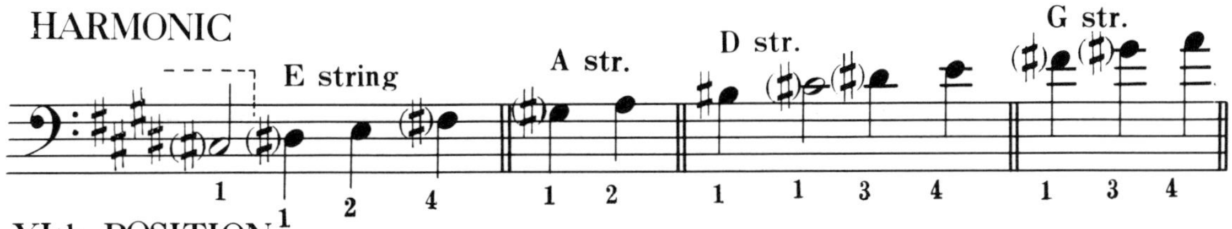

XIth POSITION

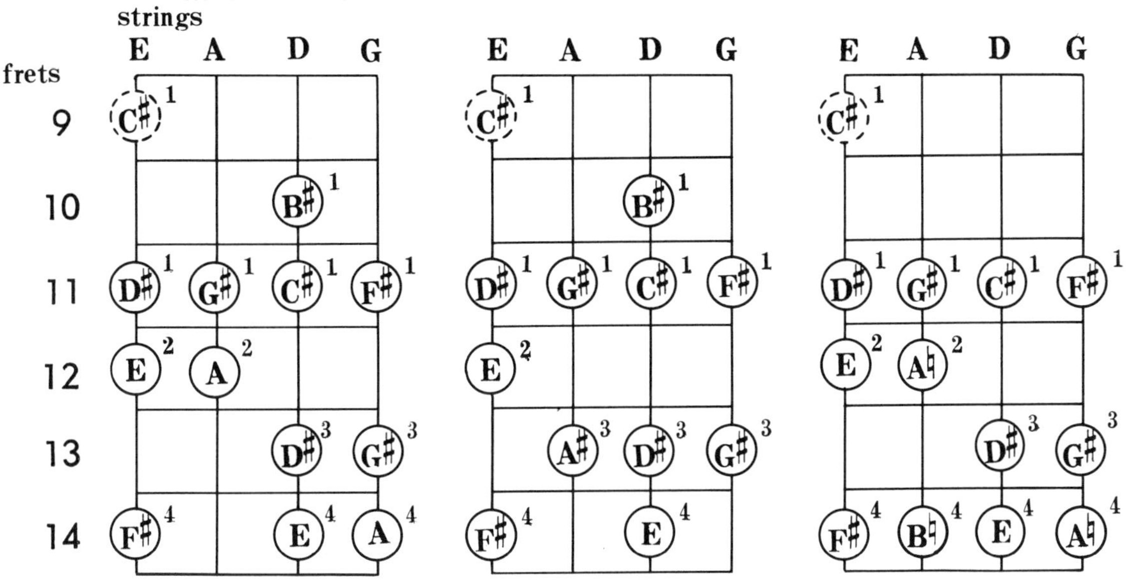

Harmonic — Melodic ascending — Melodic descending

This form is the same as the natural form, and except for mode or feeling, it is the same as the relative major (E).

MELODIC

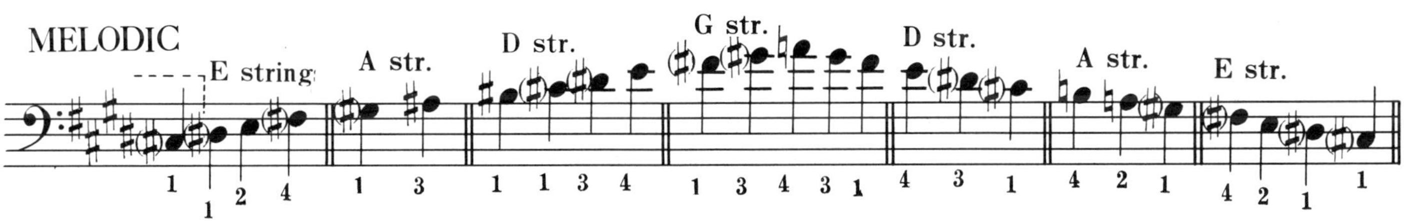

ARPEGGIOS

C♯m — F♯m — G♯7

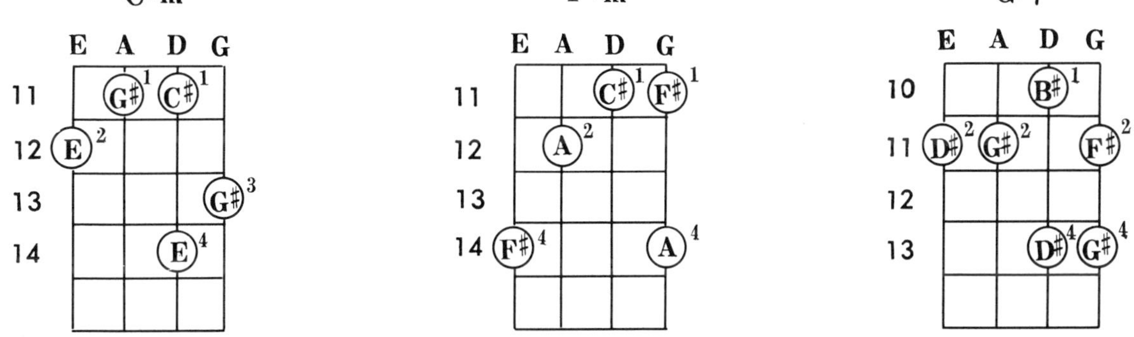

Tonic — Subdominant — Dominant 7th

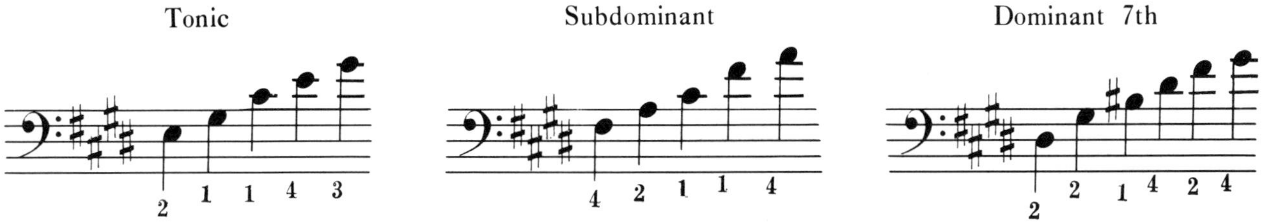

SECONDARY FORMS

B♭ MINOR

HARMONIC

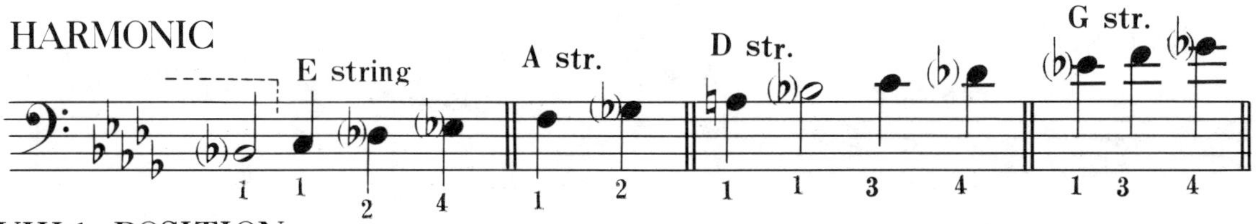

VIIIth POSITION

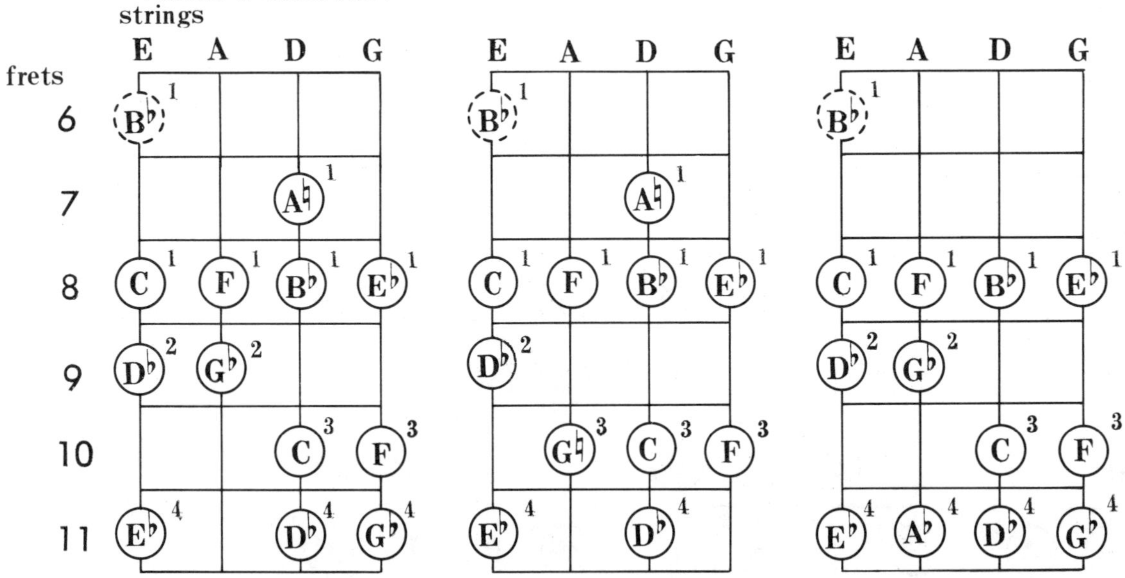

Harmonic | Melodic ascending | Melodic descending

This form is the same as the natural form, and except for mode or feeling, it is the same as the relative major (D♭).

MELODIC

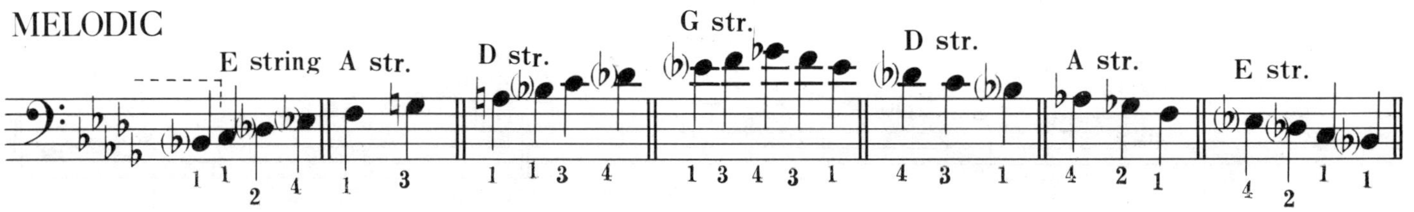

ARPEGGIOS

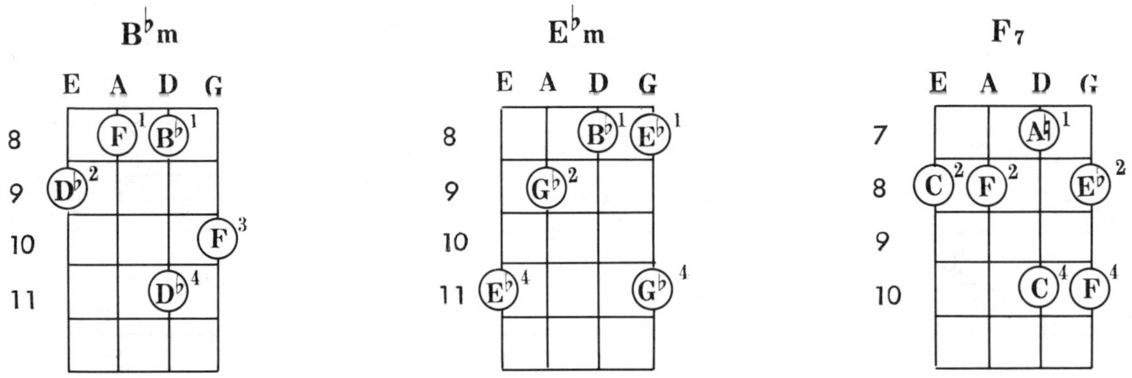

Tonic | Subdominant | Dominant 7th

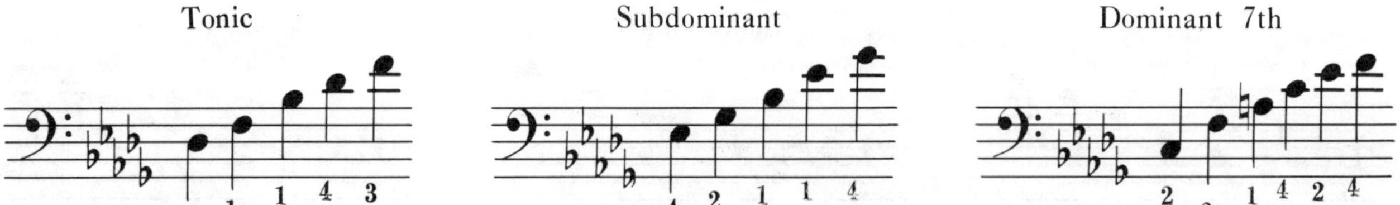

SECONDARY FORMS

G♯ MINOR

HARMONIC

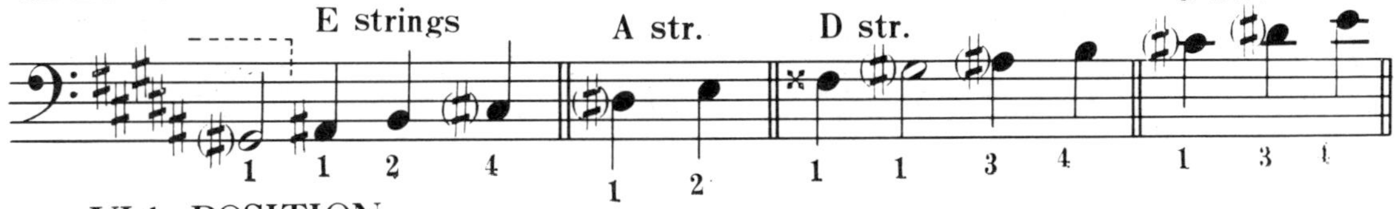

VIth POSITION

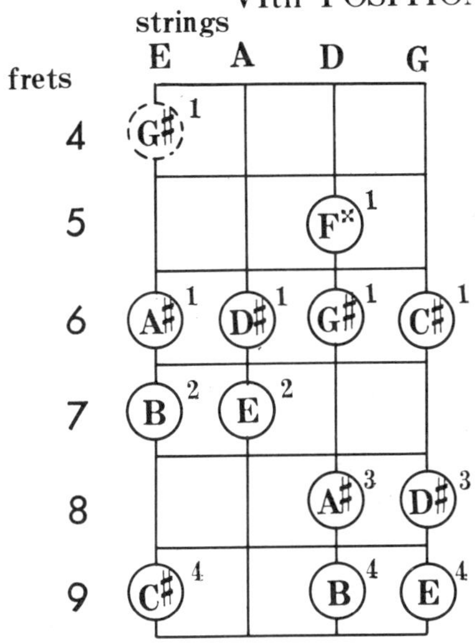

Harmonic

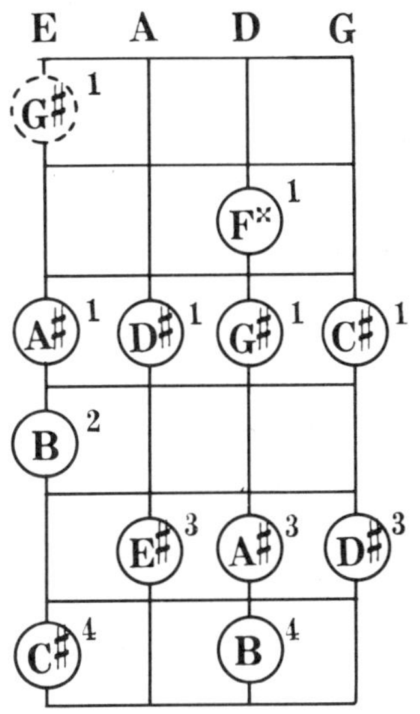

Melodic ascending

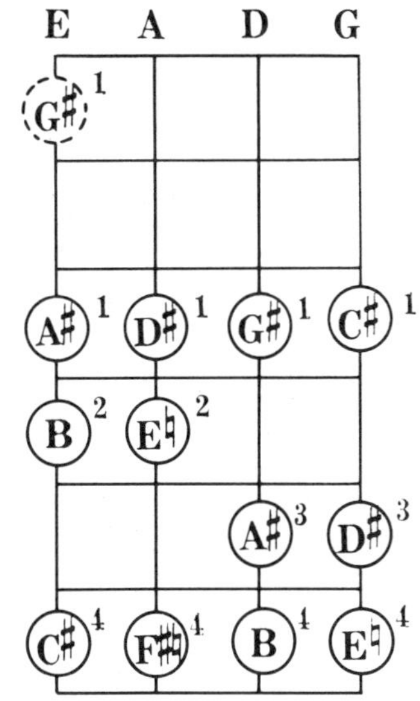

Melodic descending

This form is the same as the natural form, and except for mode or feeling, it is the same as the relative major (B).

MELODIC

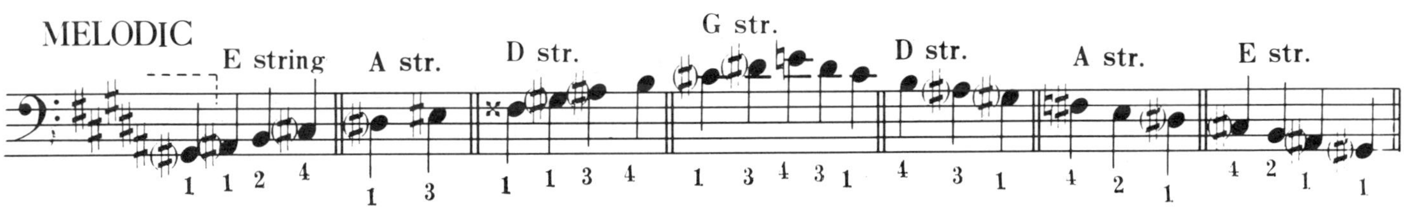

ARPEGGIOS

G♯m

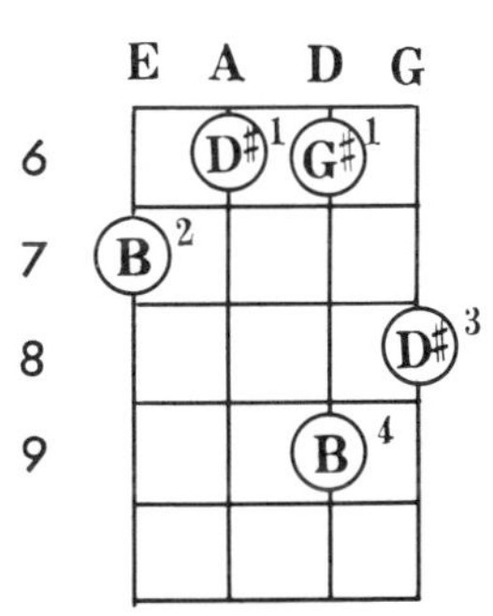

Tonic

C♯m

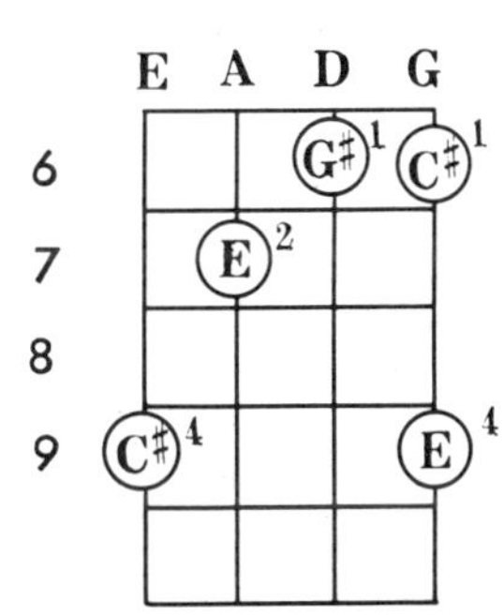

Subdominant

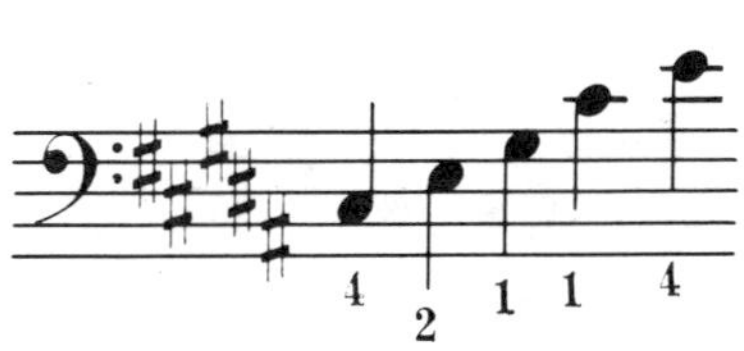

$D^{\sharp}_{7}$

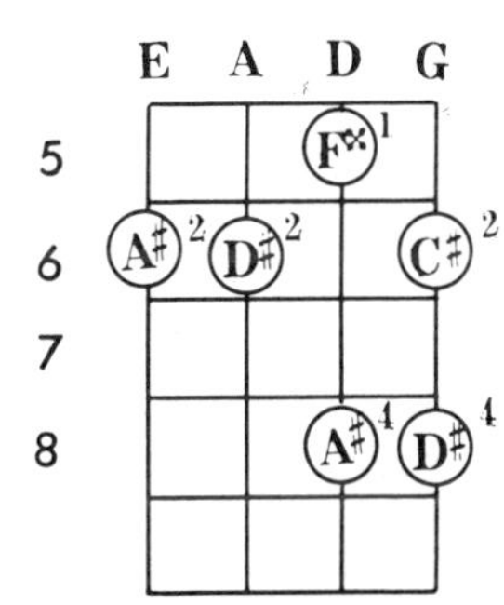

Dominant 7th

SECONDARY FORMS

E♭ MINOR

This key is enharmonically equivalent to D♯ Minor (P 61)

HARMONIC

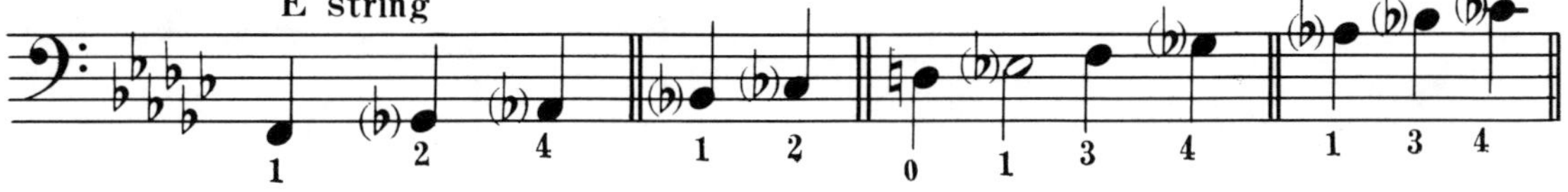

Ist POSITION

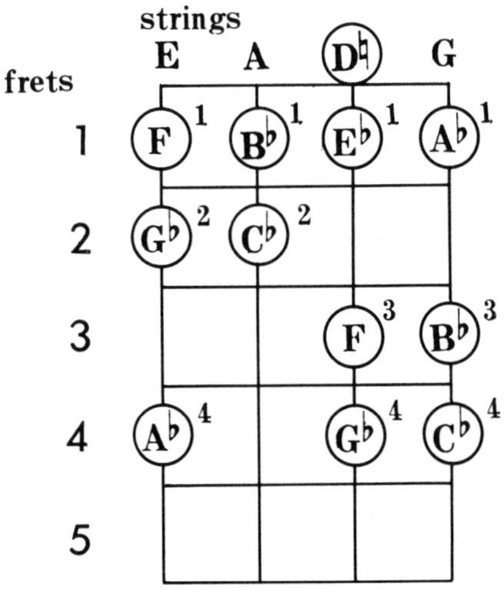

Harmonic

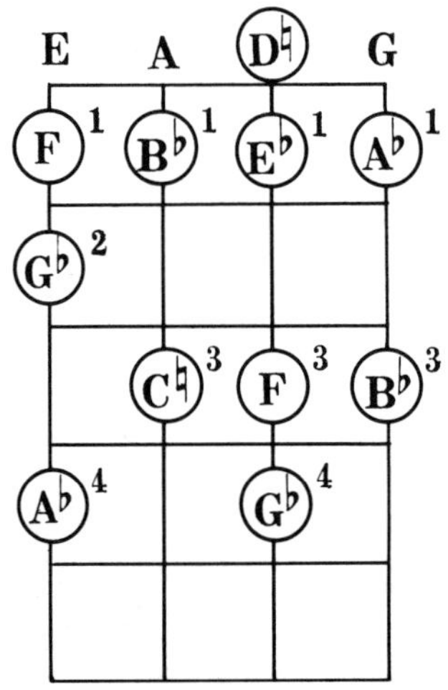

Melodic ascending

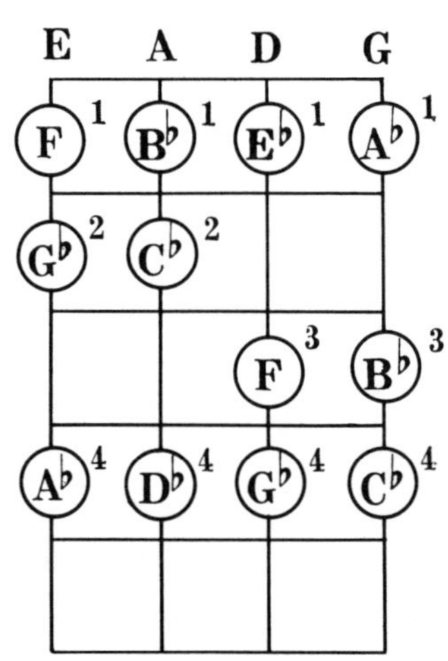

Melodic descending

This form is the same as the natural form, and except for mode or feeling, it is the same as the relative major (G♭).

MELODIC

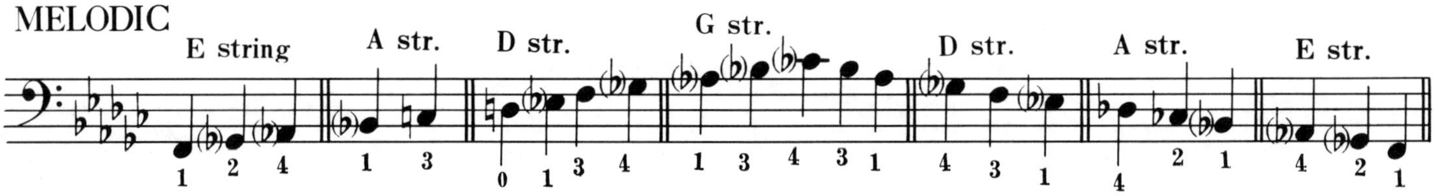

ARPEGGIOS

E♭m

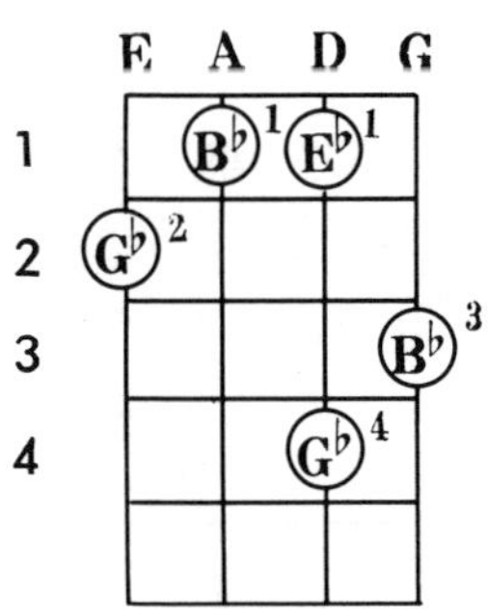

Tonic

A♭m

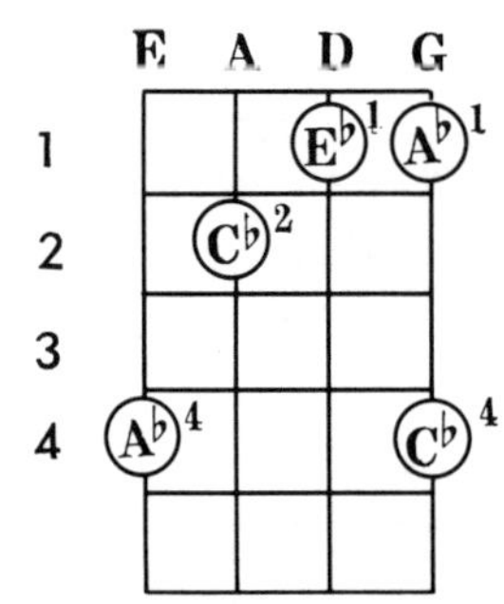

Subdominant

B♭7

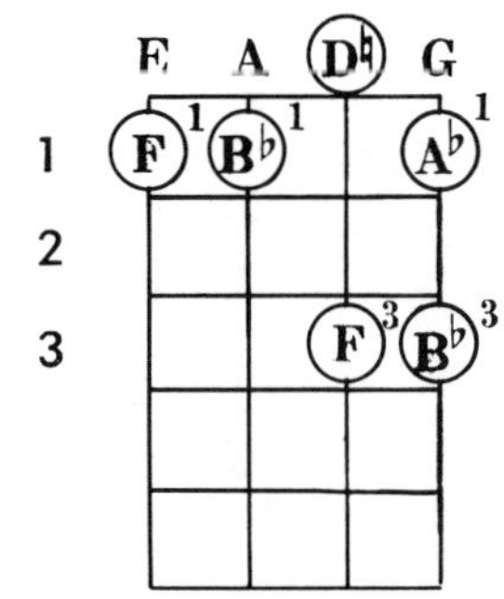

Dominant 7th

SECONDARY FORMS

D♯ MINOR

This key is enharmonically equivalent to E♭ Minor (p. 60).

HARMONIC

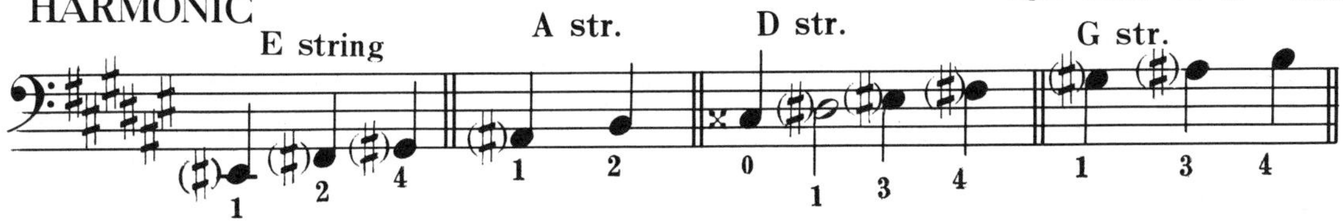

Ist POSITION

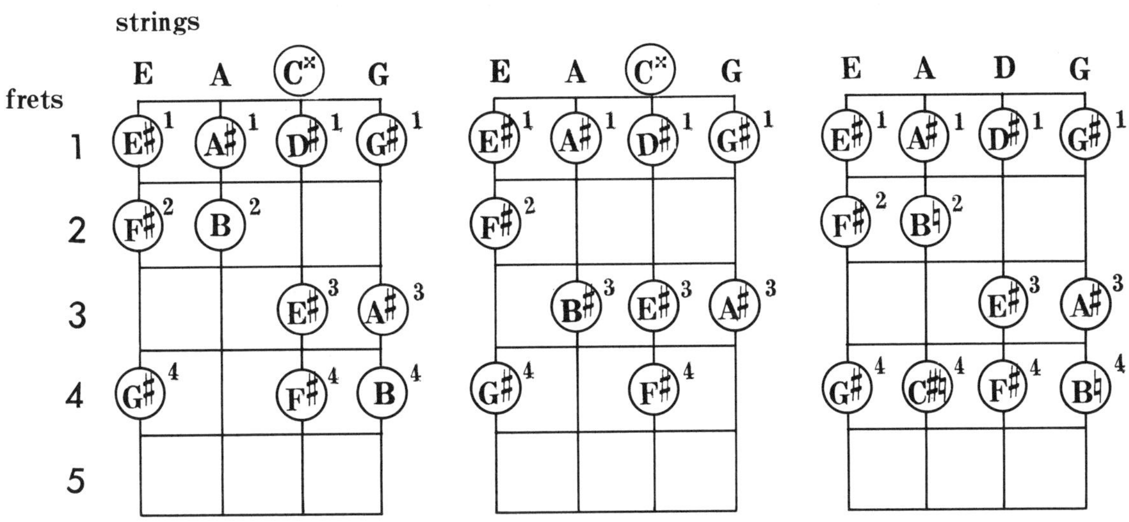

Harmonic | Melodic ascending | Melodic descending

This form is the same as the natural form, and except for mode or feeling, it is the same as the relative major (F♯)

MELODIC

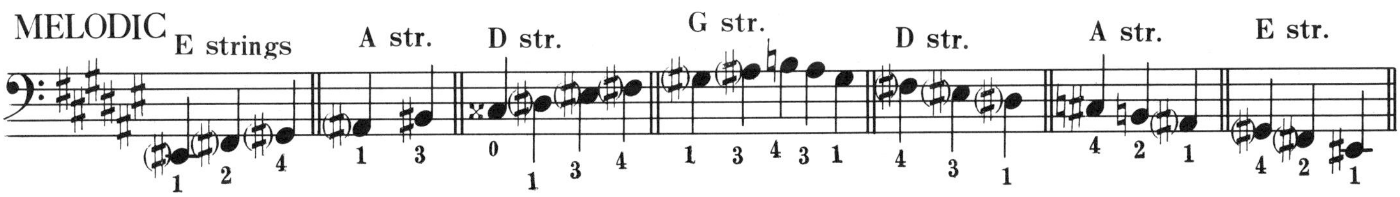

ARPEGGIOS

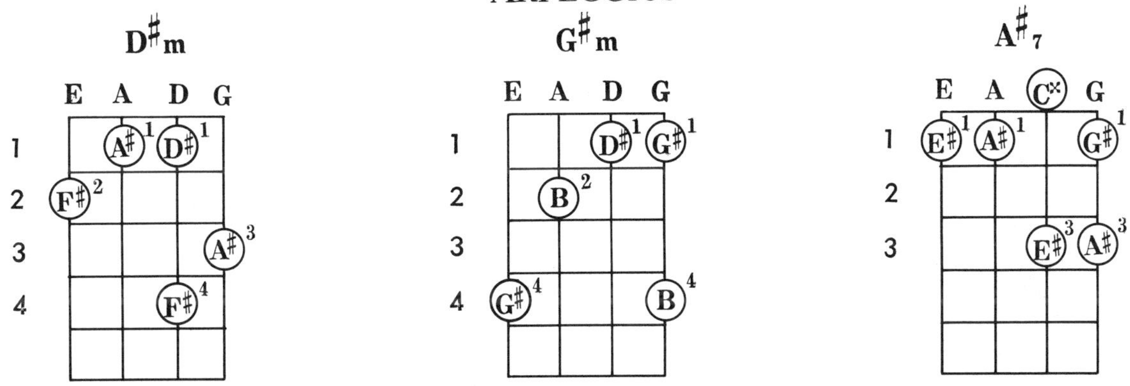

TERTIARY FORMS

A MINOR

HARMONIC

Vth POSITION

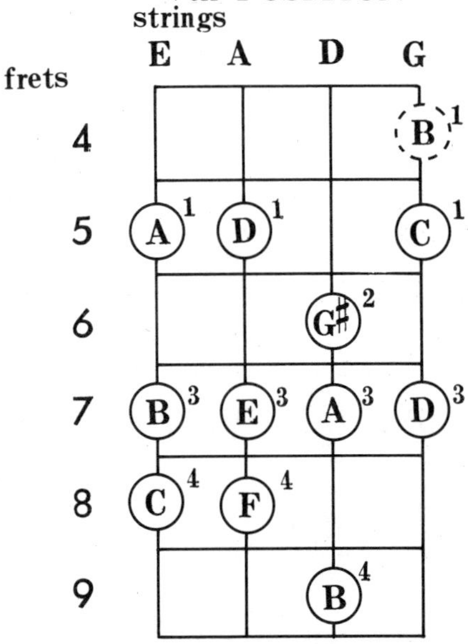

Harmonic

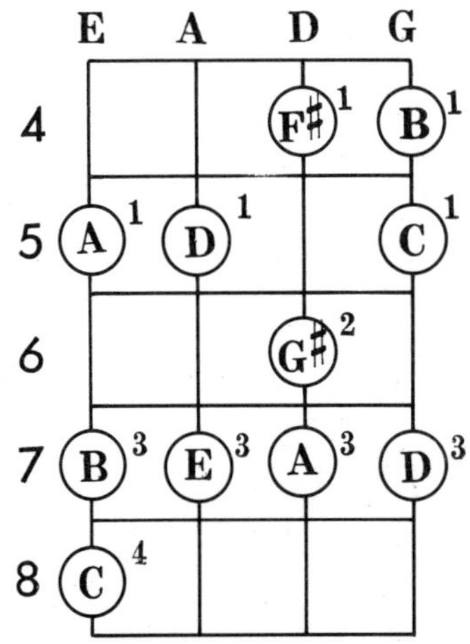

Melodic ascending

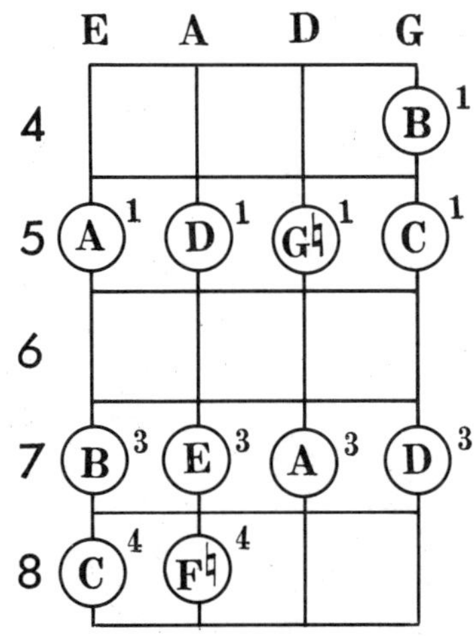

Melodic descending

This form is the same as the natural form, and except for mode or feeling, it is the same as the relative major (C)

MELODIC

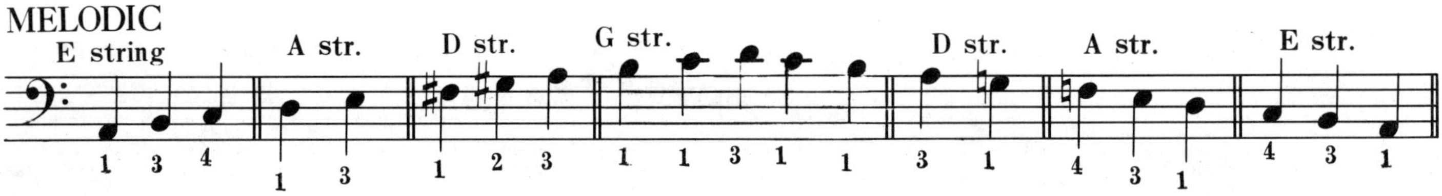

ARPEGGIOS

Am

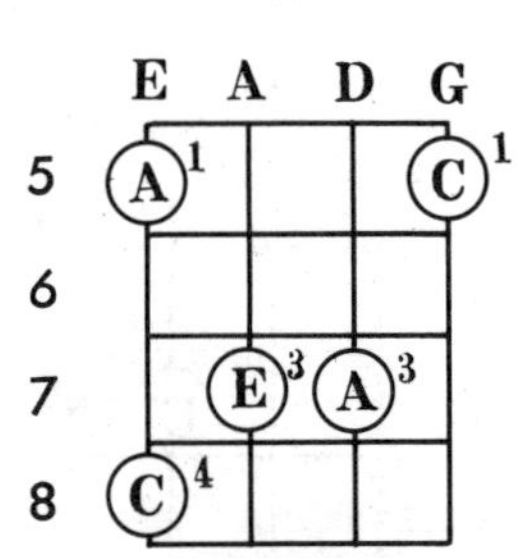

Tonic

Dm

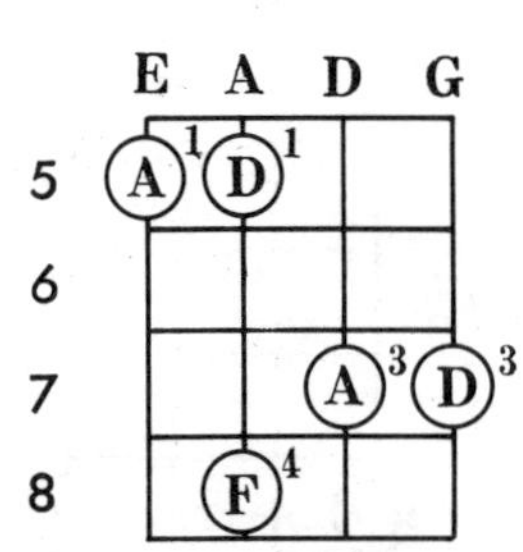

Subdominant

E7

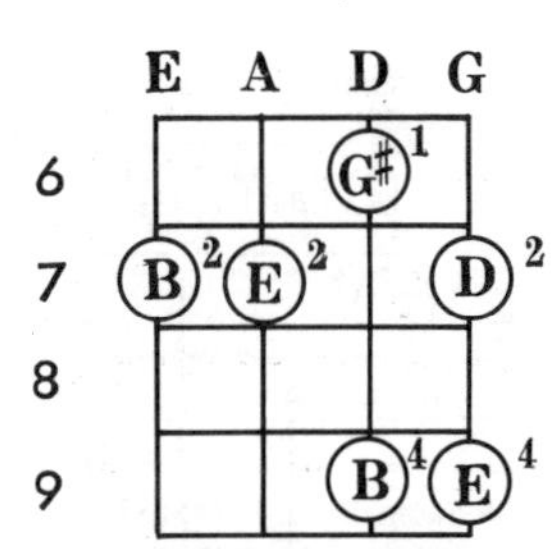

Dominant 7th

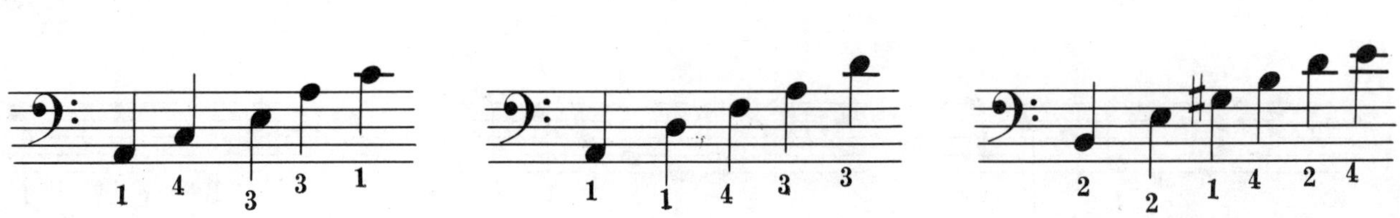

TERTIARY FORMS

D MINOR

HARMONIC

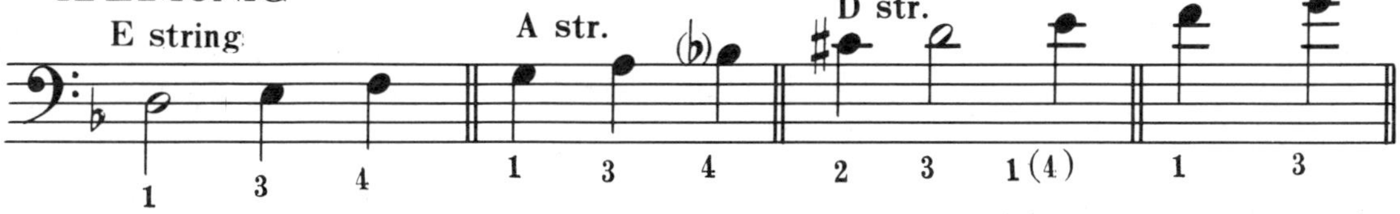

strings Xth POSITION

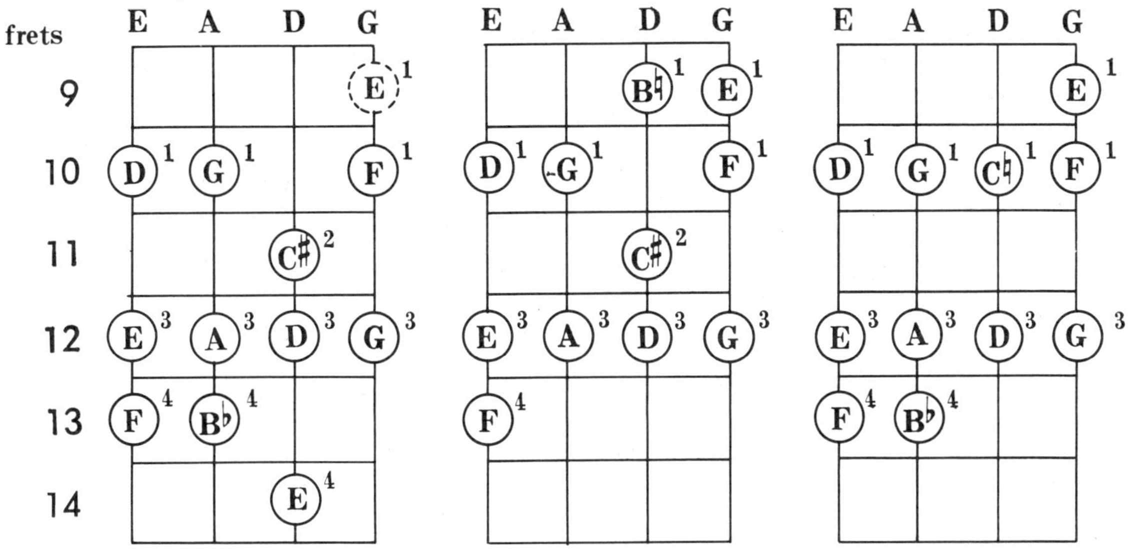

Harmonic — Melodic ascending — Melodic descending

This form is the same as the natural form, and except for mode or feeling, it is the same as the relative major (F).

MELODIC

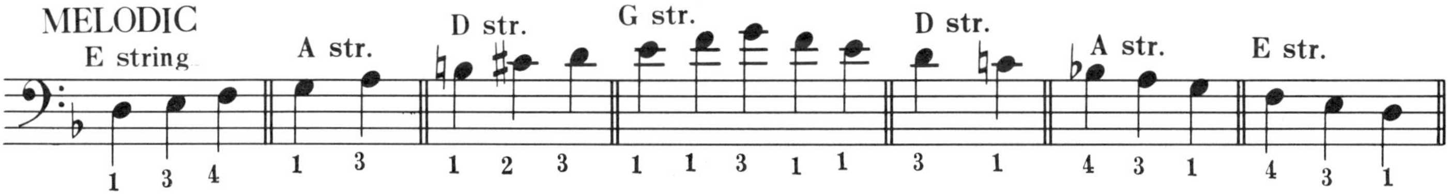

ARPEGGIOS

Dm

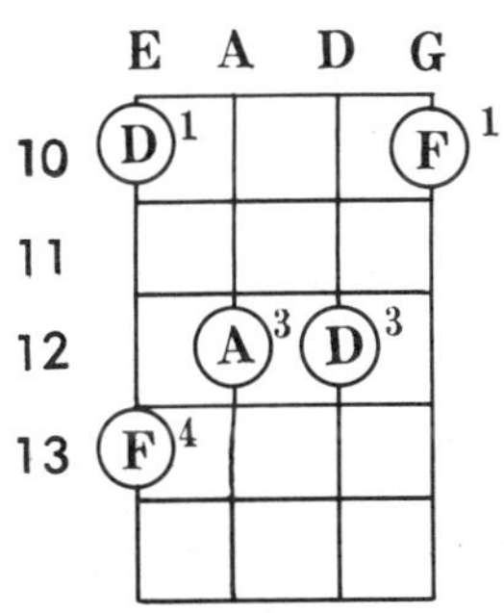

Tonic

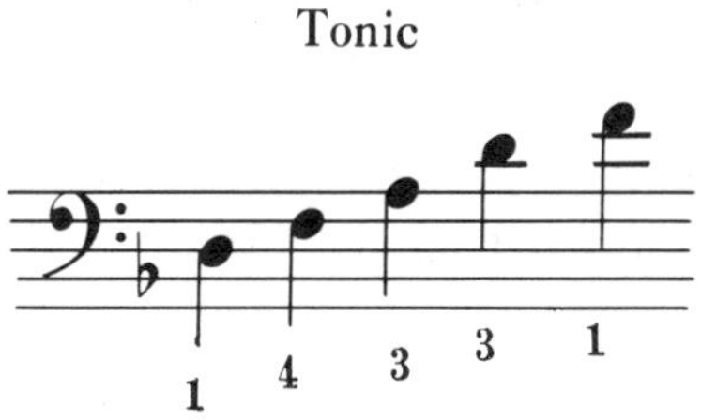

Gm

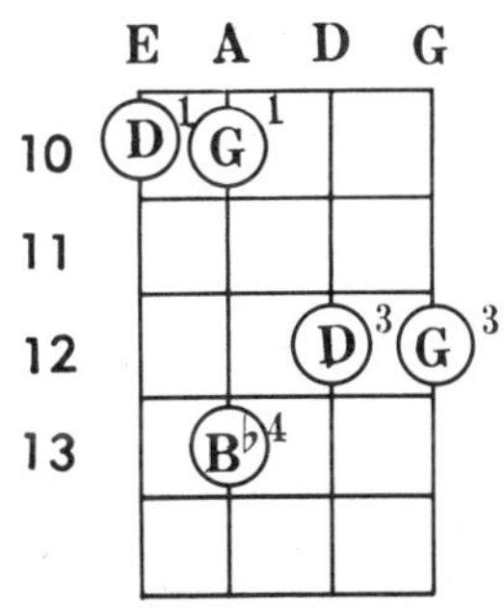

Subdominant

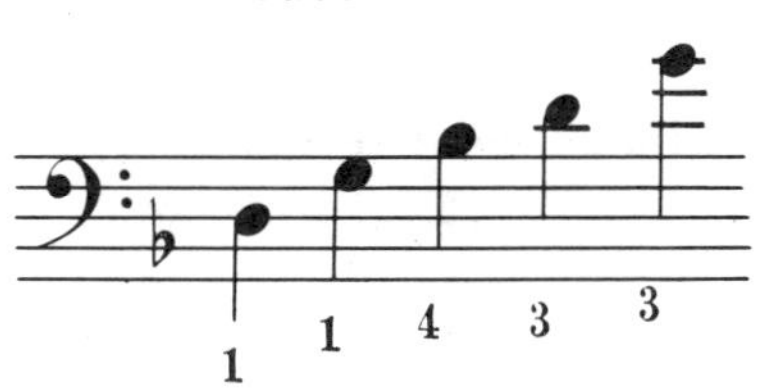

A7

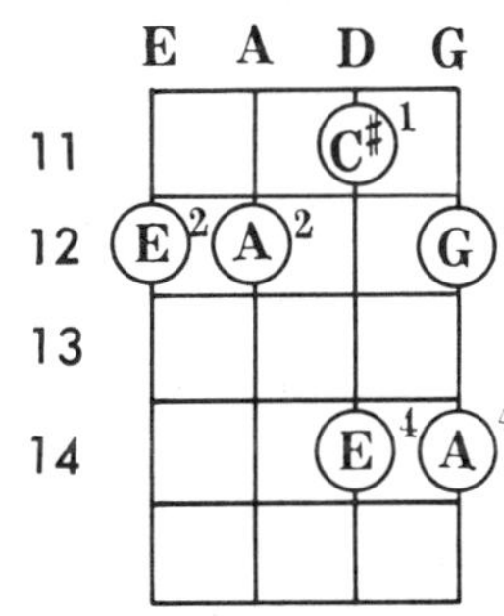

Dominant 7th

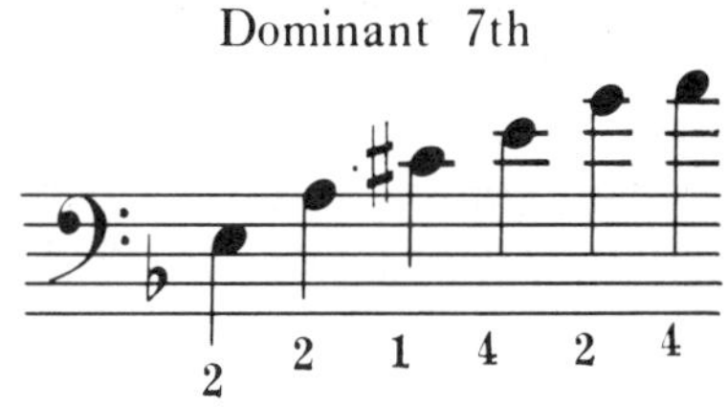

TERTIARY FORMS

E MINOR

HARMONIC

OPEN POSITION

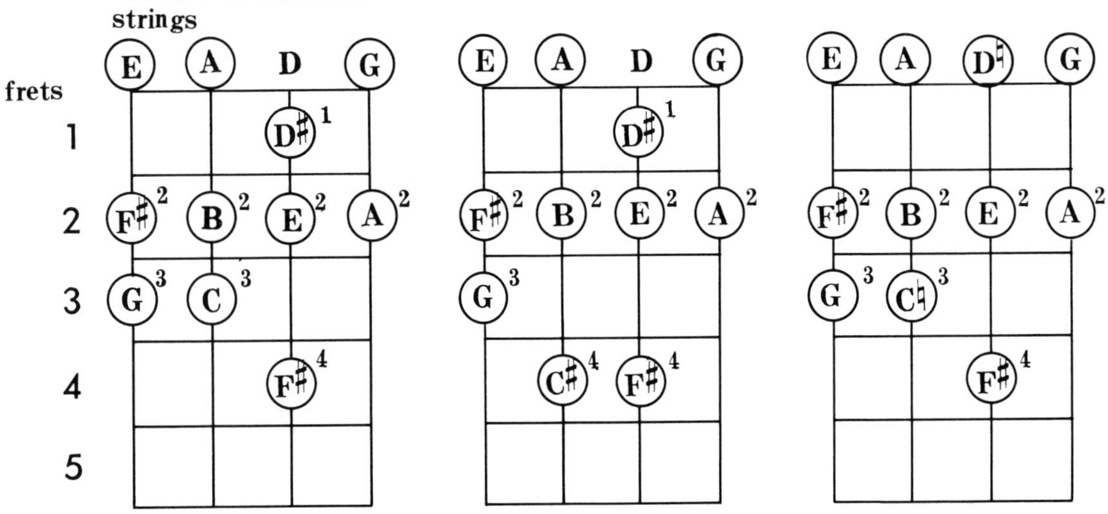

Harmonic

Melodic ascending

Melodic descending

This form is the same as the natural form, and except for mode or feeling, it is the same as the relative major (G).

MELODIC

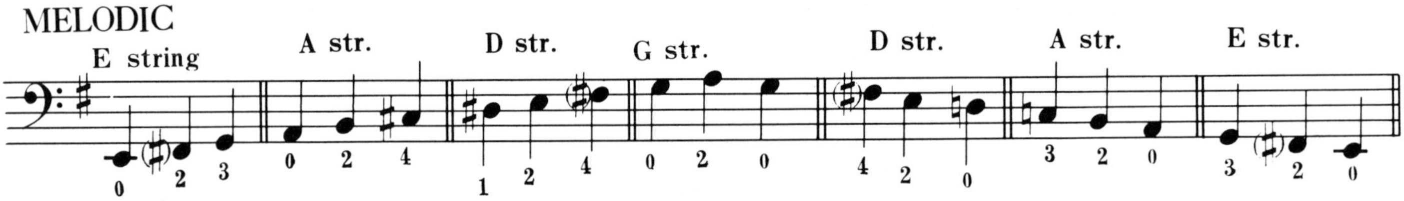

ARPEGGIOS

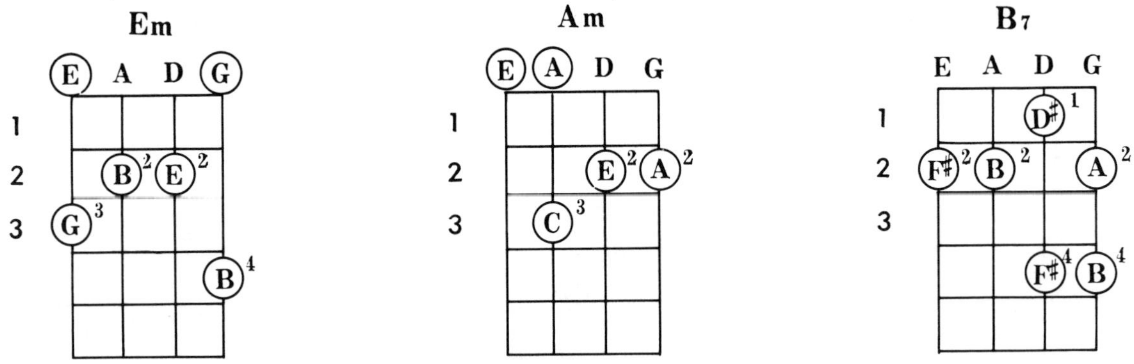

Tonic

Subdominant

Dominant 7th

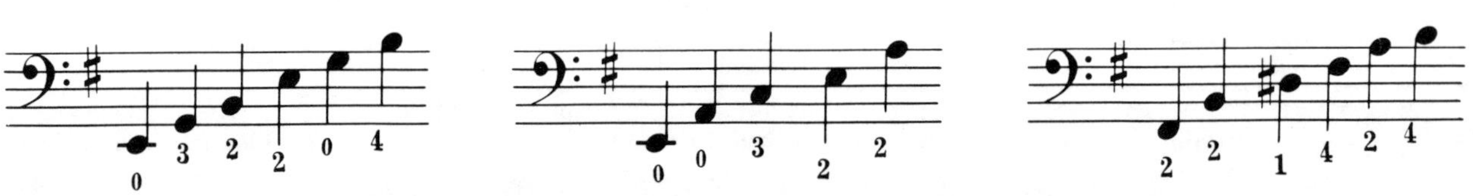

Note that this form departs from the normal tertiary form because it is played in the open position. The tertiary form for E Minor is played precisely as other tertiary forms 1 octave higher in the 12th position.

TERTIARY FORMS

G MINOR

HARMONIC

IIInd POSITION

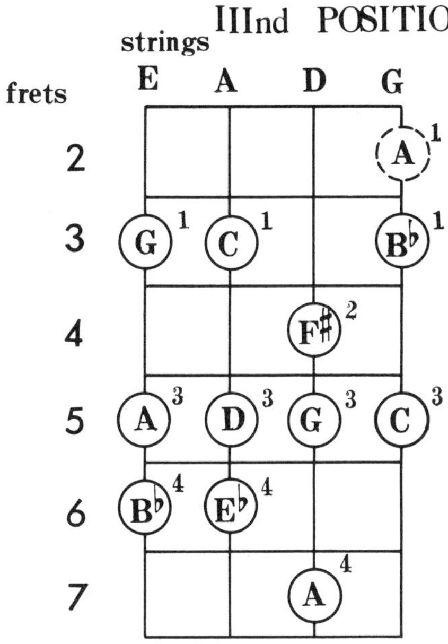

Harmonic

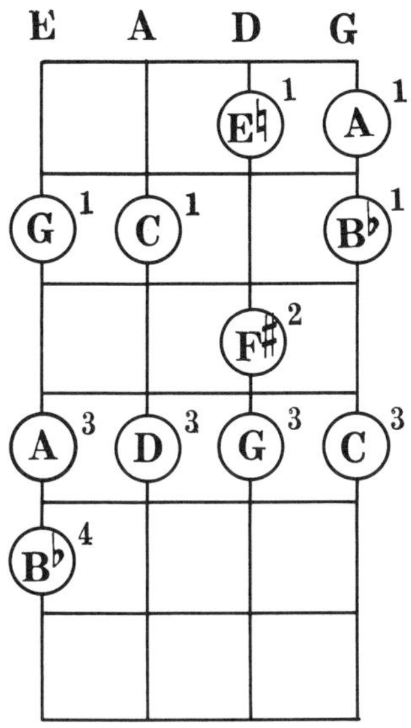

Melodic ascending

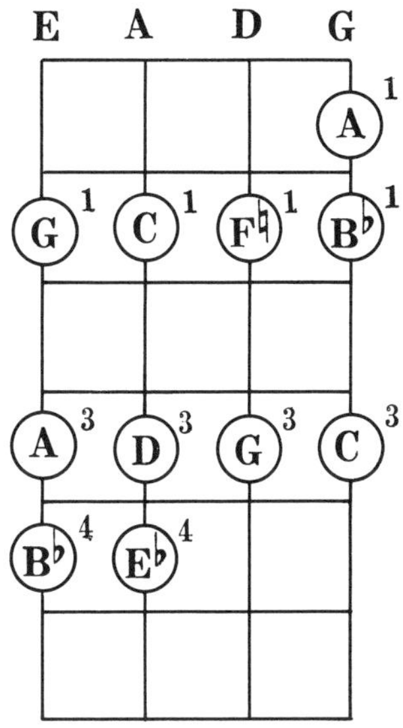

Melodic descending

This form is the same as the natural form, and except for mode or feeling, it is the same as the relative major (B♭)

MELODIC

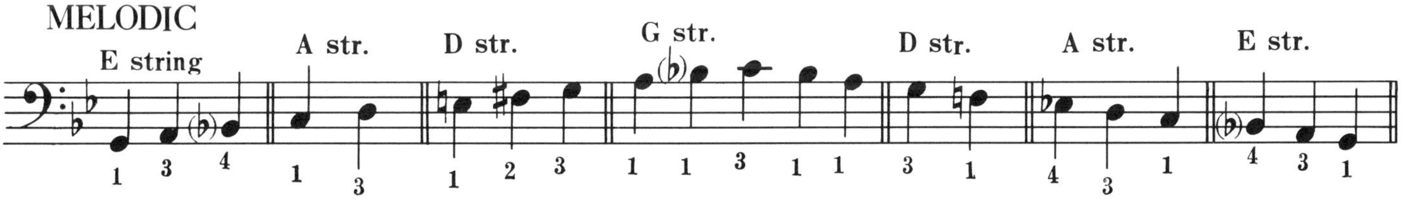

ARPEGGIOS

Gm

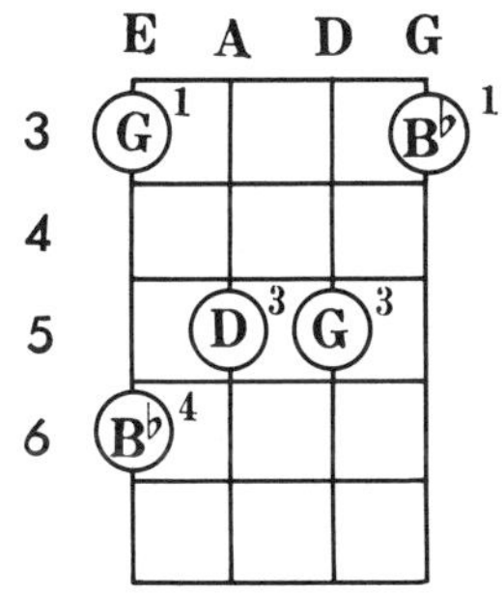

Tonic

Cm

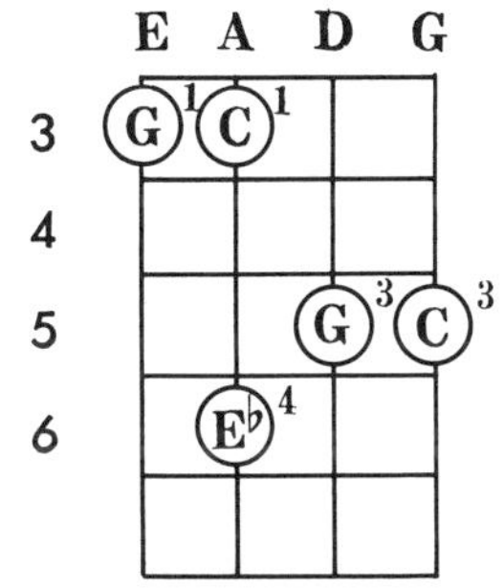

Subdominant

D7

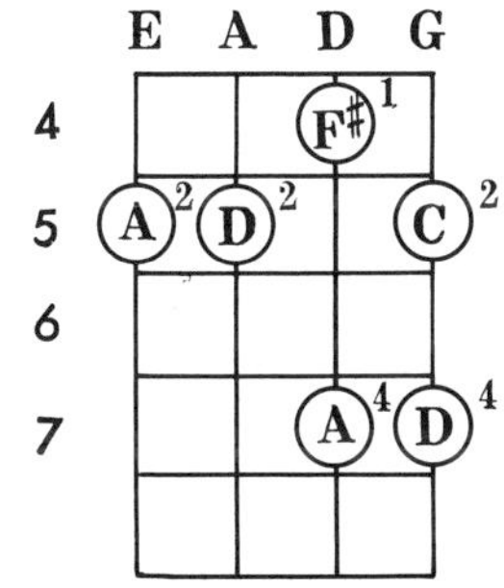

Dominant 7th

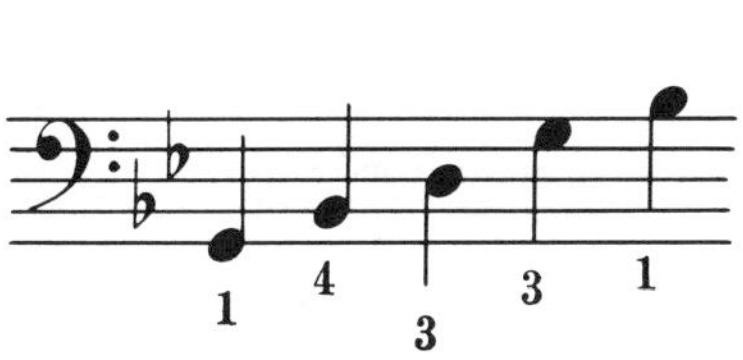

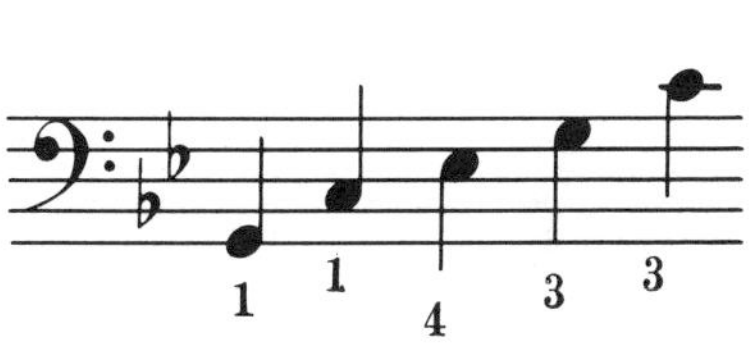

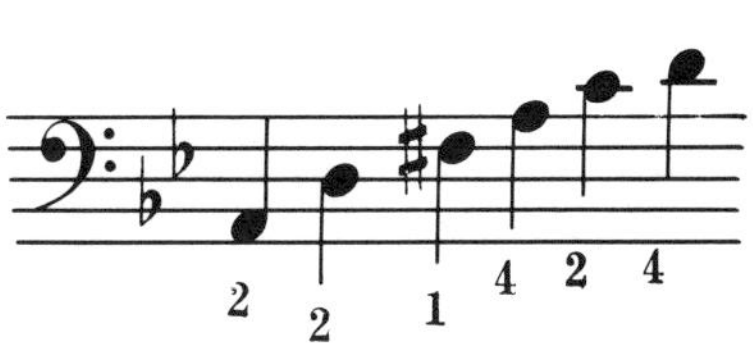

TERTIARY FORMS

B MINOR

HARMONIC

VIIth POSITION

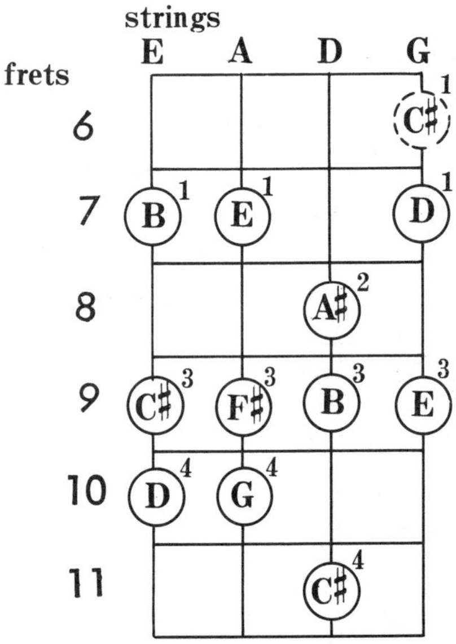

Harmonic

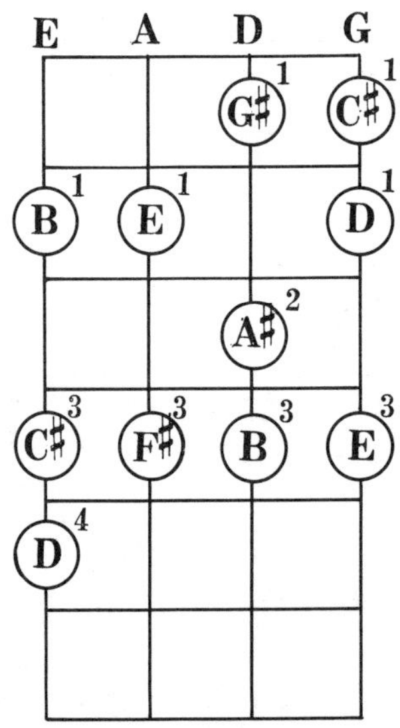

Melodic ascending

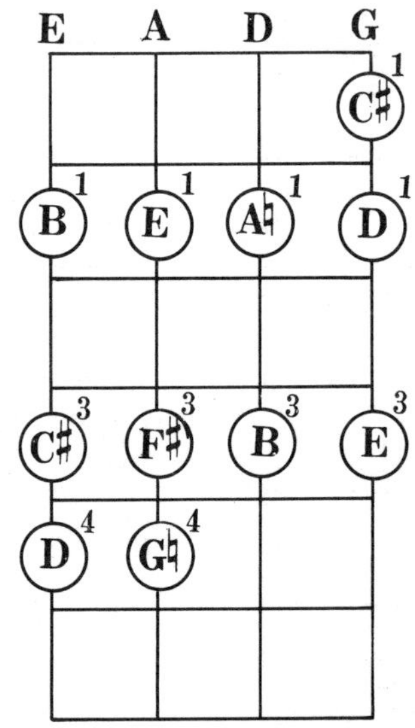

Melodic descending

This form is the same as the natural form, and except for mode or feeling, it is the same as the relative major (D).

MELODIC

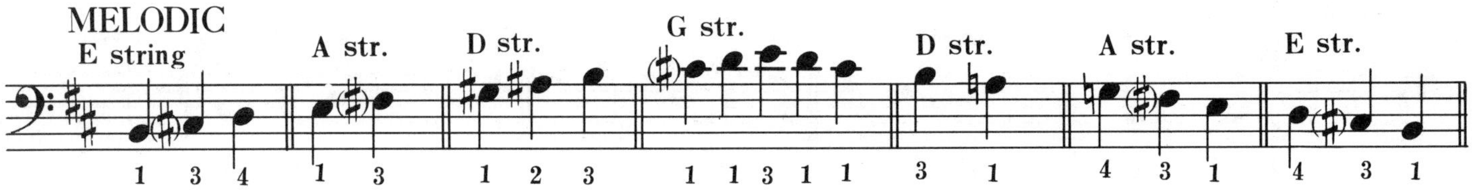

ARPEGGIOS

Bm

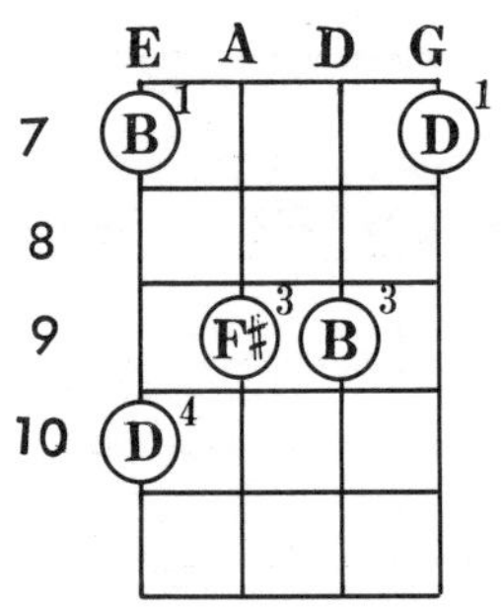

Tonic

Em

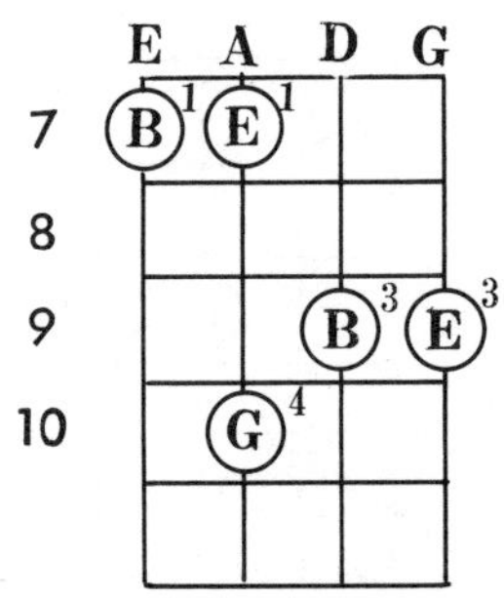

Subdominant

F♯7

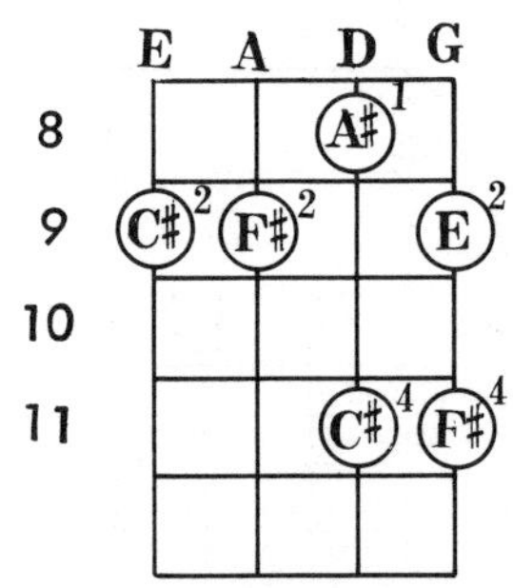

Dominant 7th

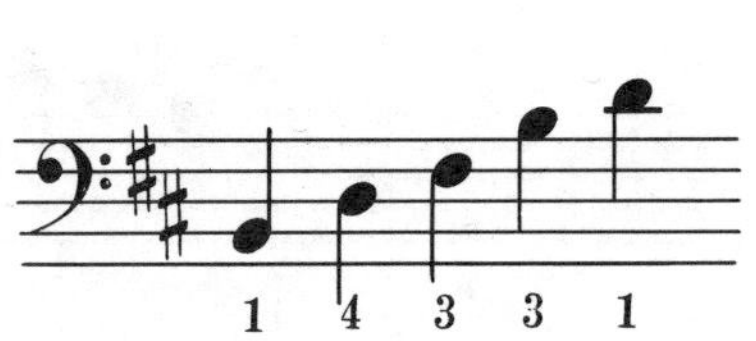

TERTIARY FORMS

C MINOR

HARMONIC

VIIIth POSITION

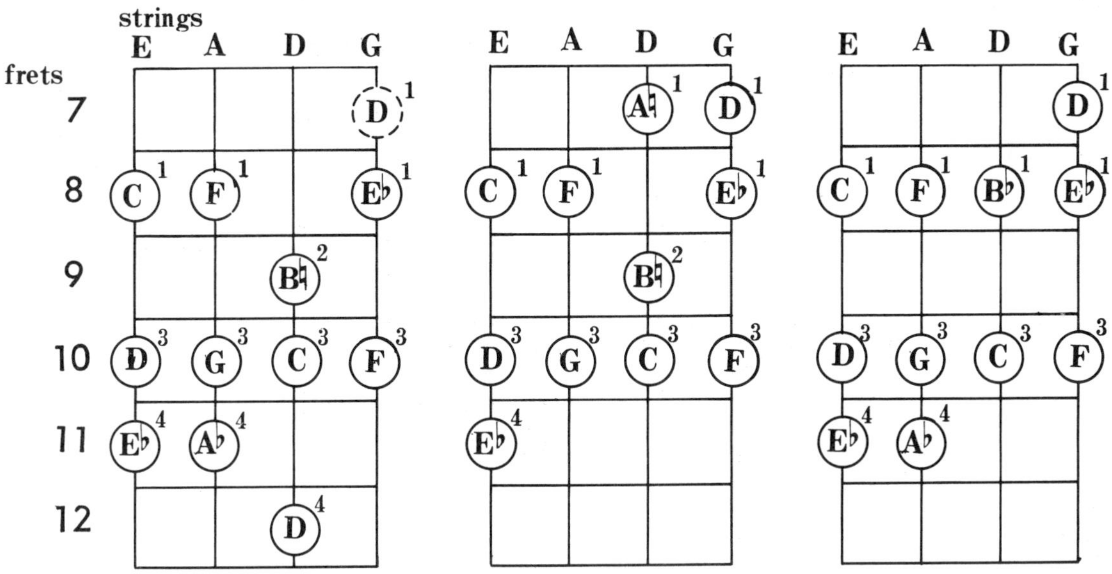

Harmonic | Melodic ascending | Melodic descending

This form is the same as the natural form, and except for mode or feeling, it is the same as the relative major (E♭).

MELODIC

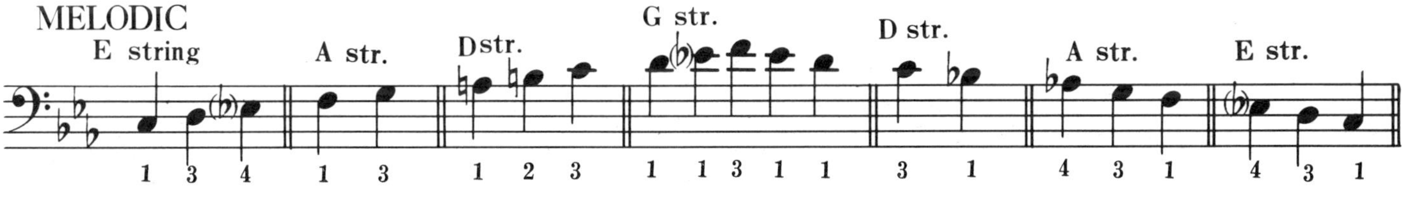

ARPEGGIOS

Cm | Fm | G7

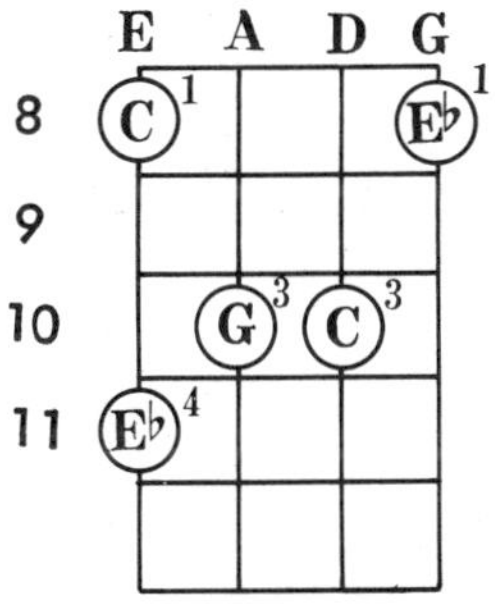

Tonic

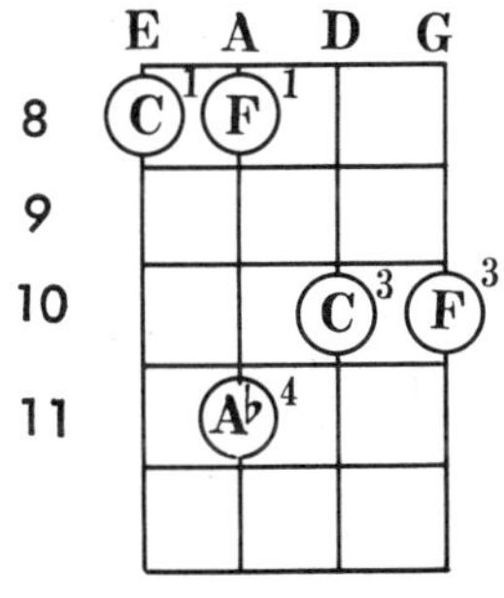

Subdominant

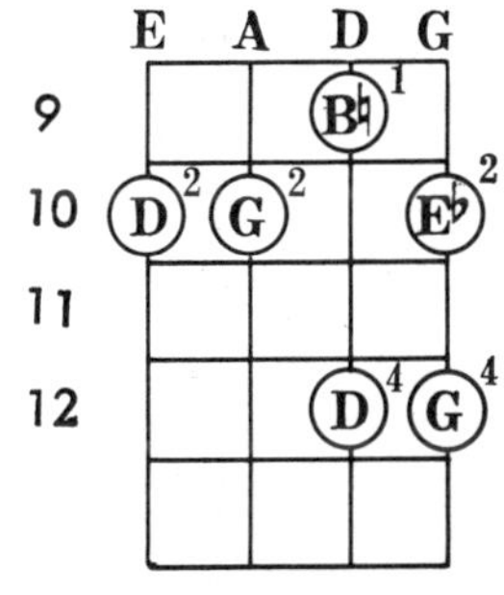

Dominant 7th

TERTIARY FORMS

F♯ MINOR

HARMONIC

IInd POSITION

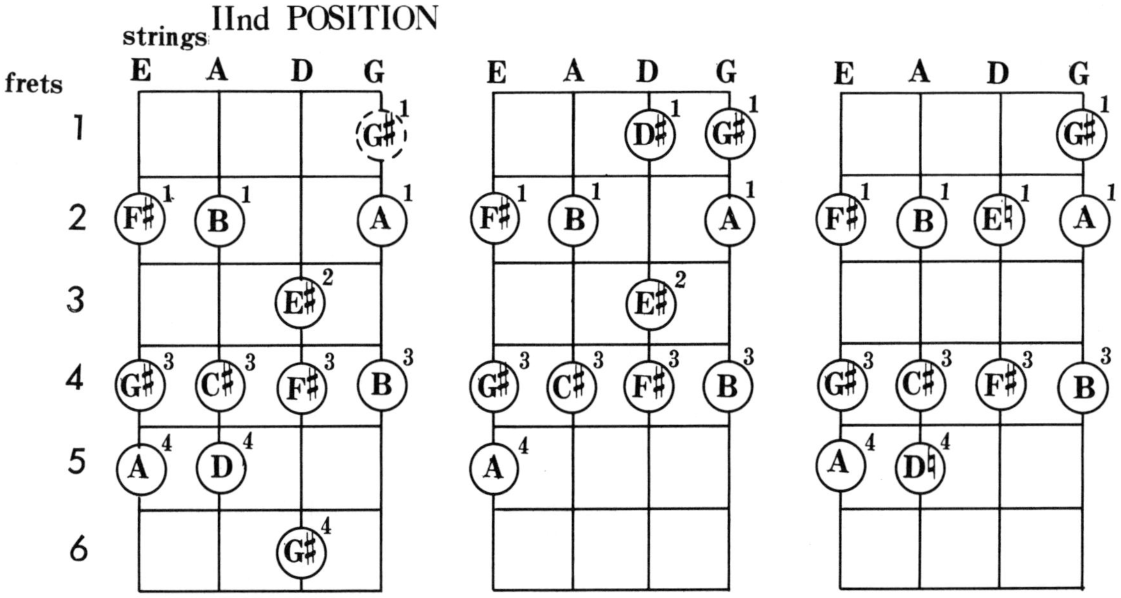

Harmonic | Melodic ascending | Melodic descending

This form is the same as the natural form, and except for mode or feeling, it is the same as the relative major (A).

MELODIC

ARPEGGIOS

F♯m | Bm | C♯7

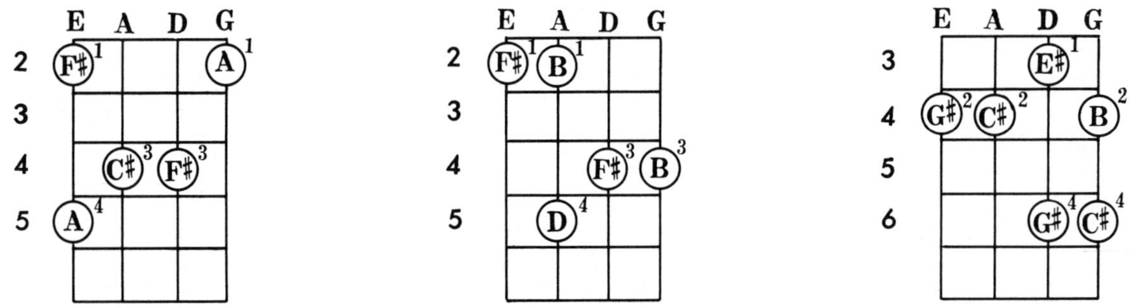

Tonic | Subdominant | Dominant 7th

TERTIARY FORMS

F MINOR

HARMONIC

Ist POSITION

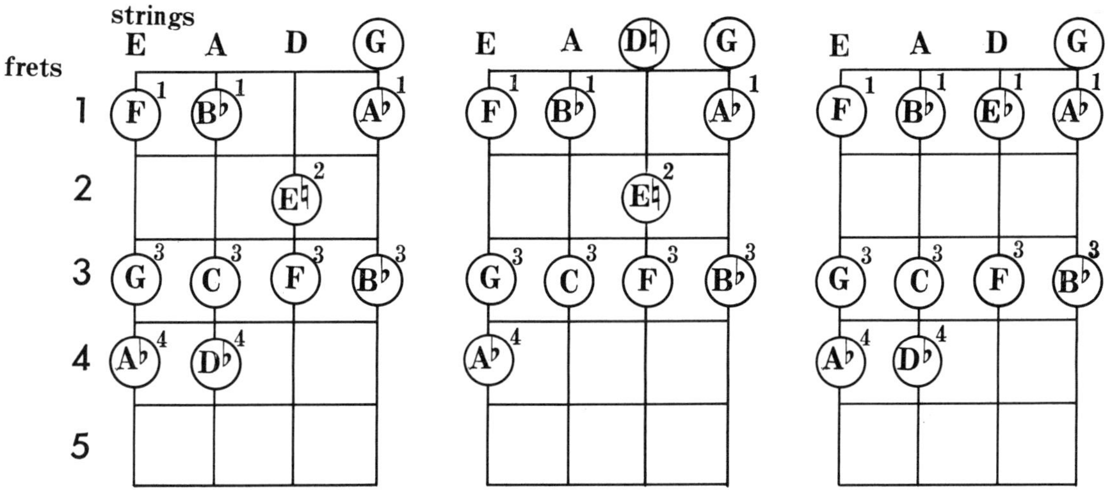

Harmonic

Melodic ascending

Melodic descending

This form is the same as the natural form, and except for mode or feeling, it is the same as the relative major (A♭).

MELODIC

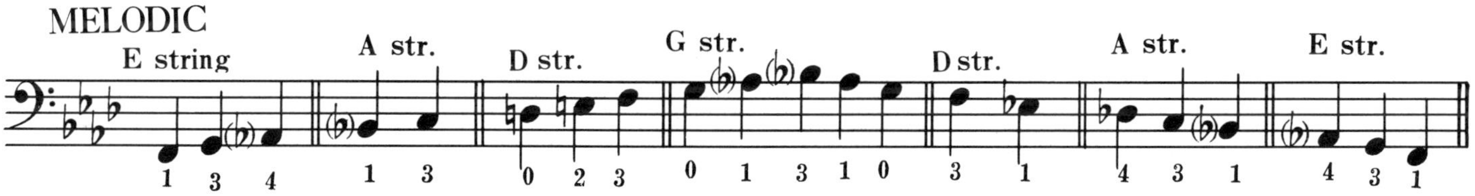

ARPEGGIOS

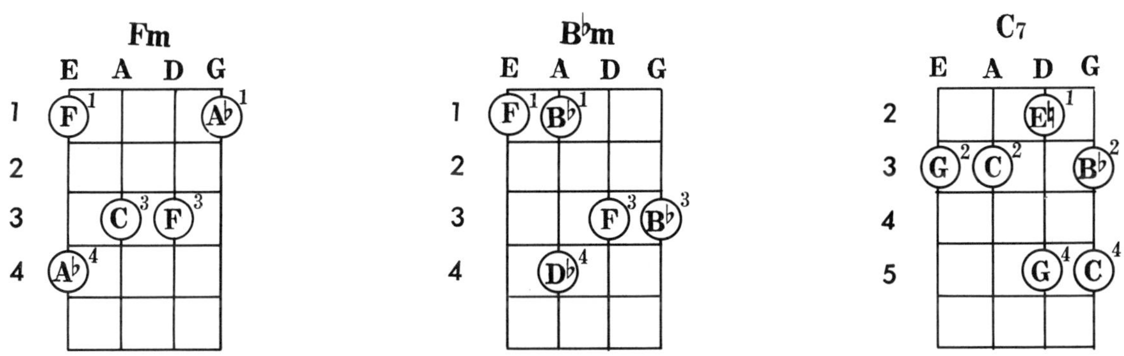

Tonic

Subdominant

Dominant 7th

TERTIARY FORMS

C♯ MINOR

HARMONIC

IXth POSITION

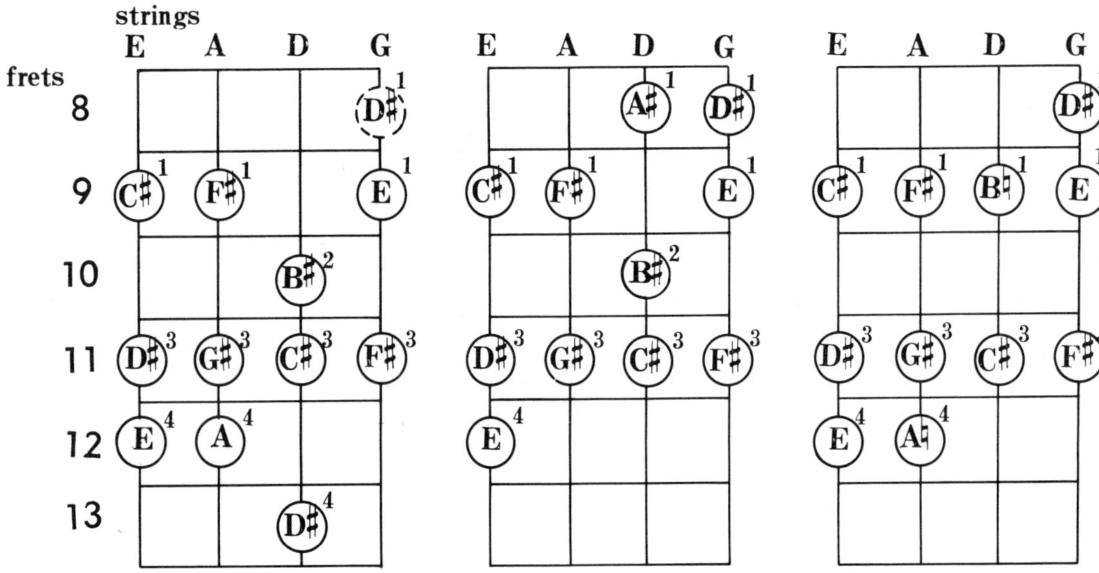

Harmonic

Melodic ascending

Melodic descending

This form is the same as the natural form, and except for mode or feeling, it is the same as the relative major (E).

MELODIC

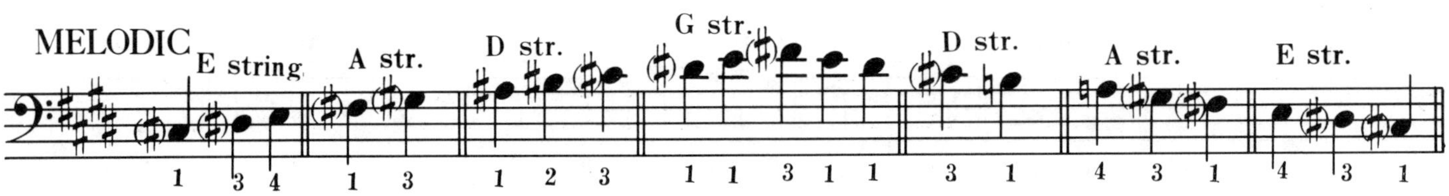

ARPEGGIOS

C♯m

F♯m

G♯7

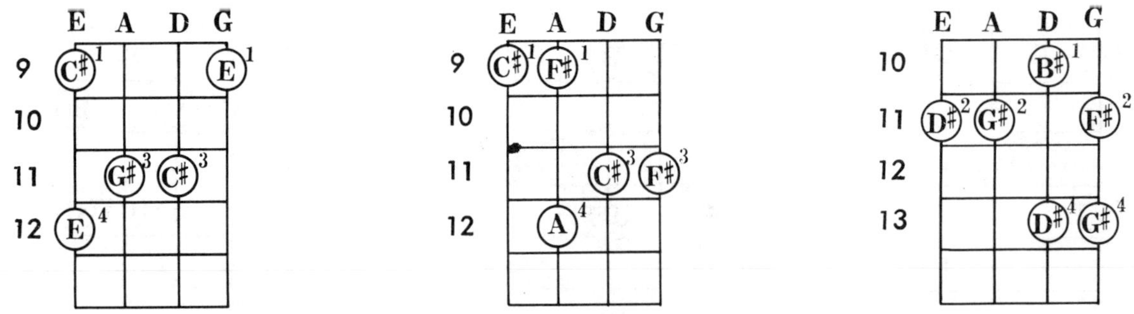

Tonic

Subdominant

Dominant 7th

TERTIARY FORMS

B♭ MINOR

HARMONIC

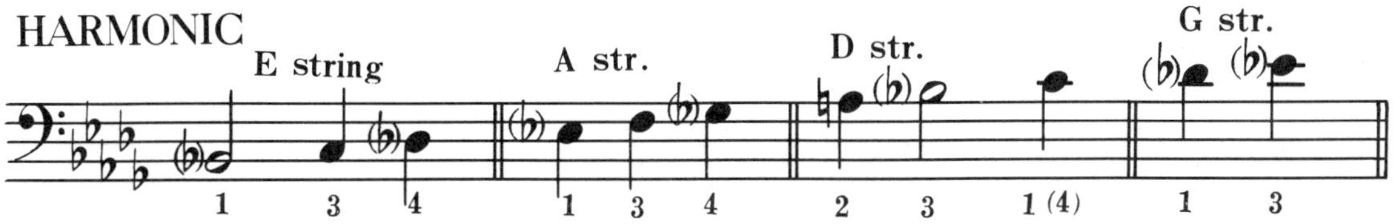

VIth POSITION

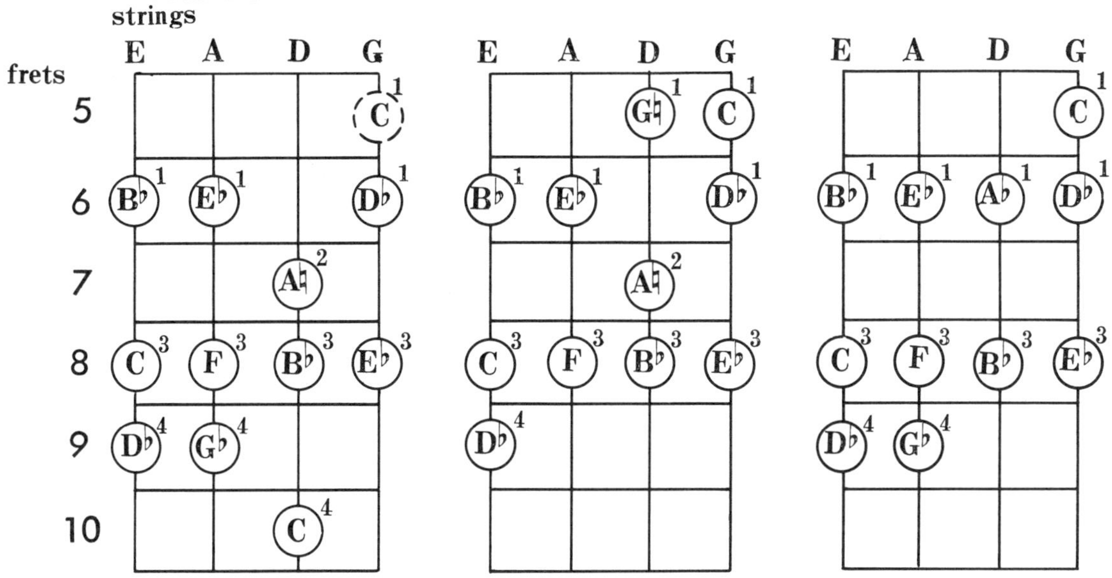

Harmonic — Melodic ascending — Melodic descending

This form is the same as the natural form, and except for mode or feeling, it is the same as the relative major (D♭).

MELODIC

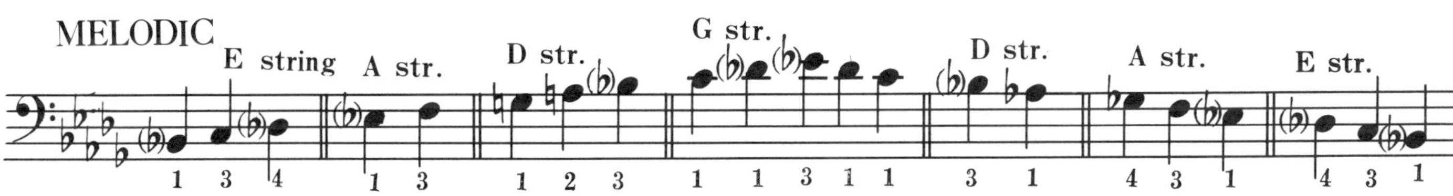

ARPEGGIOS

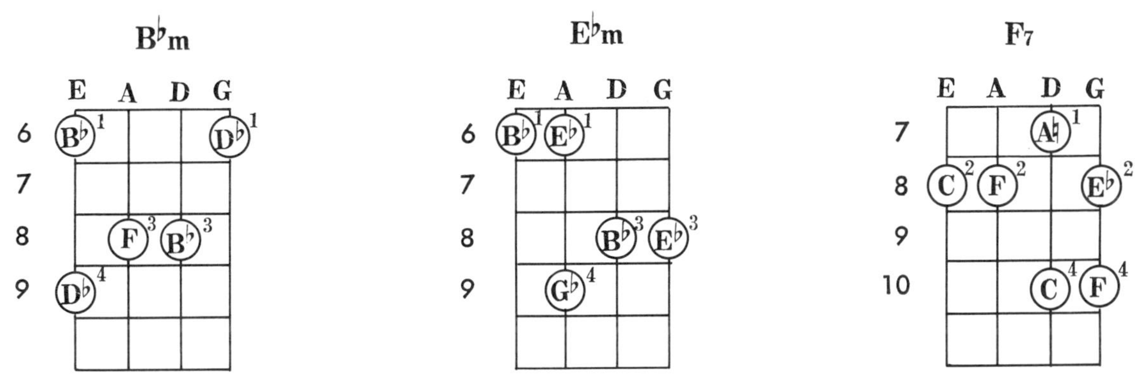

Tonic — Subdominant — Dominant 7th

TERTIARY FORMS

G♯ MINOR

HARMONIC

IVth POSITION

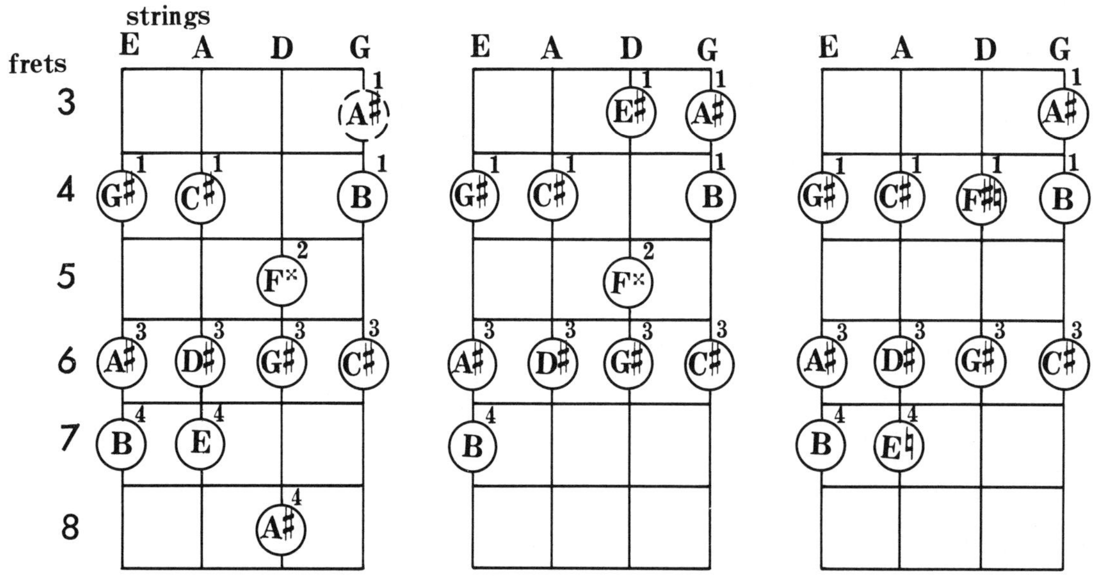

Harmonic — Melodic ascending — Melodic descending

This form is the same as the natural form, and except for mode or feeling, it is the same as the relative major (B).

MELODIC

ARPEGGIOS

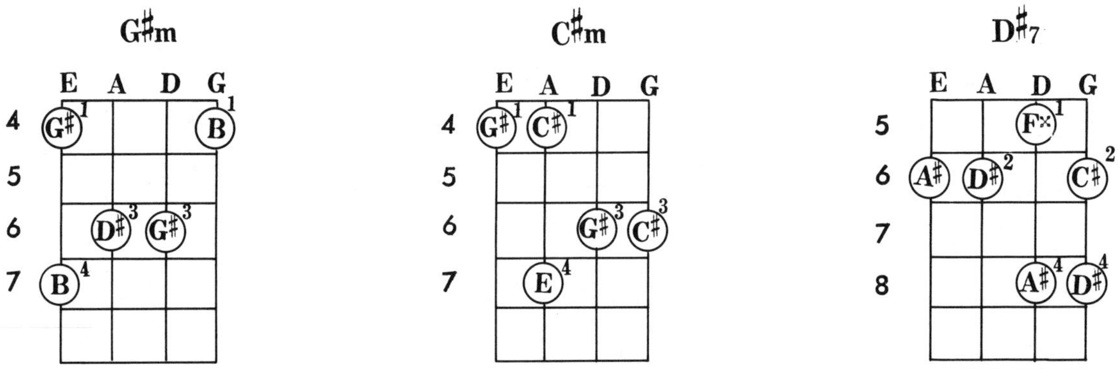

Tonic — Subdominant — Dominant 7th

TERTIARY FORMS

This key is enharmonically equivalent to D♯Minor (p 74).

E♭ MINOR

HARMONIC

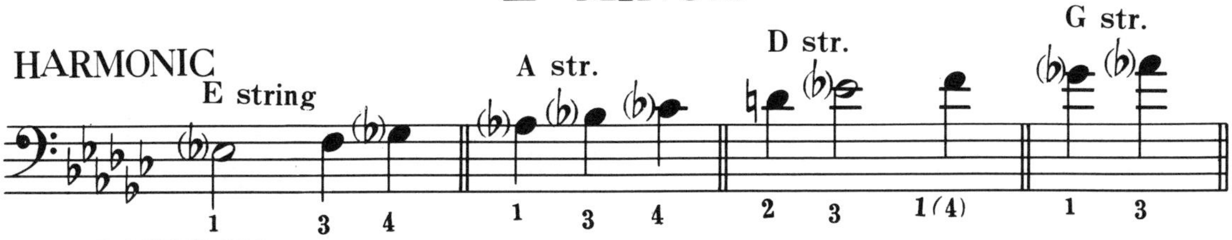

XIth POSITION

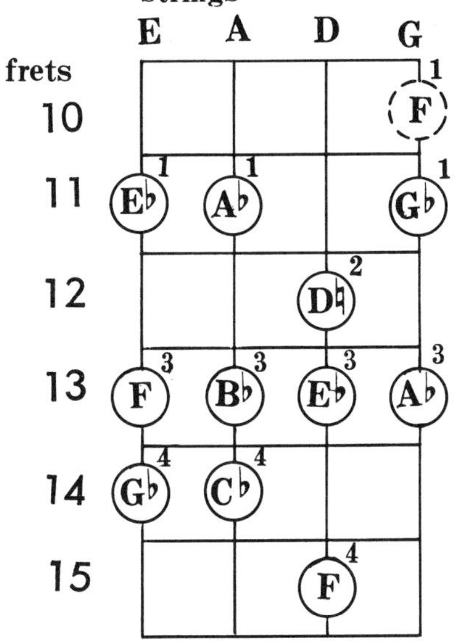

Harmonic

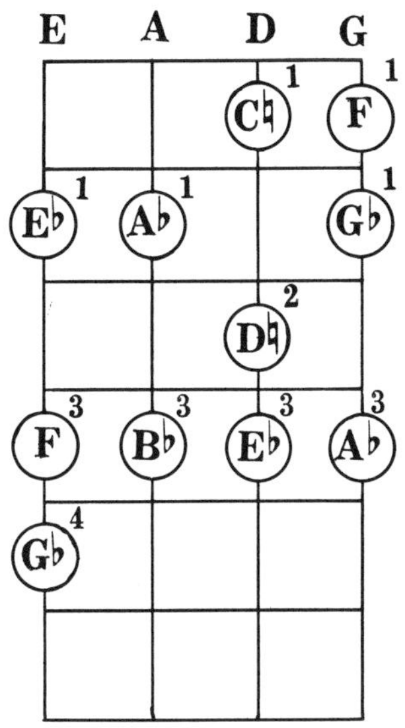

Melodic ascending

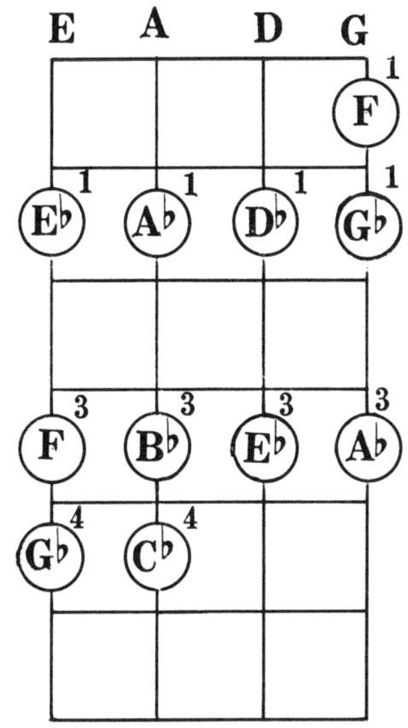

Melodic descending

This form is the same as the natural form, and except for mode or feeling, it is the same as the relative major (G♭).

MELODIC

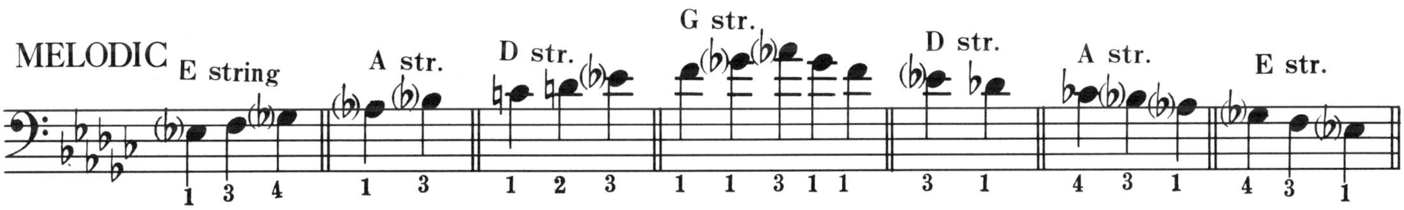

ARPEGGIOS

E♭m

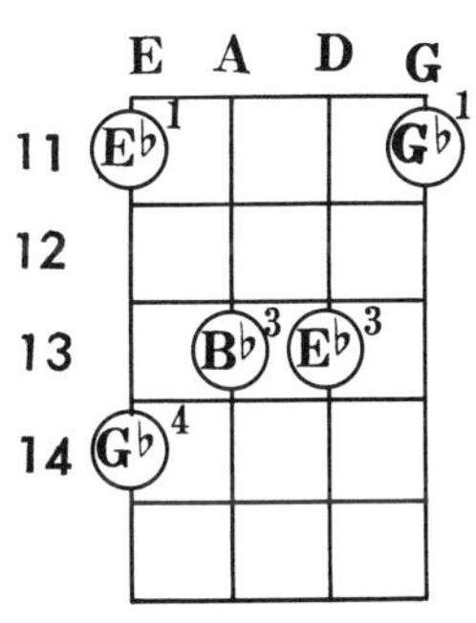

Tonic

A♭m

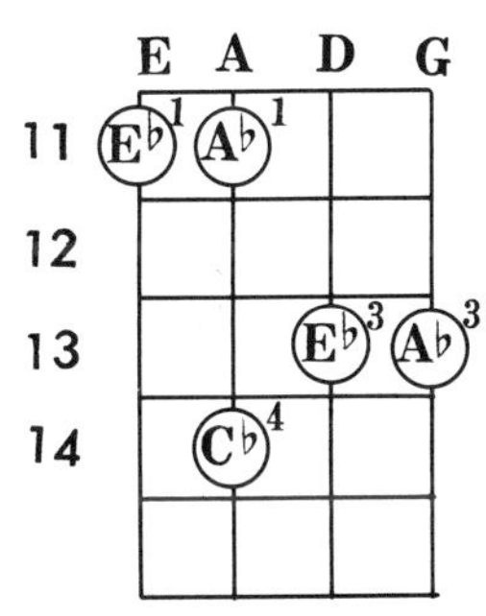

Subdominant

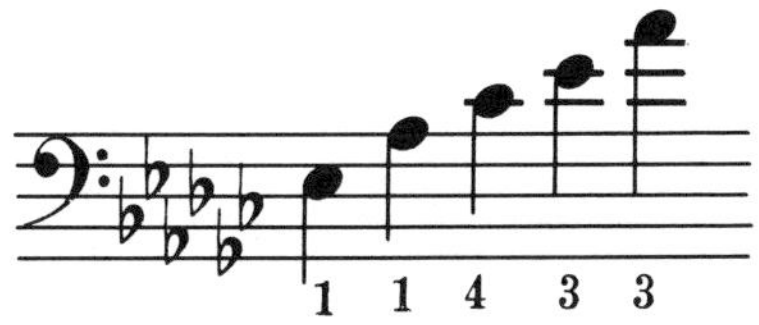

B♭7

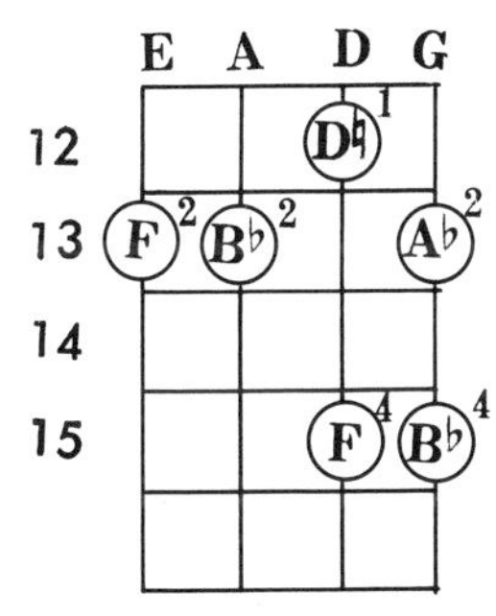

Dominant 7th

TERTIARY FORMS

D♯ MINOR

This key is enharmonically equivalent to E♭Minor (p 73).

HARMONIC

XIth POSITION

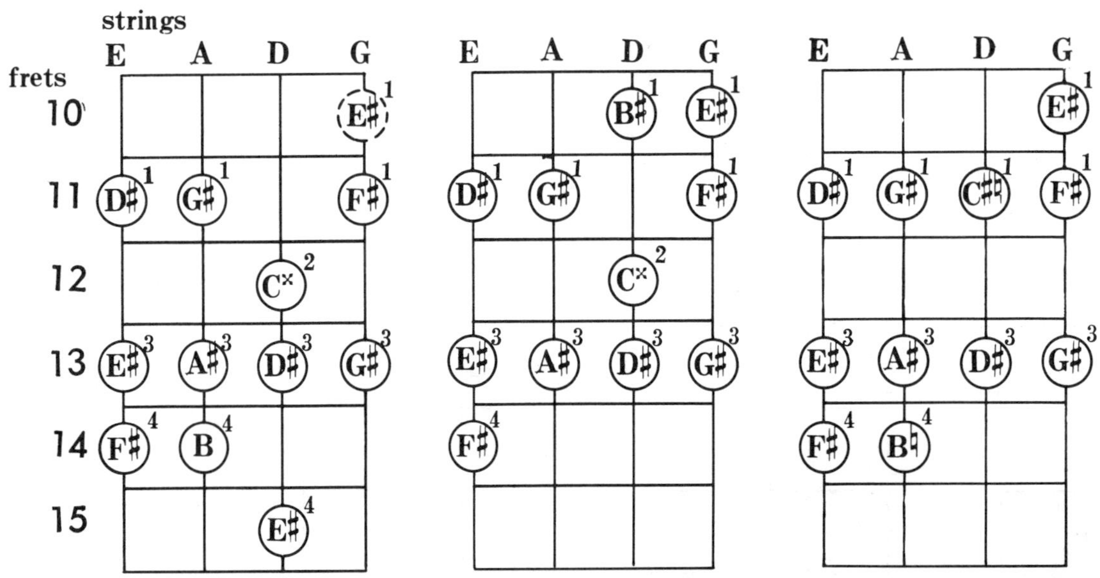

Harmonic — Melodic ascending — Melodic descending

This form is the same as the natural form, and except for mode or feeling, it is the same as the relative major (F♯).

MELODIC

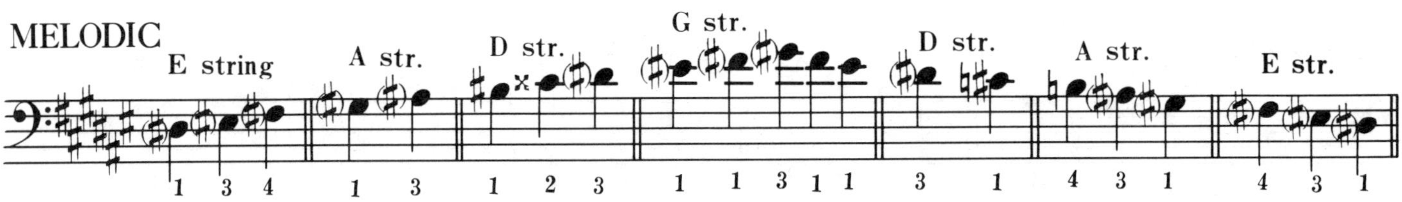

ARPEGGIOS

D♯m

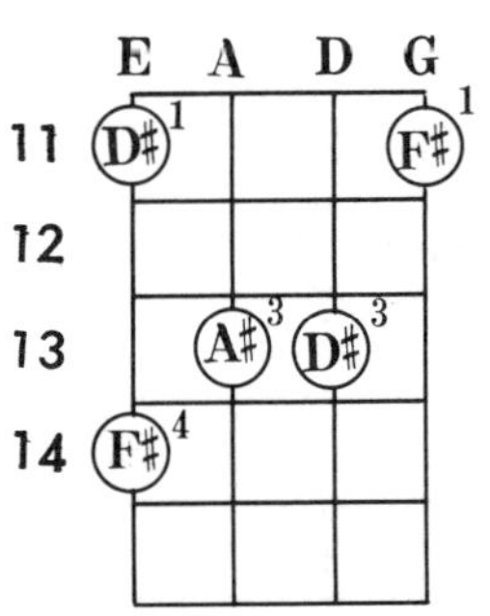

Tonic

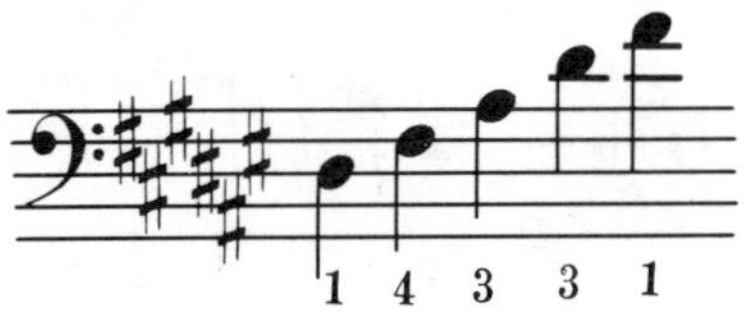

G♯m

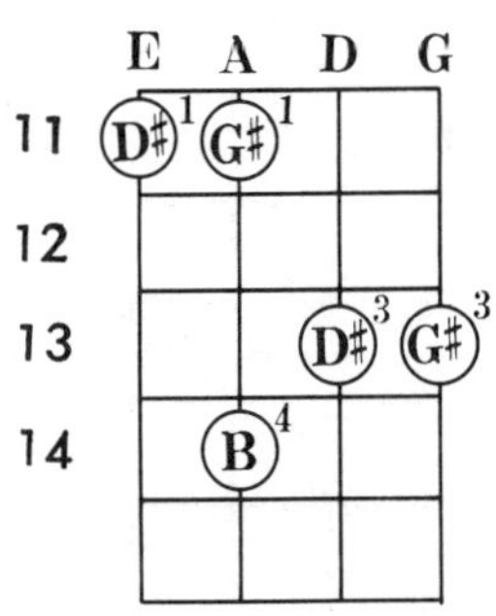

Subdominant

A♯7

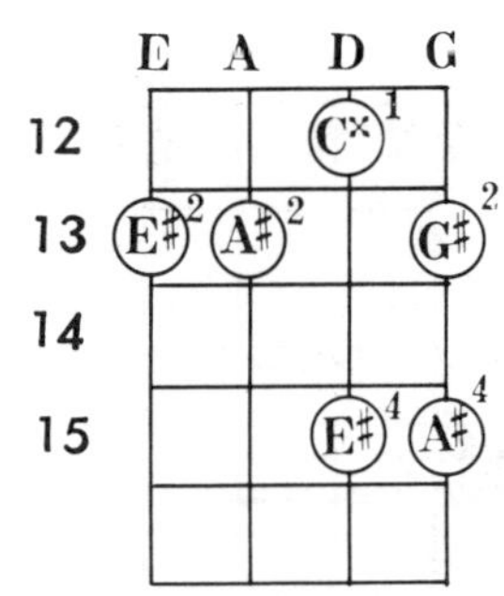

Dominant 7th

QUATERNARY FORMS

A MINOR

HARMONIC

IInd POSITION

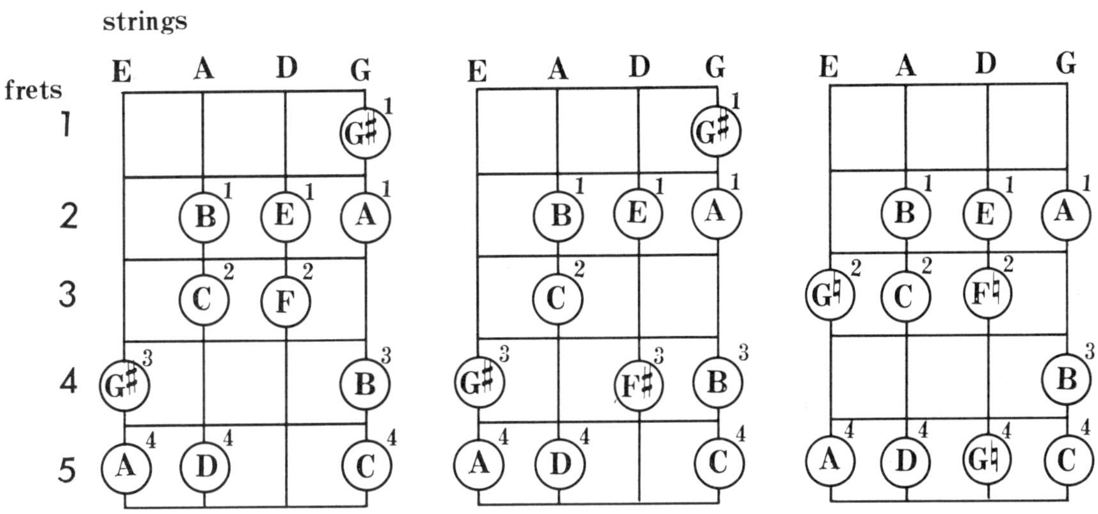

Harmonic Melodic ascending Melodic descending

This form is the same as the natural form, and except for mode or feeling, it is the same as the relative major (C).

MELODIC

ARPEGGIOS

Am

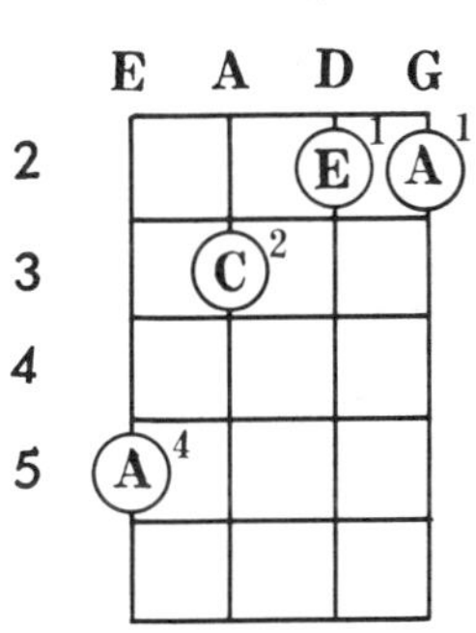

Tonic

Dm

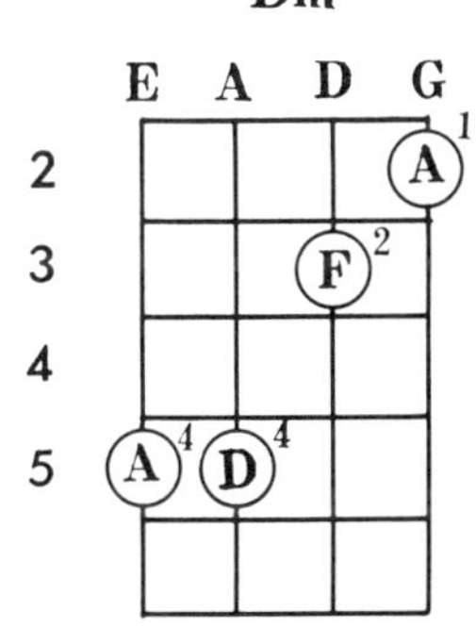

Subdominant

E7

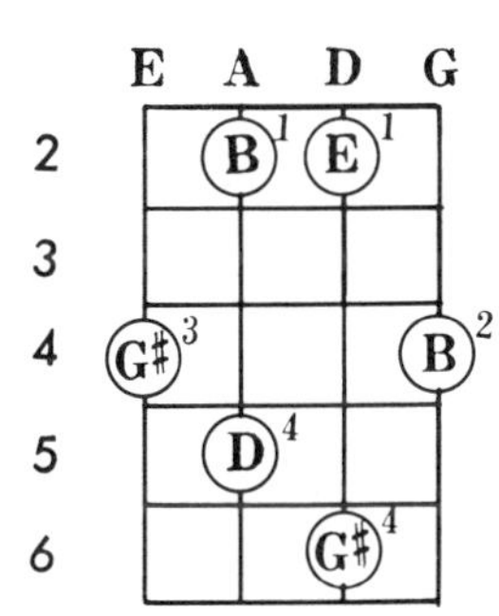

Dominant 7th

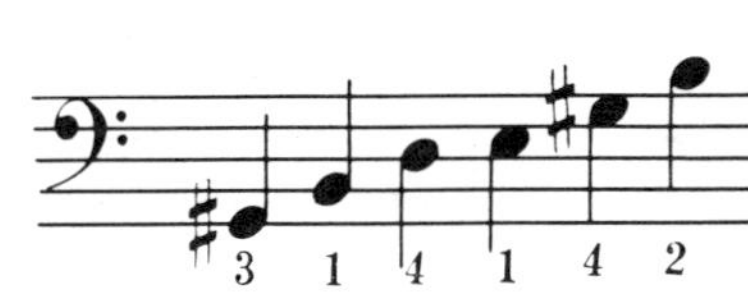

QUATERNARY FORMS

D MINOR

HARMONIC

VIIth POSITION

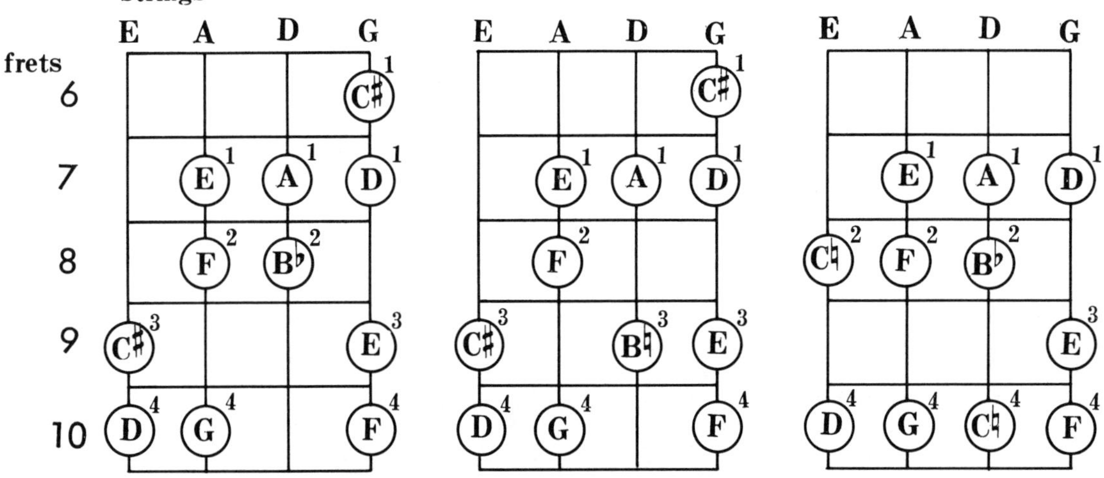

Harmonic   Melodic ascending   Melodic descending

This form is the same as the natural form, and except for mode or feeling, it is the same as the relative major (F).

MELODIC

ARPEGGIOS

Dm

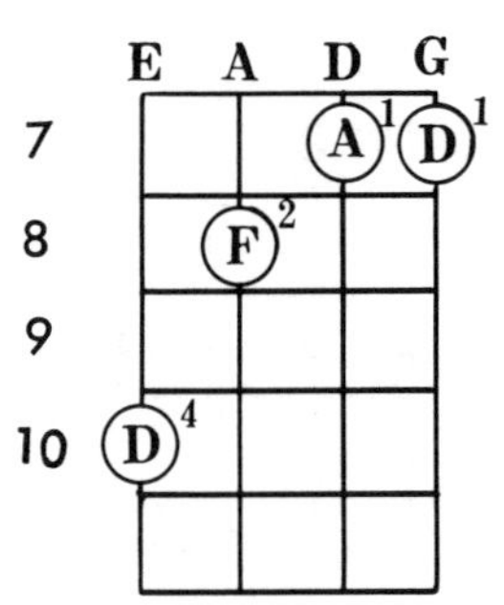

Tonic

Gm

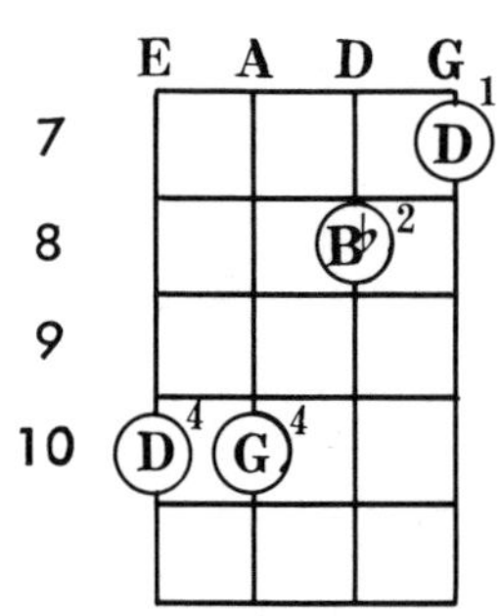

Subdominant

A7

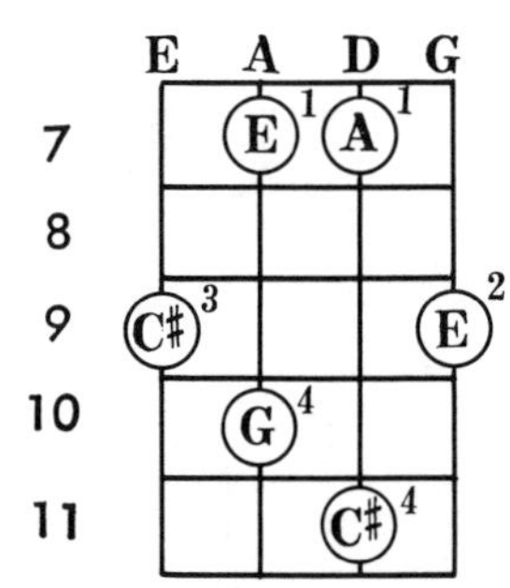

Dominant 7th

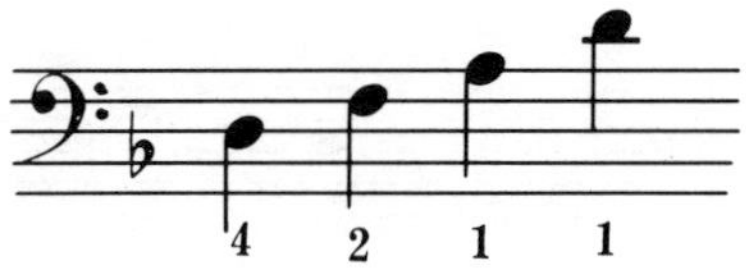

QUATERNARY FORMS

E MINOR

HARMONIC

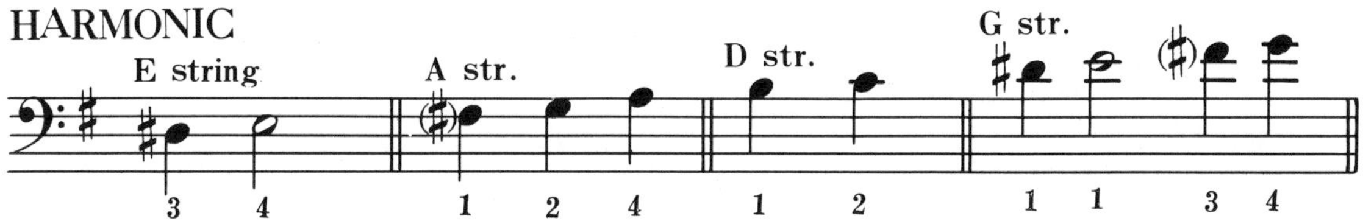

IXth POSITION

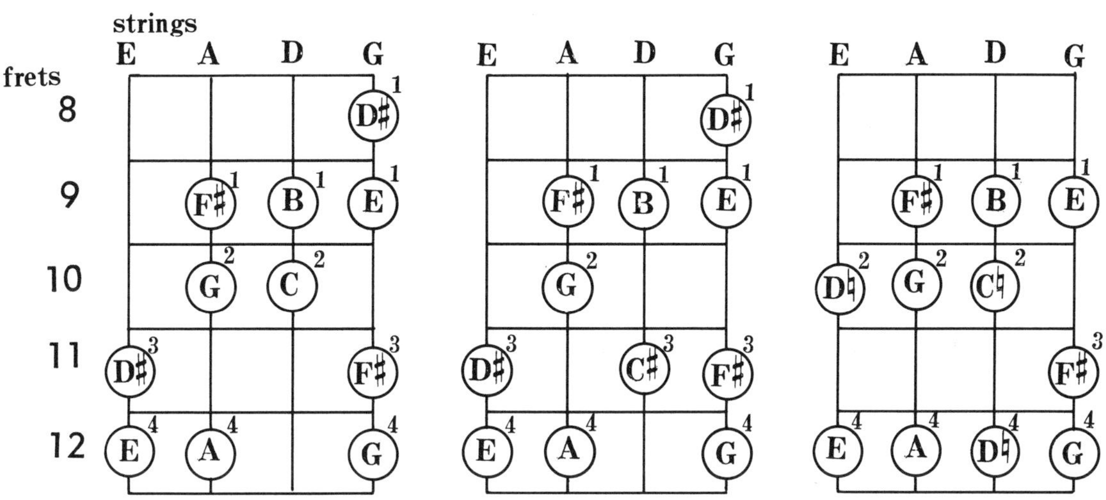

Harmonic

Melodic ascending

Melodic descending

This form is the same as the natural form, and except for mode or feeling, it is the same as the relative major (G).

MELODIC

ARPEGGIOS

Em

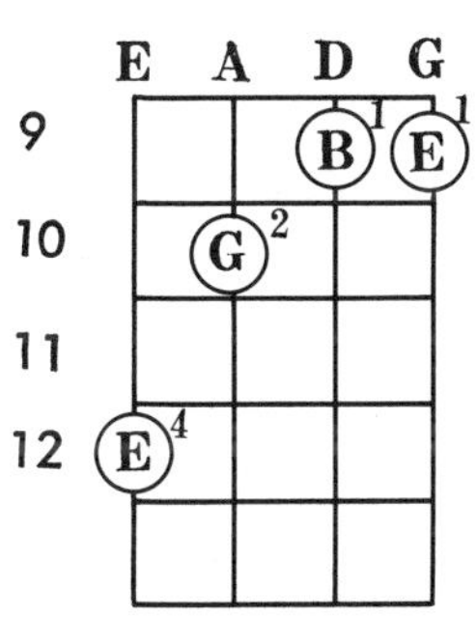

Tonic

Am

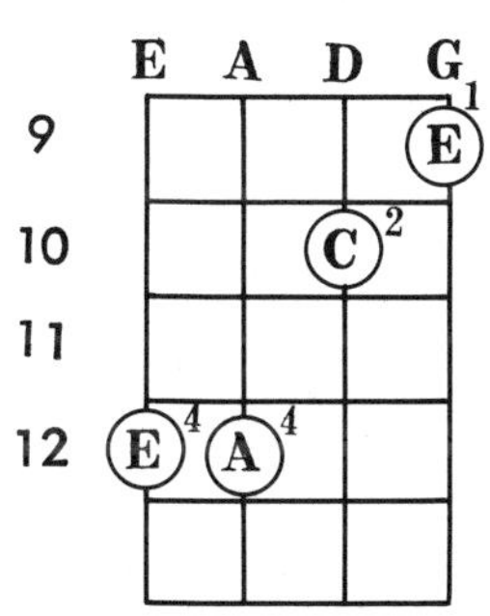

Subdominant

B7

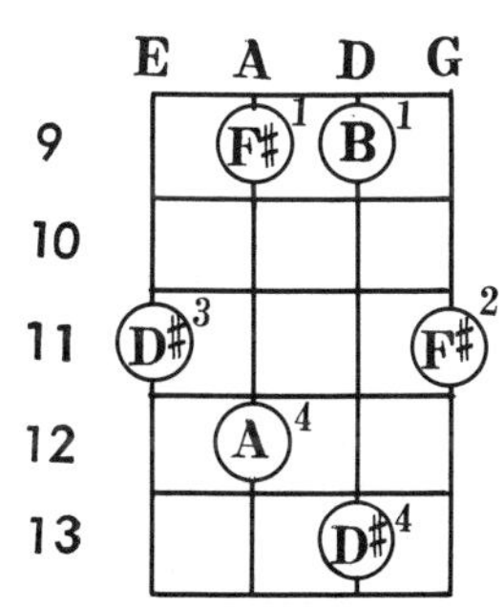

Dominant 7th

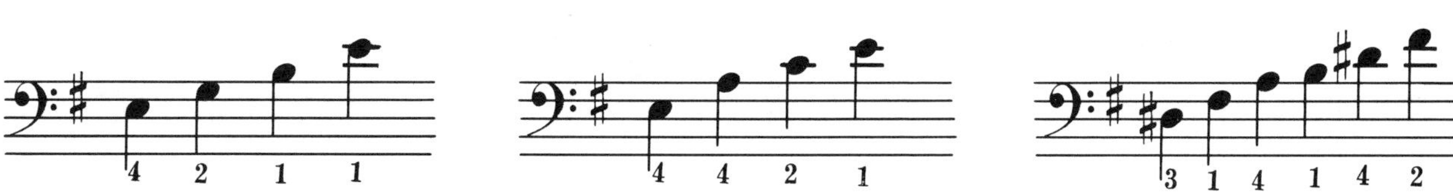

QUATERNARY FORMS

G MINOR

HARMONIC

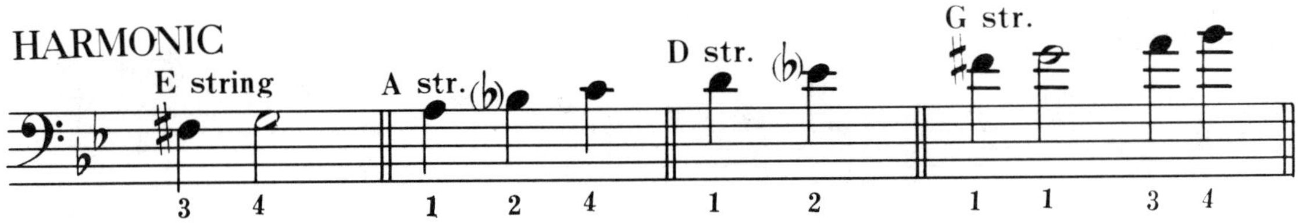

XIIth POSITION

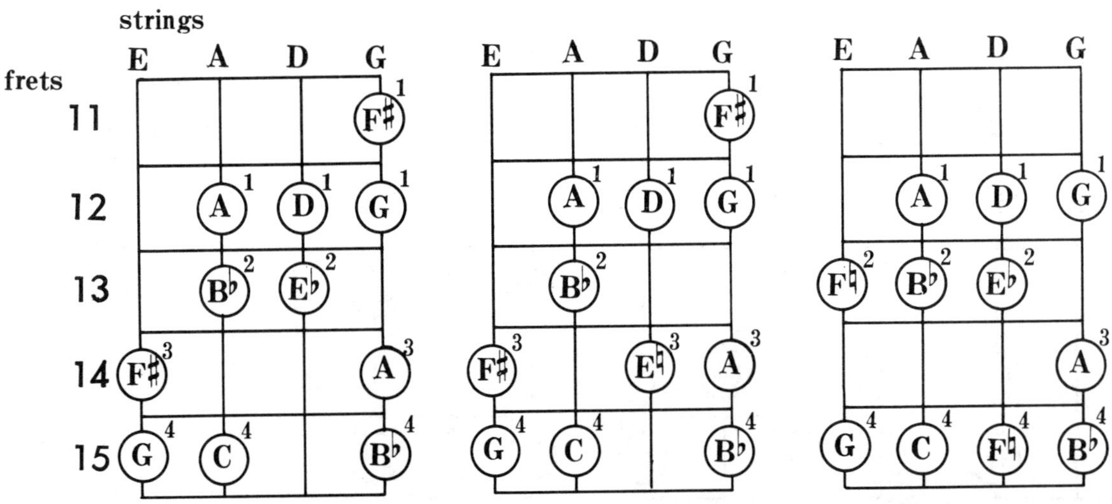

Harmonic — Melodic ascending — Melodic descending

This form is the same as the natural form, and except for mode or feeling, it is the same as the relative major (B♭).

MELODIC

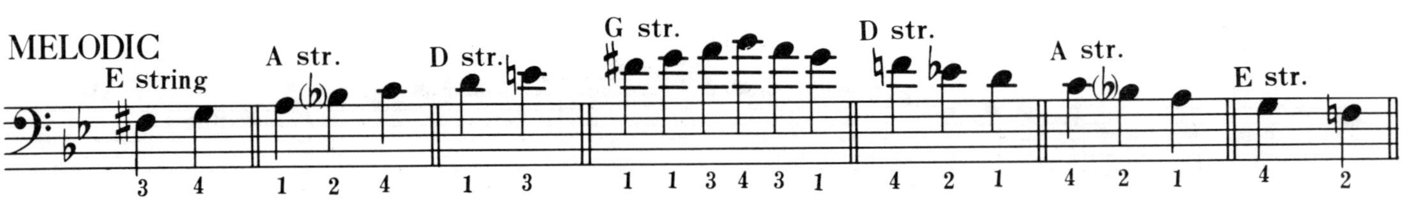

ARPEGGIOS

Gm

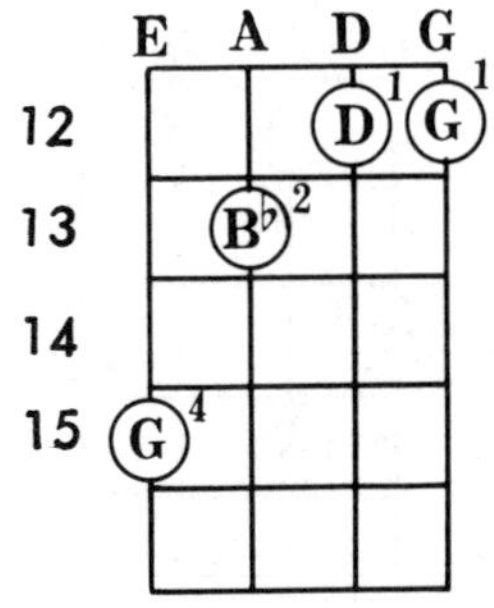

Tonic

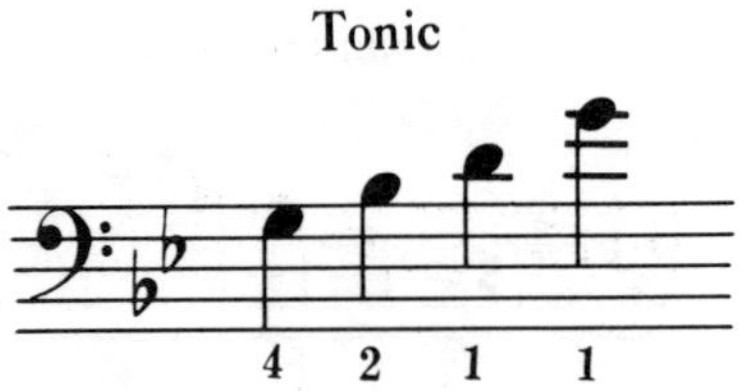

Cm

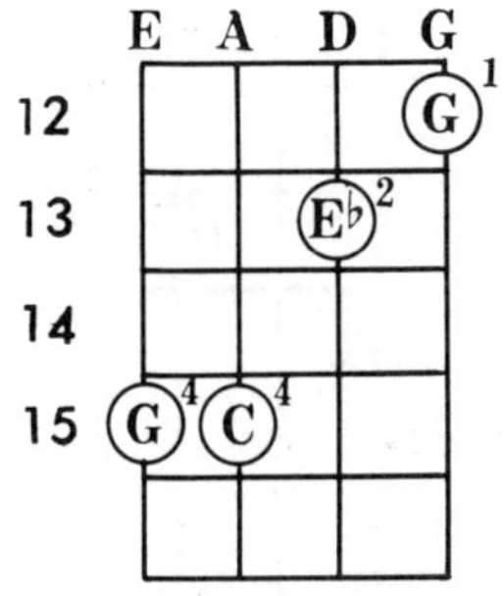

Subdominant

D7

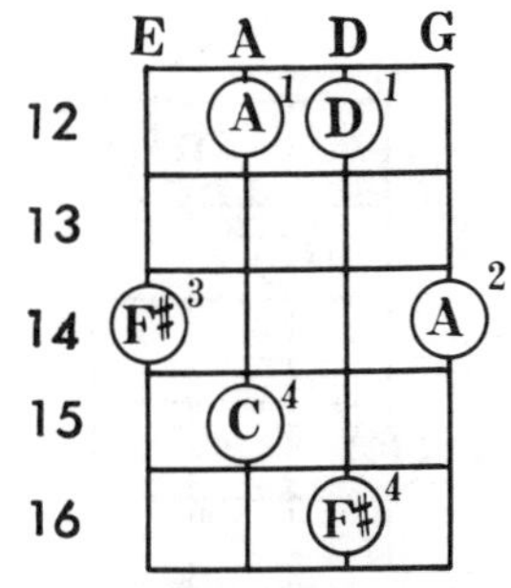

Dominant 7th

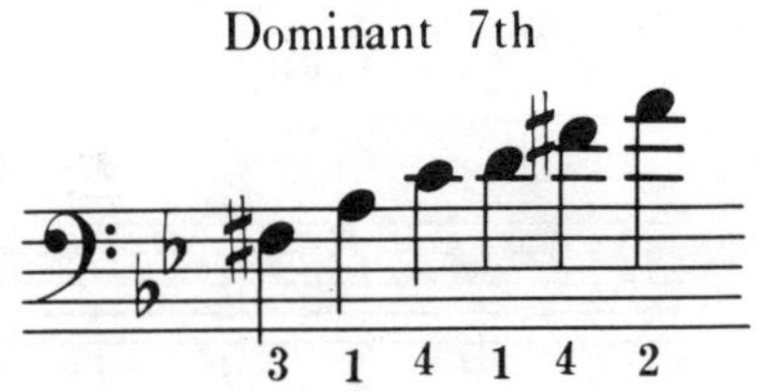

QUATERNARY FORMS

B MINOR

HARMONIC

IVth POSITION

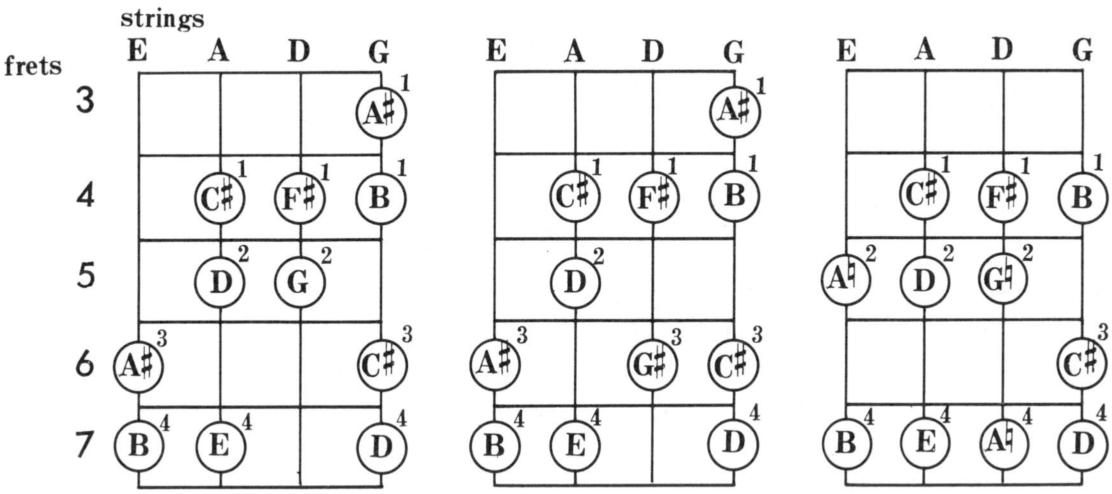

Harmonic Melodic ascending Melodic descending

This form is the same as the natural form, and except for mode or feeling, it is the same as the relative major (D).

MELODIC

ARPEGGIOS

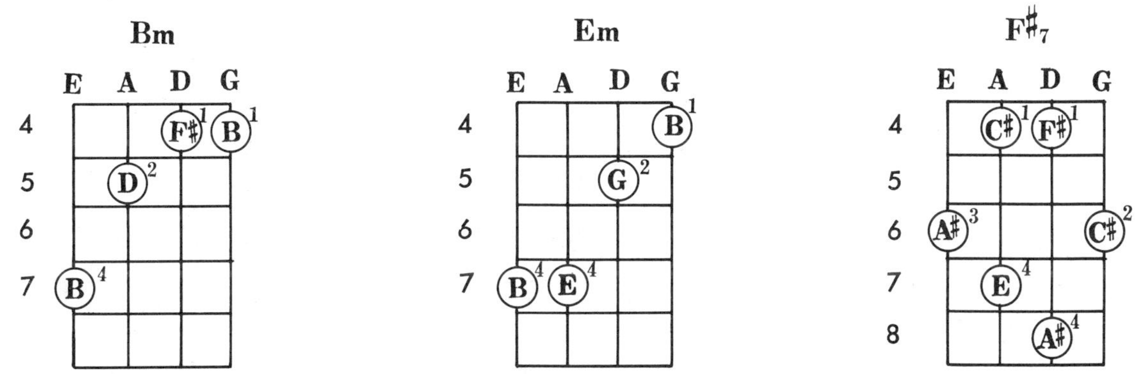

Tonic Subdominant Dominant 7th

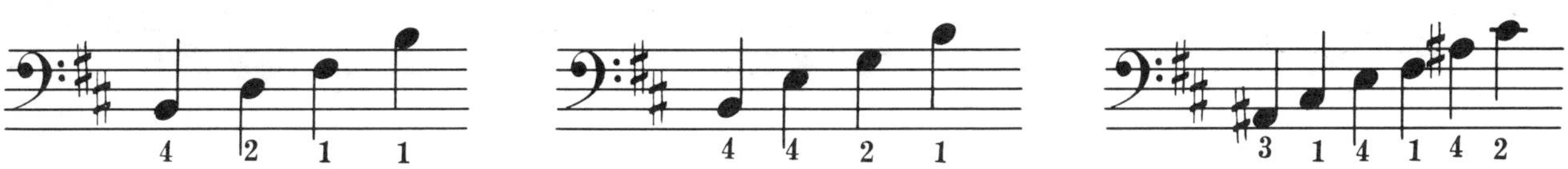

QUATERNARY FORMS

C MINOR

HARMONIC

Vth POSITION

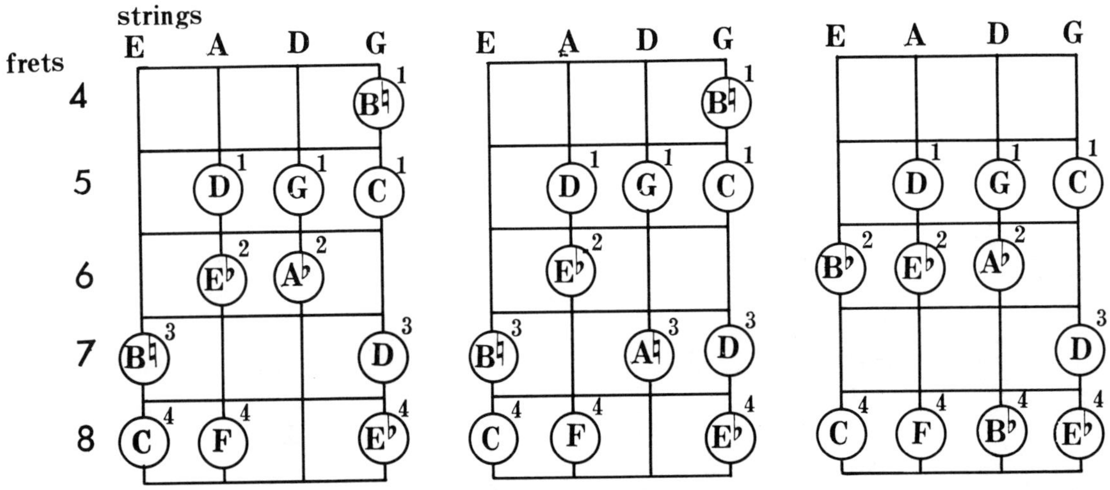

Harmonic Melodic ascending Melodic descending

This form is the same as the natural form, and except for mode or feeling, it is the same as the relative major (E♭).

MELODIC

ARPEGGIOS

Cm

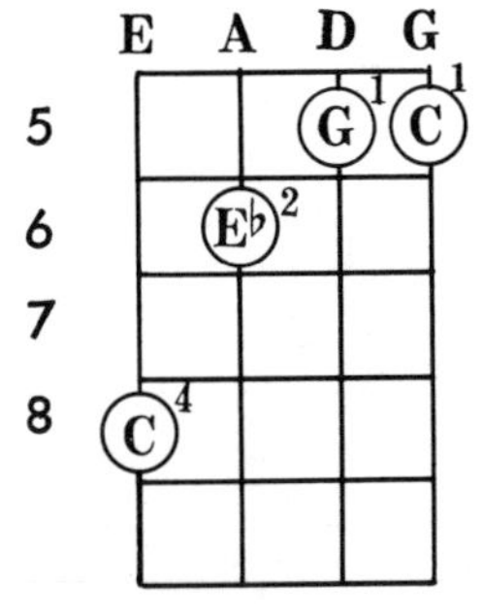

Tonic

Fm

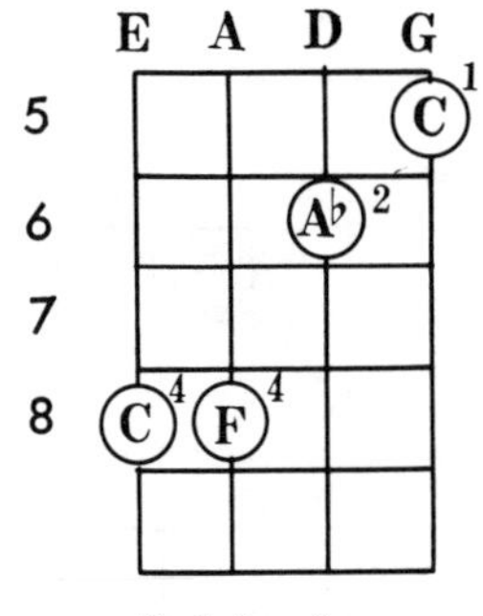

Subdominant

G7

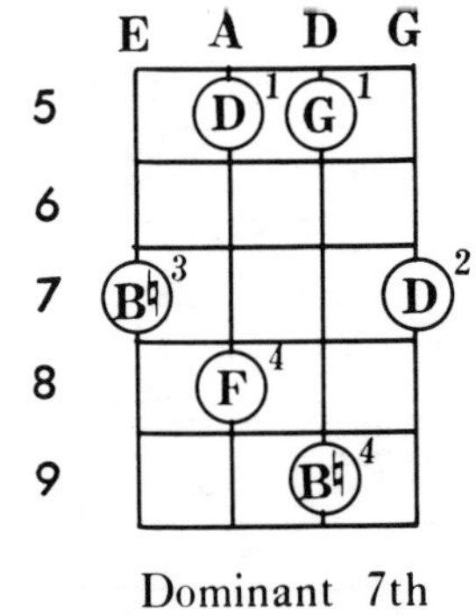

Dominant 7th

QUATERNARY FORMS

F♯ MINOR

HARMONIC

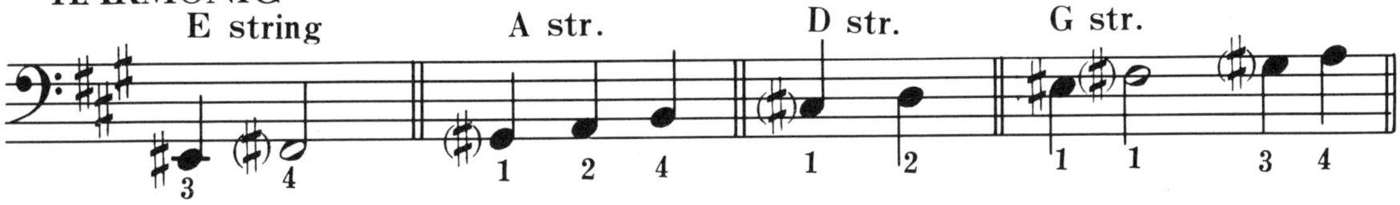

XIth POSITION

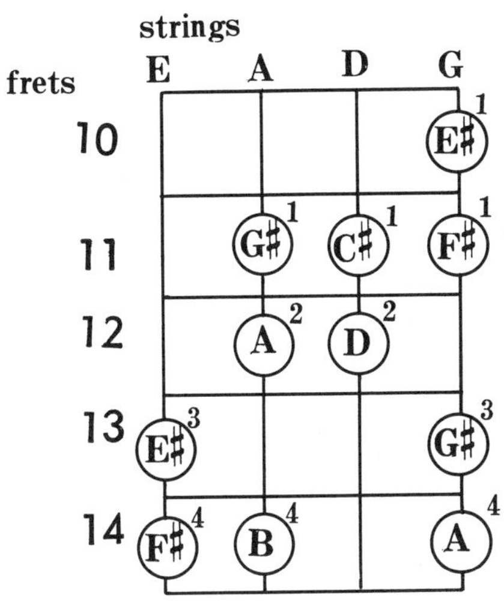

Harmonic

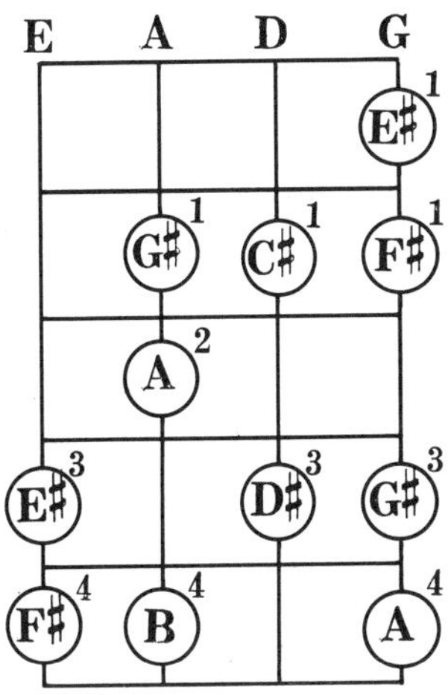

Melodic ascending

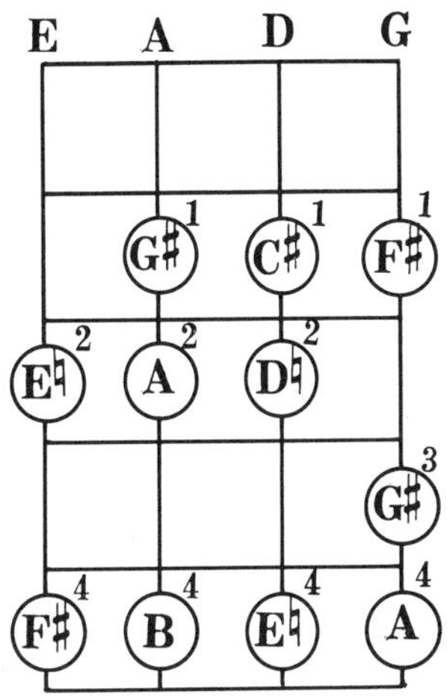

Melodic ascending

This form is the same as the natural form, and except for mode or feeling, it is the same as the relative major (A).

MELODIC

ARPEGGIOS

F♯m

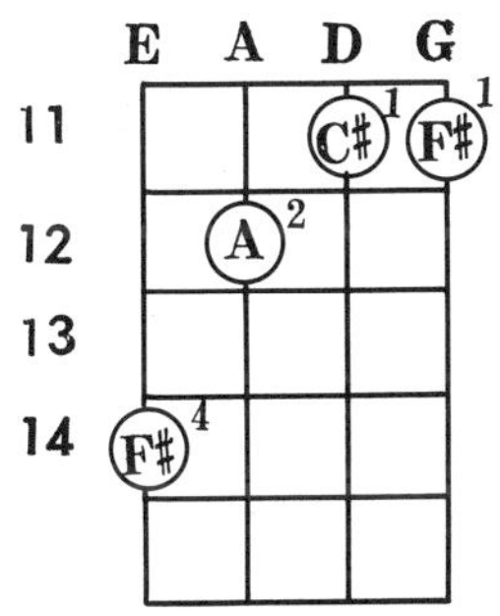

Tonic

Bm

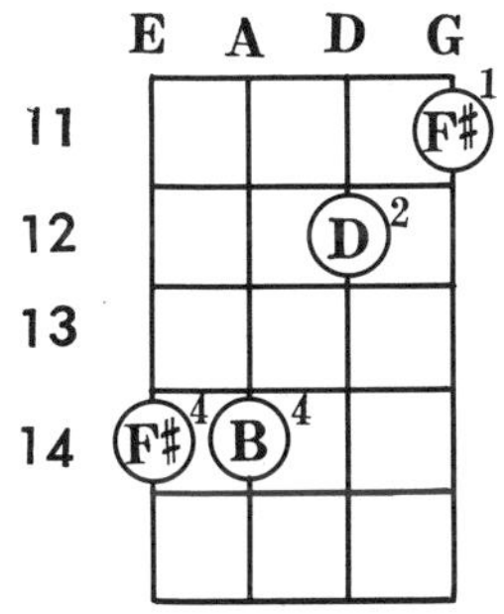

Subdominant

C♯7

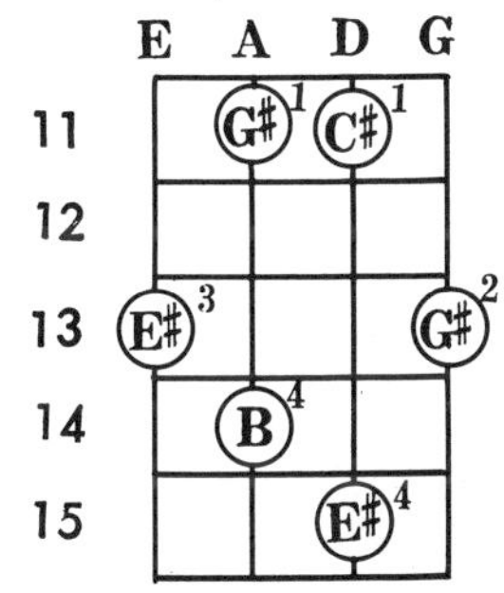

Dominant 7th

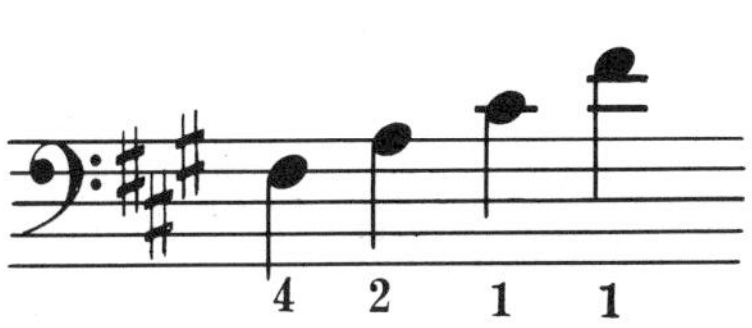

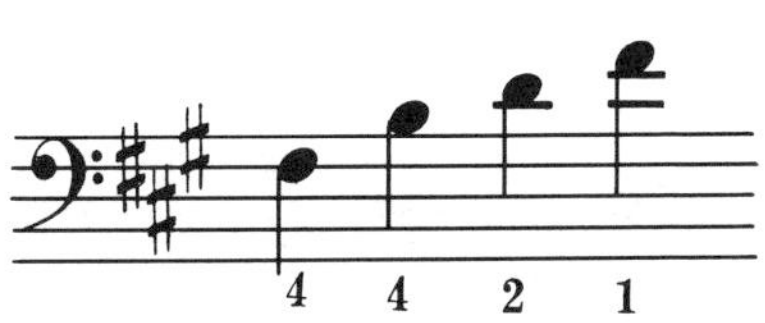

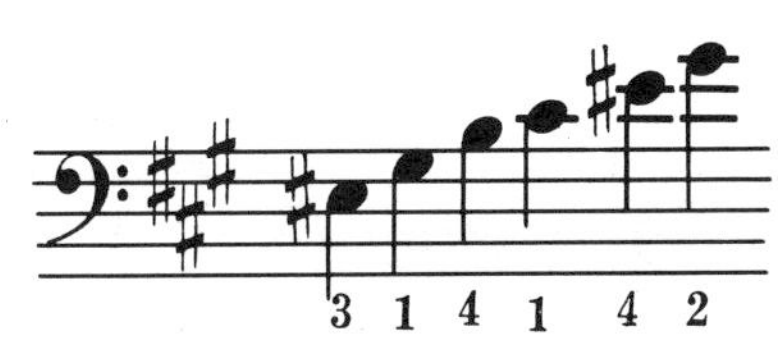

QUATERNARY FORMS

F MINOR

HARMONIC

Xth POSITION

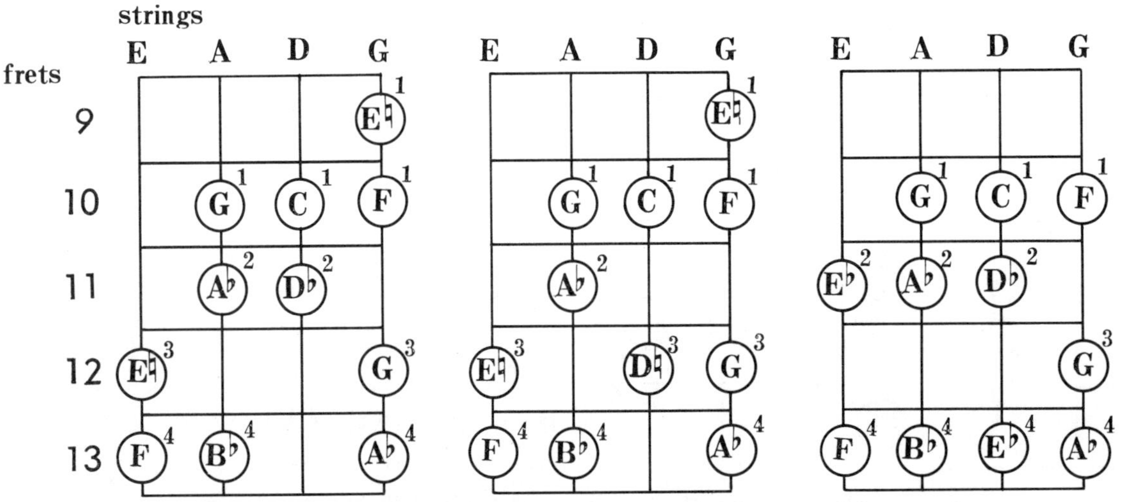

Harmonic — Melodic ascending — Melodic descending

This form is the same as the natural form, and except for mode or feeling, it is the same as the relative major (A♭).

MELODIC

ARPEGGIOS

Fm

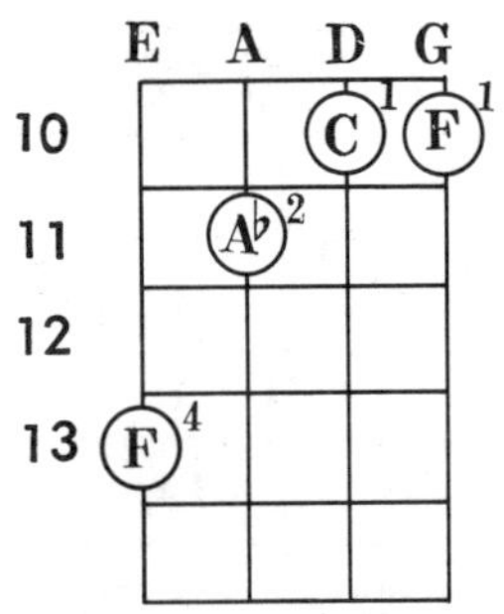

Tonic

B♭m

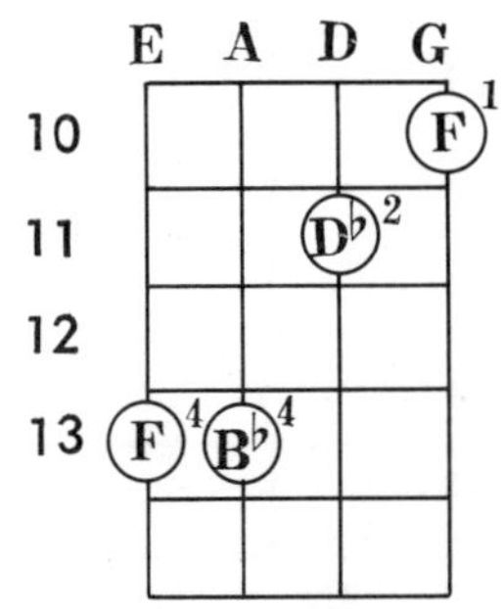

Subdominant

C7

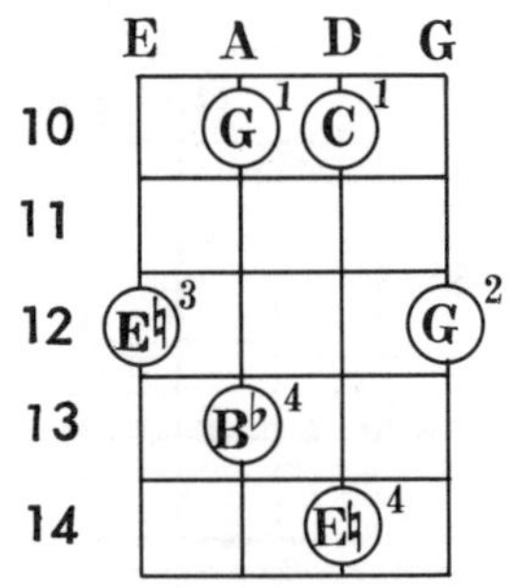

Dominant 7th

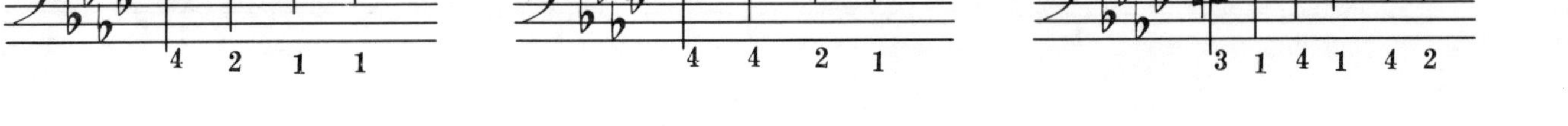

QUATERNARY FORMS

C♯ MINOR

HARMONIC

VIth POSITION

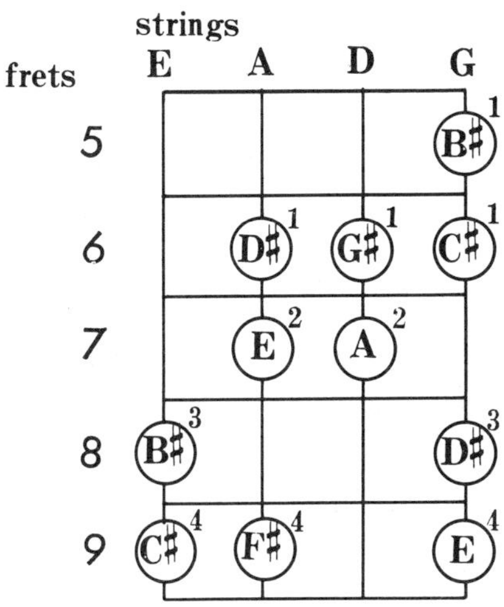

Harmonic

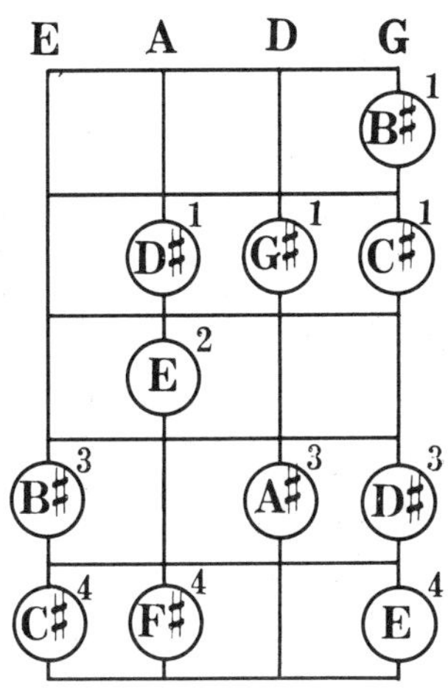

Melodic ascending

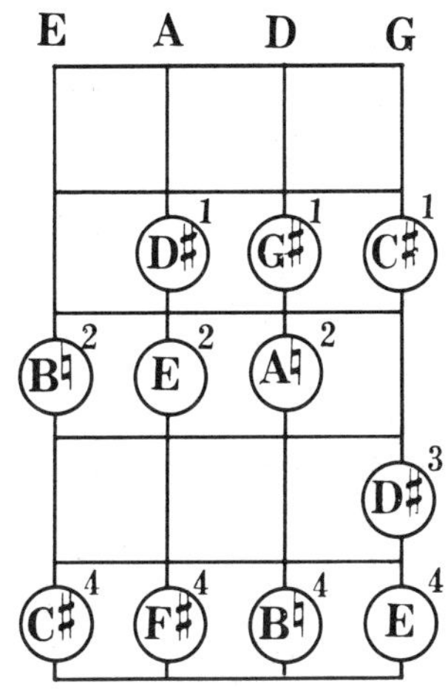

Melodic descending

This form is the same as the natural form, and except for mode or feeling, it is the same as the relative major (E).

MELODIC

ARPEGGIOS

C♯m

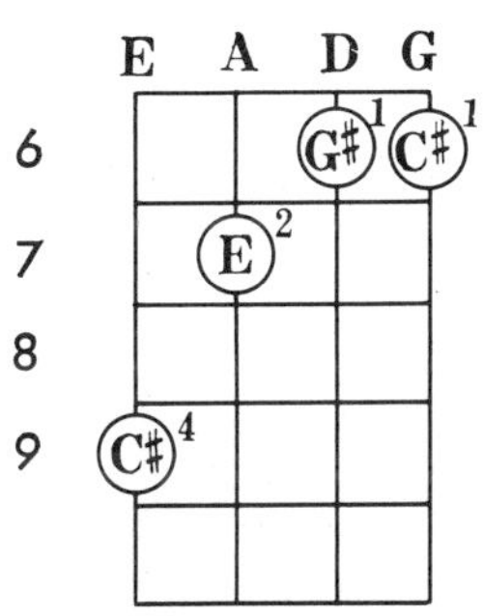

Tonic

F♯m

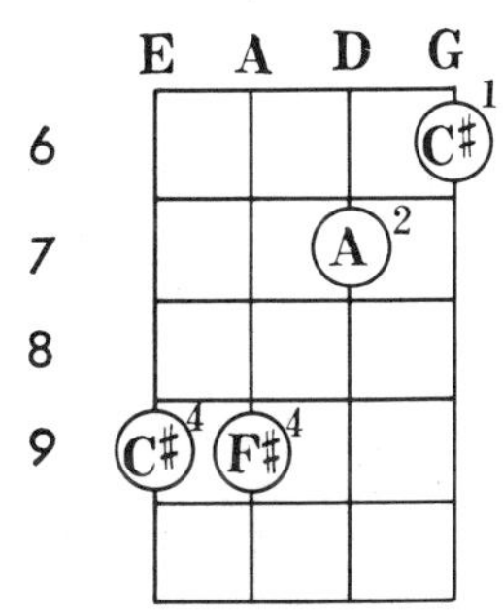

Subdominant

$G♯_7$

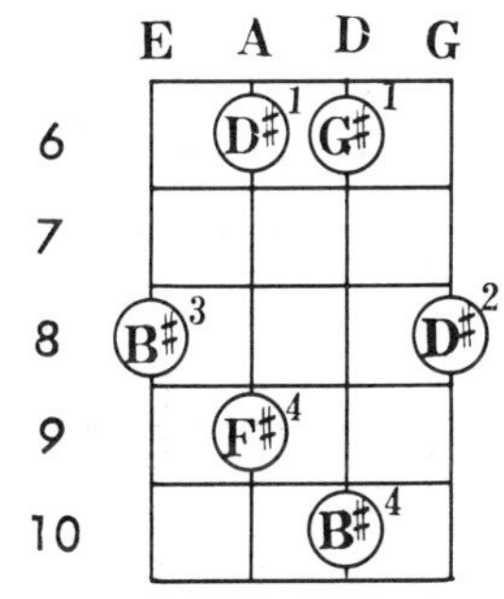

Dominant 7th

QUATERNARY FORMS

B♭ MINOR

HARMONIC

III rd POSITION

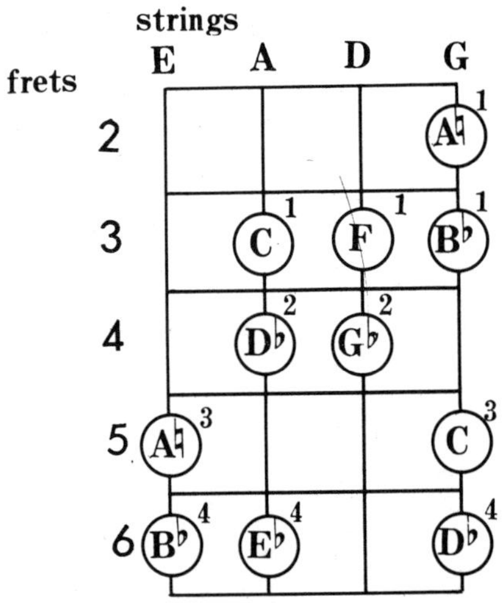

Harmonic

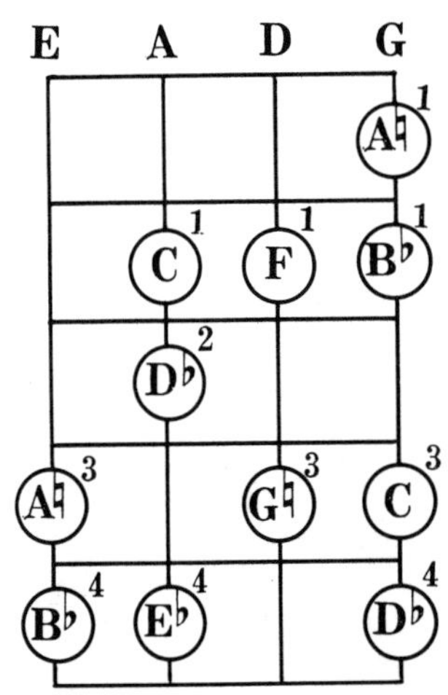

Melodic ascending

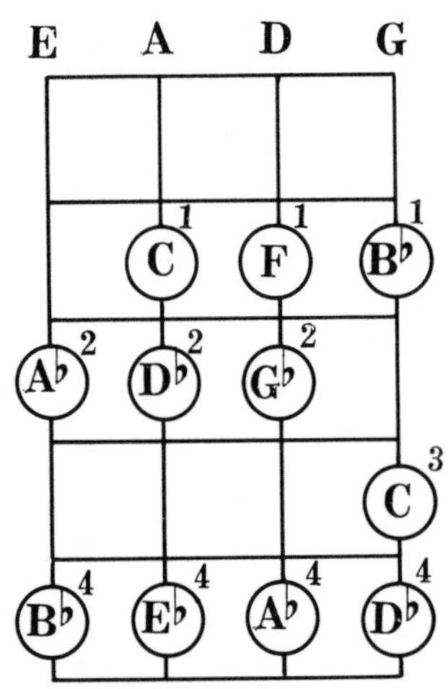

Melodic descending

This form is the same as the natural form, and except for mode or feeling, it is the same as the relative major (D♭).

MELODIC

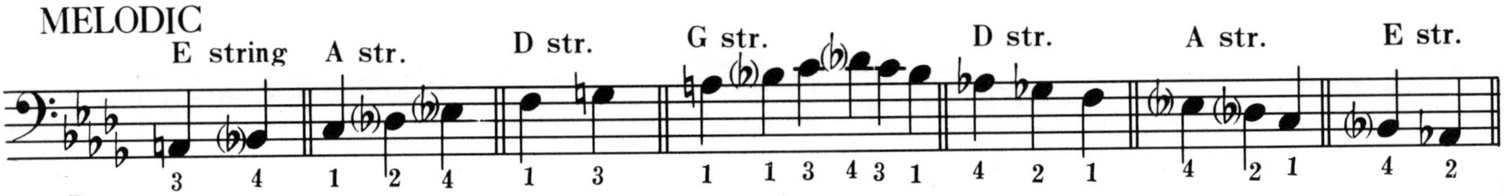

ARPEGGIOS

B♭m

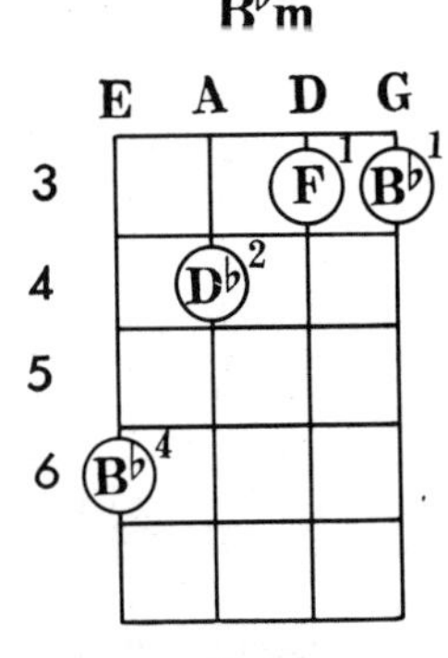

Tonic

E♭m

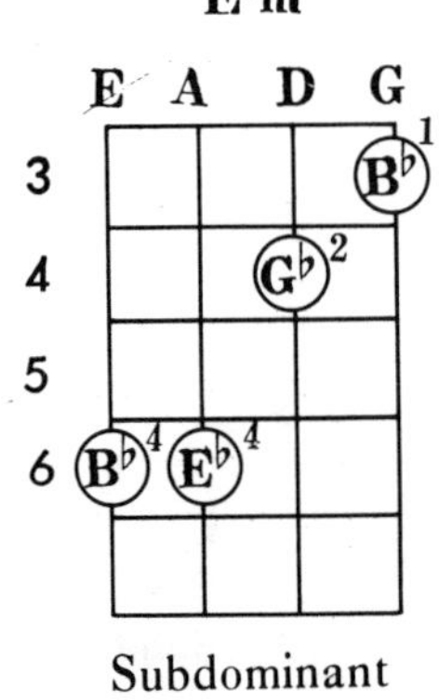

Subdominant

F7

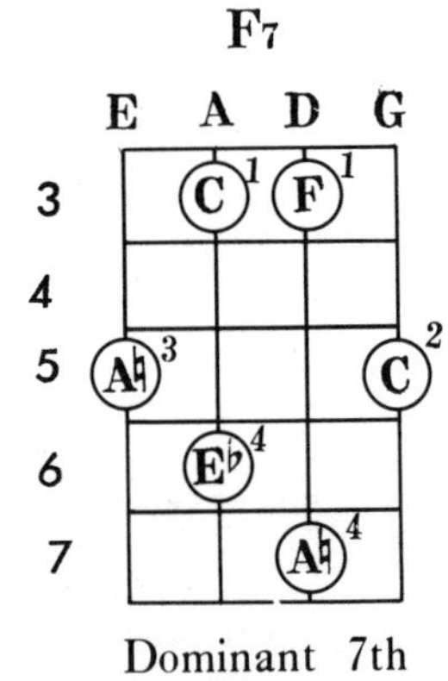

Dominant 7th

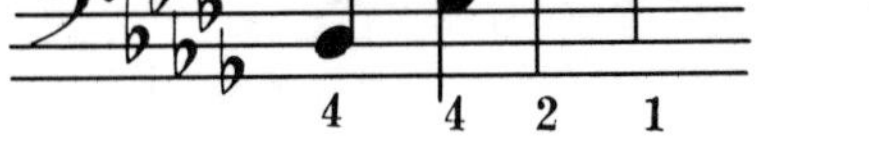

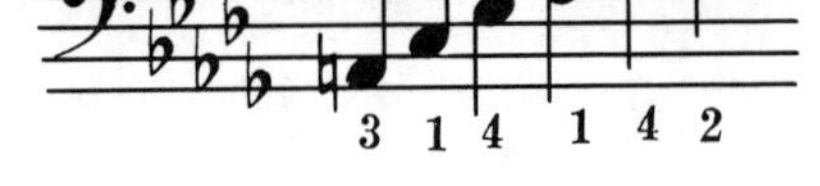

QUATERNARY FORMS

G♯ MINOR

HARMONIC

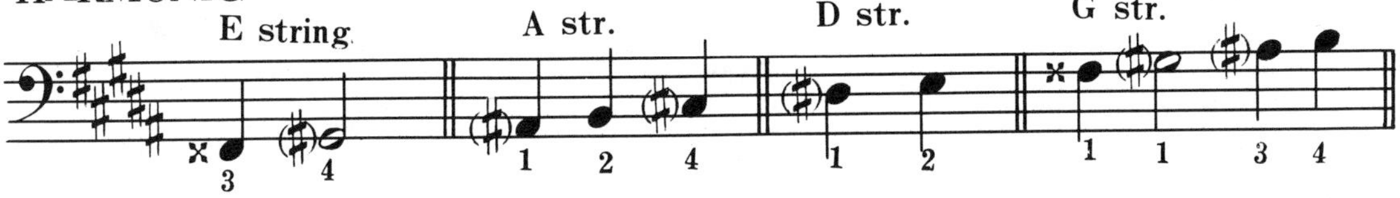

1st POSITION

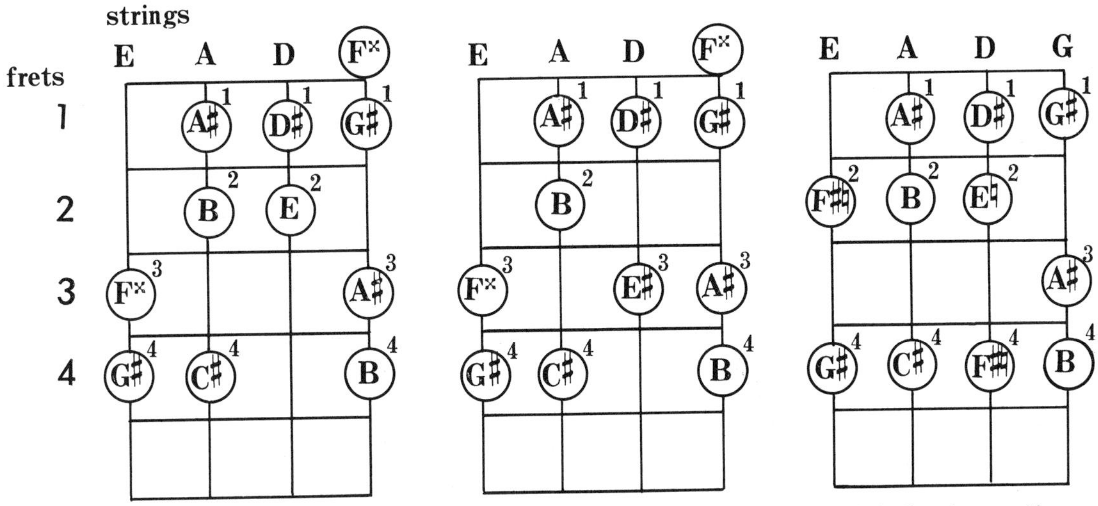

Harmonic   Melodic ascending   Melodic descending

This form is the same as the natural form, and except for mode or feeling, it is the same as the relative major (B).

MELODIC

ARPEGGIOS

G♯m

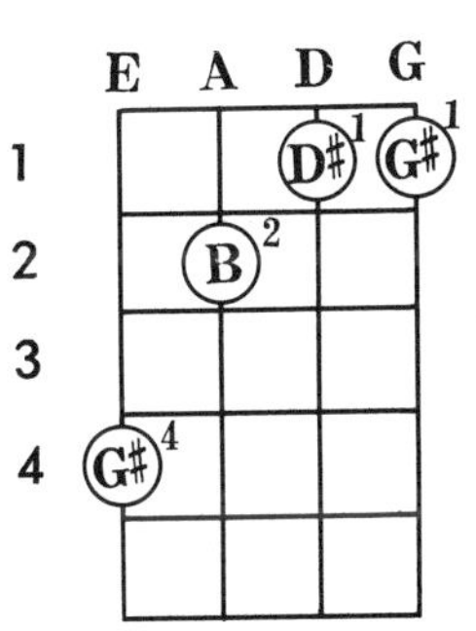

Tonic

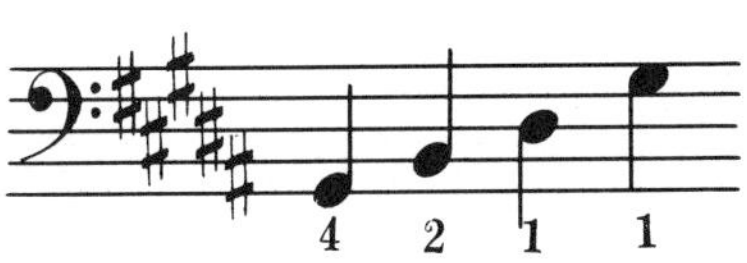

C♯m

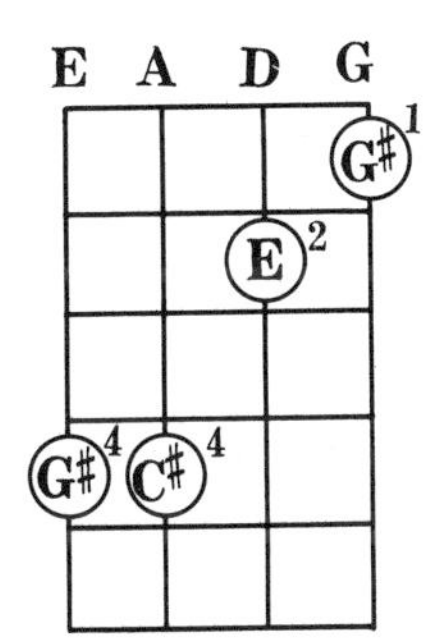

Subdominant

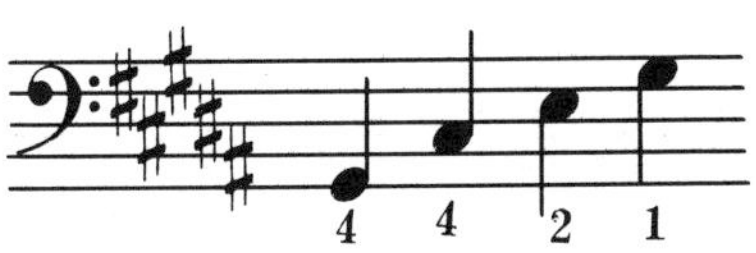

D♯7

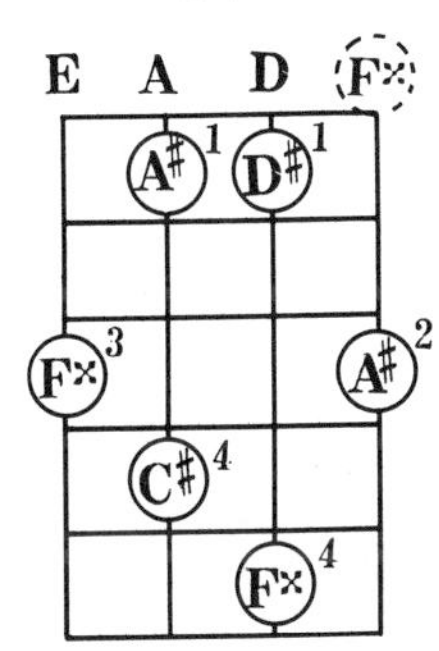

Dominant 7th

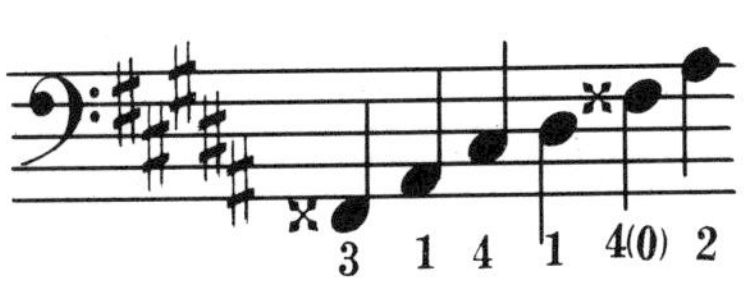

QUATERNARY FORMS

E♭ MINOR

This key is enharmonically equivalent to D♯Minor (p 87).

HARMONIC

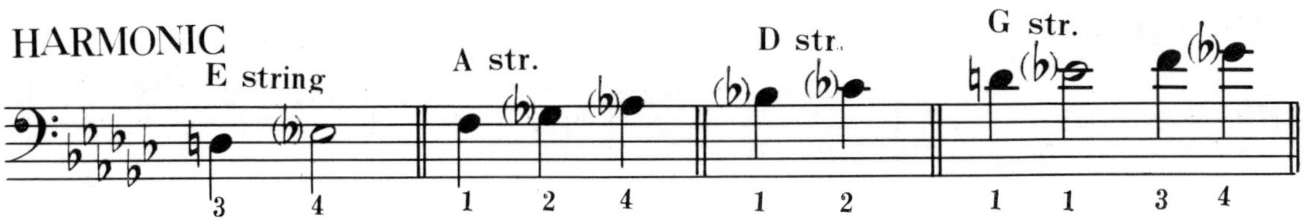

VIIIth POSITION

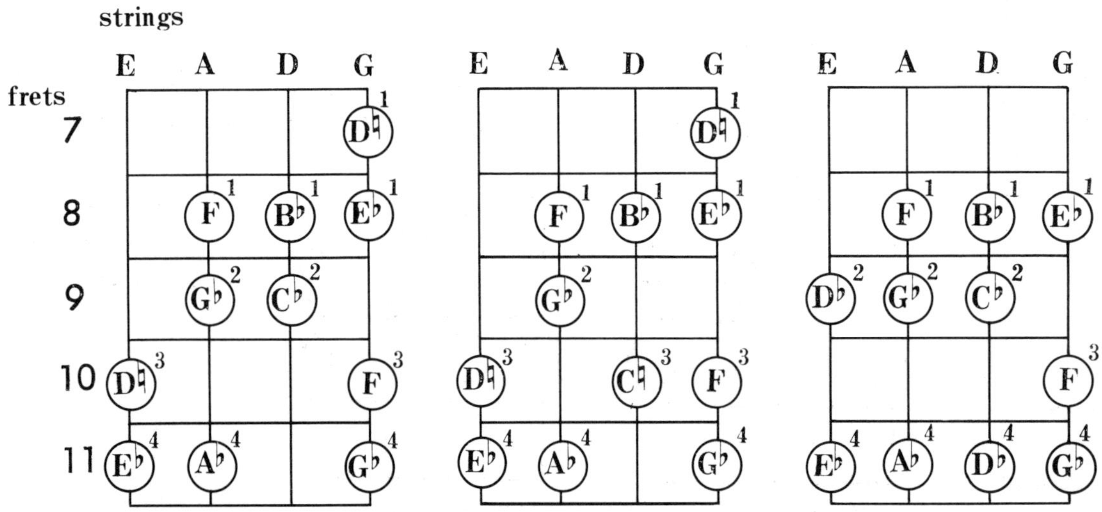

Harmonic   Melodic ascending   Melodic descending

This form is the same as the natural form, and except for mode or feeling, it is the same as the relative major (G♭).

MELODIC

ARPEGGIOS

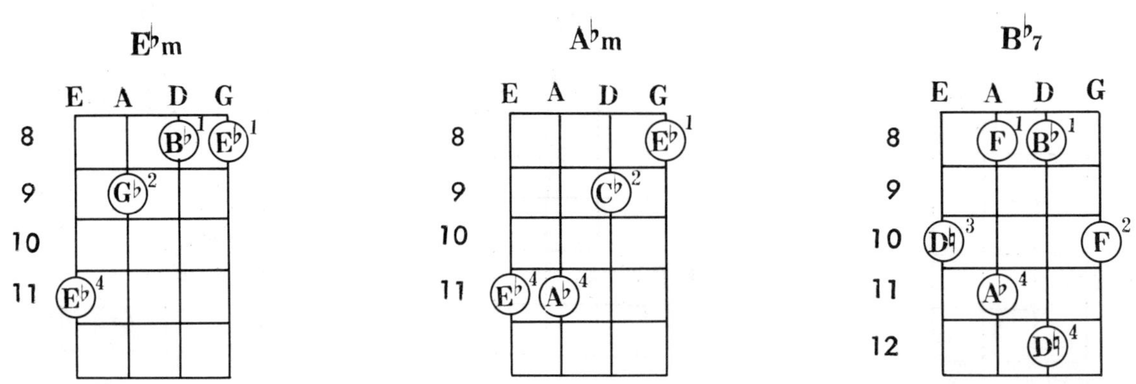

Tonic   Subdominant   Dominant 7th

QUATERNARY FORMS

D♯ MINOR

This key is enharmonically equivalent to E♭Minor (p 86).

HARMONIC

VIIIth POSITION

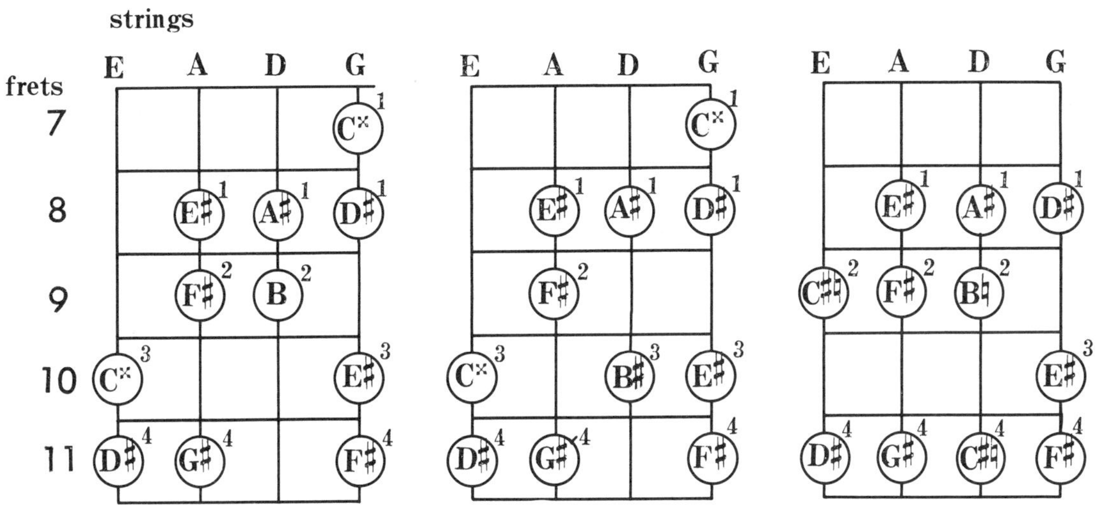

Harmonic

Melodic ascending

Melodic descending

This form is the same as the natural form, and except for mode or feeling, it is the same as the relative major (F♯).

MELODIC

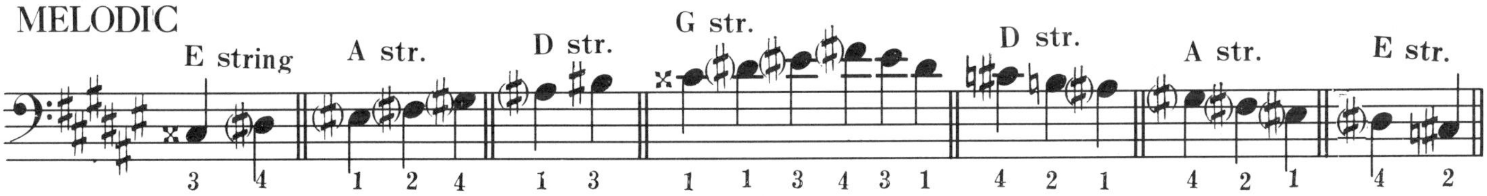

ARPEGGIOS

D♯m

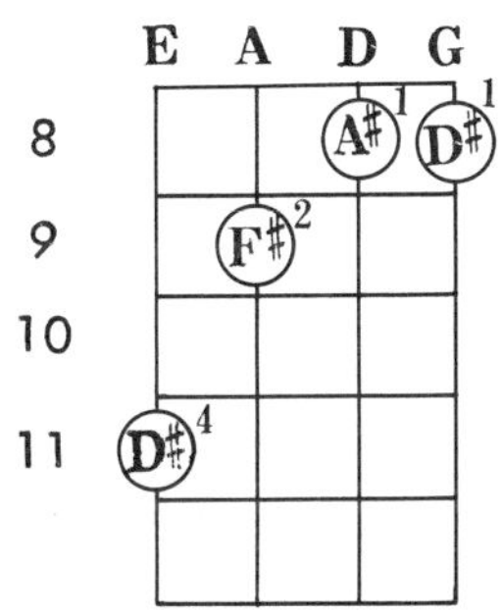

Tonic

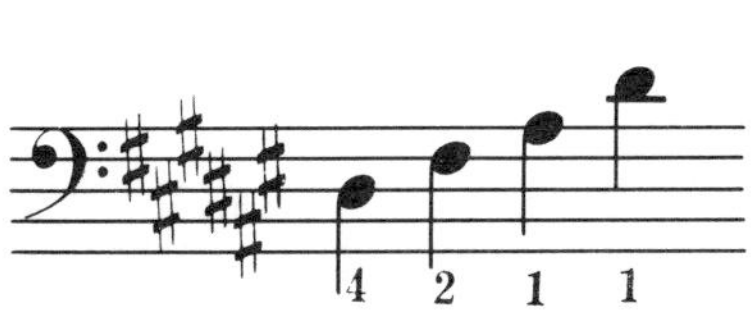

G♯m

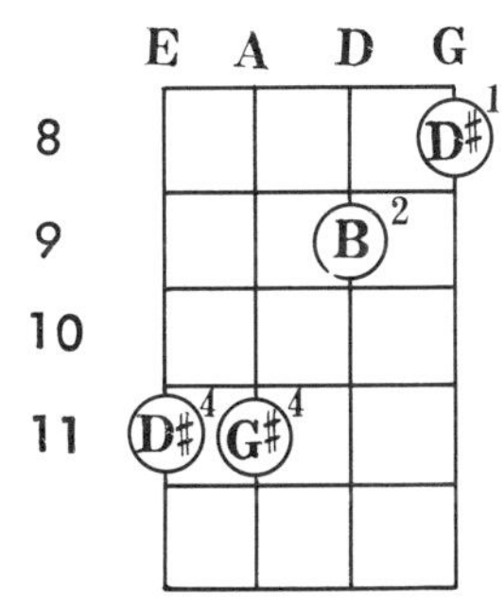

Subdominant

A♯7

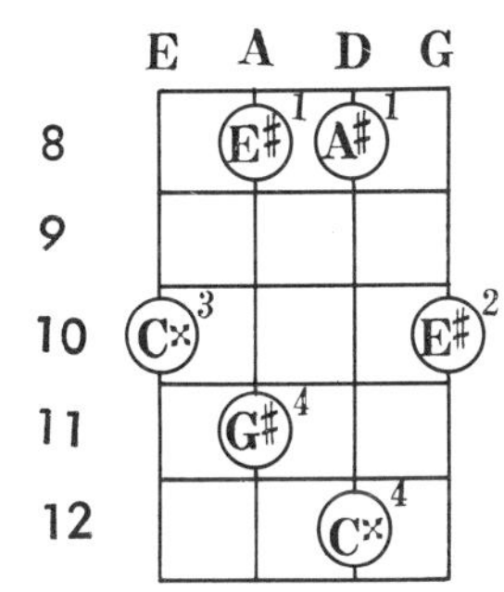

Dominant 7th

SPECIAL SCALES

CHROMATIC SCALES

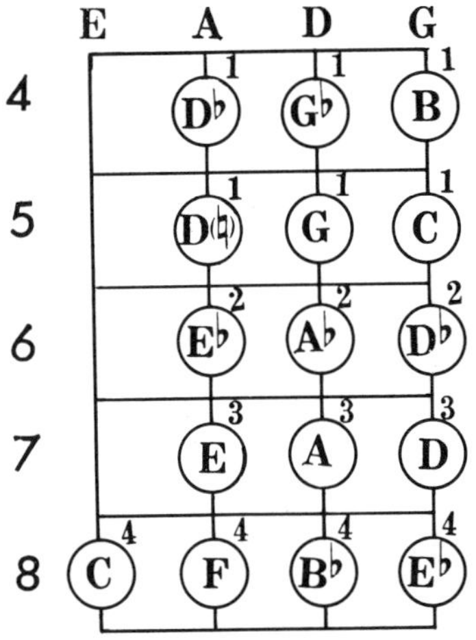

descending

The choice of fingering will depend on the context of the passage. The player must be prepared to play scales, or parts of scales, in any of the above forms.

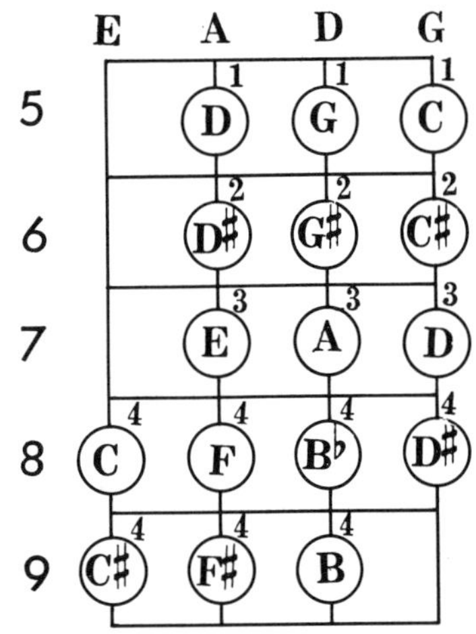

ascending

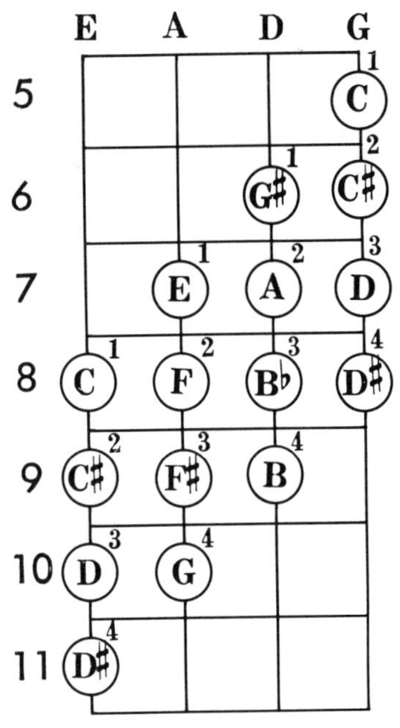

Ascending and descending fingering is the same. Note that the spelling of the accidentals should be as previously shown.

WHOLE TONE SCALE

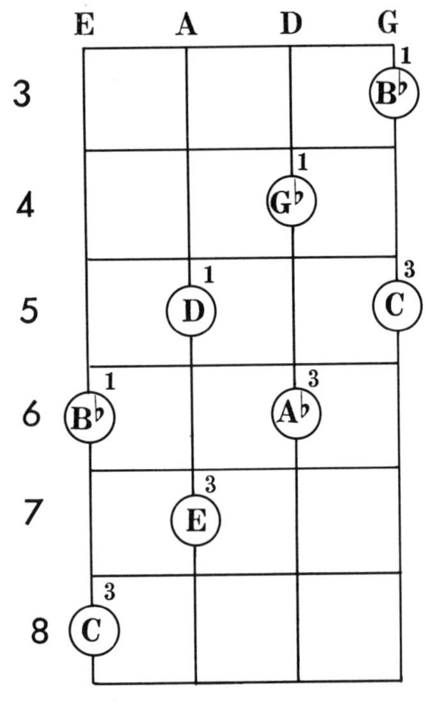

PART THREE - COMPREHENSIVE ARPEGGIOS

MAJOR TRIAD

Construct each arpeggio on the given bass using the F Major model.

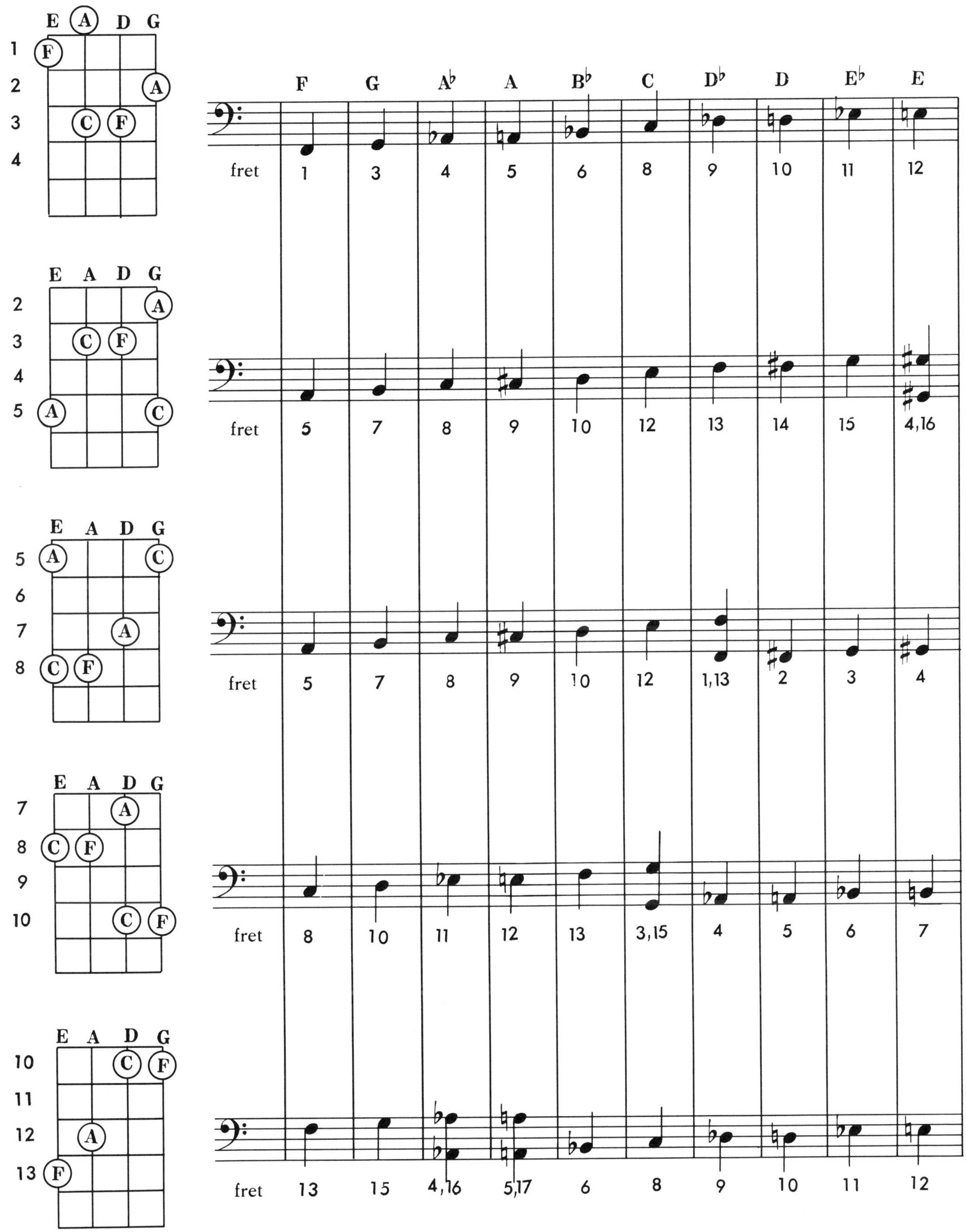

MINOR TRIAD

Construct each arpeggio on the given bass using the D Minor model.

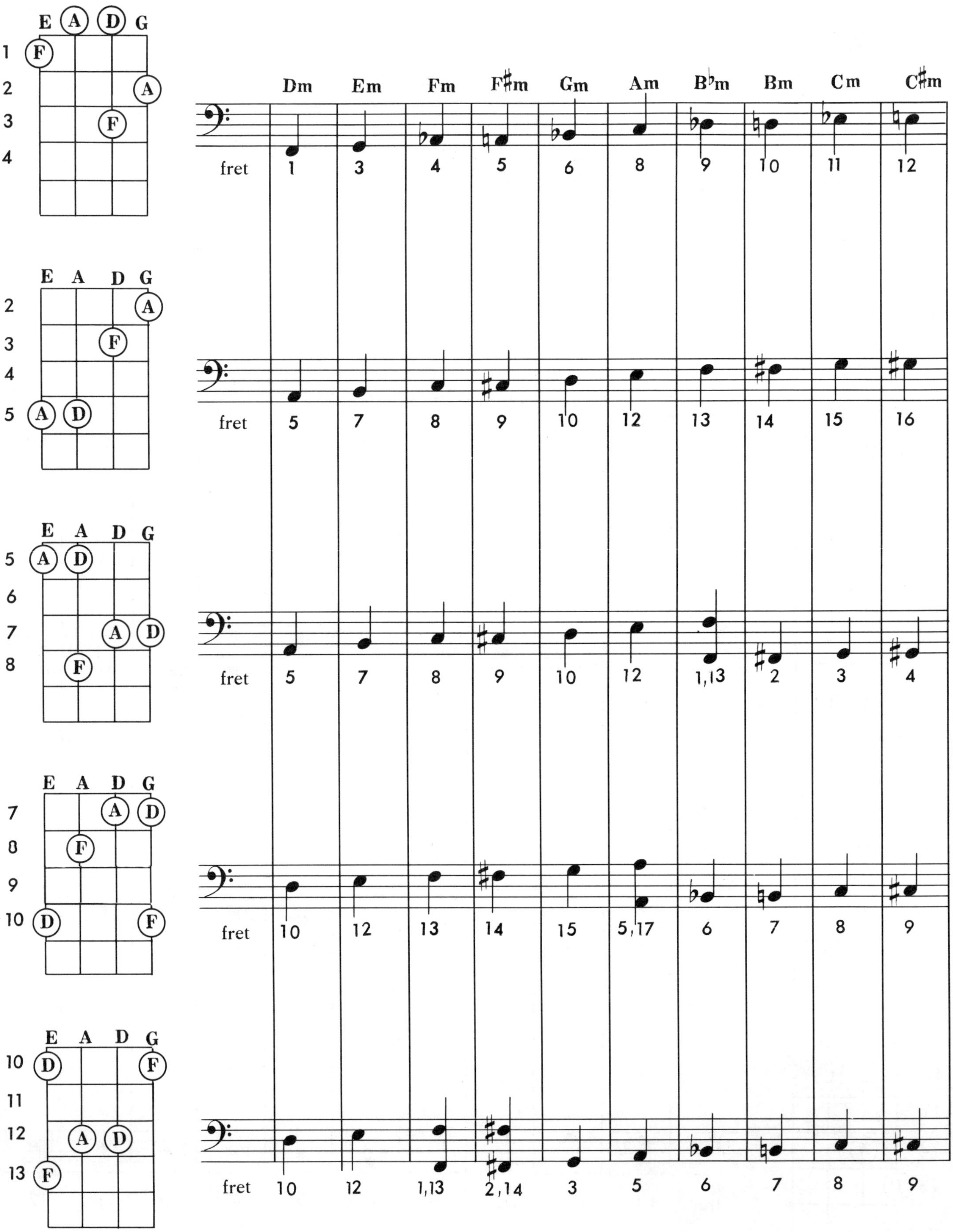

DOMINANT 7th

Construct each arpeggio on the given bass using the C7 model.

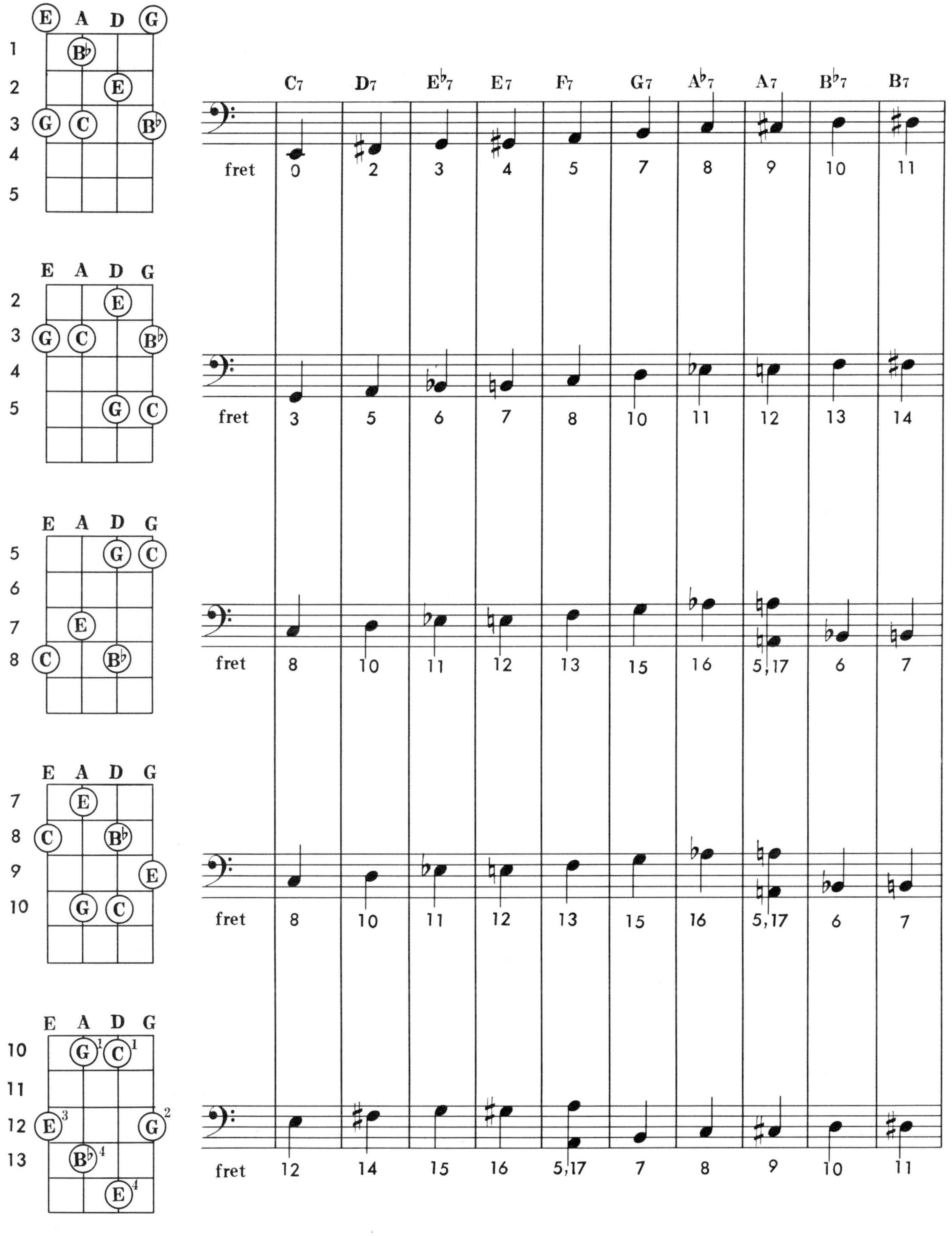

MINOR 7th or MAJOR 6th

The minor 7th arpeggio and the major 6th arpeggio (one minor 3rd higher) have the same spelling. Construct each arpeggio on the given bass using the F6-Dm7 model,

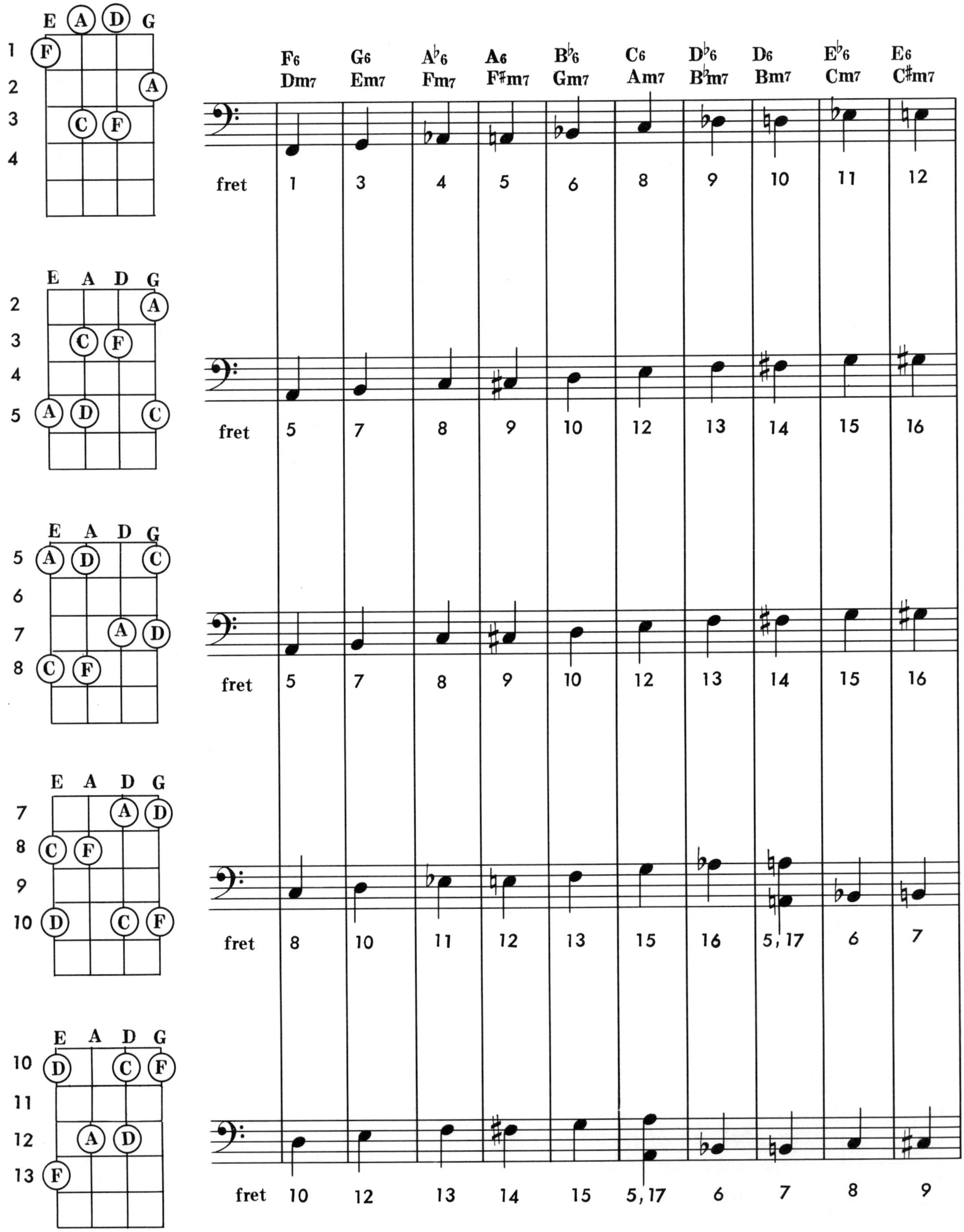

MINOR 6th

Construct each arpeggio on the given bass using the Dm6 model.

MAJOR 7th

Construct each arpeggio on the given bass using the Fmaj7 model.

DIMINISHED 7th

The diminished 7th arpeggio derives its name from any one of the notes contained in the arpeggio. Each note has an enharmonic equivalent. For example, C♭ =B, E♭♭ =D. Each diminished 7th arpeggio is repeatable every third fret ($1\frac{1}{2}$ tones) up the fingerboard.

Fdim7, A♭dim7, Bdim7, Ddim7

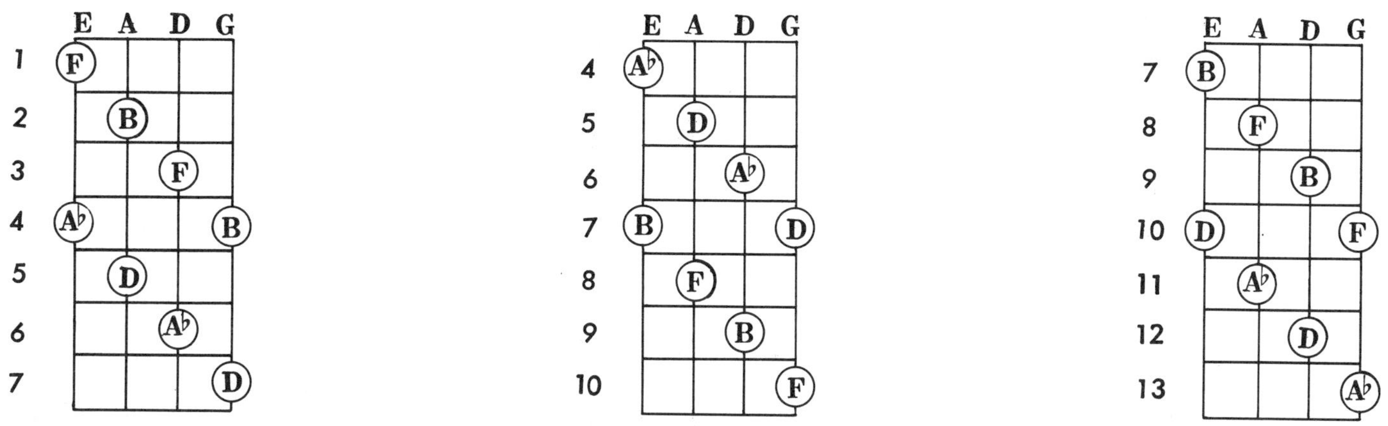

F♯dim7, Adim7, Cdim7, E♭dim7

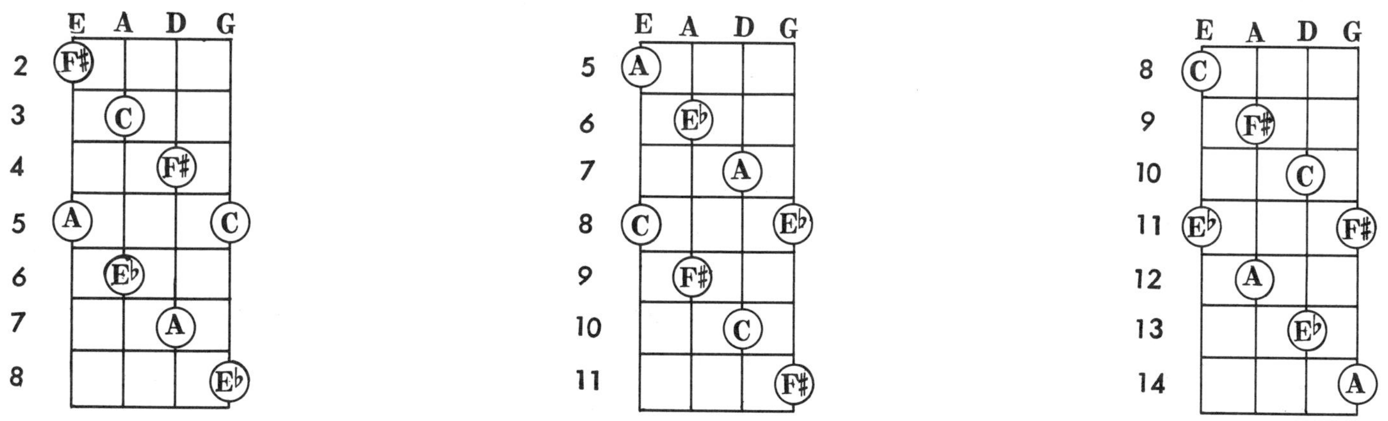

Gdim7, B♭dim7, D♭dim7, Edim7

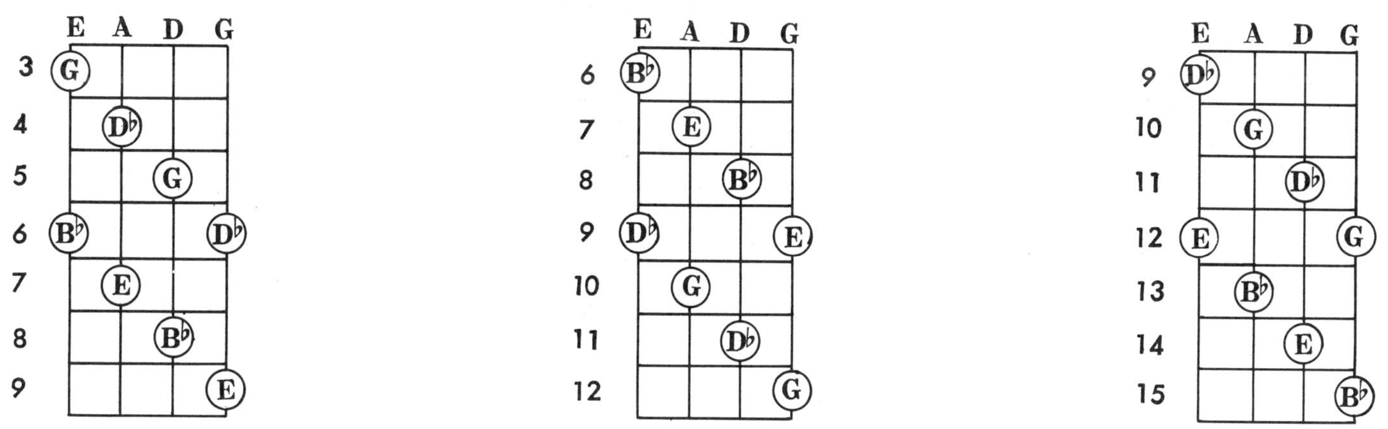

AUGMENTED 5th TRIAD

The augmented 5th triad arpeggio derives its name from any one of the notes contained in the arpeggio. Each note has an enharmonic equivalent. For example, $A^{\flat} = G^{\sharp}$, $F = E^{\sharp}$. Each augmented 5th triad arpeggio is repeatable every fourth fret (2 tones) up the fingerboard.

A♭♯5, C♯5, E♯5 *

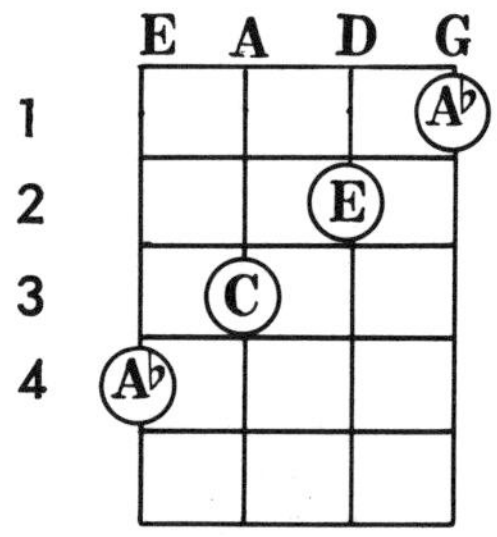

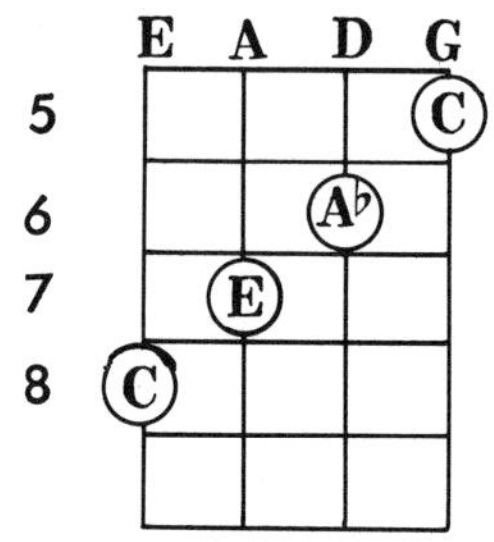

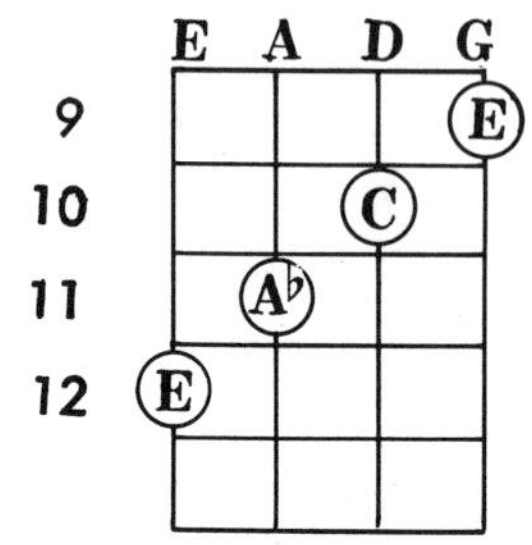

A♯5, C♯♯5, F♯5

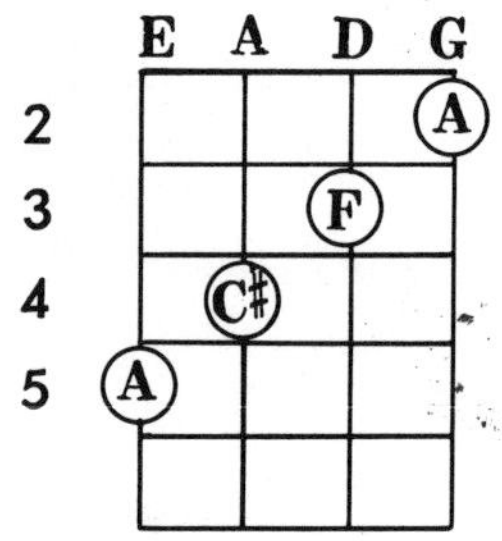

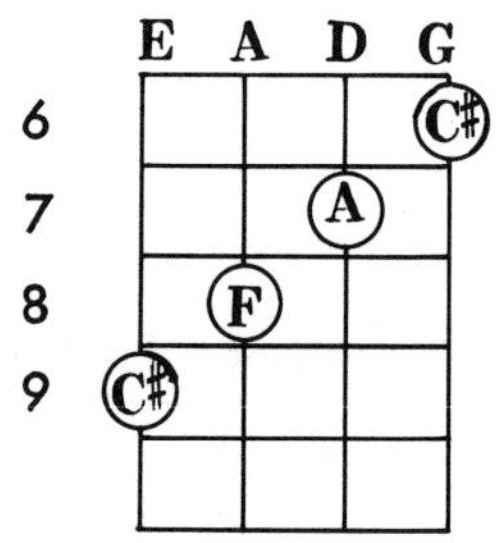

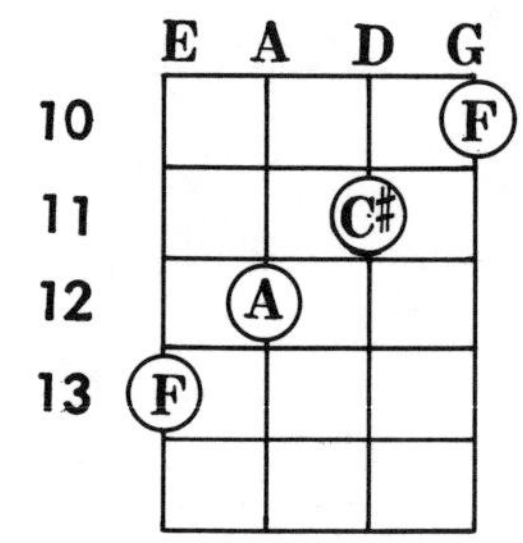

B♭♯5, D♯5, F♯♯5

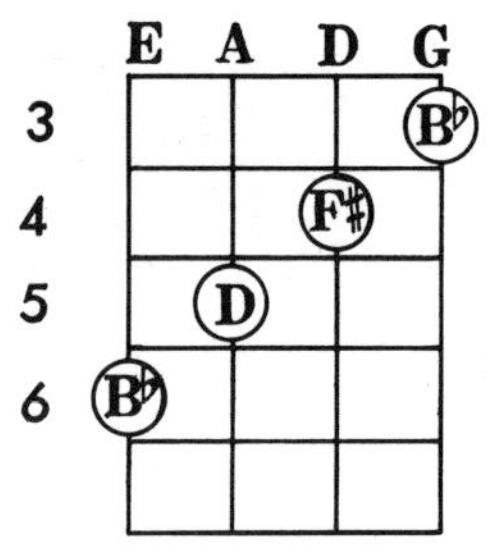

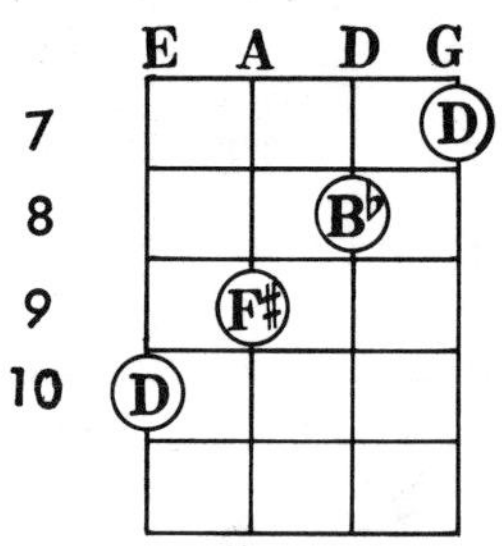

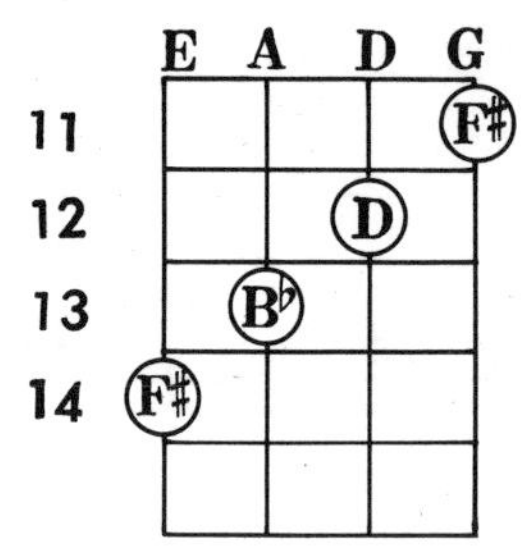

B♯5, D♯♯5, G♯5

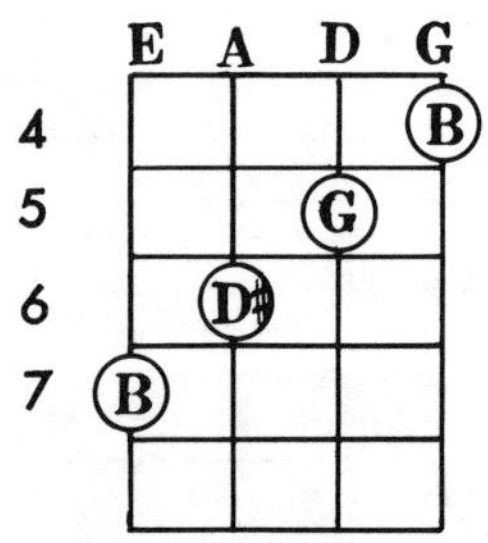

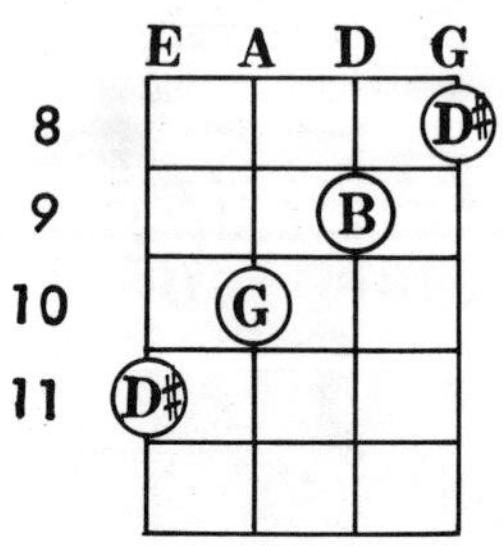

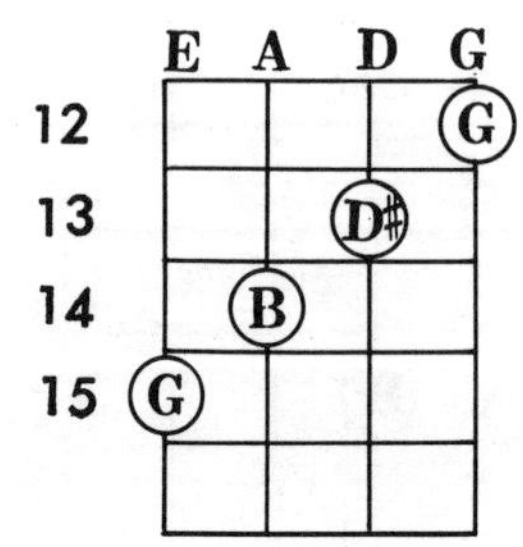

* Sometimes notated $A^{\flat}+5$, or simply $A^{\flat}+$.